# Japan's Economic Strategy in Brazil

# Japan's Economic Strategy in Brazil

*Challenge for the United States*

Leon Hollerman
St. Olaf College

**Lexington Books**
*D.C. Heath and Company/Lexington, Massachusetts/Toronto*

*Library of Congress Cataloging-in-Publication Data*
Hollerman, Leon.
  Japan's economic strategy in Brazil.

  Includes index.
    1. Japan—Foreign economic relations—Brazil.
  2. Brazil—Foreign economic relations—Japan.
  3. United States—Foreign economic relations—Brazil.
  4. Brazil—Foreign economic relations—United States.
  5. Brazil—Economic policy.   I. Title.
  HF1602.15.B6H76    1988    337.52081    87-46239
  ISBN 0-669-17428-9 (alk. paper)

Published simultaneously in Canada
Printed in the United States of America
International Standard Book Number: 0-669-17428-9
Library of Congress Catalog Card Number 87-46239

The paper used in this publication meets the minimum requirements of American National
Standard for Information Sciences—Permanence of Paper for Printed Library Materials, ANSI
Z39.48-1984. ∞™

88 89 90 91 92 8 7 6 5 4 3 2 1

*To Janet*

# Contents

# List of Tables

# Preface

I n size, resource endowment, and leadership potential, Brazil is the most important country in Latin America. Hence relations with Brazil are of strategic importance to both the United States and Japan. Their respective policies toward Brazil, however, are decidedly at odds. At the outset, if the United States actually has a foreign policy concerning Brazil—which some observers doubt—it emphasizes national security issues, in contrast to that of Japan, which concentrates on economic and political matters. Thus, potentially, the U.S. position in Brazilian markets, despite being older, wider, and deeper that Japan's, may one day be outflanked by that of the challenger.

In a broader context, as Japan seeks to reduce its dependence on the United States by diversifying and multiplying its global interests, the U.S. economy itself may be outflanked. The strategy of Japan's economic approach to Brazil far transcends its early postwar preoccupation with bilateral complementarities in trade relations. At present, with the infrastructure of its external channels and contacts in place, Japan is prepared to impose central management on a world network of joint ventures, subsidiaries, and affiliates. In doing so, it will assume the role of a "headquarters country." Japan will coordinate the relations of its foreign clients with each other as well as their relations with itself as headquarters. Coordination will be achieved through direct investments; financial, communication, and maintenance services; and Japan's global trading company facilities. Market-sharing arrangements and cartels or quasi-cartels will be organized and manipulated by managers in Tokyo.

In the first phase of their postwar rise, the "new Japans"—the newly industrializing countries (NICs), among which Brazil is numbered—were a nuisance and even a threat to Japan by virtue of the competition they mounted in its home market and in third regions. In a scenario of things to come, however, the implication of this study is that far from resisting their rise, Japan will coopt the "new Japans." This would be a logical outcome of the transposition of its domestic industrial policy to the international plane. Trade friction between Japan and the United States will disappear as Japan expatriates its low- and middle-technology industries and as its bilateral trade surplus with the United States dwindles. As the United States becomes increasingly protectionist in the low- and intermediate-technology sectors, Japan will become increasingly open. This will give Japan increased leverage for the export of its high-technology products and services to third countries. Accordingly, Japanese competition with the United States and U.S.–Japan confrontation will become increasingly indirect rather than direct. In its indirect mode, however, Japan's challenge to the United States will be more powerful than ever before.

This study refers primarily to conditions in Brazil on the eve of *abertura,* the democratic opening of March 1985, when the military regime gave way to a popularly elected government. In this critical hour of Brazil's transition, I spoke with bankers, business executives, government officials, and university professors in Brazil. Similar interviews were performed in New York, Washington, and Tokyo. In Brazil, important officials speak frankly—to a degree that would be unthinkable in Japan and scandalous in the United States. One purpose of this study is to reveal the contrasting attitudes and opinions within and among the nations studied with regard to matters impinging on each. Diverse points of view were expressed. I have made no attempt to homogenize them. My assessment, however, takes the form of the scenario sketched above.

I wish to express my thanks to Richard W. Petree, president, and Ronald Aqua, program director of the United States–Japan Foundation for a grant in support of my research for this study. Needless to say, neither they nor the United States–Japan Foundation is responsible for any of the opinions or conclusions presented here. I am also deeply grateful to the many authorities in Brazil and in Japan who generously shared their information and insights with me. They likewise bear no responsibility for errors of understanding or reporting on my part.

# 1
# The Japanese Challenge

As a framework for analysis, the present chapter takes account, first, of some trends in Japan's world environment; second, it describes the rationale of Japan's foreign economic policy; third, given its national interests, institutional arrangements, and structural constraints, it projects a scenario of Japan's global economic strategy; fourth, it identifies the place of Brazil in the Japanese strategy; and fifth, it examines the U.S. policy predicament.

## Some Trends in Japan's World Environment

Because of its great dependence on the world economy, Japan's policies are highly constrained as well as impelled by external factors. In responding to those factors, Japan is consistently pragmatic and faithful to its long-run national interests as it perceives them. A troublesome group of world trends has deep implications for Japanese policy at the present time. Among these is the anomaly of rampant nationalism in the midst of rising interdependence in the world economy. Nationalism is evident, for example, in the separatist political movements, the quarrels of the European Community, the disarray within NATO, the disharmony in the United Nations, and the xenophobia in developing countries. Pride in its achievements, together with resentment of what is perceived as foreign attacks on those achievements, has aroused nationalism in Japan itself. Second, in the major industrial nations there has been the aberration of financial market deregulation combined with growing protectionism in commodity trade. Flight capital and speculative financial deals remote from the physical production or distribution of goods now dominate world markets. Portfolio transactions have swamped the real world of commerce. In financial affairs, there has been an increasing amount of uncertainty and risk due to erratic and volatile fluctuations of interest rates and exchange rates. These sources of instability have been augmented by the rapidity, cost, and complexity of technological advance in the field of financial services. In the United States they have been compounded also by a surge in predatory financial activities—such as hostile takeovers and leveraged buyouts—that often are designed for short-term financial gains rather than long-term productive efficiency. The innovation of new financial instruments is another source of instability in financial markets, as investors switch from one type of asset to another in search of higher rates of return.

In their linkage and interaction effects, these factors have contributed to a trend toward increased economic concentration in the major industrial nations. Lacking the skills and resources to survive in the new era, minor firms and financial institutions have succumbed in large numbers. Economic concentration has increased also because of mergers for the exploitation of economies of scale in new high-technology fields. In the United States and elsewhere, economic concentration has been promoted by the watering down of antitrust laws. In 1986, the competitive impact of yen revaluation precipitated bankruptcies and accelerated economic concentration in Japan. Moreover, concentration by means of cartels has been sanctioned by governments that sponsor and enforce "voluntary export restraints." I refer to these government-to-government arrangements as "neocartels" to distinguish them from market-sharing conspiracies on the part of private enterprise. In July of 1986, a neocartel agreement for purposes of market sharing and price fixing in the semiconductor industry was signed by representatives of the United States and Japan.

Antimarket forces gained a victory in September of 1985 when the central banks of the United States, Japan, West Germany, England, and France (G-5) agreed at their meeting in the Plaza Hotel in New York to accept the principle of "management and coordination" of the exchange rate policies. In May of 1986 the retreat of the United States from a free-market position was emphasized by the proposals of U.S. Treasury Secretary James Baker at the Economic Summit Meeting in Tokyo. The communique of the meeting included an agreement on the part of the participants to coordinate their economic policies and to monitor a set of economic performance indicators for that purpose. The agreement is significant in revealing the wish of the major industrial nations to control the thermometer rather than the fever in the patient. If they were to adopt sound policies at home, there would be no need for international antimarket controls.

These partly inconsistent and chiefly antimarket trends—nationalism cum interdependence, liberalization cum protectionism, the speculative applications of financial high technology, economic concentration, government intervention, and neocartelism, as well as the vulnerability of international markets to default on the part of debtor developing nations—are among the principal factors causing politicization of economic issues in the world today. Even the liberalization of credit and finance has a politicizing and antimarket effect by promoting the growth of giant oligopoly institutions. Antimarket forces, moreover, are nourished by instability and potential instability. In its perennial quest for "comprehensive economic security," Japan is risk-averse and has an abhorrence of economic instability. It feels more threatened by instability than any other major industrial nation. At the same time, the rise of antimarket forces—which in many instances represent efforts to control instability—is highly compatible with Japan's cultural and institutional propensities. These are among the factors generating the scenario of Japan's geopolitical strategy projected below. First, however, we may consider the basic rationale of Japan's foreign economic policies.

## The Rationale of Japan's Foreign Economic Policies

Japan's dependence on the world economy is the structural basis for its international policies. More than any other major nation, Japan subordinates its domestic policies to its foreign economic objectives. This has been the case since it emerged from the "seclusion" of feudalism in 1868. Because of its unbalanced resource structure, the nation faces an external imperative: the Japanese economy is viable only by means of coordination between its internal and external sectors—a process known as "internationalization" of the economy. It is driven by Japan's dread of national isolation and the insecurity that implies. During the 1930s, fear of boycotts and hostile encirclement led Japan to internationalize by military conquest; this in turn led to the disaster of the Pacific War. Following the war, foreign distrust and discrimination reinforced Japan's sense of being a loner among nations. In the postwar period, in order to pay for essential imports, Japan progressively shifted its industrial center of gravity from traditional labor-intensive, light industry products to heavy and chemical industry products and then to high-technology products. For the purpose of reducing external dependence, this industrial policy approach sought to progressively increase the domestically value-added component of production. On the import side, Japan's industrial policy was designed to reduce its vulnerability to potential disruption of supply.

In exports, however, Japan's dependence on the world economy has increased. The ratio of its exports to its GNP, which in 1985 was 10.2 percent, does not tell the whole story. Some of Japan's major industries are dependent on exports to a striking degree. In 1985, for example, in automobiles, 55.1 percent of production was exported; in electronics and electrical machinery, 46.1 percent of production was exported; and in the steel industry, 32.7 percent of crude steel was exported.[1] Dependence also has been increased by the fact that the early postwar policy of strengthening Japan's international competitiveness throughout the entire gamut of the industrial structure has been abandoned. This reflects an intermediate stage in

Japan's shift toward "international industrial adjustment" or "agreed specialization" in the world economy. The geographic distribution of Japan's principal exports, moreover, is still relatively concentrated; hence its markets are potentially unstable. In 1985, for example, 46.5 percent of Japan's automobile exports were sold in the United States and 20.3 percent were sold in western Europe.

From a Japanese point of view, economic instability arises chiefly from external rather than domestic sources. More than any other major nation, Japan sees itself as a potential target of protectionism in a nationalistic world. In the first half of the 1980s, other dominant world trends were a further threat to Japan's economic stability. The monetary and fiscal affairs of both advanced and developing nations were in disarray. Stagflation was rife. The debt crisis of the developing nations was denied all but cosmetic treatment. Interest rates and exchange rates were misaligned and fluctuated erratically. In the capital account of Japan's balance of payments, the potentially destabilizing effect of Euroyen transactions was disturbing to the Ministry of Finance. Japan's international economic affairs, moreover, were highly politicized, especially through trade friction (*boeki masatsu*) in relations with the United States and western Europe. In the aftermath of the first oil crisis, the manager of the Industrial Research Department of the Fuji Bank made the following observation:

> Japan has succeeded in catching up in many fields to an astonishing degree. But in the process, her supply lines have become overextended and not only the logistics has gone wrong but distortions and inefficiencies have popped up almost everywhere. "Japan, Inc.," the conglomerate behemoth, turned out to be a small enterprise riding a lucky streak and ending up as an oversized dwarf.[2]

Whatever foreigners may think of the accuracy of this description, it is significant as an indicator of the feelings of skepticism and insecurity within Japan itself—feelings that are reflected in Japan's foreign economic policy.

Domestically, Japan faces destabilizing forces as well. The cyclical instability of the domestic economy has increased since the heavy and chemical industries were displaced by high-technology industries as the fulcrum of the business cycle. The shift in Japan's domestic industrial structure to emphasis on high-technology products has increased the income elasticity of demand for exports. The semiconductor industry, in particular, which has replaced steel as the key industry, is subject to greater volatility and variance in contributing to business fluctuations. The shortening of the business cycle because of accelerator effects in the demand for semiconductors is compounded on the supply side by the relatively short life of capital invested for high-technology production. Furthermore, methods by which

Japan formerly economized in the use of its resources may no longer be applicable. The "catching up" process, for example, was facilitated by the easy acquisition of technology and know-how from the West. Now Japan must produce more of its own innovations; these are on the costly technological frontier. The research and development factor that once was a subsidy to growth has become a cost of growth. Correspondingly, the cost of structural change in industry has increased enormously. Moreover, in a study of the sources of Japan's economic growth (identified as land, labor, capital, advances in knowledge, economies of scale, reduction in international trade barriers, contraction of agricultural inputs, and contraction of nonagricultural self-employment), it has been calculated that transitional factors contributed two-thirds of the growth rate during the period of the economic "miracle" and sustainable factors only one-third.[3]

Domestically, since the economic miracle, the slowdown in the growth rate of national income has been associated with a demographic transition that has an adverse impact on Japan's competitive power. The seniority wage system (*nenkō joretsu*), which is combined with the practice of "lifetime employment" (*shūshin koyo*) in major firms, raises the unit cost of labor in an aging population. Many of Japan's most important export-producing firms have a top-heavy structure of personnel in the upper wage brackets. This employment structure compounds the phenomenon of declining productivity during times of recession.[4] In terms of labor cost, newly industrializing countries (NICs) present a rising challenge to Japan in a widening spectrum of manufacturing industries.[5] At the same time, Japan has been under pressure to extend tariff preferences to the NICs and to adopt "voluntary" restrictions in its own exports to them.

Furthermore, aging of the population may induce a decline in the savings ratio. Although savings remain high in relation to domestic investment, more rather than less saving is required for purposes of capital formation in the new high-technology industries. More saving is also required for fulfillment of the overseas investment requirements of the headquarters country scenario described below. Moreover, the demographic transition has greatly increased the social security expenses of the government. The nation's medical bill has quadrupled in the past decade. The latter forms one of the three principal causes of Japan's fiscal deficits—*kome, kokutetsu,* and *kenpo* (rice subsidies, the national railroad, and health insurance).

It is difficult to maintain a constant rate of economic expansion on a growing base. In Japan, various constraints and bottlenecks have emerged that make the expansion of its smokestack industries increasingly difficult. These include environmental problems, power shortages, water shortages due to the influx of population and factories into cities, and shortage of industrial land. The rate of increase in labor productivity has declined. As a result of antipollution drives, individual firms have been forced to absorb the social costs of production (adverse externalities), hence reducing a former competitive advantage. The distribution of income and wealth has become increasingly disproportionate. Nevertheless, personal expectations have risen, and demands for equality have clashed with traditional incentives for efficiency.

Thus stability and economic security have been jeopardized by domestic as well as external difficulties. The point remains, however, that both Japan's domestic and external difficulties must ultimately be resolved in an international context. The postwar pattern of accommodation between the domestic and external sectors was established in Japan by the U.S. Occupation. Economic planning and industrial policy were introduced by the "New Dealers" of General MacArthur's headquarters. (In those days, U.S. opinion regarded government as "good" and business as "bad.") After the Occupation, the Japanese government avidly seized the baton from the Supreme Command Allied Powers (SCAP) and in the name of the national interest combined economic planning with bureaucratic careerism and comprehensive controls. Fortunately, tradition prevailed in at least one benign respect, namely, that the bureaucracy held some of the best brains of the nation. Economic planning was designed to economize on Japan's scarce indigenous resources and was implemented by means of industrial policy. Initially, that policy was conceived in terms of biased production or unbalanced growth. Economizing was performed by means of allocating resources mainly to directly productive activities rather than to infrastructure. (In this respect, while emulating Japan's postwar development, Brazil failed to follow the Japanese model.) An essential element of Japan's industrial policy was the construction of directly productive facilities in key industries. From time to time, in guiding the evolution of Japan's industrial structure, the government designated new key industries. In the early postwar period (when reconstruction depended heavily on traditional labor-intensive, light industries), coal mining and electric power were the first to be designated. Later, metals, chemicals, and machinery were sponsored. In the 1980s, key industries included microelectronics, biotechnology, and others in the high-technology field.

The key industry approach was conceived by the Ministry of International Trade and Industry (MITI) and implemented largely under its guidance. Whatever may be the merits of the argument concerning whether Japan's economic performance has been achieved by means of or in spite of intervention by MITI and the Ministry of Finance, there can be no doubt about the fact that Japan's economic "miracle" was performed under their auspices. Could the miracle have been even more splendid in the absence of government intervention? This is a sterile question. As a practical matter, the economic ministries are here to stay, and they certainly will not willingly yield their status or turf. To some extent, as an intermediate strategy, the Japanese bureaucracy relinquished some of its jurisdiction and prerogatives in the process of economic liberalization. As it has done consistently in the past, however, the bureaucracy will seek to coopt the national interest for its own purposes. Hence, apart from the "structural" dynamics of the scenario of Japan as a headquarters country, powerful bureaucratic dynamics are operating as well. By assuming a headquarters role the bureaucracy would be able to recoup losses that it sustained during the liberalization of the past two decades.

Among the instruments of industrial policy, one of the earliest was the Foreign Exchange and Foreign Trade Control Law (passed under the auspices of the Occupation in 1949 and amended in 1980). Related thereto were import restrictions by means of duties, quotas, and other nontariff barriers. Incentives were provided in the form of tax subsidies for export promotion, research and development, and other purposes. Productive efficiency and economies of scale were sought by various types of conglomeration, including government-sponsored mergers. Interest rate controls were combined with credit rationing. Low interest rates were granted to preferred borrowers by government and quasi-government financial institutions. Licensing and approval authority were used to channel scarce resources into officially approved activities and to coordinate investment in plant and equipment. One of the most important instruments was also the most amorphous, namely, administrative guidance (*gyōsei shidō*). Administrative guidance, which is nonstatutory, depends for its effectiveness on "voluntary" compliance; it takes the form of advice, suggestions, or innuendos, in many cases communicated orally. In the course of time, administrative guidance came to assume increasing importance as the targets of industrial policy changed and as some statutory instruments of control were relinquished. By its administration of controls, as well as by its resistance to liberalization of trade and capital movements, Japan, in effect, wrote the textbook for practitioners of industrial policy and economic planning in developing countries, including Brazil.

In the implementation of their industrial policy, Japanese authorities encouraged the phasing out and phasing in of industries in accordance with the changing circumstances of Japan's industrial transition. In doing so, they observed three principal criteria that were appropriate to the accommodation between the domestic and external sectors of the economy. The main criterion for selection of "sunset" industries that were to be phased out and "sunrise" industries that were to be phased in concerned their potential contribution to the balance of payments. The application of that criterion can be seen in the replacement of traditional handicraft and labor-intensive industries by heavy and chemical industries, which in turn are now being superseded by high-technology activities. Progressively, the changing industrial structure yields a growing domestically value-added component of output. Second, the accommodation can be traced in terms of the expatriation of sunset industries by means of Japanese direct foreign investment. Third, the transfer of declining industries abroad has been accelerated by means of Japan's economic cooperation programs.

Accordingly, it its rationale, Japan's foreign economic policy is essentially an extension or transposition of its domestic industrial policy. Foreign policy attempts to implement the objectives of domestic industrial policy on the international plane. Thus industrial policy has evolved into geopolitical strategy. (This helps to account for the perennial conflict between the Foreign Ministry and the MITI concerning their respective claims to economic turf.) Both industrial policy and foreign economic policy are founded on identical theoretical considerations. Starting from the concept of Japan as a workshop that processes imported raw materials and exports finished goods, both are designed to maximize Japan's comparative advantage in the world economy. Both attempt to do so by arranging a division of labor between Japan and its trade partners that will optimize their complementarity. After the Pacific war, Japan generalized this concept in relations with the whole world; it professed "friendship with all" and espoused the doctrine of "separation of economics from politics"(*seikei bunri*). The latter slogan was a declaration to the effect that the U.S.–Japan "partnership" would play no role in the determination of Japan's trade patterns. In other words, Japan's external commerce would not be subject to the dictates of the East-West conflict. Furthermore, in terms of the headquarters country scenario, "separation of economics from politics" means that economics will be bureaucratized rather than politicized in government-to-government affairs. The openly adversarial, confrontational style of Japan's present relations with the United States and the European Community, among others, will be suppressed in private deal-making sessions of the bureaucrats. A precondition for this regime will be the nature of structural evolution in the world economy. It is this structural evolution, prior to any premeditated policy, that implies the Japanese scenario itself. In a world of giant oligopolies, cartels and neocartels, allocated markets, and administered prices, the Japanese bureaucracy would be very much at home in operating behind the scenes in its traditional fashion. It would mediate, moderate, and coordinate; it would seek consensus with foreign governments on behalf of Japanese business. In collaborating with the economic development plans of countries such as Brazil, it would concentrate on opening doors for Japanese firms by organizing cartel arrangements and by promoting "agreed specialization" or division of labor, as discussed below.

## Scenario of Japan as a Headquarters Country

At this point a scenario may be outlined, based on Japan's national interests, historical experience, institutional characteristics, and structural incentives.

Among American Japanologists it is no longer fashionable to attribute Japan's economic performance to the "unique" human or cultural characteristics (values, ethics, ideology) of the Japanese people or their institutional arrangements. Instead, causality is attributed to the dynamics of "the market," with scant credit to the contribution of government and its economic planning. The latter view can be carried too far. It is apparent that planning from the top could not alone have accounted for the complex evolution of Japan's postwar economy. In Japan, however, by means of joint policy planning, consultative councils, and the community of interest between big business and the economic ministries, as well as by the actual partnership between government and business in major development projects at home and abroad, the institutional role of government is an intrinsic element in the structure of "the market" itself. Japan's potential emergence as a headquarters country is implicit in the structure of the Japanese "market" (a term by no means explained by the definition of that word in other capitalist countries) in relation to structural market factors in the United States, Brazil, and elsewhere. The functions of the Japanese government and its joint planning role with big business are key operational elements of the scenario. Assuredly, no postwar ministry has ever published a document describing plans for a world economic empire to be "coordinated" (a favorite Japanese government term) from Tokyo. It would be naive to assume, however, that the Japanese government-business bureaucracy is oblivious of structural changes in Japan and in the world economy and the trends and opportunities that such changes imply. It also would be naive to ignore the fact that the bureaucracy is more ready, willing, and able to take advantage of these trends in its own interest as well as in the national interest of Japan than is correspondingly the case in the United States. Moreover, the scenario presented here does not imply that the Japanese "headquarters" is an arrangement that could be *imposed* on other nations. It would arise from structural factors, Japanese planning, and symbiotic interests of the parties concerned.

Historically, Japan's centripetal propensity toward the headquarters form of government was revealed during the Tokugawa period when the paradox of "centralized feudalism" was contrived by the shogunate. In 1603, Tokyo (known then as Edo) became the headquarters of feudal Japan. Later, it became the headquarters of the Japanese empire, the Greater East Asia Coprosperity Sphere. After the Occupation, which attempted to disperse governmental authority, Japanese institutions of all kinds remained centralized in Tokyo to an inordinate degree. Central controls are implemented in Japan by both governmental and private authorities, but the dividing line between them is not always clear. Government influence on policies of the private sector may be imposed by either direct or indirect controls. Here again, it is difficult to define boundaries between Japan's direct and indirect controls, as well as between its statutory and informal or administrative controls. Hence there may be no basis for a distinction between government and private policies in terms of either their source or intention. (Within the private sector, it is difficult for outsiders to identify or evaluate the controls imposed by oligopoly firms—or the trade associations they dominate—on small and medium-sized satellite firms and subcontractors.) As suggested below, moreover, present trends in Japan and in the world economy imply a widening area within which Japanese business will voluntarily find a community of interests with government. The distinction between government and private controls will thus become even more ambiguous.

### The Geopolitical Approach

In general terms, Japan's national interests are those of any sovereign nation: survival, independence, continuity, stability, and economic security.[6] At the operational level, however, its attention is focused chiefly on the objectives of stability and security. While never deviating from these objectives, Japan has been highly flexible and pragmatic in its attempts to achieve them by international means.

When Japan's inperialist strategy was succeeded by the mercantilist approach, its first foreign initiatives after the Occupation were in the commercial category—it reestablished the overseas sales offices of the major trading companies. These offices served to promote the exports of Japan's traditional labor-intensive products, chiefly textiles, which at that stage were essential to economic rehabilitation. Next, in the heavy and chemical industry stage, priority in direct investment abroad was assigned to the "develop and import" (*kaihatsu yunyu*) policy, designed to assure Japan of secure and diversified sources of raw materials. This was done by means of joint venture development of mineral resources in southeast Asia, Latin America, the Middle East, and Oceania. What was especially interesting about these projects is that they yielded for Japan the virtue of the defect of its inadequate domestic resource structure. Japan achieved a competitive advantage in the cost of its raw materials not *in spite of* but *because of* its domestic deficiency. The supplies it received from abroad were of the highest quality and lowest price per unit of any in the world; they were delivered, moreover, by the cheapest form of transportation, namely, ocean freight. Since the end of World War II, by measures such as subsidies to shipbuilding and innovations in ship construction, Japan's global strategy has included the objective of keeping down the cost of world shipping. Inland transportation also was reduced, moreover, by means of the coastal siting of the principal import-processing plants. These evolving strategies reflect the parallel between Japan's industrial policy and its foreign economic policy, as well as the accommodation between the domestic and external sectors of the Japanese economy.

The transposition of domestic industrial policy to the international plane was reflected in further types of direct foreign investment. Impelled by the growing shortage of industrial sites and by environmental deterioration within Japan proper (the former was a more important factor than the latter), a beginning was made in the expatriation of Japan's heavy and chemical industries. It was spurred also by the cost of energy. While the demand for industrial inputs of imported energy and other raw materials rose at a rate exceeding the rate of growth of the GNP, the rising price of energy during the 1970s reduced the competitive power of Japan's resource-processing industries, such as aluminum smelting, steelmaking, and oil refining. Second, Japan's direct investment abroad constituted a form of "economic cooperation" with developing countries that aspired to process their own raw materials and whose "resources nationalism" was stimulating import-substitution programs. Japan's economic cooperation was thus conducive to the natural evolution of its industrial policy into a geopolitical strategy. Third, a further element of the geopolitical approach was the opportunity it provided for the export of plants and equipment from Japan and the dependency relationship (in terms of financing, maintenance, management, and distribution of output) that this established between Japan and its clients in the developing countries.

Japan's direct foreign investment has been performed in both defensive and offensive modes, by both push and pull. Defensively, its investments in developing countries have been induced by their resources nationalism, their import-substitution programs, and their infant industry protectionism. Likewise in the advanced countries, protection of declining industries induced Japan to invest for the sake of defending its established markets, especially in consumer electronics, machinery, and automobiles. In these cases, the geopolitical gambit is to *utilize* foreign protectionism on behalf of Japanese enterprises that seek shelter abroad. In its offensive mode, these same investments serve to coordinate Japan's external relations with the transformation of its indigenous industrial structure. In both its defensive and offensive modes, the rationale of Japan's direct foreign investment may include a calculated disaggregation (or "unbundling") of the production process, with some stages being assigned abroad and some retained at home. In arranging this allegedly "horizontal" distribution of production between Japan and the host country, Japan retains for itself the higher value-added operations that yield the best rates of return. In the era of its industrial maturity, this is an example of the way in which Japan maintains a balance between offensive and defensive strategies as its competitive relationships begin to outweigh its complementary relationships with developing nations such as Brazil.

"Economic cooperation" is among the means of implementing these policies on the international plane. It is to be distinguished from "economic aid," as understood in the United States. Economic cooperation includes three distinct concepts. The first refers to "satisfying human needs." In terms of the amount of funds appropriated, however, this is a minor category; it has an inauspicious future as part of the economic cooperation program. Second and third are the ambiguous concepts of "international industrial adjustment" and "international economic security" (about which more below). At the political level, the role of economic cooperation in Japan's foreign economic policy is hinted at by Miyohei Shinohara, chairman of the Institute of Developing Economies, an MITI think tank. He points out that by means of both loans and investments, Japanese government participation is needed in order to help developing countries cope with uncertainties that beset the construction of huge projects requiring enormous amounts of capital. Accordingly, in the administration of economic cooperation, semigovernmental organizations, including the Overseas Economic Cooperation Fund (OECF) and the Japan Export-Import Bank, participate in financing such projects. The nature of these projects may thus be determined by Japanese official financing agencies rather than by the host government or participating private Japanese suppliers. Shinohara warns that "should the construction of a mammoth project be agreed upon at the political level and then forced upon industry, it will run the risk of developing into a 'political boomerang.' " Moreover, it is necessary to "avoid having Japanese overseas investment projects influenced by politics and by the irresponsible statements of Japanese politicians."[7] It may be inferred that Shinohara's remarks apply to Japan's participation in the mammoth state projects of Brazil, which constitute more than half of the Brazilian economy.[8]

Concerning the international division of labor, Shinohara adds that what is needed is an "understanding" or plan of agreed specialization among nations on a regional or worldwide basis.[9] This anti–free market theme has had a long, unadvertised existence in Japanese big business, academic, and government policy circles.[10]

*The Headquarters Scenario*

In this scenario, Japan as a headquarters country is defined in terms of its institutional structure, its geopolitical strategy, and the policies by which its strategy is implemented. In Japan, domestic institutional arrangements have evolved by consensus, conditioned by the perceived interests, needs, and constraints of the Japanese nation, and in pragmatic response to its contingencies. As a result of its social, cultural, and economic institutions, Japan's national interest prevails over special private interests to a degree uncommon among nations. As a result, it seems that the whole is greater than the sum of the parts. Evidence that Japanese institutional arrangements reflect its national interest can be seen in its cultural norms (which promote stability), its methods of economizing (such as its adaptation and improvement of the inventions of others, economizing on space, and promotion of saving versus consumption), and its arrangements for coping with risk (such as the socialization of risk in the financial system). By virtue of its "external imperative," the power of Japan's domestic institutional arrangements—as in the case of industrial policy—has repercussions on the international plane. Accordingly, for structural reasons, Japan's foreign economic stategy (including the strategy of this scenario), which is determined by its national interests and its institutional arrangements, is in given circumstances almost obviously predictable.

Among the foundations of Japan's emergence as a headquarters country is the saving propensity of its people. The interaction of that propensity with the structural propensity toward a surplus in its foreign trade account results in capital outflow and the acquisition of foreign assets. (The latter propensity is induced by Japan's industrial and fiscal policies.) According to the Bank for International Settlements, (BIS), in 1985, Japan's gross domestic saving amounted to 32.1 percent of GNP, the highest in the industrial world, and its net external lending amounted to 3.9 percent of GNP. (During the same year, U.S. gross domestic saving amounted to 14.0 percent of GNP, among the lowest in the industrial world, and net external borrowing amounted to 2.8 percent of GNP.) At the end of 1985, Japan emerged as the world's leading creditor nation, with net foreign assets of $129.8 billion. (At the same time, the United States became the world's foremost debtor nation, with net foreign liabilities of $107.4 billion.) By 1990, according to forecasts of various public and private agencies, Japan's net external assets will amount to more than $400 billion. (By 1990, U.S. net foreign liabilities will probably exceed $500 billion.) The increase in Japan's foreign assets implies a rise in its political as well as its international economic power. In this context, Ezra Vogel has persuasively discussed the prospects for a "Pax Nipponica."[11]

The sources of Japan's prospective role as a headquarters country are not merely structural, or "unconscious"; they also rest on policy support. Japanese protectionism is conspicuous among the policy instruments that reinforce the structural factors. Following World War II, in accordance with Japan's industrial policy, foreign investment was entirely excluded or limited to token entry in sectors designated for development. Import competition was likewise restricted. Formerly, these policies were applied in the low- and middle-technology sectors. At present, they are being applied in the financial and high-technology fields. Lack of reciprocity is a notorious fact of life in Japan's financial sector. In 1985, after years of negotiation, four U.S. firms were allowed to buy seats on the Tokyo stock exchange. It cannot be argued that in financial services the United States "lacks persistence" or fails to supply what Japanese consumers want. Japanese nontariff barriers remain even in the construction field. In 1986, the Japanese government excluded foreign firms from bidding on the initial stages of one of Japan's major public works programs, the $6 billion Kansai International Airport in Osaka Bay. Exclusion of foreigners concentrates economic control in Japanese hands. Japanese "members of the club" are less likely to be maverick, more susceptible to administrative guidance, and more acquiescent to the protocol of Japanese government-business collaboration.[12] Moreover, even within Japan itself there are insiders and outsiders. The latter accept their circumstances. Should foreigners not do likewise?

Culturally, this acceptance is based on the Japanese principle that all men are not created equal. Japan's social and cultural conventions impose a vertical, hierarchical structure, one that distinguishes between superiors and inferiors in every human or inanimate relationship. This is the institutional basis for the Japanese passion—as individuals and as a nation—to be ranked as "number one." Rank, furthermore, has its privileges, such as the imposition of social or economic controls, including international controls. In Japan, business has been subject to both government and private-sector controls; historically, when government and business have collaborated, the government has assumed the leading role. In this context, during the liberalization of recent decades, the shrinking role of government has been an aberration.

To a degree, economic liberalization was permitted in Japan during a period of expansion both at home and abroad. An interventionist reaction set in during the mid-1980s when the rate of increase in world trade and the rate of growth of Japan's GNP were slowing down, and when growth projections were inauspicious. Neocartelism promoted by the United States, among others, contributed to interventionism by the Japanese government, thus unconsciously serving the latter's antiliberalization propensities. Neocartelism springs from the fact that its trade partners are no longer willing to accept chronic deficits as a "normal" feature of doing business with Japan. Apart from market-sharing agreements in the form of "voluntary export controls" and "orderly marketing agreements," government intervention has been induced by the fact that trade conflict has become too vicious to be resolved at the industry level; conciliation must be politically arranged. Similarly, antimarket elements of the world economy such as "national champion" firms, exchange restrictions, and the increasing prominence of state-owned trading enterprises will increasingly require government intervention in order to open doors for Japanese firms abroad. In responding to these and other changes in its external environment, Japan is wholly pragmatic and self-serving. Institutionally, it is also much better organized than the United States for policy response. Its foreign economic policy administration is centralized in two ministries, the Ministry of International Trade and Industry (MITI) and the Ministry of Finance (MOF). (Several other ministries, such as Agriculture, Transportation, and even Welfare, may make marginal contributions.) Concentration of foreign economic policy-making authority in Japan is conducive to effective implementation of the headquarters country strategy by facilitating tradeoffs in international negotiations concerning miscellaneous categories of economic and political issues. In the United States, authority for making foreign economic policy is inefficiently dispersed among various uncoordinated agencies and thus is significantly susceptible to the influence of special interests at the expense of the national interest.

Japan's strength as a nation lies in its ability to find the institutional means of compensating for its inherent vulnerability. This is also the "secret" of its economic miracle and one of the basic elements in the headquarters country scenario. Instrumentally, among the key institutions of that scenario are the *sogo shosha* (general trading companies) and the *keiretsu* (*zaibatsu* successors) with which they are affiliated. The *sogo shosha* control the greatest centralized commercial network of production, distribution, and communication facilities existing in the world today. Moreover, the *sogo shosha* are looking for new missions. In the age of high technology, they must rely less on domestic customers who order shiploads of bulk commodities and raw materials. Instead, they must expand their "third country" activities: they must provide facilities to such countries as Brazil and the United States for transactions with nations other than Japan. Japan's nine major *sogo shosha* (Mitsui, Mitsubishi, C. Itoh, Marubeni, Sumitomo, Nissho Iwai, Toyomenka, Nichimen, and Kanematsu-Gosho) have all established corporate development departments for the purpose of identifying new missions and new forms of enterprise in which they can utilize their enormous technical, financial, management, and planning capabilities. With regard to developing countries such as Brazil, they can offer their expertise in the organization and management of the traditional low- and medium-technology industries that are being phased out in Japan. They can transfer Japanese technology, organize consortiums for large-scale resource and infrastructure projects, and find markets for exportable output. They are specialists in working out the problems of shifting from one type of product to another. Within Japan, the greater the rate of change in industrial structure, the greater the role the *sogo shosha* have played. They can serve Brazil in the same way. With regard to countries such as the United States, the *sogo shosha* are providing their deal-making and market-making services in the high-technology, biotechnology, and information industies. As knowledge-intensive organizations, the *sogo shosha* make many of the decisions associated with Japan's role as an exporter of capital. Their functions include the financing of projects by raising funds outside as well as inside Japan, using multiple currencies, providing the lowest available interest rates, and bearing risk. With the assistance of the Japanese government bureaucracy, the *sogo shosha* are able to break through protectionist barriers by means of countertrade and neocartels organized at the political level. In many of their activities, they are supported by Japanese government agencies such as the Overseas Economic Cooperation Fund (OECF). In performing these tasks from Japan as a headquarters, the *sogo shosha* mark Japan as a vanguard country in the world economy.

Given these institutional instruments and technical capabilities for coping with change, what is the strategy in which they will be employed? In contemplating its strategy, the present condition of the world economy constitutes both a predicament and an opportunity for Japan. As described earlier, the predicament is largely one of instability, arising—in Peter Drucker's term—from "uncoupling" of the world economy.[13] Opportunity arises from the fact that in an uncoupled world economy there is an increasing need for the types of intermediary services that Japan is preeminently equipped to provide. In a more profound sense, however, Japan's opportunity arises from the antimarket trends that have been set in motion by the very instability that has been unleashed, for external antimarket trends enable and encourage Japan to follow its hereditary bent for management rather than liberalization of its external sector. They allow it to build on its strength as the world's leading creditor nation and leading exporter of capital: financial control augurs operational control. In the interest of reducing "excessive competition," they encourage Japan to sponsor neocartels and other external collusive arrangements that are the counterpart of its domestic trade restrictions, such as registered and unregistered cartels, "customary relationships," exclusive "channels," sole-agent franchises, and the like. Instead of acquiescing to the demands of others for "voluntary export restraints," as heretofore, Japan would take the initiative with other governments in organizing and policing trade restraints for both itself and its trade partners. In doing so, the Japanese government would enlarge the area of its partnership with business in managing and coordinating the network of Japanese branches, subsidiaries, and affiliates abroad, for the latter would be subject to the agreements as well.

In its forecast for the year 2000, the Economic Planning Agency (EPA) has estimated that 20 percent of Japan's total production will be located offshore. Within Japan proper, in the secondary sector, high-technology industries will predominate. The tertiary sector will constitute 64.2 percent of the total Japanese economy. By the turn of the century, the EPA calculates that Japan's direct foreign investment will amount to US$300 billion, exceeding the total of U.S. direct foreign investment in 1985, which amounted to US$232.7 billion.[14] Indeed at present, LDCs and NICs are competing with each other for the privilege of being "exploited" by Japan's direct foreign investment.[15]

In the headquarters scenario, Japan challenges the United States by utilizing world trends instead of resisting them. The strategy is both direct and indirect. Directly, while the United States defends its declining smokestack industries, Japan is liquidating and expatriating them. Indirectly, on this front, Japan's development assistance to Brazil is of enormous weight. Indeed, the consequences of Japan's economic activities in Brazil are greatly disproportionate to their scale. By its assistance in the construction of infrastructure and heavy and chemical industries in Brazil, Japan is strengthening Brazil's competitive power in the low- and middle-technology industries that will seek markets in the United States and in third areas where the United States is fighting to maintain its market share. The Brazilian case is thus a model of Japanese stategy in challenging the United States through the aspirations of others. Japan's policy of promoting a "horizontal division of labor" in the world economy is a euphemism for this strategy.

It can be anticipated, furthermore, that Japan will emerge one day as an *importer* of the low- and middle-technology goods that the United States urgently needs to sell. At that juncture, however, the United States will be in competition with the "new Japans" for a position in the Japanese import market. Japan's trade balance will turn to deficit; its services account—including interest and dividends on its direct and portfolio foreign investments—will turn to surplus. Japan's strategy will have contrived to smother its bilateral trade friction with the United States while promoting multilateral friction between the United States and the "new Japans." In the high-technology sector, where Japan and the United States meet in direct competition, the giant oligopoly firms of the two nations will no doubt work out a modus vivendi on a live and let-live basis.[16]

In the meantime, by virtue of the yen revaluation of 1985–1986, there was real distress among the small and medium-sized enterprises of Japan, as well as among some major enterprises in the declining industry sector. For domestic political purposes, the Japanese government commiserated with these firms and attempted to moderate the pains of their liquidation. It assisted the reallocation of resources in declining industries by means of cheap credit and other devices. Here again, the institutional means for the socialization of risk in Japan can be seen in action. However, when the Japanese government agreed in the G-5 meeting of September 1985 to cooperate in yen revaluation, it did not do so out of sympathy with the United States for its poor export performance. It did not propose to relinquish its "embarrassing" trade surplus as a philanthropic gesture toward its trade partners. On the contrary, Japan agreed to yen revaluation in accordance with its own industrial policy for phasing out sunset industries at home and for the purpose of accelerating its direct foreign investment.

Similarly, as a debating point, the Japanese call attention to the inconsistency of U.S. demands for trade liberalization while it prepares protectionist legislation specifically targeted against Japan. In reality, however, such legislation helps the Japanese government to accelerate its program for the transformation of industry. In this case, among others, the "enemy" is really the friend, albeit unconsciously so. Sophisticated Japanese bureaucrats are fully aware of this contradiction, which they deliberately exploit in order to divert pressure from themselves. Moreover, while relinquishing market share in manufactured goods, Japan is rapidly acquiring market share in the liberalized market for international financial services. In 1986, according to the Bank for International Settlements, the share of the international banking business held by Japanese banks exceeded the portion held by U.S. banks. The struggle for market share in international financial services is rapidly extinguishing minor players and promoting the economic concentration that is a prominent feature of the headquarters country scenario. Thus Japan utilizes both antimarket trends in physical trade and the promarket liberalization of international finance in the implementation of its strategy.[17]

In its broadest aspect, the headquarters country scenario transcends bilateral complementarity as a rationale for Japan's relations with other countries. Beyond this simple concept, the strategy contemplates the coordination of sets of complementary relationships among third nations. In this perspective, Japan emerges as an orchestrator of complementarities rather than as a "donkey" or "locomotive" in the world economy. Here again, Japan utilizes the virtue of its defects. As has been demonstrated, its unbalanced physical resource structure was no bar to its achieving an economic "miracle." In the Headquarters scenario, as an orchestrator of relationships among others, Japan's cultural isolation and military weakness are positive advantages: as an outsider it can remain substantially unaligned. By means of "friendship with all," its *sogo shosha* can maintain business ties even with parties (such as Iran and Iraq) that are engaged in mortal combat with each other. Not only among such adversaries but elsewhere, the *sogo shosha* control exclusive "channels" in production, distribution, and finance throughout their global networks. These will be utilized in the orchestration of complementarities among third countries. In a protectionist world, the *sogo shosha* have exceptional capabilities for the arrangement of countertrade, barter, and switch transactions that can overcome foreign-exchange controls and other types of trade restriction. In their domestic economy, the Japanese are highly aware of the strategic importance of domination of distribution networks. In the world at large, domination of distribution facilities may come to be of more strategic importance than productive efficiency. Brazil's increasing dependence on Japan lies in this framework.

Historically, from a Japanese point of view, the *sogo shosha* have served as eyes and ears of the Japanese government. Their information and communication facilities and intelligence sources surpass those of the government itself. Possessing this infrastructure, they are cast as leading players in the headquarters country scenario. In the postwar period they have worked closely with the government in the allocation and administration of its cartel arrangements. Increasingly, the *sogo shosha* and their *keiretsu* partners in Japan will serve the bureaucracy in formulating and implementing deals with foreign governments. Tie-ups by means of Japanese loans or investments, by cartels or neocartels, or by exclusive distributorships within a network of branches, subsidiaries, and other affiliates will be instruments for the maintenance and expansion of Japan's market share. For Japan as a headquarters, these networks will serve to diversify its markets and sources of supply, thus contributing to the attainment of "comprehensive economic security." As the political broker in intergovernmental arrangements, the bureaucracy will once again become indispensable to big business and will enjoy a renaissance. This, incidentally, would be in stark contrast with the adversarial relationship between government and business in the United States, where a standard complaint against Washington is that it fails to represent private firms in their attempts to make deals abroad.

The Japanese government, in contrast to the American government, will serve its own purposes as well as those of the private sector by making capital out of the politicization of economic affairs. In Japan, the community of interest between government and business will generate new bureaucratic careers, especially in the economic ministries. The government-business partnership not only will be engaged in managing, coordinating, and manipulating a world network of subsidiaries and affiliates, but also will be active in promoting cartel and quasi-cartel arrangements. International cartelism is Japan's preferred response to the paradox of a world in which protectionism is increasing while interdependence among nations increases as well. The government will take the initiative in organizing, implementing, and policing "voluntary" export and import controls. The market shares assigned in accordance with these arrangements effectively create government cartels, or neocartels. Collateral to its implementation of cartel arrangements, the bureaucracy can be of help in organizing coproduction, cofinancing, and countertrade deals between Japan and other nations. In the same context, "agreed specialization" calls for further government sponsorship and surveillance. By means of neocartelism, Japan will *utilize* the impairment of the multilateral free-market system for its own benefit and achieve a new consensus between government and business in doing so.

## Brazil's Place in the Japanese Scenario

As long-run players, the Japanese are fascinated by Brazil, "the country of the future." Brazil is already important in its own right as the leading country of Latin America. Occupying almost half the South American continent, it is the fifth largest country in the world, and it holds the sixth largest population and the eighth largest economy. Its combination of self-confidence and immaturity makes it a natural foil for the Japanese. As an official in Brazil's Foreign Ministry remarked, "Everybody in the Brazilian bureaucracy works in accordance with the assumption of 'Manifest Destiny,' although we don't use that expression."[18]

The physical appeal of Brazil attracted immigration from Japan as early as 1908, a short time after the advent of Japan's modern period under the emperor Meiji. The Japanese colony, which by 1986 numbered approximately 1 million immigrants and their descendants, is the largest expatriate group of ethnic Japanese in the world. As established and respected members of Brazilian society, they provided a base of operations for Japanese economic activities in Brazil following World War II. Without the support of the Brazilian-Japanese, Japan's business approach to Brazil would have been less readily arranged. Japan's official development assistance to Brazil also was more substantial than it would have been in the absence of the nisei community. After its major corporations established their own foothold in Brazil, however, the assistance of the Brazilian-Japanese diminished as a factor in Japan's calculations as to the benefits of economic relations with Brazil.

The prime factors in Japan's encounter with Brazil include the compatible views of the two nations and the role of Brazil in Japan's geopolitical strategy. Compatibility begins with the common passion of Japan and Brazil for economic development, as well as their pragmatic approach to attaining it. Brazil emulates Japan's development performance and the methods by which it was achieved.[19] In both countries, pragmatism includes a propensity in favor of economic controls. In their social mores, Brazilians and Japanese share the antidemocratic view that members of society are not all equal: there are superiors and inferiors. They apply this view to nations as well.

At the same time, the the conduct of their relationship, there are plenty of doubts, reservations, and complaints on both the Japanese and Brazilian sides, as discussed below. It is by no means the intention of this study to convey the impression that all is peaches and cream in Japan's encounter with Brazil. Nevertheless, their partnership has a structural foundation. That foundation is explicitly revealed in the scenario of Japan's geopolitical strategy.

In the past, to overcome the defects of its resource endowment, Japan sought foreign partners with which it could establish relations based on direct complementarity. As mentioned earlier, the headquarters country scenario transcends bilateral complementarity. In the case of Brazil, it implies support for projects such as Carajas and development of the Cerrado, which will reduce and stabilize the price of primary products, including food and minerals, worldwide. Second, it implies support for the development of Brazilian capability and competitive power in the low- and middle-technology fields. The indirect benefit to Japan of these developments will exceed the direct benefit. Key projects in these categories are supported by "symbolic" participation of the Japanese government.

In the primary products field, Eliezer Batista, Brazil's leading industrial statesman and former president of Companhia Vale do Rio Doce (CVRD), is famous for his diplomacy with the Japanese on behalf of Brazilian development projects.[20] CVRD is the world's leading exporter of iron ore. By 1988, it is expected to export 35 million tons a year. Japanese support to CVRD has certainly not been provided on the assumption that it would ship its entire output to Japan. Instead, the strategy contemplates the indirect advantage to Japan of promoting competition among Brazil, Australia, Malaysia, and other primary producers in the world at large. (In 1986, for the same purpose, Japan continued to invest in Australian mining projects even though the immediate prospects of that industry in Australia were poor.)

In agricultural products, Brazil at present competes with the United States in soybeans, frozen orange juice concentrate, tobacco, and corn. Corn and wheat, incidentally, are not exported from Brazil as yet. But merely by increasing its domestic self-sufficiency ratio, Brazil affects the world supply-demand balance in such a way as to effectively put pressure on the United States that redounds indirectly to the benefit of Japan. Similarly in the case of soybeans, Brazil supplies only a small proportion of Japan's import needs. With a view to shifting the demand-supply balance for soybeans in the world as a whole, however, after President Nixon's soybean embargo in the summer of 1973, the Japanese government helped Brazil to start its soybean expansion program. Within a decade, from virtually a standstill start, it became the world's second leading exporter of soybeans. Brazil has the world's greatest potential for repeating this feat within a wide range of primary products. According to a Japanese official who participated in his government's decision to provide funds for the soybean project, its purpose was to "keep the United States honest." This is an explicit example of the headquarters country strategy in operation. It was designed to augment the world supply and to reduce and stabilize the price of Japan's imports of soybeans from any source. Accordingly, the fact that Brazil remains a relatively minor supplier of soybeans to the Japanese market is beside the point. By the same token, in transcending simple bilateral complementarity, Japan's strategy overcomes the need for diversification of its sources of supply. This makes it more convenient for the Japanese government to manage its balance of payments affairs without reference to its logistic consequences.

In the secondary sector of Brazil's economy, the purpose of Japanese loans, direct investment, and transfer of technology is calculated to augment Brazil's role as a supplier of low- and middle-technology products and intermediate goods. Brazil is one of the NICs to which Japan is expatriating its own capacity for these products. Thus while joining hands with Japan ostensibly for its own interest, Brazil accommodates Japan's industrial policy on the international plane. In assisting Brazilian import substitution along these lines, Japan has contributed to the construction of infrastructure projects and provided the services of its *sogo shosha* for the foreign distribution of Brazilian products, including exports to the United States. The extent of *sogo shosha* export promotion in Brazil is not reportable because their statistics are not public information. Similarly, the role of the Japanese government in encouraging direct foreign investment or loans to Brazil cannot be fully evaluated because the participation of official or quasi-official Japanese financial institutions in development projects is usually purely nominal: it is intended essentially to give notice that the Japanese government approves of the project and implicitly guarantees that it will not be allowed to fail. In large infrastructure projects, symbolic participation of the government is indispensable for the mobilization of Japanese consortia. In this case, the Japanese principles of risk aversion and socialization of risk are again in evidence. This reveals also that much of the long-term thinking for which Japanese enterprise is justly praised depends partly on the leadership and planning of government agencies.

While the approach of the "Pacific Century" has inspired the United States to think of the Asian alternative to its European "special relation," Japan's strategy now extends beyond Asia to Latin America. Until the mid-1970s, Japanese direct foreign investment was mainly directed toward Asia. Recently, however, its investment activities in that region have stagnated. During JFY1984, Japan's direct foreign investment in Latin America was 22.6 percent of its total direct foreign investment (DFI) as compared with 16.0 percent in Asia. Apart from Panama (which serves as a tax haven and a country of registry for flag-of-convenience vessels), Brazil is the leading destination for Japanese DFI in Latin America. In JFY1984, the aggregate stock of Japan's DFI in Brazil amounted to US$4,274 million, or 6.0 percent of its total DFI. As a destination for Japan's aggregate DFI, Brazil ranked third after the United States and Indonesia. At the end of 1985, incidentally, the total of U.S. DFI in Brazil amounted to US$9,480 million.

Japan's collaboration with Brazil in the development of infrastructure includes projects in hydroelectric power, aluminum smelter projects in the Amazon, forest and pulp development enterprises, fisheries, steel, mining, port facilities, and irrigation programs. From a Japanese point of view, besides their long-term and indirect advantages, such projects offer immediately profitable opportunities for providing finance, technology, capital goods, and management services to Brazil. They also incur low visibility, as compared with consumer goods promotion that splashes Japanese names in neon lights across the landscape. (The absence of Japanese automobiles in Brazil helps to make it less conspicuous as an "economic imperialist.") Infrastructure projects also create contacts between the Japanese and Brazilian governments which may facilitate future political and economic collaboration.

Among other projects that enhance Japan's image as a partner in Brazilian development is the Global Infrastructure Fund (GIF) proposal announced by the Mitsubishi Research Institute in 1977. Clearly the concept was promulgated by Mitsubishi with the concurrence of the government and as a reflection of establishment thinking.[21] Among its various components, Brazil is particularly interested in the Asia port project, which aims at vastly increasing transportation capacity and reducing transportation cost for the export of primary products from South America—especially from Brazil—to the East Asian region. The Asia port concept was discussed by President Joao Figueiredo and Prime Minister Yasuhiro Nakasone on the occasion of the visit of the former to Japan in May of 1984.[22] Another project of the GIF proposal is the plan for construction of a second Panama Canal. In June of 1986, the Japan Economic Cooperation Agency opened bidding on a US$20 million study to determine the feasibility and cost of the project. The study is to be completed by 1991. (Mitsubishi Corporation was among the construction firms that filed applications.[23])

Brazil is a natural partner for Japan in the headquarters country scenario. By virtue of its mammoth state enterprises, the Brazilian economy is highly concentrated. Collaboration between the managers of that economy and those in the Japanese headquarters would promise further economies of scale in production and distribution, as well as bureaucratic aggrandizement to both. As a result of the debt crisis, more than ever before Brazilian government intervention in the nation's foreign economic affairs has become comprehensive and detailed. This expands the possibilities for negotiations between Japanese and Brazilian bureaucrats. As a consequence of the debt crisis, discussions concerning the transformation of debt into equity are being conducted at the government level. In these negotiations, the national, bureaucratic, and private-sector interests of both nations appear to be consistent; therefore, all parties can openly pursue their own interests. As seen by bureaucrats, their own "manifest destiny" is one of the motivating elements of the headquarters country scenario.

The various financial and nonfinancial consequences of the debt crisis, moreover, can be negotiated between Japan and Brazil in such a way as to accommodate both in their respective desires to reduce "overdependence" on the United States. In the outcome, liberalization would be reversed; the Japanese economy would be internationalized by other means, in fulfillment of its national and private-sector interests and in the interests of its bureaucracy. Japan's geopolitical vision would then have resolved in its own favor the paradox of increasing nationalism in a world that is increasingly interdependent. A Japanese version of "harmony" and "consensus" would prevail in the international economy.

## The U.S. Policy Predicament

In responding to the Japanese leadership challenge, the United States has been playing football against an opponent who plays judo—in which the strength of the adversary is used *against* him. (Examples are offered below.) Structurally, moreover, the open system and the individualist institutions of the United States are less well suited than those of Japan to the regime of allocated markets and administered prices in the nationalistic, protectionist, oligopolistic world that is now emerging. Although the global objectives of U.S. multinational firms may seem similar to those of Japanese *keiretsu* and *sogo shosha,* their activities are not orchestrated in terms of a headquarters strategy, they lack the collaboration, guidance, and guarantees of their government, and their strategy is relatively short term. During the past two decades, both publicly and behind the scenes, the Japanese government-business partnership has been making plans for the year 2000, while U.S. firms have been preoccupied with the quarterly expectations of their stockholders. In the Brazilian Cerrado project, for example, in which the Japanese government has sponsored the participation of private firms, the planning horizon is 30 to 50 years. Instead, as a major primary products producer, the United States has felt threatened by the Cerrado project and has relinquished leadership by taking a hostile attitude toward it. Thus from a Brazilian point of view, U.S. policies lack coherence and long-term consistency in favor of Brazilian development aspirations. Indeed, apart from its theoretical and highly compromised nondiscriminatory multilateralism, Washington has no Brazilian policy.

In style, as well as in substance, the U.S. leadership role lacks credibility from a Brazilian point of view. As seen by Brazilians, the United States attempts to coerce other countries to comply with the American prescription, as in the debt crisis, whether or not it is appropriate to their circumstances. The United States is seen as inconsistent in its practices as compared with its principles. U.S. special interest protectionism is inconsistent with U.S. principles concerning a multilateral, nondiscriminatory, free-trade system in the world economy. The inconsistency has a direct bearing on one of the key issues of the U.S.–Brazil agenda at the present time, namely, the proposal for a GATT round that would bring new areas—financial services, intellectual property, high-technology and trade-related investments—within the purview of GATT. In this as in other matters, such as the U.S. position in East–West confrontation versus Brazil's commitment to nonalignment, there is a structural conflict of interests between the United States and Brazil. In a number of these cases, Japan utilizes the U.S.–Brazil conflict to its own advantage. For example, the conflict between U.S. defense of its declining industries and Brazilian defense of its infant industries provides ideal opportunities for Japan's geopolitical strategy. Even on issues such as those concerning GATT, in which Japan is on the same side as the United States, Japan contrives to remain in the background, while the United States makes the running and serves as a target for Brazilian hostility. A staple feature of the Brazilian press is its reporting on confrontations with the United States concerning trade, debt, and investment issues, while Japan, with which many of the same matters may be under negotiation, is rarely mentioned.

Partly this can be explained by the high degree to which U.S. relations with Brazil have been politicized, while in Japan's case, that effect has been reduced to a minimum. In contrast with Japan, U.S. negotiations with Brazil are conducted openly and on the record, rather than anonymously behind the scenes. There is double jeopardy in this transparency inasmuch as the process of U.S. foreign policy formulation is administratively chaotic and haphazard. Control of economic decision making is dispersed and poorly coordinated among the various agencies (Commerce, Treasury, Defense, Agriculture, USTR, ITC, Council of Economic Advisers, White House staff) that contribute to the policy-making process. Each of these, as well as the U.S. Congress, is subject to pressure from special interests that do not necessarily reflect the U.S. national interest. From the American as well as from the foreign point of view, it is not always clear who makes U.S. foreign economic policy. (In July of 1986 there was open conflict between the U.S. Secretaries of State and Agriculture over the decision to sell subsidized wheat to the Soviet Union.) In the confusion, it is possible for foreign as well as for U.S. special interests to play off one U.S. government agency against another. On the purely legal plane, moreover, there has been some ambiguity as to whether a treaty negotiated by the executive branch or legislation passed by Congress takes precedence in the implementation of U.S. foreign economic policy. In April of 1986, the Supreme Court heard arguments on this issue, which had not been resolved at the present writing.

As a technical feature of the U.S. policy-making process, incidentally, in doing research for this study I was struck by the high degree of specialization among International Monetary Fund (IMF) and U.S. government officials concerned with Brazilian affairs. In particular, they lacked both information and opinions about matters outside the confines of their relatively narrow job descriptions. Balance of payments experts at the IMF said that they were uninformed about domestic aspects of the Brazilian economy. Statisticians were uninformed about institutional arrangements in Brazil as well as about the export consequences of foreign loans to Brazil. In the U.S. Department of Commerce, specialists on trade with Brazil were uninformed about the relation between trade and national income. The office of the U.S. Trade Representative (USTR) is exclusively concerned with trade and investment issues; it takes no account of their interaction with other U.S. foreign policy issues concerning Brazil. In the private sector, U.S. bankers were uninformed about the contribution of their loans to Brazil's export performance. In general, U.S. authorities were uninformed about the real (nonfinancial) effects as contrasted with the financial effects of the debt crisis in Brazil. They also were uninformed about Japanese economic activities in Brazil that paralleled or intersected U.S. affairs in the fields of their expertise. In contrast, in Japan I found that Brazil experts had a much wider view of the Brazilian economy and acute awareness of the implications for Japan of U.S. activities in that country. Among the various explanations for this contrast is the fact that responsibility for formulating foreign economic policy is much more tightly centralized in Japan than in the United States. In Japanese professional ranks, moreover, there are no narrowly specified job descriptions as in the United States. Furthermore, career civil servants are given rotating assignments every 2 or 3 years, which broadens their exposure and point of view.

Whereas Japan's global strategy is based on a transposition of its domestic industrial policy to the international plane, a conflict between domestic and external policy forms part of the U.S. predicament. As it impinges on Brazil, the conflict is apparent in U.S. relations with the World Bank. U.S. policy favors reducing the overhang of the world agricultural surplus, but this directly conflicts with the standard prescription of agricultural expansion as a basic economic development strategy. In the case of Brazilian agriculture, the U.S. farm lobby maintains that U.S. tax dollars are used by the World Bank to subsidize its foreign competitors. By law, moreover, the U.S. director in the World Bank is supposed to vote against a World Bank loan if it could result in injury to U.S. producers.[24] In June of 1986, however, despite the objections of the U.S. farm lobby, a US$500 million loan for restructuring Brazilian agriculture was approved by the World Bank. In the same month, over the objections of the Reagan administration, the World Bank approved a US$500 million loan to finance the expansion and modernization of Brazil's electric power facilities. Brazil's economic development plans have been resisted by the United States in the manufacturing field as well. In December of 1985, U.S. steel companies lobbied against a World Bank loan on behalf of Brazilian steel. Such a campaign on the part of Japanese steel companies would be unthinkable because it would be inconsistent with Japan's geopolitical strategy.

In these cases, the obstructive tactics of special interests conflicted with the national interest of the United States, for in each instance the proposed World Bank loans were designed to finance basic structural reforms in accordance with principles of lending conditionality that U.S. Treasury Secretary James Baker had urged the World Bank to impose. Baker's conditionality principles were calculated to increase the productive efficiency and international competitive power of borrowers in order to enable them to achieve economic growth; this is the only means by which they can become solvent enough to service their external debts.

Ironically, in its zeal for imposing U.S. conditionality rules, the Reagan administration was willing to open the door to further intervention on the part of U.S. special interests in the lending decisions of international development institutions. To enforce those rules, the United States sought to consolidate its veto power over the lending decisions of both the World Bank and the Inter-American Development Bank (IADB). In his October of 1985 plan for solving the third world debt problem, Mr. Baker proposed that in the ensuing 3 years the World Bank and the IADB should increase their lending to heavily indebted nations by 50 percent. In order to perform this task, the IADB requested an increase of US$19.9 billion in capital subscriptions from its membership. In return for its support of this request, however, in 1986 the United States insisted that the majority required for approval of individual loan proposals should be raised from 50 to 65 percent of IADB shareholder votes. The purpose—which was strenuously resisted by Latin American nations—was to make IADB loans subject to a U.S. veto in every case. Possessing such veto power, however, the U.S. government would be more vulnerable to the demands of special interests and more likely to find its own political interests amenable to acceding to such demands. Characteristically, in the United States, domestic policy transcends foreign economic policy. In this respect as well, the United States is at a disadvantage as compared with Japan.

The conflict between U.S. domestic and foreign economic policy is notoriously apparent in the agricultural field. The October of 1985 plan of Secretary Baker for resolving the debt crisis called for an internationalist, market-opening policy on the part of debtors, while the U.S. Farm Act of 1985 was openly protectionist and provided massive export subsidies. Under its so-called market loan program, the U.S. subsidizes exports of rice and cotton at prices lower than the cost of production and lower than prices available to domestic buyers. In a countervailing-duty action against U.S. exports, the Canadian Revenue Department cited seventy-five U.S. federal subsidy programs for U.S. corn growers.[25] Speaking to a World Food Council meeting in Rome, Mr. Richard Lyng, U.S. secretary of agriculture, said that the United States was "now engaging vigorously in some of the practices which we so strongly criticized in the past."[26]

The U.S. policy predicament with regard to Brazil includes an inconsistency concerning symptomatic versus fundamental reform. At the G-5 meeting in September of 1985 and at the Tokyo summit meeting in May of 1986, the United States argued in favor of international coordination of exchange rates as a means of masking the symptoms of its diminished competitive power, but in prescribing preconditions for Brazilian debt relief it demanded fundamental institutional reforms. In relations with Japan, moreover, the United States places the onus for resolution of deficits on the creditor nation, while in relations with Brazil it places the onus on the debtor.

Almost every U.S. action concerning Brazil conveys political overtones.

In general, moreover, the politicization of U.S.–Brazilian issues has re-dounded to the disadvantage of the United States. In 1974, Brazilians were deeply affronted by U.S. "interference" in their nuclear energy program. The offense was gratuitous because Brazil could not change its position on nonproliferation once the United States had politicized the issue. Withdrawal of the U.S. pledge to provide nuclear fuel reprocessing services to Brazil is better remembered there than in the United States and forms part of a foreboding background to more recent U.S.–Brazilian difficulties. Similarly, during the Carter administration, the United States confronted Brazil concerning violations of human rights. In March of 1977, President Ernesto Geisel responded by canceling a 25-year-old military assistance treaty with the United States. Recently, the United States has backed the Brazilians into a corner by making a public issue of Brazil's informatics rules. "On this matter, the Japanese do not attack the Brazilians head-on. They play it the Brazilian way."[27]

Perhaps style contributes something to the politicization of U.S.–Brazilian relations. Alternatively threatening and conciliatory statements by U.S. officials, including U.S. presidents, have served to muddy the waters. Washington's typical response to this criticism is, "Observe what we do, not what we say." (Some would remark that this is practically the opposite of Japanese diplomacy.) The net result, however, is that because of politicization of its economic relations, the United States often fails to receive credit for its positive contributions to Brazilian welfare.

Substantively, U.S. government behavior as it affects Brazil has been subject to considerable change under successive presidential administrations. Within each administration, policy has been largely ad hoc or reactive in response to exigencies of the moment either in Brazil or in the United States. In the Reagan administration, national security issues have provided the only general framework, one by which Brazil does not choose to be constrained. In June of 1986, for example, Brasilia resumed normal diplomatic relations with Cuba. In economic affairs, Brazilians regard U.S. demands for fundamental free-market reforms as self-serving on the part of the United States and politically and socially destabilizing in Brazil. Moreover, economic liberalization presents Brazil with a typical development dilemma concerning short-run versus long-run objectives. On this point, the economic assistant to Antonio Delfim Netto observed, "In theory, we should liberalize imports, promote competition, and then by means of increased efficiency expand our exports. In the short run, however, we cannot liberalize imports because it would upset our balance of payments and impair our ability to service the debt."[28]

As in the contoversy with Japan concerning economic liberalization, the U.S.–Brazilian conflict over this issue has damaged U.S. international relations. In both cases, the defect of U.S. policy has been its insistence on economic rationality from an American point of view. Ironically, since the democratization of Brazil (*abertura*) following the exit of the military regime in April of 1985, U.S.–Brazilian relations have deteriorated. Among other factors, rising nationalism inspired by the renewal of democratic institutions has made Brazilians more intolerant of U.S. economic demands. As explained by an official in the office of the USTR, democracy has generated institutional friction:

U.S. relations with Brazil have plummeted since the beginning of the Sarney administration. Since *abertura,* there has been more difficulty than before in U.S.–Brazilian negotiations. The Brazilians are not even willing to come to the negotiating table to discuss the issues. They block and stall. They stonewall. Concerning a "301" investigation, after seven months of discussion, they have finally agreed to meet with us in July [1986], but whether this will come to anything or will merely be another sterile debating session remains to be seen. [In the event, the Brazilian negotiators confined themselves to delivering a lecture on Brazil's difficulties as a developing country.]

In the "New Republic," President Sarney is not quite sure of himself, although his authority has increased since the cruzado reform of February [1986]. The ministries are jockeying with each other for power and influence. In Brazil, the informal or administrative aspects of government [as in Japan] are more important than the statutory rules, and the informal side of U.S.–Brazilian relations has become more difficult since the end of the military regime. Formerly, the method of getting things done was to call up some influential friend who had a direct pipeline to the implementing procedure and who could make it work. Now, under Sarney, there are more players in the game. You have to struggle with the whole bureaucracy. And for the first time in 20 years, there is a Congress to contend with.

The generals still occupy positions of power in various ministries, especially in informatics. In outlook, they are mercantilist. They talk about "indigenous technology" and "tropical technology." They are hard-liners and opposed to liberalization. This rubs off on bureaucrats in fields other than informatics where technocrats—who may occupy the same positions as before under Figueiredo—are intimidated and feel that they cannot make concessions. In informatics, the Brazilians resist joint ventures with foreign despite the fact that the law does not prohibit it.

There is no documentary evidence that the Brazilians have followed the Japanese economic development model, but in bilateral conversations, they have often made it clear that this is what they are consciously doing. That model includes cartels and quasi-cartels, the "law of similars," market reserve, targeting, price discrimination, foreign trade and investment controls, vague laws with ad hoc implementation, and a Byzantine labyrinth of licensing requirements. You put in a request for a license and you never know what has happened to it.

However, the Brazilians would rather deal with American businessmen than with Japanese. The Brazilians regard the United States as a paper tiger and American businessmen as pushovers. The Japanese are tougher. They can get a better deal than the U.S. businessman. Furthermore, the Japanese, like the French, practice brinkmanship and make deals behind the scenes. But the United States is transparent. All of our proceedings are reported—we lay it all out in the open, in public registers. Therefore we cannot accomplish what the Japanese accomplish in dealing with Brazil.[29]

Ironically, despite the "open" character of U.S. foreign economic relations, its contributions to the welfare of others may be less well perceived than its derelictions. As Paul A. Volcker has observed, "Over the past four years, the United States, directly and indirectly, has provided a disproportionate share of the incremental demand to the world economy. We have made room for most of the external adjustments of the debtor countries as well. In fact, Japan and western Europe essentially have had no increase in imports from Latin America since 1982, while the United States has shared disproportionately in reduced exports of manufactured goods to that area."[30] Between 1981 and 1984, Brazil's trade surplus with the United States increased almost tenfold from US$560.1 million to US$5.4 billion. In 1985, Brazil's trade surplus with the United States was US$4.3 billion. In 1985, moreover, the United States bought more than 25 percent of Brazil's total exports.

Thus the U.S. policy predicament with regard to Brazil is a compound of Japanese, Brazilian, and American elements. The national interests of the three parties are divergent in the short run. However, by means of its long-term global strategy, will Japan's encounter with Brazil bear more fruit than that of the United States? Given the Japanese challenge, what are the priorities for U.S. policy at the present time? For Brazilians, external debt is clearly the leading issue by which its relations with the United States will be shaped for years to come. For them, moreover, the debt issue reverberates with the charge of the "dependency" school of thinking that emerged in the 1960s and 1970s, namely, that the domestic affairs of Latin American countries are dominated by their international linkages. The debt crisis that exploded in 1982 suddenly made Brazilians feel that their fate was in the hands of others, especially the United States. (Probably this has contributed to Brazilian intransigence concerning the informatics issue, which again raises the specter of "domination" by others.) Many of the difficulties that have been mentioned—such as problems of perception and style, micro-macro interactions, repercussions between internal and external policies, and management of long-term versus short-term change—are not open to facile remedies. The debt problem, however, lies explicitly within the domain of U.S. administrative leadership. This matter is discussed further in Chapter 6. As an offset to the Japanese challenge, the effective exercise or default of U.S. leadership with regard to the debt issue will be important in either reconciling or further alienating the United States and Brazil. The debt issue, of course, is only one item in the U.S. policy predicament. The predicament is not that the United States has failed to "learn from Japan" or that U.S. cultural and institutional arrangements are not Japanese. It lies in the failure of the United States to fulfill its national interests within the context of its own culture and institutions. A full response to the Japanese challenge would have to be as comprehensive as the challenge itself.

## Notes

1. Industrial Bank of Japan, *Quarterly Survey*, No. 65, 1986-I.
2. Tokuo Yasui, "Demand Management and Corporate Policy," *Fuji Bank Bulletin*, February 1975, p. 21.
3. Edward F. Denison and William K. Chung, *How Japan's Economy Grew So Fast* (Washington, D.C.: The Brookings Institution, 1976), p. 116.
4. As of 1982, however, for workers who retired from their "lifetime" employment at around age 60 and who then found other employment, wages amounted to only about two-thirds of the wages of workers aged 40. The Japan Institute of Labor, *Japan Labor Bulletin*, January 1984.
5. Japan formerly relied on cheap labor in the backward sector of its dual economy. The latter has been largely liquidated during the past two decades.
6. According to a former representative of the Reagan administration, national interest is defined as "protecting the United States against aggression, maintaining the domestic bases of U.S. national defense, guaranteeing access to raw materials of vital strategic importance, and ensuring the survival of a world of independent nations." Ambassador Jeane J. Kirkpatrick, Ninth Annual Francis Boyer Lecture, delivered in December of 1985 as part of the American Enterprise Institute's Public Policy Week.
7. Miyohei Shinohara, *Industrial Growth, Trade, and Dynamic Patterns in the Japanese Economy* (Tokyo: Tokyo University Press, 1982), p. 83.
8. As of January 1984, there were 317 state-owned corporations in Brazil, which included most large enterprises not owned by foreigners.
9. Miyohei Shinohara, *Industrial Growth, Trade, and Dynamic Patterns in the Japanese Economy* (Tokyo: Tokyo University Press, 1982), p. 83.
10. A rare reference to it may be found in Kiyoshi Kojima, "An Approach to Integration: The Gains from Agreed Specialization," in W. A. Eltis, M. F. G. Scott, and J. N. Wolfe (Eds.), *Essays in Honor of Roy Harrod* (Oxford: Clarendon Press, 1970).
11. Ezra Vogel, "Pax Nipponica?" *Foreign Affairs*, Spring 1986.
12. The high-technology information era has afforded the Japanese government new opportunities for intervention and administrative guidance. Under the sponsorship of MITI, a "law on the promotion of information processing" was passed in May of 1985. It authorizes MITI to decide when it is "necessary and fair" for an industry to make concerted efforts to construct industry-wide systems, such as interfirm information systems and joint data base systems. Specific guidelines are then issued by

MITI to promote these projects. The guidelines are formulated by the ministry with the help of recommendations from the Information Processing Promotion Council, an MITI advisory body. In 1986, in accordance with the law, standardization of information-processing procedures and industry-wide data base systems was established in the steel industry.

13. Drucker refers to the uncoupling of the world's primary-products economy from its industrial economy, uncoupling of production from employment in the industrial economy itself, and attenuation of the linkage between capital movements and physical trade. Peter F. Drucker, "The Changed World Economy," *Foreign Affairs*, Spring 1985.

14. Economic Planning Agency, *2000 nen no Nihon* (Japan in the Year 2000), and U.S. Department of Commerce.

15. For example, "Peking is still putting pressure on Japan to increase investment in China while the Japanese maintain that Singapore, Taiwan, and South Korea are a far more attractive proposition." *Financial Times*, June 24, 1986.

16. In July of 1986, as mentioned earlier, the United States and Japan had already worked out a market-sharing agreement in the field of semiconductors. The U.S. deficit in electronics trade with Japan, which amounted to $15.2 billion in 1984, increased to $17.9 billion in 1985.

17. Even some conservative observers believe that the deregulation of financial markets has gone too far. Henry Kaufman argues that the removal of constraints on financial innovation creates economic instability. Henry Kaufman, *Interest Rates, The Markets, and the New Financial World* (New York: Times Books, 1986). Whatever the future of financial deregulation may be, the Japanese have shown enormous aptitude for thriving on it as it presently exists in international markets.

18. Interview with Foreign Ministry official in Brasilia, July 12, 1984.

19. In May of 1986, Brazil's federal House of Deputies passed a bill concerning internationally owned air cargo agencies operating in Brazil. Service by such firms was limited to those in which 80 percent of the capital was held by Brazilians. As a model for the bill, its backers cited Japanese legislation barring international investments in air cargo transport in Japan. *Journal of Commerce*, May 28, 1986.

20. In March of 1986, Batista left the presidency of CVRD to take charge of CVRD's new overseas holding group, Companhia Rio Doce Internacional, with headquarters in Brussels.

21. Saburo Okita, former foreign minister of Japan, is among those who have referred favorably to the GIF project.

22. Japan-Brazil Joint Press Release issued on the occasion of the state visit to Japan of H. E. Joao Figueiredo, president of the Federative Republic of Brazil, May 27, 1984.

23. *Japan Economic Journal*, June 28, 1986.

24. Concerning imports into the United States, the Department of Commerce determines whether dumping or subsidization has occurred. (Before being transferred to the Department of Commerce in 1979, this function was performed by the U.S. Treasury, to the dissatisfaction of Congress.) If so, the International Trade Commission (ITC) determines whether injury has been inflicted. ITC's decision is rendered by a vote of the members of the commission.

25. *Wall Street Journal*, July 3, 1986.

26. *Financial Times*, June 19, 1986.

27. Interview with an official in the office of the USTR, November 20, 1985.

28. Interview with Akihiro Ikeda, special secretary for economic affairs, Ministry of Planning, in Brasilia, July 12, 1984.

29. Interview with an official of the USTR, June 10, 1986.

30. Statement by Paul A. Volcker, chairman of the Board of Governors of the Federal Reserve System, before the Committee on Foreign Affairs of the United States House of Representatives, June 18, 1986.

# 2
# Brazil's Economic Strategy

I n order to interpret the U.S–Japan relationship in interactions with Brazil, it is necessary to sketch the Brazilian context in which it occurs. I will attempt to convey not only facts, but also conflicting as well as concurring opinions of observers with whom I held discussions in Brazil, Japan, and the United States during 1983–1986. Thus the study aims to raise questions as well as to answer them.

## Formulation of Goals

Primary among Brazil's aspirations are its goals of overcoming external dependence, realizing the vast potential of its natural resource structure, and achieving "greatness" (*grandeza*) among nations. Possessing a land equal in scale to that of the United States, Brazilians feel that they shoud be equally rich and influential. The Brazilian people demand growth. As I was told by a Brazilian diplomat, "Brazilian policy can be defined in terms of one word— *development*. Development is the only concept that can unite all Brazilians." Ironically, in maintaining growth by means of foreign rather than domestic savings, Brazil has become more rather than less dependent on the world economy.

There may be consensus on the desirability of growth, but there is no consensus on policies to achieve it. There are opposing schools of thought about the optimal rate of growth, about balanced versus unbalanced growth, about the priority of long-term versus short-term objectives, about the relative merits of import substitution as contrasted with export promotion, about the relative merits of installing infrustructure rather than directly productive facilities, and about the merits of direct versus indirect approaches to distribution of the benefits of growth. Mario H. Simonsen and Antonio Delfim Netto were prominent adversaries on these issues. Simonsen was minister of finance under President Ernesto Geisel (1974–1979) and briefly minister of planning under President Joao Figueiredo (1979–1985). Delfim

Netto became minister of planning in August of 1979. Opposing policy proposals have been based purely on pragmatism: like the Japanese, Brazilians have no ideological preconceptions. On this point, the civilian and military authorities were agreed.

One of the basic controversies has concerned protectionism versus the role of the free market. Pragmatically, in the 1950s, Brazil pursued industrialization by means of import substitution *cum* protectionism. Between 1947 and 1963, there was no growth in exports whatever. In 1964, export promotion became favored as the principal stimulus to growth. In changing its policy, the government argued that economies of large-scale production could be achieved more quickly by penetrating foreign markets than by waiting until a mass market had been developed at home. The narrowness of the middle class gave plausibility to that argument. (In July of 1986, Minister of Finance Dilson Funaro, in referring to President Sarney's "compulsory consumer loan" development program, estimated that it would affect only 10 percent of the population. Inasmuch as the program was specifically targeted on the middle class, it may be inferred that the middle class can be estimated to constitute 10 percent of the population.) At the same time, in observance of Japan's development strategy, Brazil continued to maintain home market defenses while seeking markets abroad. In 1964, the government was supposedly in favor of free enterprise, but it promoted the establishment of state (here synonymous with *federal*) enterprises, some of which in the course of time became barriers to private enterprise.

Brazilian impatience for growth is reflected in the policies of both its private and public sectors. In general, the private sector does not take a long-term view. It invests in projects that promise a quick return. As joint-venture partners in the private sector, Brazilians have often disappointed the Japanese, who typically take a long-term view. In the public sector, the military regime tended to take a longer-term view. However, after starting the most impressive economic boom that Brazil had ever seen, the military allowed industry to become too dependent on oil—one of the few natural resources in short supply—thus reinforcing the very external dependence that in theory it deplored. After the oil crisis of 1973, the military increased the external debt in order to avoid inhibiting growth. This ill-fated decision was followed by the debt crisis that compounded Brazil's dependence on the world economy. In 1984, Brazil became the world's leading debtor nation, overtaken only by the United States in 1985. Scarcity of resources for leadership is another Brazilian bottleneck. The military, which provided one of Brazil's few strong governments since independence, failed in its development mission and was succeeded in office by the civilian regime that was inaugurated in March of 1985.

As a vast country with enormous potential, it is perhaps natural that Brazil should have a predisposition to be inward-looking. The collapse of world coffee prices in 1929 was followed by efforts to promote import-substituting industrialization. Disruption of exports during World War II gave further impetus to that policy. It is interesting that during the 1950s and early 1960s, in defiance of the traditional economic law that prescribes specialization in accordance with comparative advantage, both Brazil and Japan attempted simultaneously to industrialize across a broad spectrum. In the case of Japan, however, industrialization was designed to promote exports, and it succeeded with the help of the undervalued yen. Moreover, Japan achieved an optimal combination of import substitution and export promotion during its postwar reconstruction period./In Brazil there was likewise a virtuous circle, for the most part serially rather than simultaneously, in which import-substitution growth of the 1950s created an industrial base that facilitated the export boom following 1964. The latter, in turn, created productive facilities that could be shifted into import substitution when external markets dried up. In rapid and overlapping sequence, by measures dating from the end of the 1960s, import substitution began with consumer goods, then capital goods, and finally energy. One of Brazil's difficulties in shifting from import substitution to export promotion was the lack of synchronization between the gestation period of investment and the fluctuations of world business. However, plant capacity that was constructed in the import-substitute industrialization period of the late 1950s and early l960s, which had been idle during the economic adjustment of the mid-1960s, was operated at close to full capacity during the "miracle" years of 1968–1973.

After the first oil shock of 1973, the government maintained its structure of export incentives intact but shifted its primary emphasis once more to import substitution. The latter was supported by an ambitious program of public-sector investments that had been initiated before 1973. During the mid-1980s, import substitution remained the basic model, while exports increased—chiefly to the United States—almost inadvertently as a result of the overvalued dollar. This might be described as export opportunism rather than export promotion. By 1985, owing to the restriction of imports during previous years, many import substitutes had become well established. Consequently, even if the quality of these products was somewhat below world standard, the authorities were willing to liberalize import restrictions to a moderate degree.

## Economic Planning

Given the nature of Brazilian economic goals, the next question concerns the shape of the planning system that attempts to fulfill those goals. From August of 1979 until March of 1985, under President Figueiredo, the planning system was essentially embodied in the person of Delfim Netto. As minister of planning, Delfim controlled both monetary and fiscal policy, including money supply, interest rates, taxes, budgets, and subsidies. In the opinion of Richard Huber, senior vice president of Citibank, "In substance, Delfim definitely used a Japanese development model."[1] In terms of objectives ("comprehensive economic security") and controls, there were clear similarities. In terms of planning institutions, however, there were similarities and differences. Institutionally, the Planning Ministry of Brazil differed from the Economic Planning Agency of Japan, which has no control authority whatever. In Brazil, the formalities of planning were performed by the Institute of Applied Social and Economic Research (IPEA) under the direction of the minister of planning. Its published documents, however, show that the planning process was very perfunctory. For example, no quantitative planning targets were formulated by the Planning Ministry.[2]

In the opinion of many observers, Delfim's Ministry of Planning during the administration of President Figueiredo did no planning at all. Delfim was a planning minister who disliked planning. Essentially, his "planning" was limited to specifying priority sectors that would be chosen to receive subsidies. The first priority was infrastructure, the second was exports, and the third was energy.[3] Another view of the matter was expressed by an American observer in Brazil who described Brazilian planning as simply a coordination process performed by Planning Ministry, which reconciled and accommodated the antagonisms of rival ministries (principally Finance, Commerce and Industry, Interior, Transportation, and Labor) and rival state enterprises.[4] For a further opinion, I asked a member of the government, "Is export promotion connected with economic planning?" He answered, "In theory, yes; in practice, no."[5]

In contrast with the industrial policy approach attempted, for example, by Reis Velloso under President Geisel, Delfim and his "boys" practiced short-term pragmatism, changing their minds frequently. Delfim's directives were not merely pragmatic and nonideological, they were also highly personal. His *boletinhos* (notes of instruction scribbled on pieces of paper and bestowed on petitioners like a doctor's prescription) were the means by which many of his economic policy decisions were imposed. Delfim also was not impressed with the value of long-term research. Brazil's principal agency for long-term research in science and technology is the National Research Council, which Delfim starved of funds. His principal tool was monetary economics, to which he was partial by virtue of his successful experience as minister of finance under President Costa e Silva.

In 1984 I asked a famous Brazilian economist, "What is the economic strategy of the Brazilian government?" He replied, "I doubt there is any strategy at all."[6] Another economist, subsequently an important member of the Sarney government, observed, "There is no unified Brazilian policy in practice; it exists only in the minds of some people."[7] In comparing planning in Brazil and Japan, an official of the Mitsubishi Heavy Industries Company in Tokyo said, "Brazilian planning is not good. Global planning does not exist."[8]

In style, Delfim's use of the Japanese development model reflected the practices of MITI and the Ministry of Finance during the early period of Japan's postwar reconstruction. It was a pragmatic, nonideological assortment of direct and indirect controls and overt constraints combined with incentives. It combined formally enacted legislation with administration guidance, the latter being wholly informal and lacking in "transparency." In Brazil, Delfim, who had contempt for the congress, instigated a steady stream of "decree laws" issued by President Figueiredo. He was also unconcerned by inconsistency. While practicing open as well as covert intervention, Delfim professed to be a "free market" man. Perhaps this, too, was meant in a Japanese sense.

In an American sense, the free market does not prevail in Brazil. Nor is there any Brazilian commitment to it in principle. A government official informed me, "A free economy would not have produced industrialization in Brazil."[9] This assertion was spelled out in remarks by Roberto Fendt, Jr., director of studies and research at the Fundacao Centro de Estudos do Comercio Exterior (FUNCEX):

> "First, you must understand the basics. Japan has been an example to Brazil since the 1970s. In terms of economic planning, MITI prepares explicity "visions" of the Japanese economy. The United States is also explicit: it espouses a free market economy, social mobility, equality of opportunity, and efficiency. But Brazil is less explicit. The goal is to make Brazil an industrial nation. This has been the goal since 1889 when the Republic was established.
>
> Up to 1822, Brazil was a colony of Portugal, which was not a modern nation. The Brazilian goal is to modernize by means of industrialization. We reject rural society. Rural society is despised in Brazil, but nobody will tell you this.
>
> The first of two important landmarks were the 1930 revolution of Getulio Vargas, which became a dictatorship (the Estado Novo) in 1937, and which created the foundation of a central government. Second was the 1964 military revolution. Both tended to create a unitary republic in Brazil. Prior to 1930, Brazil was a federation of autonomous states. This autonomy was an obstacle to modernization and progress. Unification promoted a centripetal tendency, toward the center. Thus the question arose, can we combine the market with central planning, as Japan has done? Since the 1960s and early 1970s, however, we had a bright future, like Japan in the late 1950s. We were growing so fast that it appeared we would reach

the economic size of the EC countries. So we said, "Let's do it even faster! If Okita could see it in his lifetime, why couldn't Geisel see it in his lifetime?" Brazil was en route, by the "third way."

The method by which this was attempted was to combine state and private enterprise, like Japan. And to have MNCs involved as well, as in the automobile industry, but under the control of the state and indigenous interests. We attempted to maintain national control, which is a very basic matter. We rejected interdependence. Interdependence would bring denationalization, as in the case of Luxembourg. We felt we would be dominated by others.

So we say, "Let's do what Japan did!" There have been more Brazilian efforts for rapprochement with Japan than Japanese efforts for rapprochement with Brazil. Closer ties with Japan would reduce our overdependence on the United States. In some respects we emulate Japan and in other respects we are the opposite. We say that we practice a market economy, but in a peculiar sense. Social and political problems require the opposite of a free market. Brazil is one of the most protectionist countries in the world. However, we want access to the markets of the developed countries. In this sense, we are still LDC. In Brazil, central controls are pervasive and affect all major economic and political decisions. The government controls more of the economy than it owns. Funds for investment come from private international sources or from international agencies as well as from domestic sources. But profit is not on OK word in Brazil. It is un-Brazilian to say, "I am maximizing profit." That would mean you are exploiting the poor. As a centrally planned economy, we love and hate the market. We love and hate the United States and Japan.[10]

## Federal Enterprises

One respect in which the Brazilian development model differs from the Japanese is that in Brazil the public sector is large; in Japan it is relatively small. Brazil's state enterprise system is sometimes described as the "third way" between socialism and capitalism. It was strongly stimulated during World War II. The grandiose or "pharaonic" projects were conceived largely during the economic "miracle" period of 1968–1973, at a time when the government professed to be "procapitalist." In 1983, the number of federal (often referred to as "state") enterprises was approximately 550, mainly in mining (metallic minerals), petroleum, steel, chemicals, transportation[11] (shipping, railroads, aircraft), public utilities, and banking. Basic industry is monopolized by the government. Private-sector firms, which include only a handful of major enterprises, remain dominant in traditional fields such as food, sugar, alcohol, lumber, and textiles. Private firms are also found in capital goods and electronics. In 1982, federal firms produced about 60 percent of industrial output. In the same year, they performed about 60 percent of total investment in Brazil.[12] On the whole, their financial results were negative. In 1980, their operational deficits (total expenditures minus internally generated revenue) accounted for 66 percent of the total federal budgetary deficit. According to the Central Bank of Brazil, in the year ending March 1984, state enterprises accounted for about US$65 billon of Brazil's US$100 billion foreign debt.

With the slowdown in the growth rate during the mid-1970's, the private sector became critical of the "statization" of the economy. From a Japanese point of view, however, the increasing centralization and concentration of the Brazilian economy provided an environment conducive to large-scale Japanese economic involvement in Brazil. In particular, the possibility of forming joint ventures with huge federal-sector enterprises or their satellites constitutes one of the attractions of Brazil for Japanese big business.

Brazil's federal enterprises are as controversial as they are formidable. Many came into existence haphazardly as a consequence of entrepreneurial default and aversion to risk in the private sector. The government's rationale in promoting them has included the intention of imposing government control on natural monopolies, achieving economies of scale, promoting external economies, providing employment, and creating infrastructure as a foundation for accelerated industrialization in the private sector. Nationalistically, another purpose was to forestall the preemption of significant sectors of the Brazilian economy by foreign multinationals. (Nevertheless, partnership in state-owned enterprises has been offered to foreign investors, such as Japan, that could provide capital or advanced technology.) These are precisely the principles that prompted MITI to promote the rise of *keiretsu* groups, including key industries and major firms—in the private sector—in Japan during the 1950s and 1960s. In many cases, the Brazilian government became the owner of enterprises (including many service companies) involuntarily. This has occurred as a result of foreclosure or rescue of firms that were unable to pay their debts to BNDES (National Bank for Economic and Social Development), which is Brazil's principal institution for long-term financing and practically the only source of term credit for small and medium-sized firms. Hotels, insurance companies, and real estate agencies are among the types of enterprises that have been acquired by the government in order to prevent their bankruptcy. The government's heterogeneous economic, political, and social criteria for maintaining the federal enterprises is one source of confusion in the arguments concerning whether their performance has been good, bad, or indifferent. There are also arguments concerning the extent to which the public-sector firms complement, conflict, or compete with the private sector.

In their statistical study concerning the period 1970–1980, Mooney and Newfarmer conclude, "Our central argument is that the public sector by and large complements the private sector in Brazil rather than competes with it."[13]

Similarly, on the basis of data though 1980, Thomas J. Trebat concludes, "The Brazilian public enterprise experience, in sum, has demonstrated that state ownership of basic industries can be an effective substitute for private enterprise in stimulating rapid and sustained economic growth."[14]

In Brazil there is apprehension concerning the growth of the state enterprises, and reservations are expressed concerning their efficiency. Sergio Correa da Costa, Brazil's ambassador to the United States, told me that "there can be no doubt that private enterprises are more efficient than state enterprises. As exceptions, Petrobras and Vale do Rio Doce (CVRD) have been superbly managed, but they were milked by the government. They were obliged to borrow money they did not need, which was siphoned off by the government for its own purposes." A member of the Japanese embassy in Brasilia remarked, "Some are good, but they are poorly organized. According to the World Bank, the Brazilian power sector has been well organized and managed." However, an American business consultant in Brazil asserted that "the government has no control over the state enterprises. Therefore, their policies are not coordinated."[15] Indeed, in an address at the annual meeting of the board of governors of the Inter-American Development Bank, the president of the Central Bank of Brazil stated,"Brazil has also committed its share of errors, particularly in terms of the institutional rigidities expressed by the excessive presence of the State in the economy. Paradoxical though it may seem, the essentially political problem of finding an adequate means of establishing government control over the State enterprises has, in practice, been shown to be much more complex than the task of imposing indispensable rules on the operations of the private sector."He added that it was necessary to institutionalize "more effective mechanisms of control over the state enterprises through the Secretariat for the Control of State-Owned Enterprises (SEST), which operates under the authority of the Secretariat of Planning of the Presidency of the Republic."[16] SEST was established in October of 1979 for the purpose of controlling the budgets, imports, and borrowing of state-owned enterprises. During the military regime, one of the main reasons for lack of goverment control of the state enterprises was the "old-boy network" of former generals who dominated many of them and who had a direct pipeline to the person of the president himself, thus shortcircuiting control procedures. Following the *abertura* of April of 1985, about 13,000 to 14,000 retired military officers retained administrative positions in major firms and influence in the government. Among other abuses, IMF investigations occasioned by the debt crisis uncovered remarkable fringe-benefit arrangements, perquisites, and "payments" to privileged members of the state enterprises.

In the past, in accounting for the success, as measured by profitability, some of the state enterprises, including some in petroleum, mining, and electricity, it has been noted that they possessed advantages not available in the private sector. Among these were greater freedom to raise prices, exemption from federal income tax (until 1975), easier access to long-term foreign loans from international lending agencies, greater ability to obtain financing through the domestic stock market, and the absence of indexing on public-enterprise debts to private firms. Moreover, joint ventures between government firms and multinationals facilitated imports of high-technology capital goods that were not available to potentially competitive firms in the private sector.[17] According to a professor of economics at Catholic University, "When the major state enterprises are in deficit, the Ministry of Planning simply tells the Central Bank to supply them with funds. There is no legislative content to these instructions."[18]

The absence of comprehensive financial control in the public sector has been a major inflationary factor in the Brazilian economy. Despite SEST, budgetary restrictions on state enterprises and "autonomous institutions" have been haphazard. Some of the ministries nominally in charge of major state enterprises have been weaker and more poorly staffed that the firms under their jurisdiction. With regard to investment budgets, a large proportion of "budgeted" expenditures were left to be covered by a line item designated as "resources to be defined." This led to continual demands on the budgetary authorities for supplementary transfers from the Central Bank. Moreover, by virtue of the relatively strong borrowing capacity of major enterprises, they were induced to borrow foreign currency funds, which were then appropriated for general balance of payments purposes. The domestic credit operations of the state enterprises were largely unregulated. As an offset to foreign borrowing or investment projects which they were induced by the government to undertake but which were unwarranted from a business point of view, the state firms would be compensated by federal tax and credit accommodation.

The financial situation of the state enterprises is largely a consequence of the investment strategy adopted after the first oil shock of 1973. In an effort to protect Brazil from future external shocks, major import-substitute projects were inaugurated in the fields of capital goods, basic inputs, and nonferrous metals. The projects included investments in nuclear and hydro-electric power, steel, cellulose, and petrochemicals. Since Brazil lacked the domestic savings to finance these projects, they were financed by foreign borrowing. The combined domestic and foreign borrowing of the ten principal state enterprises amounted to almost ten times their equity capital as of December 31, 1981. This ratio reflects not only financing required for their own operations, but also financing that was channeled through these firms for general balance of payments purposes. The role of the ten major state enterprises in the Brazilian economy may be evaluated from the fact that they accounted for between 17 and 22 percent of total fixed investment in Brazil during the period 1978–1981.[19]

As a result of recently imposed price controls, the state enterprises have been unable to raise their prices to the full extent of inflation. Fictitiously, they have been able to show profits in their balance sheets because by law they are allowed to include as revenue the effect of inflation on the difference between the nominal value of their fixed assets and their net worth. If these inflationary "profits" were eliminated, all the major enterprises except Petrobras and CVRD would show a loss. Even in the latter cases, given their monopoly advantages, how much more should they have accomplished?[20]

Major federal enterprises were given independence (or "autonomy") on the theory that they would then be free of politics and could act entrepreneurially and efficiently. It has not worked out that way. Instead, many have been monopolistic and inefficient and have caused misallocations of resources. Moreover, they have become heavily involved in politics. Domestic suppliers of capital goods, for example, constitute a lobby behind Petrobras. Much of the government bureaucracy is potentially controlled by the federal enterprises. Many of these enterprises have been physically located in inappropriate regions for political rather than economic purposes. Some major federal projects are located in Brazilian states where opposition political parties are in office. In such cases, there is an increasing amount of conflict between the state governments and the national government.

On November 22, 1985, the Brazilian government admitted for the first time that a substantial part of its foreign debt, which at that time amounted to US$104 billion, had been wasted on ill-conceived federal projects that will never yield a return and are being written off. Formerly, the government had always insisted that unlike other debtor countries, the Brazilian debt had been incurred for productive purposes that would eventually justify the expenditure. As of November 1985, US$60 billion of the US$70 billion public debt was owed by state companies. According to Henri-Philippe Reichstul, head of the State Companies Division of the Planning Ministry, as much as a quarter of this amount, or US$15 billion, had been "irrevocably lost." Among the projects responsible for this loss were the nuclear program (US$5 billion), the steel railroad designed to run from the interior of Minas Gerais state to the coast near Vitoria (US$3 billion), which has been abandoned, the Acominas integrated steelworks (US$3 billion), a project misconceived from the start, and the Caraiba Metals copper mine and refinery.[21]

The political and economic power of the state enterprises constitutes a force impelling the private sector to follow their lead. Thus although under Delfim the government "plan" was fluid or nonexistent, to the extent that the government's intentions were reflected in the policies of the state enterprises, the private sector could be effectively mobilized behind them. As a supplier to government enterprises, which are in many cases their principal or sole customer, private-sector firms play the government game.

The nuclear energy program, which began as a political project of President Geisel, has been criticized as an egregious misallocation of resources in Brazil, a country enormously well endowed with hydroelectric potential. The state enterprises that are developing the program, however, argue that it is important for Brazil to engage in it for the sake of the technological spin-offs and educational benefits the program affords. "It helps us to understand the things that are going on elsewhere." The government of President Jose Sarney contains many new leaders who formerly as opposition critics were the foremost opponents of the state enterprises. Formerly, for example, Professor Luciano Coutinho as an outsider "frequently attacked the previous governments's expensive infrastructure projects, such as hydroelectric dams." Now, as the new secretary general of the Science and Technology Ministry, "he is considering launching a few of his own. . . . 'Professors have the luxury of thinking,' says Coutinho. 'Now I must do.' "[22]

For fiscal reasons, however, it is not likely that the Sarney administration will sponsor a new boom in state enterprises. More than a decade ago, after the first oil shock, it became clear that the government was vastly overextended in its commitment to state firms. In 1976 it issued a decree requiring presidential approval for the establishment of new state firms or for creation of subsidiaries of then existing firms. When the Figueiredo administration entered office, restrictions were further tightened. The theory (as distinguished from the practice) of that administration was explained to me by Akihiro Ikeda, special assistant to Delfim Netto in the Ministry of Planning. He said, "The Brazilian dilemma is that we have to copy technology from abroad; we have to solve the balance of payments problem; we have to learn how to make industry more efficient, more competitive. In theory, this means that we must get rid of the state enterprises."[23]

In July of 1979 President Figueiredo established a Ministry for Debureaucratization, which was assigned the task of reducing government red tape and divesting the government of state enterprises where possible. The mandate of SEST (Secretariat for the Control of State-Owned Enterprises), created in October of 1979, also included "destatization" among its secondary objectives. In September of 1981, a Special Commission for Destatization (CED) was established for the principal purpose of privatizing, reorganizing, or dissolving state enterprises. During the 4 years prior to March of 1985, the government managed to eliminate 133 state-owned companies by merger or sale to the private sector.[24] Without exception, however, these have been minor enterprises, the disposition of which has made no appreciable difference to Brazil's fiscal position. Brazil's private enterprise sector lacks the capital to make any substantial acquisition of major state enterprises, and for nationalistic reasons, there is reluctance to allow foreigners to acquire them. Proposals for the conversion of foreign debt to foreign equity have scarcely taken hold.

## Dualism and the Economic "Miracle"

Whether by predisposition or design, it is a coincidence that dualism has played a role in both Brazilian and Japanese economic growth. Institutionally, moreover, a hierarchical distinction between "superiors" and "inferiors" is recognized in the political economy of both countries. This helps Brazil and Japan to "understand" each other.

Historically, Brazilian dualism has been explained as a legacy of its colonial experience. The nation was founded by exlplorers whose motive was to exploit the country for the benefit of Portugal, the home country. The founders imposed a dualistic, hierarchical system on the native society, and power of economic initiative was reserved to the government. The Catholic Church contributed to dualism in its vast aggregation of latifundia. In contrast, the United States was founded by colonists who came to develop rather than to exploit the land. British imperialism was soon shrugged off. Consequently, the institutions of the United States became more democratic, progressive, and entrepreneurial than those of Brazil. In the United States, there was less dependence on the government to take the lead; there was no vacuum that only state enterprises could fill.

Besides state versus private capitalism, Brazilian dualism takes other forms as well. It exists in the form of a sharp imbalance in the distribution of income and wealth, imbalance between rural and urban welfare, sectoral imbalance between agribusiness and subsistence agriculture within the rural sector, imbalance in production techniques, inequitable educational opportunities, and unbalanced levels of regional development. In a phrase coined by Roberto Campos, Brazilian dualism has been described as "Belgium in India."

The persistence of a highly inequitable distribution of income is documented in Brazil's census statistics. The data show that in relative terms, inequality increased between 1960 and 1970. Between 1970 and 1980, there was no appreciable change. During the latter decade, there was a large rise in rural incomes in relation to urban incomes. Within the rural sector, however, there was a large increase in the degree of inequality of agricultural income. These offsetting changes account for the stability in the overall degree of income inequality between 1970 and 1980. During that decade, the lowest 40 percent of income earners received less than 10 percent of total income, while the upper 10 percent of income earners received approximately 50 percent of total income. In 1986, approximately 10 million peasant families were landless.

When the generals took over the government in 1964, they followed the textbook prescription for economic growth: export promotion, with emphasis on new industrial products; inflow of direct foreign investment to supplement domestic savings; restraint of inflation; and accumulation of capital by means of restrictive wage and tax policies. These policies were implemented in such a way as to reinforce dualism. Upon arrival in office, the military instituted a tax reform that gave the government enormous new revenues, but the "reform" was imposed in such a way as to accomplish a massive expropriation of wages for the benefit of the state sector. Under President Emilio Medici and his minister of finance, Delfim Netto, the economic "miracle" (1968–1973) was also an exercise in physical, social, and political repression that denied both voice and the fruits of progress to the backward sector of the dual economy. According to Celso Furtado, "The so-called 'Brazilian miracle' was based on gigantism and paranoia, and ruined the Brazilian economy."[25] In effect, growth was accomplished without development.

Within agriculture, for example, "support programs were usually regressive. Generally the largest farms planted cash crops; they benefited disproportionately from credit subsidies and tax breaks. They also gained from export incentives and economies of scale, and had easier access to new technology, marketing infrastructure and the capital required to buy easier access to new technology, marketing infrastructure and the capital required to buy machinery and fertilizer."[26] The Figueiredo administration, inaugurated in March of 1979, attempted to reduce inequalities through the tax structure, the pattern of incentives and subsidies, and the wage indexation system. When it left office in March of 1985, however, the imbalance remained largely intact.

In postwar Japan, the role of dualism was different from its role in Brazil. In Japan, in the 1950s and 1960s, it was employed in the service of development, whereas in Brazil, it was a drag on development. Structurally, Japanese dualism was characterized chiefly by the exploitative relation between big business in the modern capital-intensive sector and small and medium-sized labor-intensive firms in the traditional-goods sector. The latter was squeezed by the former in subcontracting relationships. The backward sector of Japan's dual economy absorbed the surplus labor force, thus performing an important social as well as economic function. In the course of Japan's economic "miracle," however, which was accompanied by a demographic transition reducing the excess labor supply, the productivity rose in both the backward and modern sectors, wages rose, and contrary to the practice in Brazil, the wage structure throughout Japanese industry became fairly uniform, with small differentials between the top and bottom of the hierarchy. Thus, in the course of Japan's economic miracle, the dual structure of industry was liquidated as backward firms became modernized and independent. Above all, by virtue of Japanese economic communitarianism, the fruits of progress were widely distributed and the middle class was rehabilitated. Unlike Brazil, Japan lacks visible extremes of coexisting wealth and poverty. It was the existence of a large middle class in Japan, a country with approximately the same population size as Brazil, that made it possible for economies of large-scale production to be achieved within the domestic market, without reference to external demand.

In Japan, moreover, it was the savings of the middle class that provided the capital for economic development. Japan did not have to rely on imports of capital for long-term investment. By means of industrial policy, the government gave astute guidance in the allocation of the nation's capital resources, which remained in the private sector. As in the case of Brazil, it provided incentives and subsidies, largely through the tax system and by control of money and credit. Liquidation of the dual economy in Japan and the prosperity of the middle class have provided Japan with an economic basis for political consensus, which Brazil sorely lacks.

After the oil shock of 1973 and the world recession that it precipitated, Brazil's immature middle class could not provide a domestic market large and dynamic enough to replace external demand. The consequences of economic dualism, accordingly, can be seen in the implications of the import-substitution program that was adopted at this juncture, replacing the export-promotion policies of the Medici regime. Import substitution, implemented by central planning and financed by foreign borrowing, was the program of President Ernesto Geisel, who succeeded Medici in March of 1974. Characteristically, the import-substitution program emphasized state-sponsored construction, chiefly in the areas of infrastructure and basic industry. It was intended that the construction program would keep internal demand at a high level, would subsequently provide support for directly productive activities in the private sector, and would eventually make Brazil independent of the world economy. Brazilians believe that this trick might have worked if not for the second oil shock that occurred in 1979.[27] This assumes that during the period of gestation of the infrastructure projects the middle class could have expanded sufficiently to provide a mass market for the subsequent output of Brazilian industry.

Interactions between the imbalance of the state and private sectors and the imbalance between the privileged and underprivileged components of society have compounded the dualism of Brazil's economy. These imbalances defeated the import-substitution policy that was adopted following the economic "miracle." Although Geisel had good intentions, his "pharaonic" projects required a long gestation period; by 1986, some of them still had not matured. Here Brazilian strategy diverged sharply from that of Japan. In the postwar reconstruction of their economy, the Japanese deliberately skimped on the construction of infrastructure in favor of investment in directly productive facilities. Early rehabilitation of the Japanese middle class provided a domestic mass market favorable to the achievement of international competitive power and the promotion of exports. Brazilian policies, on the contrary, despite some conspicuous export subsidies, have been interpreted as containing an antiexport bias since the mid 1970s.[28] The bias was offset following the outbreak of the debt crisis in 1982 by special efforts to export and by the ease of exporting to the United States due to the overvalued dollar. Brazil's propensity to import, meanwhile, cannot be fulfilled unless it exports or borrows more. Despite its aspiration to achieve greatness in the world community, Brazil has a profound and immature predisposition to be inward-looking. Its antiexport bias has created a natural opportunity for Japan's general trading companies, the *sogo shosha*, which possess unrivaled economies of scale in external distribution, to offer their services to Brazil.

## Notes

1. Interview in New York City, June 13, 1983.
2. Interview with Joao Carlos do C. R Cavalcanti, chefe do Dept. de Operacoes com Organismo Internacionais, Banco Nacional de Desenvolvimento Economico e Social (BNDES), in Rio de Janeiro, August 16, 1983.
3. Interview with Joao Carlos do C. R. Cavalcanti, chefe do Dept. de Operacoes com Organismo Internacionais, Banco Nacional de Desenvolvimento Economico e Social (BNDES), in Rio de Janeiro, August 16, 1983.
4. Interview with Daniel G. Sydenstricker, diretor-presidente, Cia. Auxiliar de Empresas de Mineracao (CAEMI), in Rio de Janeiro, August 12, 1983.
5. Interview with Brian Michael F. Neele, head, Trade Information Division, Ministry of External Relations, in Brasilia, July 11, 1984.
6. Interview with Professor Francisco Lafaiete Lopes, Department of Economics, Catholic University, in Rio de Janeiro, July 20, 1984.
7. Interview with Professor Luciano G. Coutinho, Department of Economics, University of Campinas, in Sao Paulo, August 2, 1983.
8. Interview with Jose H. Kojima, manager, Machinery Headquarters, Mitsubishi Heavy Industries, Ltd., in Tokyo, July 12, 1983.
9. Interview with J. A. de Macedo-Soares, chief, Commercial Division, Ministry of External Relations, in Brasilia, July 12, 1984.
10. Interview with Roberto Fendt, Jr., director of studies and research, Fundacao Centro de Estudos do Comercio Exterior (FUNCEX), in Rio de Janeiro, July 20, 1984.
11. The excellent national airline, VARIG, is private. Public transportation is government-owned, except for buses, which are operated by small private firms.
12. Data from Ilona A. Beer, manager Citibank, in Rio de Janeiro, July 18, 1984.
13. Joseph Mooney and Richard Newfarmer, "State Enterprise and Private Sector Development in Brazil," June 1981 (processed), p. 1.
14. Thomas J. Trebat, *Brazil's State-Owned Enterprises: A Case Study of the State as Entrepreneur* (Cambridge: Cambridge University Press, 1983), p. 241.
15. Interview with Robert H. Blockers, president, Blocker Assessoria de Investimentos e Participacoes, S.A., in Sao Paulo, July 3, 1984.
16. Carlos Geraldo Langoni, "The Lessons of the Crisis," in Central Bank of Brazil, *Discourses* No. 2, March 1983, p. 5.

17. J. R. Mendonca de Barros and D. H. Graham, "The Brazilian Economic Miracle Revisited: Private and Public Sector Initiative in a Market Economy," *Latin American Research Review*, Vol. 13, No. 2, pp. 5–38; as cited in Dennis J. Mahar, "Destatization in Brazil," in Howard J. Wiarda and Janine T. Perfit (Eds.), *Changing Dynamics of the Brazilian Economy* (Washington, D.C.: American Enterprise Institute for Public Policy Research, Occasional Papers Series No. 5, February 1983), p. 44.

18. Interview with Professor Francisco Lafaiete Lopes, Department of Economics, Catholic University, in Rio de Janeiro, July 20, 1984.

19. The major ten state enterprises are the following: Eletrobras (electric power), Siderbras (steel), Telebras (telecommunications), RFFSA (railroads), Acesita (speciality steels), Itaipu (hydroelectric power), Petrobras (oil), CVRD (mining), Nuclebras (nuclear power), and Portobras (ports).

20. The preceding three paragraphs are based on an interview with Luiz Paulo Giao, chief of division, Department of Economics, Central Bank of Brazil, in Brasilia, July 10, 1984.

21. *Financial Times,* November 25, 1985.

22. *Business Week,* June 17, 1985, p. 54.

23. Interview with Akihiro Ikeda, special secretary for economic affairs, Ministry of Planning, in Brasilia, July 12, 1984.

24. *Journal of Commerce,* March 4, 1985.

25. *Gazeta Mercantil,* June 6, 1983, p. l6.

26. Bryce Ferguson and Ilona Beer, *Brazil: A Strategy for the 1980s* (Brazil: Citibank, December 1981), p. 65.

27. Severo Gomes, Geisel's minister of industry and commerce, was one of the principal advocates of widening and strengthening the domestic market. In my conversation with him, he maintained that Brazil's economic "miracle" has been "primarily dependent on domestic demand." Interview in Brasilia, August 10, 1983.

28. See William G. Tyler, "The Anti-Export Bias in Commercial Policies and Export Performance: Some Evidence from the Recent Brazilian Experience," *Weltwirtschaftliches Archiv,* March 1983.

# 3
# The Brazilian Approach to Japan

The national priorities of Brazil and Japan have dovetailed, but they also have shifted repeatedly during the postwar period. Accordingly, in the course of time, the initiative for bilateral collaboration has passed back and forth between them. When Kakuei Tanaka was prime minister, the Japanese "miracle" was at its peak, and his attention was directed toward liberating Japan from its natural-resource constraints. Domestically, he published his plan for "remodeling the Japanese archipelago." Externally, for the same purpose, Tanaka visited Brazil in September of 1974 and promised President Ernesto Geisel Japan's cooperation in various categories, including development of hydroelectric power for aluminum smelter projects in the Amazon, forest and pulp development projects, and agricultural and fishery projects (Table 3–1).

After the oil crisis of 1973, Brazil embarked intensively on a renewed import-substitution program as a means of coping with the price of oil and reducing Brazil's dependence on a world economy that had become depressed. In September of 1976, in the first trip of a Brazilian president to Japan, Geisel affirmed the "complementary relationship" and asked for help in performing his grandiose import-substitution projects. On this occasion it was agreed that Japan would provide economic assistance in the amount of US$3 billion. Prime Minister Takeo Miki, who received Geisel, promised to cooperate in the construction of an aluminum complex in Belem, support for a pilot project in the agricultural development program for the Cerrado, help in the construction of the first stage of the Tuberao steel mill, cooperation in the Praia Mole port construction project, support for the Cenibra and Flonibra forestry and pulp resources projects, help in the expansion of the Usiminas steel mill, assistance in the development of Brazilian iron mines such as Capanema, and support for the Nibrasco joint venture for export of iron pellets to Japan.

It was agreed that the two nations would cooperate in science and technology, that Japan would provide export credits for the financing of Brazilian purchases of equipment and capital goods from Japan, and that

## Table 3–1
## Postwar Chronology of Japan–Brazil Relations

| | |
|---|---|
| 1949 | Under auspices of the Occupation authority (Supreme Command Allied Powers), a Japanese trade mission visits Brazil. |
| 1951 | Kanematsu-Gosho, Ltd., establishes a local office in Brazil. |
| 1952 | Japan–Brazil peace treaty and trade agreement is signed. |
| 1953 | Immigration of Japanese into Brazil is resumed. |
| 1955 | Toyobo Company establishes Japanese manufacturing operation in Brazil. This is followed by the "first rush" of Japanese firms into Brazil, centering on cotton spinning, fishery, and machinery production. |
| 1958 | Japan–Brazil joint steel venture, Usiminas, is established. |
| 1959 | Shipbuilding company, Ishibras, is established. |
| 1960 | Large-scale private Brazilian trade mission arrives in Japan for the first time after World War II. |
| 1962 | Japan–Brazil civil aviation agreement is signed. No. 1 blast furnace of Usiminas is kindled. |
| 1964 | Military revolution takes place in Brazil in March. |
| 1967 | Japan–Brazil tax treaty is concluded. A "second rush" of Japanese firms is inaugurated with the entry into Brazil of Toshiba Corporation, Nippon Electric Company, and others. |
| 1971 | Doko mission visits Brazil. Other missions follow, and the "Brazil boom" is in full swing. |
| 1972 | $58 million loan is granted by Japan for Japan–Brazil shipbuilding program. |
| 1973 | Last Japanese emigration ship arrives at Santos Port. (Thereafter, emigrants leave Japan by air.) "Oil shock" takes place in October. |
| 1974 | Private-level Japan–Brazil economic committee holds inaugural meeting. Prime Minister Kakuei Tanaka visits Brazil and promises cooperation in large aluminum, paper pulp, and other projects. |
| 1975 | Brazilian distrust of Japan is aroused by postponement of Amazon aluminum smelting plan. Nagano mission and also Prime Minister Takeo Fukuda visit Brazil. Japan–Brazil economic cooperation is reaffirmed. |
| 1976 | President Ernesto Geisel visits Japan in September. "Complementary relationship" of the two nations is affirmed. Japan offers economic cooperation in the amount of $3 billion. Second Japan–Brazil joint economic meeting is held. |
| 1977 | Japan–Brazil joint-venture pulp plant, Cenibra, begins operation. |
| 1978 | Seventieth anniversary of Japanese emigration to Brazil is celebrated in June. Japanese banking syndicate extends $700 million loan to Tuberao steel mill. |
| 1979 | Meeting of Japanese and Brazilian cabinet officers is held. The "Asia port" concept is introduced. Japanese Foreign Minister Sunao Sonoda visits Brazil in August. |
| 1980 | Japan's Federation of Economic Organizations (*Keidanren*) inaugurates the Carajas cooperation committee. Construction of Tuberao steel mill begins. Japanese mission for trade promotion visits Brazil and arranges procurement in the amount of $700 million. Japan participates in Brazil's oil development projects. |
| 1981 | Large Japanese steelmakers reach agreement in April to buy 10 million tons of Carajas iron ore annually. Decision is made to begin construction of Amazon aluminum smeltery. Japanese Minister of International Trade and Industry Rokusuke Tanaka visits Brazil, followed by Foreign Minister Sunao Sonoda. |
| 1982 | Prime Minister Zenko Suzuki visits Brazil in June. The prime minister points out that Brazil is the country to which the largest amount of Japanese investment and financing has been directed. |
| 1984 | President Joao Figueiredo visits Japan in May. An agreement on scientific and technological cooperation is signed. |

long-term commercial contracts would be arranged for the expo Brazilian raw materials and food to Japan. It was also agreed tha Brazilian government would issue yen-denominated (*Samurai*) bonds i Tokyo market. In May of 1984, President Joao Figueiredo visited Japan and received a pledge of US$1.32 billion in further financing. Since World War II, relations between Japan and Brazil have evolved in every international dimension except the military and strategic. Brazil's approach to Japan has been made by means of contacts at the private-company level, through Japan's Federation of Economic Organizations (*Keidanren*), through contacts at the government ministerial level, and through contacts with the prime minister. As stated by a member of the Asian Department of Brazil's Ministry of External Relations, it is the mission of that ministry to act as a coordinating agency and to give a "political meaning" to these contacts.

## The Milieu for Capital Inflow

Diverse opinions are expressed by informed persons in Washington, Tokyo, and Brazil concerning the congeniality of the Brazilian milieu for foreign investment. An official of the World Bank declares that "Brazilians have an easy working relationship with foreigners." The political officer at the Brazil desk of the U.S. State Department remarks that "Brazil is still reluctant to accept direct foreign investment. They want foreign loans."[1] The official and economically rational position on foreign investment does not necessarily reflect Brazilian sentiment concerning foreign capital.

Formally, in contrast with frequent and drastic changes in supplementary laws and administrative regulations, the basic laws concerning foreign investment in Brazil have remained intact since 1964. The chief statutes governing foreign investment (Law 4131 of September 3, 1962 and Law 4390 of August 29, 1964) declare that foreign investment will receive essentially the same treatment as domestic capital. Various fiscal, financial, and import "incentives" are legally available to foreigners as well as to Brazilian investors. In fact, however, specified markets are reserved for Brazilian nationals. These include armaments,[2] public utilities, the information media, petroleum exploration and refining (other than by means of a risk contract with Petrobras, the government oil monopoly), marine insurance and reinsurance, specified types of ocean shipping, and areas of informatics as broadly defined. In sectors such as banking, petrochemicals, mining, telecommunications, pharmaceuticals, and aircraft, foreigners are subject to restrictions. Among other industries, foreigners are not welcome in the alcohol fuels program.

According to the U.S. Embassy in Brazil, sectors in which foreign capital is wanted include those contributing to import substitution, export expansion, and capital goods manufacturing and those related to priorities such as agroindustry, essential consumer goods, and major projects such as the Carajas project and the Cerrado agricultural development project. In addition, Brazil offers regional development and incentive programs in the Northeast, the Amazon, and the free-trade zone in Manaus.[3] Under pressure of the debt crisis, two measures were recently adopted, namely, Decree Law of December 29, 1982 and Ministry of Finance Order Number 1383. These were intended to provide income tax incentives conducive to the conversion of foreign loans into equity investment. However, very little conversion has occurred.

The government's ambivalence toward foreign investment is evident. For example, it wants foreign investment that contributes to industrial development and economic growth, as well as for balance of payments reasons, but at the same time it clearly prefers joint ventures with majority interest on the Brazilian side. It welcomes transfers of technology, but since 1975 it has restricted foreign entry into markets such as informatics, in which domestic technology is both inadequate and immature. Moreover, a good deal of administrative discretion exists in implementation of the laws, which are not necessarily interpreted in favor of foreigners. In particular, the Brazilian elite is not pro-United States. In general, because of Brazil's financial dependence, they are anti-OECD as well. In a mechanical sense, there may be a coherent Brazilian government policy toward MNCs, but in practice, according to an American banker in Rio de Janeiro, there is no consistency in the way various agencies and officials apply it. The rules of the game are not well defined.

The bias against foreign equity capital became explicit during the brief administration of Joao Goulart (1961–1964). Prior to 1963, in the absence of "conditions" for the entry of equity capital, the inflow was uninhibited. Thereafter, despite the "outward-looking" policies of the military regime that took office in 1964, borrowing from abroad predominated over accepting foreign direct investment. On the Brazilian side, the nationalist attitude was conveyed by Senator Severo Gomes (formerly minister of industry and commerce under President Geisel), a proponent of government control of the economy. "The law for foreign investment permits great liberty to foreigners to do what they want—with some exceptions," he said. "But we need more control to harmonize these investments, especially in the long term. This would be in the interest of the MNCs themselves."[4] At the beginning of the century, foreign capital enjoyed industrial dominance in Latin America in fields such as public utilities. Brazilians are wary of allowing this to happen again.

In emulation of Japan's "catching up" accomplishments following World War II, Brazilian authorities would like to achieve technological advance by acquiring foreign technology and know-how without acquiring foreigners.

An American investment consultant in Brazil remarked, "Brazil wants U.S. capital and technology, but not Americans."[5] Accommodation of this attitude is reflected in the fact that some Brazilian firms are only facades for foreign companies. There is a difference, however, between Brazil today and Japan following World War II. At that time, as a crippled supplicant, Japan was able to "presume upon the indulgence" (*amae*) of its patron. Today, greatness is Brazil's manifest destiny. For that reason, despite its nationalistic technology policy, many major foreign technology companies maintain token branches in Brazil. Are they willing, however, to foster Brazil's high-technology competence without being permitted to sell final products of a high-technology type in the Brazilian market? This, evidently, is what the government hopes for in its relationship with Japan. Accordingly, a great deal of importance was attached by Brazil to the science and technology agreement that was signed during President Figueiredo's visit to Japan in May of 1984. In the meantime, as remarked by Senator Severo Gomes, "We must inhibit payment of royalties for things that are not real technology transfers."[6]

## The Nature of Capital Inflow

The foremost period of foreign investment in Brazil was 1960–1980. During those decades, investment by the United States was predominant. Foreign investment entered the automobile, chemicals, metals, and mechanical fields. Japanese interest was initially focused on procurement of raw materials for export to Japan. Next it concentrated on loans for the construction of infrastructure that would promote the production of raw materials and on direct investment for raw materials supply. In the Cerrado project, the Japan International Cooperation Agency (JICA) and the Brazilian Ministry of Agriculture made a technical study concerning the production of soybeans, which turned out to be of better quality than those of the United States. After 1974, foreign financing was primarily in the form of loans. Direct investment was substantial, however. It accounts for approximately 10 to 15 percent of total industrial production in Brazil. As a result of economic instability and the U.S. capital shortage, a big slump in direct foreign investment occurred in 1983. To the extent that it occurred, foreign investment in Brazil was largely in the form of involuntary reinvestment of profits. In an interview with Ana Maria Jul at the IMF, I was told that while statistics concerning foreign direct investment in Brazil by industry and statistics concerning investment by country of origin were readily available, no foreign investment statistics of country of origin by industry or industry by country of origin had been compiled.[7] This makes it difficult to quantify the extent to which direct investment by Japan and the United States, respectively, has been aimed at the Brazilian domestic market rather than exports. According to Senator Gomes,

"The United States and Japan have both mainly looked at the domestic Brazilian market. This is a big country, and it has a big domestic potential."[8] Paulo Rabello de Castro, editor of *Conjuntura Economica,* had a similar opinion. "U.S. MNCs came here," he said, "to cash in on domestic Brazilian growth and to target the domestic market, not the export market. Now they are trying to export for political reasons. The Japanese, however, came later, and they did try to export, primarily raw materials to Japan."[9] A Brazil expert in the Mitsubishi Heavy Industries Company in Tokyo made a remark, which, if biased, at least reflects a Japanese point of view. "U.S. firms in Brazil," he said, "are mostly in the soft industries, which are characterized by mass production and by short-term horizons with regard to profit returns."[10]

## Administration of Policy

There are all sorts of reasons why the prescriptions of textbook development economics may fail to work and many reasons why development may occur—as in Japan and South Korea—as a result of policies that defy the textbooks. In the Brazilian case, the results of comprehensive economic controls have not shown the textbooks to be invariably wrong. Despite its magnificent natural endowment, Brazil's masses visibly live in poverty. Economic controls have not removed bottlenecks; instead, they impose inappropriate institutional arrangements that perpetuate dualism and backwardness. By analogy, the debt problem has been seen by the IMF as merely a liquidity problem rather than as a solvency problem. This view is based on the proposition that Brazil's resources are in place. If resources are not available for use, however, in effect, they do not exist. Brazil's predicament is a problem of institutional organization, which is a structural matter and therefore a solvency problem. Institutional arrangements, such as corporatism, centralization, and the manifold devices of government intervention, determine how Brazil's economic and social system functions. They also determine the extent to which relations with the United States and Japan are functional or dysfunctional, "solvent" or "insolvent."

Corporatism is a system in which, by mutual agreement and at the expense of the general welfare, industry, labor, and government operate the economy for their own benefit. Brazil's corporativist system was modeled on that of Fascist Italy. In Brazil's private sector, there are confederations representing various professional, industrial, and commercial groups. A typical and important example is the Federation of Industries of Sao Paulo (FIESP). Throughout Brazil, there are thousands of minor "FIESPs," known pejoratively as "unions of individualists." Members of particular occupations or professions feel obliged to join their respective corporatist federations, which "represent" them. Economists, physicians, livestock producers, and engineers all have corporatist affiliations. The federations apply political pressure by vocalizing to the Congress and to the press. They apply political pressure to the banks, for example, regarding allocation of scarce credit. They bargain with the government concerning price controls, subsidies, and quotas.

Even before the revolution of 1964, comprehensive direct controls were employed in Brazil. They proliferated further under the military regime, in contrast to the political liberalization that eventuated in *abertura*. According to the director of the Mitsui trading company (Mitsui Brasileira, Ltda.) in Rio de Janeiro, "There is much more government control here than in Japan."[11] Government intervention dominates production, finance, pricing, and distribution. Through its federal enterprises, the government is the buyer of last resort. Typical restrictions include performance requirements for domestic and foreign investors, discretionary and duplicative import licensing procedures, market reserve policies, restrictive government procurement, quotas, foreign exchange controls, registration of loans, registration of software, mandatory use of a central gateway for transborder data flows, and export restrictions. Among the agencies that control activities of foreign businessmen in Brazil are the Central Bank, which imposes control on money and credit, as well as registration of capital and remittances; the Monetary Council, which controls the entry of foreign investment (under the chairmanship of the Ministry of Finance, one-third of its membership is from the private sector); the Economic Development Council (CDE); the Industrial Development Council (CDI), which screens and controls industrial projects; the Special Fund for Industrial Finance (FINAME); the Superintendency for the Development of the Northeast (SUDENE), which guides the nature of investment and administers special taxes and subsidies; the Foreign Trade Department of the Bank of Brazil (CACEX), which coordinates and carries out Brazil's foreign trade policy and supervises almost all operations related to external trade; the Special Secretariat for Supply and Prices (SEAP) of the Ministry of Planning, which (instead of CACEX) controls exports of agricultural products and which has monthly meetings with FIESP concerning the regulation of prices in the domestic market; the Brazilian Coffee Institute (IBC)[12]; the Department of Foreign Capital Supervision and Registration (FIRCE); the Institute of Industrial Property (INPI), which controls patent, trademark, and licensing agreements, including the amount of royalties that can be remitted to foreign countries; the Special Secretariat for Information and Technology (SEI); and many others. In terms of its impact on American and Japanese business, "The government's regulation of the economy is even more oppressive than the preemptive role of monopolistic state enterprises. Every day we read the newspapers backwards: we start with the financial page to find the latest government regulations before reading the 'news' on the front page."[13] Moreover, "If you don't do what the government wants, they can get back at you. Everything in Brazil works by means of licenses, by which they can restrict your credit at the bank, your imports, and every other move you want to make."[14]

Regulatory discipline in Brazil is confused by the fact that the Central Bank is both a central bank and a development bank. The government's control of its own finances is disrupted by the fact that a substantial part of the federal government's expenditures are performed outside the Treasury budget. Since 1964, the government has maintained three separate annual budgets. First is the fiscal budget, controlled by the Planning Ministry. It includes the federal tax revenues and expenditures based on them. Second is the budget for federally owned enterprises. Third is the monetary budget, which consolidates Central Bank and Banco do Brasil operations. This budget is proposed by the Central Bank and submitted for the approval of the National Monetary Council, after which it is managed by the Banco do Brasil. A decade ago, Professor Allan Meltzer looked for causes of inflation in Brazil and was puzzled to find that there was no fiscal deficit and no source of inflation in the balance of payments. Then he discovered the monetary budget. This system is highly inflationary, while the federal budget itself may ostensibly be balanced. Moreover, the three-budget system in the past has made it impossible to find the exact amount of public spending—often to the government's benefit in dealing with the IMF. Beginning in 1986, there has been a progressive and now virtually complete integration of the monetary budget into the federal fiscal budget.

The budget system has been conducive to the government becoming overextended (*estatizacao*). This, together with the overcentralization of the economy, has multiplied the effects of institutional confusion. In financial markets, the system has been highly segmented, and selective credit controls have been applied. In contrast with the successful regime of segmentation in the Japanese banking system, however, in Brazil it has stultified the economy. Central control, incidentally, has had a particularly adverse effect on small and medium-sized businesses, which are the chief victims of bureaucracy and red tape. This problem is worst at the state government level, where permissions to be obtained, forms to be filled out, and lengthy procedures hinder the establishment of new firms. The federal government proposed the reduction of red tape that restricts the formation of small businesses, but Leonel Brizola, the socialist governor of Rio de Janeiro, opposed this because he feared it would cause his state to lose revenue. Most states depend on the federal government for 70 to 90 percent of their budget expenditures. No state can autonomously impose an income tax, for example. Dependency of the states on the federal government may politically motivate the perpetuation of overcentralization in Brazil.

In addition to the overextension, overcentralization, and institutional disarray of the federal government, the business milieu in Brazil is marked by ambiguity between administrative and legislative authority. "Decree laws" proclaimed by the president and "resolutions" issued by federal agencies are among the most important rules of the nation. "In Brazil, administrative controls are more important than legal controls."[15] For example, tax rates, import and export licenses, interest rates, price controls, and the degree of "monetary correction" (indexation for inflation) are administratively rather than legislatively determined. Indeed, the Brazilian Federal Constitution gives the President of the Republic exclusive authority to initiate laws dealing with economic or financial matters or increasing payrolls or public expenses. However, bills proposed by the President of the Republic may be amended by the federal Congress, provided that no increase in expenditures is involved. Thus while the Congress may *pass* bills on economic or financial matters issued by the President, the Congress cannot *propose* such bills.[16] In addition to his control over foreign trade and foreign investment, which are "economic or financial matters," the President controls informatics by classifying it as a "national security" matter.

The preeminent role of the bureaucrats induces the practice of administrative guidance—with encouragement from the Japanese example—whereby administrative instructions are not even written down. This practice relieves the bureaucracy of the burden of abiding by precedent and widens its discretionary scope. Its actions are also more flexible by being removed from public scrutiny. In the administration of licensing, it is especially convenient for the government to impose restrictions in verbal rather than written form. Restrictions imposed by administrative rather than statutory measures, moreover—again, as in the case of Japan—are "deniable," or they may escape international attention. Thus they may forestall retaliation or at least make it more difficult. In foreign trade, because of Brazil's informal administrative guidance, the effective level of its protectionist barriers cannot be readily quantified. Within the bureaucracy, moreover, it is the top ministers who decide everything of importance. This is contrary to practice in Japan, where the staff works out the answers and the minister merely nods his approval.

Even when laws are written down, national policy is often unclear and subject to the interpretation of various government agencies that participate in implementing it. Characteristically, new rules are promulgated by means of circulars, legalistically formulated. In practice, however, one department chief explained that in cases where his office is directly concerned, he negotiates the manner in which a new rule will be implemented by making personal contacts and commitments among other concerned agencies, Japanese-style.[17]

Although the government may deny it, according to a professor at the Getulio Vargas Foundation, by means of administrative guidance it does play a role in the relations of state and private Brazilian firms with foreign entities. Moreover, there is little judicial recourse in Brazil from arbitrary administrative decisions. For example, according to the same observer, the executive branch typically starves the judiciary of funds, thus crippling its ability to perform.[18] Another consequence of administrative discretion in implementing the law is that many laws are simply not enforced. The Constitution contains an antimonopoly provision, but it is not observed in practice. Price controls are widely violated.

Is the regulatory climate changing in the course of Brazil's economic tansition, especially under the impact of the debt crisis? As of August of 1983, according to Senator Severo Gomes, "It is not changing yet. But it is going to change. I hope it will be controlled by the Congress and not by the bureaucracy."[19]

## Policy Instruments

After the revolution of 1964, Brazil's instruments of economic control in the external sector were largely designed to promote its import-substitution and export-promotion policies. The import-substitution policies were designed to benefit indigenous firms. Since the advent of debt crisis, external policies have been chiefly concerned with Brazil's balance of payments difficulties, with emphases on capital movements and commodity flows.

The following is my translation of an undated intramural Japanese memorandum prepared by Mitsubishi Heavy Industries, Ltd.[20] It comments on various regulations concerning foreign capital in Brazil.

### Capital in Brazil

A. Pre-Geisel legislation:

1. Uniform Labor Law
   Decree Law No. 5452, May 1, 1943
   In foreign enterprises, two-thirds of the capital and two-thirds of the employees must be Brazilian.

2. Foreign Capital Law
   Decree Law No. 4131, August 29, 1964
   Fundamentally, this law says that no discrimination is to be made against foreign capital. But at the same time, it restricts profit remittance to overseas and forbids loans by public banking agencies to foreign enterprises. Also, it restricts the remittance of royalties to the parent company abroad.

3. CREA Law
   Decree Law No. 5194, December 24, 1966
   This law is designed to ensure jobs for engineers and technicians. CREA

qualifications require graduation from a Brazilian university or similar background. Such persons may register as CREA engineers. It is possible for foreigners to register, but the procedures are intricate. A CREA engineer must be employed for the establishment of certain types of companies.

4. Engineering Consultant Law
   Decree Law No. 64345, April 1, 1969
   Decree Law No. 66717, June 15, 1970
   Decree Law No. 73140, November 9, 1973
   Enterprises that declare themselves to be professional engineering consultants must at their founding have the majority of their shareholders registered as CREA engineers. In addition to this condition, enterprises eligible to submit a bid involving public enterprises must be controlled by Brazilian nationals.

5. Law of Industrial Property Rights
   Decree Law No. 5648, December 11, 1970
   Decree Law No. 5772, December 21, 1971
   In addition to restrictions on royalty payments specified in Decree Law 4131, various further restrictions apply to the remittance of royalties and similar transactions between the subsidiary and the parent company.

B. Post-Geisel legislation:

1. Law of Technical Aids
   INPI Ato Normativo 15, September 15, 1975
   Before 1975, foreign capital was generally unregulated by means of laws and ordinances. Instead, control usually took the form of administrative guidance. The present law strengthens control of technical assistance in wide range and detail. For foreign capital, this control was made extremely strict.

2. Overall Industry Policy
   CDE Resolution 9, March 31, 1977
   This law is a basic protection measure for domestic manufacturers; it is something the domestic capital goods manufacturers have been waiting for. After it was announced, however, domestic manufacturers said that it fell short of their expectations and demanded a more definitive law to regulate foreign capital. Its main contents are:
   a. Government organizations will give preference to domestic business.
   b. BNDES and other public financing agencies will give preference to domestic projects.
   c. Joint ventures with domestic majority ownership will be encouraged. This means offering necessary funds, promoting technology transfer, and promoting basic as well as applied engineering. Main contractors are to be domestic enterprises; home manufacturers of components are to be strengthened.
   d. Concerning the capital goods industry:
      i. Government organizations will give priority to domestic goods in their procurement.
      ii. Government organizations and public financing agencies will cooperate

to promote specialization of enterprises in order to avoid an excessive increase in the number of enterprises.

iii. The level of domestic production of components will be raised.

iv. In the formation of consortia, leading domestic firms will be given priority.

e. Government organizations cannot purchase goods manufactured in projects that have not been approved by CDI, INPI, and others.

3. Law on Rate of Domestication
CDI Resolution 49, May 27, 1977
This law is designed to increase in stages the percentage of domestic production of every product, both mass-produced goods and capital goods. The percentage and the schedule for domestication are to be registered with FINAME and reported to CDI. This makes it possible for CDI to also check which manufacturers make what products.

4. Rate of Domestication
FINAME Circular 30, March 18, 1977
The rate of domestication, which was targeted at 65 percent in special programs, has been raised to 85 percent.

5. Restriction on Remittance of Licensing Fees
INPI Ato Normativo 30, February 2, 1978
Remittance of technology fees in the automobile industry is forbidden, with exceptions in special cases. There has been a suggestion to the INPI director to extend this practice to other categories in the future.

6. Advance Inspection Law
INPI Ato Normativo 32, May 10, 1978
Provides for advance inspection on technical aid contracts. This makes it possible to exercise control more strictly.

7. Foreign Capital Registration Law
FINAME Circular 35, May 21, 1978
Foreign capital is to be registered only after various restrictions have been enforced:
a. Ban on remittance of royalties.
b. One type of machinery more than four firms. [This may mean that no foreign capital will be registered if more than four domestic firms produce machinery similar to the production proposed.]
c. CDI permission required.

8. Telebras Foreign Capital Regulation
NORMA 145, May 1977
In placing orders, Telebras will give priority to domestic producers.

C. Points not legislated but given administrative guidance:

1. CDI:
a. At the time of investment, foreign capital shall bring in 75 percent of its total expected expenditure as a risk fund.

  b. Payment of technology licensing fee shall not be linked to the output of a specific product.
  c. Export of output will be made obligatory. The objective is to export double the amount of the import components.
  d. Restriction on types of eligible machinery.
  e. Advance application is required for permission to alter the stock share ratio or organization [of the foreign firm].
  f. Ban on competition with domestic manufacturers. Limit on the number of manufacturers.

*Note:* As of December 7, 1979, CDI lost 90 pecent of its previous function. What will happen to CDI in the future is unknown. [The preceding items refer to the situation prior to December 7, 1979.]

2. FINAME:
  a. There were various discriminatory acts against foreign capital at the time of registration. For example, the registration list might not be announced, or registration might be reserved.
  b. Ban on substantial remittance of royalties.

*Note:* Since December 7, 1979, various subsidies and special privileges have been decreased. There has also been a change in the FINAME financing pattern.

3. Ministry of Justice, Ministry of Labor: Restriction on the issuance of visas to foreigners. The details are not clear, but it is especially difficult to obtain a visa for clerical employees.

4. CADE: This is similar to the Japanese Fair Trade Commission. It is concerned with surveillance of the abuse of economic power. It was formed at the time the left wing was in political office. For a time it seemed to have been inactivated. Subsequently, however, it intervened in the heavy electrical equipment manufacturers cartel matter and the tire manufacturers resale price matter, and there have been other actions giving an impressing of targeted attacks on foreign capital.

5. General: In specified categories, takeover of Brazilian enterprises by foreign capital has been strictly forbidden since around 1973.

The restrictions referred to in the preceding memorandum replicate the smothering restraints imposed on foreign capital in Japan during the first several postwar decades. The "law of similars," The policy of market reserve, and the foreign exchange control laws of Brazil could be described as very Japanese in spirit, prior to the era of liberalization. The "law of similars," in effect since 1967, is not statutory. It has the flavor of common law and is enforced by administrative guidance. As a protective device, it has been used to mobilize tariffs, exchange regulations, quotas, or outright import embargoes in cases where domestic producers can supply a product "similar" to a proposed import.

Whereas the "law of similars" restricts imports of competitive products, the policy of "market reserve" goes further: it prevents foreigners even from producing competitive products within Brazil. From the point of view of the U.S. government, Brazil's market reserve policy is the "most restrictive"of its external policies.[21] In Brazil, the executive vice president of the American Chamber of Commerce stated that the market reserve policy constituted "the largest challenge the Chamber of Commerce faces. It is detrimental to Brazil and to the United States. The Chamber of Commerce has many allies among the Brazilians in this matter."[22]

One branch of the market reserve policy is the "empty space" approach, likewise of Japanese origin. (It was reflected in official Japanese policy until May of 1973 when the Fifth Capital Investment Liberalization Program opened all but twenty-two industries to 100 percent foreign equity control.) It encourages Brazilian (usually state) enterprises to enter and monopolize any empty space in the commodity chain in order to prevent foreign multinationals from preempting it. Thus Brazilian state companies monopolize many new industrial areas. Another branch of the market reserve policy, as in the case of informatics, purports to be warranted for "national security" reasons, thus replacing foreign "information imperialism" with Brazilian nationalsim in the information field. Market reserve in informatics was inaugurated by the military authorities in the early 1970s. Among others, foreign entry into heavy industry, energy, mining, engineering construction, pharmaceuticals, and biomedical computer equipment has likewise been increasingly restricted. Proponents of these restrictions argue that exclusion of foreigners is essential for the achievement of economies of scale in indigenous enterprises, especially in fields such as electronics. My Brazilian government informants pointed to Japan's success as having been accomplished by the same method. At present, Japan and the United States are the principal targets of Brazil's market reserve restrictions, especially in the informatics field.

*Informatics,* in accordance with other aspects of Brazilian administrative procedure, is not strictly defined. It might cover any branch of high technology. Administrative discretion in extending the boundaries of technological protection is thus quite flexible. A *national company,* however, is officially defined. It refers to a company organized under Brazilian law, 100 percent of which is owned by a Brazilian national and subject to effective national control. The later phrase means that the firm is domestically autonomous in terms of voting control and independent of foreign sources of capital and technology. Until October of 1984, informatics was subject to the policy-making authority of the Special Secretariat for Information Technology (SEI), a branch of the National Security Council. On October 3, 1984, Congress passed a national informatics law making SEI subordinate to a new body, known as the National Council for Information Technology and Automation (CONIN), headed by the President, with membership including ten government officials and eight industry representatives. SEI continues to be an advisory and executive agency. The new law provides for federal controls on the import of computer equipment until 1992. Until that time, only national companies may build micro, mini, and supermini computers. Foreign multinationals, however, including IBM and Hewlett-Packard, may continue to manufacture mainframe computers in Brazil, as they have been doing hitherto.

Article 9 of the new informatics law states that CONIN "shall adopt temporary restrictive measures for the production, operation, marketing and importation of informatics goods and services." The same article provides exemptions from restrictions on manufacturing and marketing for national companies using national technology and for informatics goods manufactured without imported components. *National technology* and *tropical technology* are popular terms in Brazil's protectionist vocabulary.

Politically, the informatics restriction, which was initiated by the military, is supported by a coalition between the left and the right. The right wing is led by the Servico Nacional de Informacoes (SNI), the internal security arm of the military. The left wing is led by the Party of the Brazilian Democratic Movement (PMDB). National producers of computer equipment, represented by the Brazilian Association of Computer Manufacturers (ABICOMP), are a third factor. They are motivated by a desire to exclude foreign competition and also to copy foreign hardware and software without paying royalties. In this they have the acquiescence of SEI. Apple Computer and IBM applied to SEI to register their copyrights and patents, but they were unable to receive clearance. Although legally provided for, in practice neither patent nor copyright protection is currently available to foreigners in Brazil. This anomaly contains a Japanese nuance. Typically, when a Japanese government agency takes a negative view of an application, it does not *deny* the application; it simply refrains from giving approval. The Brazilian government thus connives with the private sector in the practice of pirating foreign property. This may have a bearing on the government's reluctance to agree to proposals for placing such matters under the jurisdiction of GATT. Politically, it gives the government a basis for arguing that it intervenes in the economy for the benefit of private industry, not at its expense. While pirating may promote the prosperity of individual firms, however, it does not invigorate the international competitive power of Brazilian economy.

A fourth source of support for the informatics restriction comes from bureaucrats whose careers have been built on it. The combination of right wing, left wing, labor, business, and bureaucratic support for the informatics restriction creates a powerful lobby in its favor. In addition, there is a good deal of popular sentiment in support of developing domestic capability free from the "domination" of foreign companies. Hence the policy is not likely to be changed soon. Various foreign firms in the informatics field have been forced to sell out to Brazilian interests. In the hope of some possible future change in policy, many high-technology companies continue to maintain at least token branches in Brazil. In the meanwhile, the combination of import restrictions and informatics restrictions is a hindrance to Brazilian users of high-technology equipment.

This situation provides an interesting example of the Brazilian predicament with regard to economic development. Analyticaly, it can be described by the proposition that the aggregate of private interests is not necessarily equivalent to the interests of the nation as a whole. In arguing the contrary, proponents of informatics restrictions cite the example of Japan's successful infant industry protectionism. A visiting delegation from Washington under the leadership of Richard Smith, U.S. State Department assistant secretary for finance and international development, was told in Sao Paulo that Brazil's policy of market reserve was patterned directly after Japan's policy of the 1950s and 1960s for the encouragement of indigenous enterprise.[23] It was a policy established "in the national interest."[24] The Japanese, however, started with a technological tradition and a reservoir of scientific and technical manpower that Brazil lacks. Furthermore, when Japan's "catching up" effort began, informatics was in its infancy. During that period, it was possible to "learn by doing." At present, the sophisticated level of high technology and the speed of its advance in leading industrial countries make it virtually impossible for beginners to reproduce the Japanese feat. Japan's infant industry efforts occurred at a time when high-technology competition was less intense and the stakes much lower than they are today. In helping Japan as a beginner, moreover, the United States felt less threatened about its own position in world-class high-technology competition than it does at present. American firms were willing to license technology and know-how more freely than they are today. Indeed, Brazil's delinquency in providing patent and copyright protection makes it unlikely that it will receive the sort of help from abroad that Japan was able to buy. It would seem that the distance between Brazilian accomplishments and those of leading industrial nations in the informatics field is bound to widen.

Regardless of the debt crisis, there has been no remission of the market reserve policy in Brazil. Some of the prohibitions, moreover, are enforced in a rather erratic manner. A foreigner, for example, cannot buy land in Brazil. Nor can a Brazilian company owned by a foreigner buy land in Brazil. But a Brazilian company owned by another Brazilian company which in turn is owned by a foreigner *may* buy land. As mentioned earlier, there are administrative restrictions against foreign companies that are not written down. For example, there is no statutory restriction against the establishment by foreigners of new commercial banks. In practice, however, foreigners are not allowed to open new commercial banks, nor are existing commercial banks owned by foreigners alowed to establish new branches.[25]

Beyond the specific types of interventions and protectionism referred to earlier, the Brazilian government maintains a battery of foreign trade and foreign exchange controls that have a sweeping impact on foreign commerce and investment. In the opinion of a Citibank official with personal experience of both countries, "Brazil's foreign exchange controls are all-encompassing and worse than Japan's, except perhaps for Japan in the 1950s."[26] The foreign exchange controls are administered by the Exchange Department (DECAM) of the Central Bank, and control over foreign capital is administered by the Department of Foreign Capital Supervision and Registration (FIRCE) of the same institution. In principle, these controls are applied on behalf of Brazil's import-substitution and export-promotion policies and in the interest of debt management. For many years, in order to encourage capital inflow, the government kept the cost of borrowing from abroad below the cost of domestic funds, and credit ceilings were imposed on domestic borrowing. The consequences were counterproductive.

Resolution 851 (July 29, 1983) centralized all foreign exchange payments in the hands of the Central Bank. It required all foreign exchange proceeds to be surrendered to the Central Bank in exchange for cruzeiros. (Exchange centralization was partly rescinded in March of 1984.) It also established a foreign exchange allocation system. Foreign currency can be officially obtained only for authorized transactions. Applications for the purchase of foreign exchange must be accompanied by appropriate and voluminous documentation. (However, an illegal "parallel" market is tolerated by the authorities; the parallel rate of exchange is quoted daily in the newspapers.) All importers must be registered with CACEX, and imports can be transacted only by registered firms or persons. CACEX also issues import licenses, without which no import is permitted. Exports do not require a license, but they do require an export certificate issued by CACEX as evidence of compliance with trade and exchange regulations. Importers are required to submit an annual import program to CACEX as a basis for requesting import licenses. External financing of an import must be registered with FIRCE, which is conditional upon a prior ruling by CACEX that the proposed import commodity is not available from domestic sources. Many "superfluous" imports are not eligible for licensing by CACEX.[27] Most exports require prior approval of CACEX; exports of specified comodities (including some raw materials consumed domestically) are prohibited or conditional on prior domestic sales. Some exports are subject to an annual quota. Exports of coffee are subject to authorization by the Brazilian Coffee Institute (IBC). According to Central Bank Resolutions 799 and 800 (February 21, 1983), export taxes ranging from 9 to 20 percent were levied on a wide range of mainly unprocessed agricultural, livestock, and forestry products.[28] These coexist with subsidies for exports of manufactured goods.

Controls on capital movements are designed to restrict capital outflow and promote capital inflow. Prior approval from the Central Bank is required for practically all foreign currency loans received. The interest rate on such loans must be certified to correspond to the interest rate in the country of origin. Loans executed or proceeds received after January 1, 1984 must be for a minimum period of 9 years, and repayment can begin only after 60 months. The Central Bank will recognize only foreign currency remittances that have been made through authorized banking channels and are exchanged into cruzeiros at the official rate of exchange. With minor exceptions, foreign currency payments for current invisibles require the approval of DECAM or FIRCE. Purchases of foreign exchange are subject to a financial transactions tax of 25 percent. (Petrobras, the oil monopoly, and Brazil's largest firm, is exempt from this tax.) Remittance of dividends and repatriation of equity capital are subject to prior compliance with capital registration and approval procedures. Tax penalties for profit remittance constitute one of the principal factors discouraging to U.S. direct investment in Brazil. Remittance of dividends is subject to high withholding taxes on dividend rates above a fairly low level. Remittance of interest is likewise subject to withholding taxes. Royalties may not be remitted by a Brazilian subsidiary to its foreign parent when 50 percent or more of the local firm's voting capital is held by the foreign principal firm. Foreign investments made by Brazilians are subject to the approval of the Central Bank.

Brazil's protective stance in the external sector is compounded by subsidies for export promotion and other types of incentives. The variety, subsectoral dispersion, and interacting effects of Brazilian subsidies make it difficult to evaluate their quantitative impact. Exports are subsidized not only at the point of export, but also at the level of production for export. Agricultural loans, for example, are provided at negative real interest rates. Thus even the definition of an export subsidy is complex. A subsidy, moreover, could be a favor having no observable financial dimension. Regulations for the granting of subsidies are by no means invariable.[29] In practical terms, most subsidies are given to big business. About two-thirds of government subsidies are disbursed in Sao Paulo and the southern part of Brazil, thus reinforcing regional dualism.[30] Moreover, most agricultural subsidies go to rich farmers, not the poor, reinforcing the dualism of income distribution. In a sardonic comment concerning subsidies and incentives, Delfim Netto remarked, "Private enterprises are sucking the government's nipples."[31]

The subsidy system for exports includes both fiscal and financial incentives. It was established during the economic liberalization of 1964–1967 and reinforced in later years. Fiscal incentives include (1) exemptions from indirect taxes (such as import duties) and (2) subsidies to compensate for such export disincentives as overvaluation of the exchange rate. The first of these includes mainly duty drawback privileges; the second includes the export tax credit (*credito premio*), exclusion from corporate income tax of profits made on export sales, and other exemptions. The *credito primo* was finally eliminated in 1985, and agricultural credit subsidies were cut back drastically in accordance with the austerity measures of 1983–1984. The Special Program of Fiscal Incentives for Exporters (BEFIEX) was established in 1972. Washington opposes BEFIEX as a violation of GATT. It is of importance mainly to a few large exporters in the automotive field. The BEFIEX subsidies are determined on an individual company basis in negotiations between individual beneficiaries and the BEFIEX administration. Typically, in return for adherence to long-term export targets on the part of the firm, they include substantial duty and tax reductions on imports of products to be used in the production of goods for both the domestic and export markets. During 1978–1980, about 20 percent of industrial exports were performed with the benefit of BEFIEX. The export tax credit, introduced in 1968, has been the most important subsidy to exports. (It was scheduled to be terminated at the end of 1985.) "In the transport equipment industry, the amount of tax credit received in 1979 was more than four times the amount of export profits." This and similar data for other industries suggests that "export incentives were concentrated in industries with the least comparative advantage."[32] It may be noted that Ford and General Motors are among the principal beneficiaries of BEFIEX. In 1980, the adjusted average rate of Brazil's fiscal export incentives (including the export tax credit, income tax reduction, BEFIEX, drawback, and others) was equivalent to aproximately 9.3 percent of the total value of exports.[33] Under a December 1982 bilateral understanding with the United States, no new BEFIEX contracts are to be approved. It remains to be seen whether this understanding will hold water.

As distinguished from fiscal export incentives, financial export incentives include those provided by the Fund for Export Financing (FINEX) and the Central Bank Resolution 674 program. The former provides preshipment and postshipment financing; the latter provides preshipment financing. The subsidy element provided by financing under Resolution 674 has been estimated as 12.7 percent of the value of manufactured exports in 1981.[34] In addition to these visible subsidies, invisible subsidies are provided to favored firms in the form of negotiated electricity and energy rates. According to an estimate cited by the senior vice president of Citibank in Sao Paulo, invisible subsidies to Brazilian exports are approximately 25 percent of the magnitude of visible subsidies.[35]

## Discrimination against Foreigners

Discrimination against foreigners takes place in the distribution of subsidies as well as in other respects mentioned earlier. According to an official of a major Japanese capital goods producer, "The Brazilian government directs many kinds of discrimination, both legal and illegal, against foreign companies. However, discrimination against Japan is not greater than against the United States or other countries. As an example concerning the United States, General Electric Company makes locomotives in Brazil, but the national manufacturers of locomotives persuaded the government not to purchase locomotives from them."[36] According to a minister of the Japanese Embassy, the Brazilian government "applies pressure on Japanese companies to use Brazilian national company inputs in their manufacturing activities."[37]

In the field of banking, for more than a decade, foreigners have been denied entry into commercial banking and have been confined to investment banking.[38] As borrowers, foreign firms are not eligible for loans at subsidized rates of interest from Brazilian investment banks, from the National Bank for Economic and Social Development (BNDES), or from the Bank of Brazil. (This creates an inducement for foreign firms to take a minority position in joint ventures with Brazilian firms.) Moreover, to accelerate the inflow of foreign currency, the Brazilian government restricts access by foreigners to indigenous banks. U.S. and Japanese firms receive very little accommodation at Brazilian financial institutions. As of July 1984, the latter were subject to the rule that the sum of their loans to MNCs and Brazilian state enterprises must not exceed 30 percent of their total lending. Japanese firms do not borrow from Brazilian banks for their investments in Brazil. In the debenture market, according to an unwritten rule of the Securities Commission (CVM), foreign firms can seek funding only to the extent of 50 percent of the capital they brought into Brazil.

In "national security" industries, apart from those from which foreigners are totally excluded, foreign firms are required by law to be minority shareholders. Accordingly, Japan's NEC was obliged to reduce its equity in a Brazilian electronics firm from 100 to 49 percent. In the high-technology field, foreigners are discouraged by inadequate patent protection. The life of a patent is 15 years from the date it was applied for. However, the government may take from 6 to 9 years before deciding to grant a patent. Will the milieu for foreign direct investment improve as a result of the debt crisis? According to a first secretary at the U.S. Embassy in Brasilia, "I doubt it very much. The United States has made a little progress in a few areas— science and technology, nuclear, and military-industrial production. But not much progress has been made in the economic area. The United States has put no pressure on Brazil, except to come to an agreement with IMF."[39]

Prior to a new rule announced in June of 1984, Japanese trading companies (*sogo shosha*) were not eligible to attempt to qualify for national treatment under the Brazilian trading company law. Qualified firms receive important benefits that had been denied to the Japanese. According to the new law, a qualified trading company must have the form of a corporation (*sociedade anonima*) rather than the form of a limited-liability company (*sociedade por quotas de responsabilidade limitada*). Mitsubishi Trading Company, which according to my Mitsubishi informant has a "strong relation" with the Brazilian government, was the first to become eligible. Prior to the new law, Mitsui Trading Company did not have enough capital investment in Brazil to make the corporate form worthwhile; thereafter, however Mitsui was planning to comply with the conditions.

An intramural memorandum in Japanese of Mitsubishi Heavy Industries, Ltd., dated June 2, 1980, was made available to me in Tokyo. The memorandum comments on "examples of opposition to foreign capital group enterprises in Brazil" in the heavy industry field. It identifies several leading pressure groups, the Brazilian Industrial Machinery Association (ABIMAQ) and the Brazilian Basic Industry Development Association (ABDIB). ABIMAQ is associated with the Industrial Machinery and Equipment Syndicate of Sao Paulo (SIMESP). These organizations represent the Brazilian heavy industry and machine manufacturing sector. The memorandum describes a dozen cases in which government restrictions imposed at their instigation frustrated the business efforts of foreign firms in Brazil. The latter included the following: Krupp, IBM, Demag, Kawasaki, F.L. Smidth, Dow Chemical, G.E. Philips, Westinghouse, Toyo Soda Co., Michelin, and CBC. The memorandum identifies ABDIB as the principal source of nationalist discrimination in the heavy industry field. It refers to ABDIB's way of thinking as expressed in a meeting held on July 26, 1978. At the meeting, ABDIB declared that "the independence of our nation must include political, economic, and technical dimensions." In commenting on this statement, the Japanese memorandum remarks that "it might be compared to the mood of the Meiji Restoration in Japan."

The Japanese memorandum classifies the types of discrimination against the foreign firms just specified in the heavy industry field in Brazil as follows:

1. There were cases in which the Industrial Development Council (CDI) disapproved of projects proposed by foreign firms, but the details of the disapproval were not revealed.

2. There were cases in which CDI gave its approval, but conditionally.

3. There were cases in which disapproval was instigated by the oposition of domestic firms.

4. There were cases in which there was disapproval of proposed takeovers.

5. There were cases in which the reason for disapproval was that domestic manufacturers should be given preference.

6. There were cases in which the foreign equity participation was considered to be excessive.

7. There were cases in which the issue concerned the technology-transfer law.

8. There were cases in which by administrative guidance the Central Bank disqualified loans and profits for the purpose of foreign capital registration, even if they were reinvested. The memorandum points out that the Central Bank attempts to reduce the amount of reinvestment as much possible in order to promote the inflow of fresh capital from abroad.

These observations are consistent with the comment of the economic consul of the American Consulate at Sao Paulo, namely, that "import substitution is designed to benefit indigenous firms. Discriminatory policies are applied in their favor."[40]

## The Brazilian View of Japan

Brazilian perceptions of Japan are reported from various sources: Brazilians in Brazil, Brazilians abroad, Japanese in Brazil, Japanese abroad, Americans in Brazil, and Americans abroad. According to a professor at the Fundacao Getulio Vargas, "Japan has no cultural impact on Brazil. In the cultural field, the United States is the winner. I would never think of sending a student to Japan to study. What institution would I send him to? In my ten years at Vargas no Japanese professor has ever visited this institution. However, we have received visits from U.S., European, and even Chinese professors. Fifty percent of the music people listen to is from the United States. American and European movies play in Rio, but no Japanese movies. (Of course there are Japanese theaters in the "Little Tokyos" of Brazil.) Culturally, in planning a trip abroad, a Brazilian would think of going to New York ten times before thinking of going to Tokyo once."[41]

Despite its contact with Japan through immigration, for historical reasons Brazil is more aware of western Europe—especially of Germany and increasingly of France—than of Japan. As measured by press coverage, for example, Japan is hardly of consequence to the Brazilian at large. In the media, there is practically no reflection of the role of Japan in Brazilian affairs. Instead of being innocuous, however, from the point of view of a Chase banker highly conversant with Brazilian matters, "Brazilian–Japanese relations are not good." Why? "I don't know."[42]

Some perspective on the banker's comment may be found in remarks of the chairman of the Brazilian–American Chamber of Commerce in New York:

> In the background is the fact that during 1943–1944, Japanese were in a position of power in Brazil. But during World War II, U.S. propaganda

against Japan was very strong in Brazil. From a Brazilian point of view, the Japanese were more the enemy than the Germans or the Italians. Brazilians became suspicious of the Japanese. A residual of that suspicion still exists today. This enters into the problem of doing business. Brazilians find it difficult to do business with the Japanese. Their values are different from Brazilian values. Brazilians talk to Americans and Europeans and they can understand one another. But it is difficult to understand what a Japanese is thinking. Dialogue is difficult with them. They talk very little, They don't make waves. Concerning negotiating style, the Japanese come in three and fours. They have no power of decisionmaking. In this regard, the United States is similar: they send an employee who has no decision-making power. In the private Brazilian sector, on the other hand, it is a one-man show. The boss is the owner. He can make decisions. It would be more convenient if he could meet his counterpart—a single individual—who likewise would have decision-making power.

In a larger context, Japanese policy is planned strategically. Brazilians perceive the private sector as working in terms of the Japanese government plan. Thus they don't have the flexibility of the U.S. private sector. The Brazilians "tolerate" the Japanese. Notwithstanding, the Japanese private sector is perceived as much more helpful to Brazil than the U.S. private sector. The United States does not export from Brazil to the United States because they don't want to upset the markets for their domestic U.S. plants. The Japanese trading companies, however, market Brazilian products all over the world. In Brazil, when leftists pejoratively refer to "multinational companies," they are referring to American companies, not Japanese companies.[43]

In Tokyo, I asked the Brazilian ambassador for his comments on Japanese relations with Brazil. He observed that whereas U.S. firms are broadly diversified in Brazil, the Japanese take an approach that is "too narrow. Brazil's complaint against Japan is that it should be able to export a more diversified list of products to Japan. In terms of product categories, Japan's imports from Brazil are more narrowly concentrated than those of any other country. Second, Brazil wants more exchange with Japan in science and technology." The ambassador's first secretary amplified this in saying that Japan "does not bring in front-line technology to Brazil. It brings in second-class technology that is obsolete in Japan. Therefore the products of Japanese firms in Brazil are not competitive in advanced countries; they can be exported only to LDCs in Africa and the Middle East."[44]

In Brazil I was interested in the impressions of officials who had had negotiating experience with the Japanese. A senior official at the Central Bank made some ambivalent comments:

The Japanese negotiating stance is different from that of any other country— the eyes, the face, the color. They are talking and I don't know what they are thinking. They smile. . . . The Japanese government establishes a defensive position with regard to Japanese interests. They have a fixed objective. The Japanese are not the first to support a project. They come in only after others have made a commitment. Japanese banks lend money to Brazilian enterprises only with certain restrictions, and they lend only to projects in which they themelves are interested. U.S. banks lend to anybody. The Japanese are very careful. Very deliberate. There is always the calculating machine in the hand, and making the numbers. And also the photographic machine. In what they do, the Japanese are very solid. The United States is more quick; they take less time to sign. But after the accord, the United States changes its thinking a little. The Japanese do not change.[45]

In the business sector, similar remarks were made by the chief manager for international finance of the Companhia Vale do Rio Doce, (CVRD), the enterprise that is the cutting edge and by far the principal partner for Japan's economic activities in Brazil:

In negotiations, the Japanese are very cold. They go into detailed minutiae of the contract. Brazilians do not do this. They do the opposite. Brazilians are generalists. After the agreement has been signed, the Japanese observe it scrupulously. They always make payments on time. Also, they remain in contact. They establish an office here in Rio where any problems or differences can be ironed out promptly. They establish a "complete relationship" with the Brazilian party.[46]

The traditional Japanese characteristic of maintaining established relationships was mentioned in remarks by Jose Carlos P. M. da Fonseca, director of BNDES. "To keep contacts open," he said, "Japanese delegations come to this office as usual, even though they are not active in making loans to Brazil at present."[47]

Jose Botafogo Goncalves, a senior member of the Planning Ministry, expressed the Brazilian point of view as follows: "Technically, the Japanese are internationally competitive. In terms of management, they are very strict in detail, very careful in planning projects, and they are expert in financial control. Japanese global planning is applicable in Brazil, but Japanese labor-management methods are not exportable to Brazil."[48] He did not elaborate on the latter point.

In the actual operation of foreign enterprises in Brazil, an official at Citibank observed that "U.S. companies are strongly staffed with Brazilian executives, but Japanese companies are mainly staffed by officers from Japan. If they had more Brazilian executives, they would be more profitable."[49]

In foreign commerce, the Brazilian Ministry of Foreign Affairs performs some functions that in Japan are a prerogative of the Ministry of International Trade and Industry (MITI). Because of the rivalry between MITI and the

Japanese Foreign Ministry, this discrepancy in the jurisdiction of Brazilian and Japanese official counterparts may be a source of friction at the bureaucratic level. Hence it also might help account for the difference in opinion of various Brazilian officials concerning Brazil's economic relations with Japan. In the Brazilian Foreign Ministry, I spoke with two officials who had decidedly different opinions concerning Japanese relations. The chief of the Department of Trade Promotion, which deals with day-to-day practical matters, was critical of Japan's "protectionist policies and secrecy in matters of technological exchange."[50] An opposite opinion was expressed by the official concerned with trade policy, which takes a conceptual approach to international exchange:

> We acknowledge that we don't know how to manipulate the Japanese system. However, we have very few trade problems with Japan. They made a special effort to have a clean docket before Figueiredo's visit to Tokyo in May 1984. It should be added that although we have few product-specific conflicts with Japan, we do diverge on other matters. We don't want a new GATT round. We perceive Japan as hiding behind the United States in Latin-American trade issues. Japan is also a hard-liner in East-West matters, but with a low political profile. In relations with Japan, we have little trouble because in contrast to the U.S. system, it is not their practice to hire a lawyer and start a legal process. We have many complaints against the United States. The U.S. system is to go to the courts or appeal to the ITC for sanctions. Then the lawyers fight it out. Instead of open confrontation in the courts, the Japanese parties—MITI, the Foreign Ministry, and the association of producers of a particular product—coordinate their efforts and work out a solution with us in private. In Japan, there is less public confrontation. The difficulty or problem never comes to the attention of the press. The difference between Japanese style and American style is not merely a matter of form—it is a substantive matter.[51]

At the official level, compatibility between Brazil and Japan was affirmed in remarks of other respondents. Minister Oto Maia, a Japan specialist in the Division of Asia and Oceania of the Foreign Ministry, made the unqualified statement that "Japan has been cooperative with Brazil." He added that during the previous 18 months of his current assignment, "there has been no incident of conflict or potential conflict between the United States and Japan in matters concerning Brazil."[52] In discussing the debt crisis, Akihiro Ikeda, economic assistant to Delfim Netto, acknowledged that "on the financial side, Japan's actions concerning Brazil have been OK." Reflecting on his negotiating experience in trips to Japan, Ikeda's observations were piquant. "They have no theory of administration," he said. "Their administration is poor; it is very slow. There is much confusion in Japanese administration. There are a lot of papers on the tables. There is a lot of talking on the telephone. There is no clear leadership."

"And what is the Brazilian system?" I asked.

"A Brazilian minister can decide any question by himself. In Japan, a minister can decide nothing. Even in private firms in Japan, the chairman can decide nothing. In Brazil, the chairman makes decisions. Japan is a country of coordination, not of decision making. Brazil is the opposite. It is more like the United States."

I followed this up by asking, "And what is the role of the Congress in the Brazilian system?"

"Congress may interfere in Brazilian development in the near future," he said. "Last Year, there was a public-sector deficit. We are fighting it. But Congress passed a law giving more money to state and local governments. This was an amendment to the Constitution, so the President could not veto it."[53]

Just as the Japanese feel that it is important to diversify their markets and sources of supply, the Brazilians feel that it is important to diversify the sources of foreign investment in Brazil. From a Brazilian point of view, however, what is the Japanese motive for investing in Brazil? Perhaps the Brazilian attitude toward Japan can be summarized in the remark of the chief of International Operations of the Central Bank of Brazil. "The Japanese always have a strategy," he said. "I don't know what it is."[54]

## Selected Interviews

As a means of conveying representative attitudes that affect Brazil's economic relations with Japan and the United States, the following is my record of selected interviews conducted in Brazil. The remarks are not necessarily coordinated. They reflect the course of the conversation. It will be noted that here as elsewhere in this account, conflicting statements may be found.

*Interview with an Official of C. Itoh do Brasil, S.A., in Sao Paulo, August 5, 1983*

During 1970–1979, our investment in Brazil increased very much. We have twenty joint ventures in Brazil. We hold only minority equity positions in these joint ventures. As a trading company, we get little benefit from our joint ventures. And there is no repatriation of dividends, due to foreign exchange restrictions. As a foreign trading company, we receive no export subsidy from the Brazilian government. The joint venture companies of C. Itoh are eligible for Brazilian government subsidies when they export directly by themselves, so that is what they do. If they should export through us, we would not receive the tax rebate subsidy. Therefore, our business is primarily indent business: we act as an agent for C. Itoh in the United States and for C. Itoh in Japan and in other countries. Up to several years ago, most of our exports from Brazil were traditional products, and we imported heavy industrial equipment. But now it is difficult to import from Japan because of quota and foreign exchange restrictions. Therefore, we have changed our activity from being mainly an importer to being mainly an exporter. Ninety percent of our activity is exports from Brazil to Japan and to third countries.

Until three years ago, our main exports were coffee, iron ore, and soy beans. Our major activity has been exporting traditional products, but now also light industry products, such as textiles, staple fiber, cloth, cotton yarn, pulp and paper, cellulose, iron products, and light machinery. We export Brazilian textiles all over the world, principally cotton textiles. This is just as we did in Japan 25 years ago. Japan went from light industry to heavy and chemical industry, but Brazil started in heavy industry right away. So Brazilian industry has a lot of problems to solve. Sixty percent of Brazilian industry is in the public sector, the state companies. It is not competitive. Ten percent of Brazilian industry is in the domestic national sector, indigenous enterprise. It is not competitive either. So 70 percent of Brazilian industry is not internationally competitive. Twenty percent of Brazilian industry is in the hands of the MNCs. They are internationally competitive. Concerning the indigenous domestic private sector, the mentality of the owners is individualist. It is to make a profit for the family, not for the company. They squeeze the profit and put it in their pocket.

Unlike *sogo shosha* in Japan, we do practically no domestic trade in Brazil. We do some exporting for U.S. companies in Brazil, in speculative commodities such as soy beans, wool, and coffee. We sell to the C. Itoh New York office. They coordinate the world market. The *sogo shosha* tell the Brazilian government that they must change the trading company law so as not to discriminate against foreign trading companies. But they are slow to do this. They are afraid that the *sogo shosha* will take over the entire trading company business of Brazil. If we were eligible for the export subsidies that are received by Brazilian trading companies, we could do the invoicing ourselves and take the risk ourselves. As providers of indent service, we cannot take risk. Foreign importers abroad would like to buy directly from C. Itoh as invoicers, as principals. This is because we have an established name. As an indent agent, we merely make a commission. As an invoicer, or principal, we would make a profit. Moreover, acting merely as an agent, we cannot make the fullest use of our international information.

There are very few companies in which a foreigner holds a majority position. Until 1973–1974, foreigners could control 100 percent of the capital. Since then, it has not been allowed. But without majority control, we can't manage. U.S. companies came to Brazil before 1973–1974, so they were able at the time to become 100 percent shareholders. At present, due to inflation and recession, operating profits are poor, so U.S. companies are attempting to make financial profits with the use of their financial resources.

The *sogo shosha* are taking an interest in the movement in advanced countries away from heavy industry toward soft, or high-technology, industry. The soft industries are more profitable. In the meantime, Japan could give its old technology to Brazil without payment. Together with cheap labor, this may help Brazil to export more and thus to solve its debt problem. A severe problem for the Brazilian government at present is the transfer of technology. At present, Brazilian manufactured products lack international competitive power. In return for providing Brazil with technology, the *sogo shosha* should have the privilege of exporting the products produced with that technology.

Besides the problems of Brazilian management, there is also a lack of loyalty on the part Brazilian workers. Every young Japanese worker is thinking about rising into management. This is because of lifetime employment. But in Brazilian companies, management is a family monopoly. There is no chance to get into management if you are not a family member. Therefore, if a Brazlian worker sees a better opportunity elsewhere, he moves readily. In the case of a Japanese company, we have 1,000 open eyes. In a Brazilian company, there is only one open eye and 999 closed eyes.

Originally, import substitution was the reason for industrialization in Brazil. Afterwards, capacity was excessive and they had to export the products of the import-substitute industries. But the import-substitute industries were located in the wrong places for exporting. Also, there were poor loading and discharge facilities at the ports. And transportation to the ports was expensive. And the availability of vessels was insufficient. Thus even if the FOB price at the factory was competitive, the CIF price at the port was not competitive. Furthermore, the Brazilians have no after-care mentality. There is no thought about repeat business after the sale. It is common for discrepancies to occur between the sample and the merchandise that is delivered. But they do not satisfy claims. C. Itoh guarantees identical specifications in the sample and in the delivered merchandise. That is why foreign buyers prefer to do business with C. Itoh.

The Brazilians do not reinvest their profits, and they continue making the same products with the same machines. We had personal experience with this. Before 1973, there was a worldwide paper shortage. At that time, the quality of Brazilian paper was very poor. But in spite of the poor quality and despite the long distance, Japan bought paper from Brazil. So Brazil received a big profit. We Japanese feared that there would be an increasing shortage of primary products. So I came here to buy a paper company. I checked the balance sheet. I expected to see a big profit. But there was no profit. The family that owned the paper company had squeezed the profit. And there was no reinvestment. Their machinery was very old. The speed of their machines was only one-third the speed of machines of Japanese paper companies. After that, the world supply and demand of paper became balanced. When the price of paper came down, Japan wanted to export paper to Brazil. But the Brazilian government imposed import restrictions, and the family that owned the paper company I had investigated raised their prices and received much profit. They sent their profits to Switzerland. This explains the lack of international competitive power in Brazil. Family enterprises cannot be world competitive. Only MNCs can achieve international competitive power in Brazil. This problem cannot be cured by the IMF policy for Brazil. The IMF wants Brazil to remove its protectionst barriers. This would only cause bankruptcy.

## Interview with an Official of the Ministry of External Relations, in Brasilia, August 9, 1983

Japan is my pet hate. I am speaking to you very frankly.

There is a difference of opinion concerning Japan among the ministries in Brasilia. There is an internal Japan lobby here. In particular, there is a lobby of prejudice in favor of Japan in the Planning Ministry, with regard to mineral resources; in the Agriculture Ministry, with regard to the Cerrado project; and in the CVRD, which is powerfully represented in Brasilia. In the Planning Ministry, Akirhiro Ikeda, special adviser for economic affairs to Delfim Netto, is a key member of the Japan lobby.

However, I think that we should put pressure against Japan because of its trade practices, among other reasons. For example, the Foreign Minister made a demand last March for off-season remission of agricultural import restrictions by Japan, but it was ungraciously received. My bad will to Japan is because it is an unfair trade partner. Japanese trade is highly administered. The Japanese government colludes with Japanese industry to restrict trade. In addition to that, the employment effects of selling our natural resources to Japan are small.

The agricultural projects of the Japanese in Brazil are also unfair. In the Cerrado, the Japanese are learning about how to perform savannah agriculture; this is giving them knowledge they will apply later in Africa. This is a one-way flow of technological know-how. They are learning from their experiments in the Cerrado, but they keep the information secret and do not share it with us. The real scientific research of the Cerrado project is being hidden from Brazil. For example, what percent of aluminum or other additives have to be put into the soil to get the desired results. In the Cerrado, there is scientific exploitation of Brazil. In civil construction, the Japanese are performing services that should be supplied by national companies. The Japanese are participating in petrochemicals; they have an intention of participating in Carajas. They participate in Usiminas, but they have complained about the delays in payments from Usiminas.

The Brazil–Japan relationship is *not* healthy. Brazil should put increasing political pressure against Japan. In the Brazilian government, there should be fewer nisei in key positions. Sales from Brazil to Japan are not market-oriented. They are MNC-organized. For example, there are Ford and IBM sales from Brazil to Japan. The MNCs dominate the modern sectors of the Brazilian economy. A new dependency position is being generated. Brazil is being used by the MNCs to export goods from Brazil to Africa. Thus the relationship between Africa and Brazil resembles the dependency relationship between Brazil and the advanced countries. A way of neutralizing this effect of Brazil as an export platform for the MNCs would be to require a partnership between the MNCs and private Brazilian national firms, plus the Brazilian government. This trilateral relationship would be a means of adjusting the MNC operations in accordance with Brazilian national aims.

The Japanese trading companies are not given national trading company treatment under the trading company law. That is, they do not receive export incentives. Therefore, what they do is associate themselves with

Brazilian national trading companies that do receive the export incentives. Thus the Japanese trading companies do receive some of the benefits of the export incentives that are intended for Brazilian national companies. In the meantime, the Japanese trading companies perform the actual trade operations and the Brazilian national companies do not improve their trading technology and cannot compete with the Japanese. Interbras, for example, operates through C. Itoh or Nissho Iwai.

Concerning your particular questions: Do Brazilian bankers agree with the IMF prescription? Not necessarily. They have acquired many industrial enterprises, farms and real estate through foreclosure. But they are afraid that by becoming proprietors of these businesses that they are more liable to being nationalized.

Japan's financial stake has been more conservative than that of the United States. However, the Bank of Tokyo was involved in a scandalous joint venture with Lume, a speculative financial organization. The joint venture collapsed.

Would the cutback of state enterprises have a more adverse effect on the United States or Japan? It would be more adverse to Japan. Japan has always favored "package" deals. They involve the lending of money by Japan on condition that orders are placed with Japanese suppliers. The United States has not favored package deals, except during the last two months of Ambassador Motley's period here in Brasilia. He arranged a protocol for hydroelectric plants, for which Brazil would buy the equipment from the United States. There would be no public tender. However, this might not be legal from a U.S. point of view. Europeans and Japanese are masters in the art of arranging negotiated deals of this sort, without public tender. However, the initiative in these matters has shifted. We used to say "I will buy $1.00 of your equipment if you will give me a loan of $1.50." Now the foreigner says, "I will lend you $1.00 if you will buy equipment from me." Because of the failure of the United States to arrange package deals, there are almost no major projects throughout the world economy that are being undertaken with American technology.

How is the regulatory climate changing? The number of controls is increasing. More regulation naturally occurs during a time of crisis.

The Brazilian bureaucracy. Yes, there is overlapping authority in the bureaucracy. The amount of "debureaucratization" is trivial. It is negligible.

What are the controls on the use of funds borrowed from abroad? The Brazilian state companies made many syndicated loans from foreign banks. The foreign banks, however, knew that these were not project loans; instead, they were balance of payments loans. The New York banks were confederates with the Brazilian government in this deception. The way it worked was that the state companies would borrow money that was ostensibly for the projects they were undertaking. The loans were indeed guaranteed by the government. But when the proceeds of the loans were received by the Central Bank, which was supposed to make them available to the state companies, in many cases they never were used for the projects at all but were simply retained by the Brazilian government for its general purposes. The Japanese were naive about this before they learned the facts of life. They made a US$700 million loan to the Brazilian government that was supposed to go into the Tuberao project, but the money never went there.

Concerning administrative controls versus legal controls. There is a growing tendency to abuse administrative controls and to evade the Congress.

Concerning conflicts between the state governments and the national government. There are many conflicts. This is especially the case with regard to fiscal jurisdiction and with regard to local security. The concept of national security hs been expanded, against the interests of the local authoritities.

Is the role of the MNCs increasing? The role of the MNCs and the role of the national government are both increasing. The relation between the MNCs and the national government is becoming more cooperative rather than more adversarial.

Concerning financing. The Japanese have loaned both to state enterprises and to the private sector. However, they prefer the double guarantee of lending to state enterprises because these loans then become an obligation of both the state enterprise and the Brazilian government. Despite OECD rules, public financing by Japan is more competititve than that of the United States. The Japanese make arrangements for parallel financing, parallel trade, or compensation of one sort or an another.

In what fields is there U.S.–Japanese competition or cooperation in Brazil? There is competition in the fields of telecommunications and petrochemicals. There is no cooperation between the United States and Japan in Brazil.

What is the ratio of domestic debt to foreign debt? Nobody knows.

What is the ratio of private debt to public debt? Public debt is overwhelmingly greater.

To what extent was Brazil's economic "miracle" dependent on export demand as compared with domestic demand? The economic miracle was based primarily on pharaonic projects fueled by easy money from U.S. bankers.

Changing forms of foreign enterprise in Brazil? The Japanese are attempting to enter the construction business in Brazil.

My reaction to Japanese bureaucrats? Kakuei Tanaka was the most boring man I ever met. Incredibly boring. I was riding in the car with him. He had nothing to say.

Are Japanese firms better able to cope with Brazilian government regulations than U.S. firms? To some extent, U.S. firms engage in practices in Brazil that they would not attempt in the United States. Things that are illegal in the United States.

Do Japanese trading companies do business domestically in Brazil, or only in export business? Export business only.

What is the relation between CACEX and the Ministry of Foreign Affairs in the regulation of foreign trade? We have a love-hate relationship with each other. This is because the Ministry of Foreign Affairs is in control of trade in military goods. CACEX controls most of the rest.

## Interview with Senator Roberto Campos, Federal Senate of Brazil, in Brasilia, August 11, 1983

There are two devils in Brazil: the IMF and MNCs. Brazil has a deep aversion to the MNCs. But the process of venting frustrations is not concrete; it is vague. Japan's profile is less objectionable than that of the United States because it is lower. Japan is distant. The Japanese colony here also makes things easier.

What are the supposed sins of the MNCs? Transfer pricing: understating exports and overstating imports, in order to transfer profits. Brazilian firms may do the same, in order to put dollars abroad. But in this matter, the MNCs are more exposed. Their documentation is more complete and more verifiable. If they step out of line, their leftist accountants will expose them. Actually, concerning competitive strategy, in some industries, foreign presence is the only way to keep up to date. For example, in pharmaceuticals. No Brazilian company in that field can support the R&D necessary to keep up to date.

Concerning foreign exchange controls. The national company is much more forcibly hit than the foreign company, which can obtain intracompany loans. Foreign exchange controls are very harmful to the competitive power of indigenous Brazilian companies. Price controls are likewise more disadvantageous to the Brazilian firm than to the foreign firm.

The market reserve policy is a nationalistic overreaction that will condemn us to technical retardation. The big fight at present is in informatics. To stay in Brazil, the major foreign computer companies have been compelled to sell 51 percent of their equity to Brazilian nationals. But despite becoming national companies through having accepted 49 percent minority positions, they are forbidden to combine informatics and telematics. Automobile companies remain wholly foreign owned. Ford and GM insist on 100 percent ownership. They say this is the only way to have a globalistic approach. But politically, this is unwise. In the future, they might be nationalized. When we feel humiliated, nationalism and xenophobia are reasserted. You came here at the most acute point of xenophobia.

What are the necessary policies? In the short term, we have to be deflationary. In the long term, overexpansion of the public sector has to be adjusted. But the government doesn't say, "Growth and development have to pause; inflation has to be reversed." It merely says "We are in a crisis." The theology of growth continues, despite the reality of restrictionism that is being imposed.

As a solution, it is impractical to convert loans into equity because remittance of dividends is more restricted than remittance of interest.

How is the pattern of trade shifting? It is shifting away from the United States toward the EEC and Japan.

Economic concentration: it is increasing in the domain of Brazilian state enterprises, not in the domain of the MNCs. Cartelization is increasing because it is promoted by increased competition in a shrinking market. There are several ingredients of cartelization. First, we have an antititrust law and an Antitrust Council with enormous powers, but the law has never been applied. Second is our market reserve policy. Third, we overindulged in fostering the growth of state enterprises. All of this is cartelization.

In economic policy, the Ministry of Finance, the Ministry of Planning, and the Central Bank are now united. But the other ministries are not.

Are there any Japanese or U.S. pressures on Brazil in an attempt to take advantage of the debt crisis? There are no U.S. or Japanese pressures on Brazil except in informatics.

There is a logistic problem in exports. Large iron ore carriers can overcome the high cost of oil in transportation to Japan. But wood pulp and other products cannot be transported in such large quantities.

Is foreign investment screened to see whether or not it conforms with Brazilian national economic plans? Yes, too much screening is being done.

Do Brazilian bankers agree with the IMF austerity prescription? Yes, they accept the IMF line. The businessmen are deadly enemies of the banks. So the banks may be nationalized. Their profits are extortionate. The government is pressing on the banks: they are the only type of business that has to pay income tax *in anticipation* of their profits.

How is the regulatory climate changing? It is changing for the worse. There are more foreign exchange controls. There is too much overlapping of authority in the Brazilian bureaucracy.

To what extent does the private sector follow the government plan in making its investments? The government seeks to guide private investment by means of incentives rather than by targets. The private sector is also guided by prohibitions.

How does the Brazilian government control the use of funds that have been borrowed from abroad? Two-thirds of the debt has been incurred by the government itself, so this is channeled directly. Rio Doce was induced to borrow more than they needed, so as to accommodate the government. Also Petrobras in some cases.

What is the relation of administrative controls to legal controls? Some controls are *illegal*. The informatics and telematics regulations are illegal. But the MNCs are tame, and therefore they comply.

What is the degree of compliance with the regulations of the national government? The MNCs are the most compliant. They are the least disobedient to the government. Small Brazilian companies are less obedient. Next is big business: they are even less compliant. The most disobedient are the federal enterprises. They are totally uncontrolled. There is, for example, the phrase, "The Republic of Petrobas."

Is the role of the MNCs relatively increasing or decreasing? It is decreasing. There is a certain amount of U.S. disinvestment: Remington, ITT, and Firestone are trying to pull out. Consulting engineering companies such as Morrison-Knudsen are pulling out because of market reservation. At present, direct investment in Brazil by foreigners is being made only in autos and in minerals (bauxite, aluminum, gold). Also investment is continuing where further investment is unavoidable because of previously planned projects. However, the annual amount of new direct investment has declined drastically.

Is the relation between the MNCs and Brazil becoming more cooperative or more adversarial? It is becoming more adversarial.

What are the possibilities for socialism or communism in Brazil? Do I fear the possibility of communism? I am worried about something worse— the gray area between them. We used to associate unemployment with illiteracy. Now educated people are unemployed. There are unemployed intellectuals. Even new engineers are unemployed. I am worried about the hybrid product of an effete capitalism and an undisciplined socialism. Worse than communism is the hybrid product of a capitalism without incentives and a socialism without discipline.

Socialism has not been discredited in Latin America. This is the last place in the world in which the myth survives. We are the last deluded people. We underestimate the imposed uniformity of socialism.

*Interview with Eliezer Batista, President, Companhia Vale do Rio Doce (CVRD), in Rio de Janeiro, August 13, 1983*

As an introduction to Mr. Batista, it should be remarked that he was the only president of a major state company (apart from Ozires Silva, president of Embraer, the state-owned aircraft firm) to be retained in office following the change in regime from the military government to civilian government in Brazil in March of 1985. He personally is almost exclusively responsible for the close association of the Japanese government and Japanese private business with the greater Carajas project in the southeast Amazon and the Cerrado grains project in west central Brazil. The greater Carajas project is composed of various agromineral and industrial developments and covers an area of 1,900 square miles. It contains the world's largest iron ore reserves. CVRD controls the Carajas project. Batista has been president of CVRD since 1979. The company is the most outstanding success of all state companies in Brazil. Fifty-one percent of its shares are owned by the Brazilian government. Japan is the biggest outside investor in CVRD subsidiaries, in the amount of US$467 million, with US$300 million provided by the Export-Import Bank of Japan and a consortium of Japanese steel companies. As Roberto Fendt remarked, "It is easy for the Japanese to work with CVRD because it is government controlled," (interview, July 20, 1984). Carajas is the most dynamic factor in Brazil's economic relations with Japan. Batista has been described as Brazil's "unofficial ambassador" to Japan. In June of 1985, he was awarded the Grand Cross of the Order of the Sacred Treasure by order of Emperor Hirohito. By courtesy of an introduction from Saburo Okita, I interviewed Mr. Batista at his home on a Saturday morning.

The U.S. steel industry is obsolete. U.S. steel lost their best managers to other industries, and now they want to survive by means of protectionism. The U.S. approach reflects the "discounted cash flow" mentality. The new president takes over and wants to show big progress in five years time. The shares may go up, but at the end of five years the company may be broke. No R&D, no reserves, no investment for the future. The United States should anticipate and prevent difficulties rather than merely attempt to correct the mess afterwards.

U.S. protectionism is retrogressive. It is also inconsistent. Minnesota and the Canadians complain about Brazil, while Sweden is dumping pellets in Europe. Why don't U.S. unions complain about [Ian] MacGregor [National Coal Board chairman]? In the open market, Brazil has to close down its inefficient industries. So the United States should close down its own declining industries as well. But the United States only says that Brazil must close down it inefficient state enterprises. The IMF prescription is too global: it does not discriminate among real projects. You may do more harm than is necessary. As a result of the debt crisis, the productive as well as the nonproductive projects are being stopped. This is one of the *real* effects of the debt crisis.

Brazil is poorly capitalized. We have more room for U.S. investment. Carajas is an ideal focal point for U.S. and Japanese cooperation with Brazil. Carajas is the most important link between Japan and Brazil, and it could be a link between the United States and Brazil as well. It may be even more important for the metals industry of the United States than for Japan. Carajas can provide cheap minerals plus energy to both the United States and Japan. Carajas is the opposite of OPEC. It is designed to reduce, not raise, the price of raw materials to make steel. This will make it more competitive with other materials. If you want cheap steel in the United States, this is complementary with the United States. We don't want to price steel out of the market and induce the entry of substitute materials. It wouldn't do us any good if we find our mountain of raw material is not wanted. The same principle applies to the stabilization of agricultural prices and the prices of other minerals. This is our objective. U.S. farmers, on the other hand, want to raise prices.

Thirty-five years ago, the Rockefeller Foundation showed the importance of the Cerrado as an alternative to the Argentine pampas. The Cerrado is as big as the U.S. midwest, or bigger. But the United States takes a competitive view of Brazil; the Japanese take a complementary view. U.S. Secretary of Agriculture Block has spoken of Brazil recently. He says that Brazil subsidizes agriculture. But the Cerrado has better logistics than U.S. agriculture. Cerrado can produce economically without subsidies. The Japanese have suggested the logistics of combining Cerrado grain with iron ore in transportation. They proposed the construction of giant carriers for combining the shipment of minerals with the shipment of grain. We are already shipping grain and ore together. Contrary to Block's thinking that the Cerrado is competitive with the United States, by stabilizing world trade it could benefit the United States as well as Japan. The Japanese, in contrast to the United States, see the multilateral benefits of the Cerrado and the Carajas projects. In this way, the Japanese are more congenial with us than the United States.

Carajas will stabilize world mineral prices. Cerrado will stabilize world agricultural prices. We will stabilize prices at a lower level, not at a higher level, as done by the OPEC cartel. We will develop offsetting regions, so that drought in one region will be offset by crops in another. This will reduce the fluctuation in prices by physical means rather than by means of the financial risk takers in the commodity markets. We will reduce the crazy oscillations of world market prices. We will reduce the need for speculators who assume the risk of commodity price fluctuations. There will be no need for grain commodity exchanges. Because of the stabilization of prices, there will be no need for intermediaries, and long-term contracts could be made between producers and consumers. This would further stabilize the market. This is more efficient.

The secret of our success is that we sell infrastructure services efficiently. By means of our system of storage, railroads, ports, we control our production cost and our logistic cost; thus we control the CIF price. We control every element of the system. We have large production, good logistics, and good shipping. Therefore, we manage the risk on a system basis, not on a commodity grain exchange speculative basis. In the future, this will result in the disappearance of the commodity exchanges. The commodity exchanges cause overcompetitiveness.

As a possibility for multilateral collaboration, Brazil could use U.S. large-scale techniques in agriculture. U.S. firms could take part in the Cerrado, along with their interests in the United States. Japanese companies are here and they are not competing with each other in Brazil. Carajas is another Malaysia. It is for everybody's benefit. Carajas will be the biggest producer of pulp and pulp products and tropical-equatorial products. Here we compete with Malaysia. We have the cheapest cost of pulp and forest products in the world. The U.S. south is quite efficient. Southern U.S. pulp can compete with us, but our pulp is cheaper. We are much cheaper than Canada.

Rio Doce is the most efficient company in Brazil. Efficiency is the most important matter. Politicians confuse power with efficiency. This is the mentality of the state companies. If bigness were the test, the elephant would be the owner of the circus. We are finishing Carajas with 30 percent less dollar cost than the original estimates. Because of the recession, the cost of production in Carajas had gone down in real terms. The debt problem does not affect Carajas because it is fully financed.

Most important companies in Brazil are public companies. There are three kinds. First, the CVRD type: no subsidy, it competes internationally and survives independently, by itself. It is highly efficient. Second is the Eletrobras and Petrobras type: they have administered prices, like utility companies. Price equals cost plus a margin. They have no international yardstick. Some of these companies may be good. Third are public companies in the social and development area, such as universities. They work like a ministry. They have no criteria.

What are the lessons of our experience? The main lesson is that there should be high-level cooperation, in terms of multilateral rather than bilateral interests; there should be complementarity of economic interests. Banks should look into the structure of the projects they finance and not act merely as money sellers. They should analyze the project, not merely the balance sheet. But they don't know physics and are not equipped to do this. Bankers analyze only ex post, not ex ante.

Another lesson is that market reservation is a mistake. I don't believe in it. We will invent the wheel all over again.

The "romantic" idea of Brazil as leader of the third world is ridiculous. This is an error of strategy. We need more cooperation with developed countries. We should be complementary with the developed countries, especially with the United States and Japan. We should help the third world by our collaboration with the United States and Japan. We can supply the third world with intermediate technique, but it is a mistake to try to "conquer African markets," ignoring the United States and Japan. Brazilian–Japanese companies or Brazilian–Japanese–U.S. companies can do better in Africa than Brazil versus Africa.

Japan has complementarity with east and southeast Asia for the same products as Brazil's complementarity with Japan. So southeast Asia and Brazil are in competition for the Japanese market. Brazil has better relations with Japan than with southeast Asia. Moreover, Japan would rather buy here than in southeast Asia. Japan should invest in the production of semifinished products in Brazil to be shipped to the United States: there is room for more complementarity between Brazil and the United States and for Brazilian help to the U.S. steel industry. The United States could do what Japan does: make more highly finished products.

Politics in Brazil is worse than in the United States. The level of education of the people and of their representatives is too low. We need to control population growth. Politicians bribe the voters. Brazil must put order into the economy with proper politics, not mere "politicians." The United States has no concept of the fact that its own system cannot be exported. It is not applicable in Brazil. The alternative to the military in Brazil is chaos. Economic democracy is not possible if you have chaos.

The United States is making its own errors. It is starting to create export trading companies on the Japanese model of the 1960s. But in Japan, the 1960 *sogo shosha* model is dead! They are not making profits, either in Brazil or in Japan. Partly this is because of the emergence of international banking. In the old days, Japanese banks were less powerful and the *sogo shosha* provided financing services. This is no longer a source of strength for the *sogo shosha*. Moreover, high-technology producers do their own marketing. *Sogo shosha* don't have the personnel to sell those products. They lack technical expertise.

What are Brazil's complaints against Japan? In relations with Brazil, there has been no error. Japan's behavior has been constructive all the way. We have no criticism of Japan.

## *Interview with an Official of the Federation das Industrias do Estado de Sao Paulo (FIESP), in Brasilia, August 9, 1983*

In the long run in Brazil, Japanese businessmen will be the winners and U.S. businessmen will be the losers. Japanese businessmen are more flexible than the Americans, and they are more willing to take risks. A U.S. company that holds 25 percent or more of the voting shares of a subsidiary abroad must include that subsidiary in its consolidated balance sheet report. The U.S. manager of a subsidiary has to make sure that he does not contribute any problems to the consolidated balance sheet of his parent company in the United States. Therefore, he will not take any risks. In refraining from risk, he may ensure his own security, but he may drag his company down.

The Japanese as an individual does not take risks either. However, he works in a different system, and his system works more quickly. He communicates with Tokyo instantly, and a decision is made that he implements. Evidently somebody in Tokyo is in a position to be the risk taker. In the United States, communication is slower between the subsidiary and the home office. Moreover, the home office may understand less about the subsidiary than in the corresponding case in Japan. Not only does the Japanese firm take more risks, it is more flexible than the U.S. company. The Japanese company plays the game. If bribery is necessary, the Japanese knows how to do it. The U.S. firm is afraid of stepping out of line in terms of U.S. antibribery or antitrust laws. There is an increasing amount of corruption in Brazil at present. You have to pay under the table to get things done. This is especially true in the state sector. In that sector, whom you know is very important. It is less important in the private sector, in textiles, say, or shoes. Of course, sometimes the Japanese get caught, as in the case of goods valued at US$3.3 million that were illegally imported in May [1983] and that were seized by the federal police. In that case, NEC, National, and Sony were the culprits. In the United States, the Hitachi episode with IBM is another example of the risks they are prepared to take.

Part of the reason there is increasing corruption in Brazil at present is the uncertainty of the times and the recession. In the state sector, there is uncertainty because bureaucrats do not know whether they will keep their jobs. The Japanese will not do *more* illegal activity than their competition, but they will do as much. They will do whatever is necessary to maintain their market share within the customary boundaries of behavior. The Japanese manager does not have to worry about losing his job. The U.S. manager does have to worry about it. The Japanese manager makes his risky decision in consultation with Tokyo. The U.S. manager makes it on his own.

Therefore, the U.S. manager does not make risky decisions. In the Japanese system, the organization, the whole, is greater than the sum of the parts. As a person, the individual Japanese may or may not be very impressive. But as a member of a group, he is very impressive. The Japanese works for his company. The American works for himself. In Brazil, as well as in Japan, Japanese labor-management relations are better than those of the American companies. A good manager is not one who never makes a mistake. A good manager is one who makes correct decisions 70 percent of the time. The rest of the time he makes errors. But he makes his decisions quickly and flexibly.

I can give you a case history of how these things work in practice. In the air conditioning business, there were three companies in Brazil fifteen years ago. They were Trane, Hitachi, and Carrier. They had entered Brazil at about the same time. About ten years ago, Carrier dropped out, leaving Trane and Hitachi. When Hitachi started, it held about 5 to 7 percent of the market. At present it holds 50 to 60 percent of the market. Hitachi achieved its success by playing the game. Last year, however, Carrier came back, combining with a Brazilian company.

When Carrier dropped out ten years ago, Trane did not cut its prices to enter the vacuum created by the 30 percent market share dropped by the departing company. Instead, it *raised* its prices and lost its market share. It did this because its president had been having difficulties with the head office in the United States by running a loss. Therefore, he took this occasion to raise prices and eliminate his loss, even though by showing a "profit" he lost market share. As a result of this strategy, the American president was promoted. His company, Trane, however, became defunct and was taken over by my company. Hitachi did the opposite: it cut its prices and absorbed a large part of the market share dropped by the departing competitor.

There is no cooperation between the United States and Japan in Brazil. On the other hand, there is no conflict either. However, there is competition between them.

"In thinking about the future," I asked, "are you optimistic or pessimistic?"

"I'm optimistic", he replied, "because I have to be."

## Notes

1. Interviews, May 1984.
2. It has been reported, however, that 25 percent of the shares of Engesa, the principal military equipment manufacturer in Brazil, are owned by the Kingdom of Saudi Arabia. Engesa is a private, not state-owned, company.
3. American Embassy, Brasilia, *Semi-Annual Foreign Economic Trends Report—Brazil* (May 1984). Under pressure of the debt crisis, two measures were recently adopted, namely, Decree Law of December 29, 1982 and Ministry of Finance Order No. 1383. These were intended to provide income tax incentives conducive to

the conversion of foreign loans into equity investment. However, very little conversion has occurred.

4. Interview in Brasilia, August 10, 1983.

5. Interview with Robert H. Blocker, president, Blocker Assessoria de Investimentos e Participacoes, S.A., in Sao Paulo, August 3, 1983.

6. Interview in Brasilia, August 10, 1983.

7. Interview with Ana Maria Jul, assistant director, Atlantic Division, Western Hemisphere Department, International Monetary Fund, in Washington, D.C., June 6, 1983.

8. Interview with Senator Severo Gomes, Federal Senate of Brazil, in Brasilia, August 10, 1983.

9. Interview with Paulo Rabello de Castro, redator-chefe, *Conjuntura Economica,* Fundacao Getulio Vargas, in Rio de Janeiro, August 15, 1983.

10. Interview with Jose H. Kojima, manager, Machinery Headquarters, Mitsubishi Heavy Industries, Ltd., in Tokyo, July 12, 1983.

11. Interview in Rio de Janeiro, July 17, 1984.

12. In August of 1985, following an independent audit of IBC, its incompetence and corruption prompted the government to propose abolition of the agency. It had 7,672 people on its payroll, but only 900 of these actually performed any useful function. Similar charges were made against the Sugar and Alcohol Institute (IAA) and the National Tourism Authority (Embratur). These three agencies have been described as the "biggest, oldest, and most disorganized" of Brazil's federal agencies. *Gazeta Mercantil,* August 12, 1985.

13. Interview with Daniel G. Sydenstricker, diretor-presidente, Cia. Auxiliar de Empresas de Mineracao (CAEMI), in Rio de Janeiro, August 12, 1983.

14. Interview with Robert H. Blocker, president, Blocker Assessoria de Investimentos e Participacoes, S.A., in Sao Paulo, July 3, 1984.

15. Interview with Robert H. Blocker, president, Blocker Assessoria de Investimentos e Participacoes, S.A., in Sao Paulo, August 2, 1983.

16. Letter from Dr. J. C. Goulart Penteado, firm of Pinheiro Neto, Advogados, November 7, 1985.

17. Interview with Carlos Eduardo de Freitas, chief, International Operations Department, Central Bank of Brazil, in Brasilia, July 15, 1984.

18. Interview with Professor Antonio Carlos Porto Goncalves, Fundacao Getulio Vargas, in Rio de Janeiro, July 20, 1984.

19. Interview with Senator Severo Gomes, Federal Senate of Brazil, in Brasilia, August 10, 1983.

20. The memorandum was given to me in Tokyo in July of 1983.

21. Interview with Jon Rosenbaum, assistant U.S. trade representative (America), Office of the United States Trade Representative (USTR), in Washington, June 8, 1983. By SEI order of July 1981, eighteen product categories were subject to the market reserve policy.

22. Interview with Ercole A. Carpentieri, Jr., executive vice president, American Chamber of Commerce for Brazil, in Sao Paulo, August 3, 1983.

23. *Journal of Commerce,* January 28, 1985.

24. It may be noted that Mexico's similar policy was relaxed when in December of 1984 it was announced that IBM would be given permission to invest US$300 million in a new wholly owned factory near Guadalajara to produce microcomputers.

25. Despite its great influence, as of 1984 even the Morgan Guaranty Trust Company had not been allowed to establish a wholly owned commercial bank subsidiary in Brazil. A Citibank official expressed the opinion that even the foreign banks that were established prior to the present restrictions, such as Citibank, and which are having their innings in Brazil due to the debt crisis can expect to be "kicked out of the country in ten years time."

26. Interview with Richard Huber, senior vice president, Citibank, in New York, June 13, 1983.

27. In addition, during late 1980 and early 1981, Brazil's effective rates of tariff protection were estimated to be 60 percent for capital goods, 42 percent for intermediate goods, and 36 percent for consumer goods. World Bank, *Brazil: Industrial Policies and Manufactured Exports* (Washington, D.C., 1983), p. x.

28. Tax policy for agricultural products has been designed to promote the industrialization of agriculture. It is argued that processed agricultural products earn more foreign exchange, are less subject to price instability, and enjoy more buoyant export markets than unprocessed commodities.

29. "The Central Bank has frequently broken its own rules and regulations, waiving official requirements and granting financial aid to private-sector banks and other companies in the financial sector as the result of 'political decisions' made by senior officials and ministers," according to Deli Borges, formerly chief of the Central Bank's capital markets control division. *Gazeta Mercantil,* May 28, 1984, p. 10.

30. Interview with Helson Braga, assistant to Roberto Fendt, CACEX, in Rio de Janeiro, August 16, 1983.

31. *The Japan Economic Journal,* September 8, 1981, p. 25.

32. World Bank, *Brazil: Industrial Policies and Manufactured Exports* (Washington, D.C., 1983), p. 58.

33. *Ibid.,* p. 63.

34. *Ibid.,* p. 215.

35. Interview with Lawrence G. Smith, senior vice president, Citibank, in Sao Paulo, July 5, 1984.

36. Interview with Jose H. Kojima, manager, Machinery Headquarters, Mitsubishi Heavy Industry, Ltd., in Tokyo, July 12, 1983.

37. Interview with Jun Kawashima, minister, Embassy of Japan, in Brasilia, August 8, 1983.

38. Foreign banks, such as Mitsubishi, Sumitomo, Bank of Tokyo, and Citibank, which had engaged in commercial banking in Brazil prior to the prohibition are permitted to continue doing so. However, they may not increase the number of their branches.

39. Interview with Martha Claire Carbone, first secretary, Embassy of the United States, in Brasilia, July 9, 1984.

40. Interview with Hilton Lee Graham, consul for economic affairs, American Consulate General, in Sao Paulo, July 5, 1984.

41. Interview with Professor Antonio Carlos Porto Goncalves, Fundacao Getulio Vargas, in Rio de Janeiro, July 20, 1984.

42. Interview with Francis Mason, senior vice president, Chase Manhattan Bank, in New York, June 14, 1983.

43. Interview with Vicente J. Bonnard, chairman of the executive committee, Brazilian-American Chamber of Commerce, in New York, June 13, 1983.

44. Interview with Edmundo Sussumu Fujita, first secretary, Embassy of Brazil, in Tokyo, July 11, 1983.

45. Interview with Louis Paulo Giao, chefe de divisao, Departamento Economico, Banco Central do Brasil, in Brasilia, July 10, 1984.

46. Interview with Euclides Penedo L. Borges, chief manager, Finance, International Area, Companhia Vale do Rio Doce (CVRD), in Rio de Janeiro, July 23, 1984.

47. Interview with Dr. Jose Carlos P.M. da Fonseca, diretor, Banco Nacional de Desenvolvimento Economico e Social (BNDES), Area Internacional, in Rio de Janeiro, August 16, 1983.

48. Interview with Jose Botafogo Goncalves, secretario do cooperacao economica e tecnica internacional, Secretaria de Planejamento, in Brasilia, August 8, 1983.

49. Interview with Hiroshi F. Katayama, vice presidente, Citibank, N.A., in Sao Paulo, July 3, 1984.

50. Interview with Paulo Tarso Flecha de Lima, chefe do departamento de promocao comercial, Ministerio das Relacoes Exteriores, in Brasilia, August 9, 1983.

51. Interview with J.A. de Macedo-Soares, chief, Commercial Division, Ministry of External Relations, in Brasilia, July 12, 1984.

52. Interview with Oto Maia, minister, Division of Asia and Oceania, Ministry of External Relations, in Brasilia, July 12, 1984.

53. Interview with Akihiro Ikeda, special secretary for economic affairs, Ministry of Planning, in Brasilia, July 12, 1984.

54. Interview with Carlos Eduardo de Freitas, chief of department, International Operations Department, Central Bank of Brazil, in Brasilia, July 12, 1984.

# 4
# The Japanese Approach to Brazil

T here are several schools of thought about Japan's postwar economic accomplishments. One school attributes them to the unique human and cultural characteristics of the Japanese people. In this version, values, ethics, and ideology are considered to be the determining factors, as well as the use of traditionalism in the service of modernization. An opposing school attributes Japan's performance to its institutional and organizational arrangements. The latter school itself subsumes a conflict. Some argue that it was strategy and planning that were critical to Japan's success; others argue that Japan's adherence to the market system was the predominant organizational factor. An adequate explanation would probably include elements of each of these views. In the case of Japan and Brazil alike, it is probable that the role of government as compared with that of the private sector is relatively more important than in the United States. Analytically, the nature of the relationship among the three nations depends heavily on government policy. In their mutual relations, policy considerations include matters of initiative versus response, complementarity versus competition, long-term versus short-term objectives, and micro-macro interactions. As determined by its national interests, Japan's objectives are more fixed and clear than those of the United States or Brazil. Its planning and strategies for the achievement of those objectives, however, are subject to change in accordance with changes in the world environment.

## "Follow the Leader"

The temporal coincidence of the Japanese and Brazilian "miracles" had a powerful interaction effect in stimulating their economic relations. During the period 1955–1970, Japan's annual average growth rate was 10.2 percent in real terms. In Brazil, in real terms during 1969–1973, growth rates were more than 11 percent annually; for the period 1963–1981, they averaged more than 8 percent annually. During the presidency of Juscelino Kubitschek

(1956–1961), import-substitution industrialization encouraged Japanese investment in Brazil. In 1955, the Fuji Bank invested in the Banco America do Sul; thereafter, other Japanese banks, trading companies, and corporations in various industries followed the leader. By 1961, forty-five Japanese companies had entered Brazil with a total investment of US$158 million. A period of stagflation ensued from 1962, and Japanese investment dropped off. After the revolution of 1964, however, it became active again, entering a second stage in the early 1970s and reaching boom proportions in 1973. In November of 1972, Kogoro Uemura, the chairman of Keidanren (Japan Federation of Economic Organizations), led a delegation to Brazil. This bestowed the imprimatur of the Japanese establishment on close encounters with Brazil. By 1973, more than half of Japan's investments in Latin America were concentrated in Brazil; these amounted to US$741 million and constituted about 9 percent of Japan's total foreign direct investment. During 1955–1960, 36 investment projects were undertaken by Japanese firms in Brazil; during 1971–1975, 369 projects were undertaken.[1] In the first stage, there was a tendency for Japanese firms to attempt to acquire 100 percent equity control of their direct investments. Thereafter, minority positions became the mode.

In the second stage, starting after 1968, besides the major projects, many small and medium-sized Japanese firms were attracted to Brazil because the oil shock had dampened the economic "miracle" at home while Brazil, until 1980, was still attempting to expand. However, the Brazilian government's attitude toward foreign investors somewhat hardened after 1973, and Japanese investors began to seek indigenous joint venture partners to negotiate with the bureaucracy. In the first stage, Japanese companies had been very cautious. But in the second stage, they became emboldened by their success in Japan to take more risks in Brazil. There was also "misunderstanding" by Japanese firms concerning Brazilian entrepreneurship and a failure to recruit good partners. Many mistakes were made at this time. "In 1972–1973, Japan had little experience in Brazil. So we believed what the joint venture partners said. This was a learning period. Now we are more cool."[2] Typically, the Japanese have a tendency to go from one extreme to another, partly as a result of the "follow the leader" syndrome. In matters of direct investment, they have had cycles of fever and chill regarding Brazil. This is par for the course. More important than the cycles, however, is the long-term trend, which is rising. In the early 1970s, moreover, the reversal was precipitated by lack of experience on the part of Japanese investors as to how to operate in conditions of high inflation such as those prevailing in Brazil. After the second oil shock, Japanese trading companies were at a disadvantage because their operations in Brazil, as distinguished from their operations in Japan, are concerned primarily with exporting. But inflation was accelerating faster than the depreciation of the exchange rate. Thus the cruzeiro was becoming overvalued and Brazil was losing its international competitive power. Brazilian exporters required subsidies from the federal government in order to overcome the inconsistency between the inflation rate and the exchange rate. But Japanese trading companies were not eligible for subsidies.

The third stage began in 1980, following the second oil shock. At this point, Japan began a political dialogue with Brazil in addition to the economic dialogue that had been established. In accordance with administrative reform proposals for augmentation of Japan's diplomatic system, this dialogue was undertaken by the Ministry of Foreign Affairs. In particular, Japan and Brazil began to exchange information about other countries in which they are respectively interested. "For example, we brief Brazil about China, and they brief us about Latin America. Thus we have added a political dimension to the economic dimension of our relationship. Incidentally, the Foreign Ministry takes the most favorable attitude toward Brazil of any Japanese organization you will visit. The Keidanren people are not so favorable toward Brazil as we are."[3]

A contrast between Japan and the United States can be seen in the sequence of types of Japanese investment in Brazil within the stages outlined earlier. In the U.S. case, the banks came to Brazil first, and then the manufacturing firms followed. In the Japanese case, the trading companies (*sogo shosha*) came first, followed by light manufacturing (especially textiles) and assembly industries and banking. After World War II, Japanese banks were busy in their own domestic market because of the weak capitalization of Japanese firms at that time. Moreover, Japanese government foreign exchange controls restricted the extent to which international banking was possible. But Japanese banks strongly compete with each other; this gave rise to a "follow the leader" effect after the Fuji Bank showed the way. Despite the "consensus" process, leadership in Japan is of critical importance. If the leader goes in the right direction, the result may be an economic "miracle"; if the leadership is wrong, as in the Pacific War, the result is disaster. The step-by-step official procedure of the Japanese bureaucracy is an institutional antidote to the propensity for sharp policy reversals.

At present, Citibank in Brazil is advancing in the fields of information systems, consumer finance, and other innovations. But Japanese banks are still loan-oriented. Apart from their financing of Japanese multinational companies, Japanese banks specialize in lending to Brazilian state enterprises. According to an observer at Citibank, "This is because public-sector lending is less risky and less work." By the same token, the "spread" in Japanese bank loans is lower than that of American banks. As in the case of some trading company operations, for purposes of international coordination and control, Japanese financial affairs in Brazil are monitored in New York as well as in Tokyo.[4]

Notwithstanding its natural attractions, Japan's postwar entry into Brazil by means of direct investment would have been much more modest if not for the willing and able collaboration of the immigrants and their descendants. Prominent Brazilian-Japanese in the government have been described as constituting a "Japan lobby." In the 1960s, when it was easy to enter Brazil, small textile companies, as well as major firms, were attracted to doing so. "Even today, small or medium-sized firms that have some special know-how or expertise of their own can enter Brazil without the protection of a Japanese big business firm."[5]

There are numerous inconsistent statistics concerning the number of Japanese firms in Brazil, as well as inconsistent estimates of the number that have withdrawn in the wake of the debt crisis. According to Consul General Yabu of Sao Paulo, during the period 1970–1974, the number of Japanese companies reached a maximum of 400 firms. As of July 1983, he estimated that there were 250 Japanese firms with "child" companies in Brazil. Some of these had Brazilian top staff. In general, however, they did not have Brazilian top staff. Brazilians were rarely appointed to technical advisory positions. One difficulty in estimating the population of Japanese companies is the fact that no distinction is made in the membership list of the Brazil–Japan Chamber of Commerce between Japanese and Japanese–Brazilian companies. Recently, the number of Japanese companies in Brazil has remained steady, but the number of personnel has been reduced because of the decline in business activity. Concerning the business contraction, the case of C. Itoh Company is an instructive example. In 1972–1973, there were twenty-three C. Itoh subsidiaries in Brazil. In July of 1983, there were seventeen. But the difference is not attributable to pullouts or bankruptcies. Some firms were either merged with other C. Itoh companies or were sold to the Brazilian partner (at very low prices). Officially, there was no notice that they were withdrawing from the field. (The six companies that disappeared had been engaged in chemicals, machinery equipment, and steel structures.) This example suggests that statistics concerning the "withdrawal" of Japanese direct investment from Brazil should be treated with caution.

An enormous discrepancy exists in the record of Japan's direct investment in Brazil as compiled by the Central Bank of Brazil compared with the record as compiled by the Japanese Ministry of Finance. According to the Central Bank of Brazil, the total figure for Japan's direct and portfolio investment in Brazil as of December of 1984 amounted to US$2.1 billion dollars. According to the Japanese Ministry of Finance, the figure as of April of 1984 was US$4.3 billion, more than twice as much. The difference may partly be accounted for by the fact that the Japanese authorities record their investment figures as of the date of government approval of the project, while the Central Bank of Brazil records investments as of the date of entry of funds into Brazil. It seems doubtful that this explains the whole discrepancy. In a comparison of Brazilian figures with those of the United States, the same problem appears. According to the U.S. Department of Commerce, the total amount of U.S. direct investment in Brazil at the end of 1983 was US$9 billion, but according to the Central Bank of Brazil it was only US$7 billion.

Regardless of complementary or symbiotic relationships and bright hopes for the Brazilian future, by 1984 Japanese investment in Brazil had arrived at an impasse. Very little new investment was being undertaken, and investors were taking a "wait and see" attitude. In accordance with their temperamental extremes, Japanese investors had become more pessimistic than either the Americans or the Europeans. For the *sogo shosha*, which were in the throes of a wrenching transition of their own, this was the "winter season" in Brazil. Their business prospects were largely confined to the possibilities for using Brazil as a base for third-country trade.

The Brazilian stagflation and debt crisis gave rise to a nuance in the typical long-term thinking of the Japanese community. Because of the restrictions and high risk of their role in Brazil, the *sogo shosha* adopted an attitude that was short-term-oriented as compared with that of the Japanese manufacturers. In general, however, Japanese firms have scope for long-term thinking because their major stockholders are insurance companies and banks that make no demands for short-term dividends.

The *keiretsu* conglomerates are so large that their strategy may subsume macro as well as micro considerations. Nevertheless, like Japan itself, their resources are not unlimited and they cannot attempt everything at once. Brazil is a nexus of priorities that intersect, overlap, and conflict. In the short run, Japan's preeminent interest is in southeast Asia. In Latin America, the *sogo shosha* are waiting for the dust of the debt crisis to settle in order to see more clearly where their own long-term interest lies. Even in the short run, however, the *sogo shosha* enjoy a certain amount of leeway because of the fact that the performance of Brazilian subsidiaries is not included in consolidated company reports; therefore, losses in Brazil are not necessarily embarrassing to head offices in Japan.

Although they take an optimistic long-term view of Brazil, Japanese businessmen are not immune to short-term doubts and misgivings. Indeed, behind the cool persona, Japanese emotions are sharp and volatile. The epidemic of pessimism during the debt crisis following 1982 was reflected in comments by Kazuo Uesugi, president of the Japan Trade Center in Sao Paulo:

> We have no clear-cut strategy at present for Brazil. Frankly speaking, we are at a loss about what to do in the future. We are pushing some projects that have already been started—Carajas, Albras, Cerrado, Cenibra, and Flonibra. However, even though they are sound, there is a slowdown and reduction in scale even in these projects. Both the domestic and foreign market prospects

are poor. Brazil needs new markets, such as Communist China. There is a need to barter Chinese oil for Brazilian iron ore. Japan can import paper pulp, ferroalloys, aluminum, and chemicals from Brazil, as well as labor-intensive and energy-intensive projects. However, Japan must invest more in Brazilian manufacturing to help expand its exports to world markets as well as to Japan.[6]

Fundamentally, the nature of Japan's approach to Brazil is determined by its national interests and the rationale of its foreign economic policy. In the long run, these provide guidance for the decisions of its government and business leaders. The pace and scope of Japan's approach, however, are conditioned by economic conditions and government policies in Brazil. Indirectly, the United States "cooperates" with Japan by demanding Brazilian policy concessions or accommodations that would be of benefit to Japan as well as to itself. The combination of Japanese "coolness" and American "heat" may be of compelling effect in securing such concessions. In addition, various real (nonfinancial) factors, as discussed below, have a mixture of positive and negative effects in conditioning Japan's approach to Brazil. On balance, the real factors are generating an increasing number of long-term opportunities for direct investment in anticipation of the eventual recovery and stabilization of the Brazilian economy.

In the meanwhile, it may be noted that the Brazilian representatives of major Japanese firms, such as C. Itoh, Mitsubishi, Mitsui, and others, are the key decision makers of those firms respectively for their affiliates in all of Latin America. Their planning is reflected in Japanese business activity throughout the region. Subject to supervision from Tokyo, Sao Paulo serves as a subordinate headquarters. On the American side, there is an attempt to observe what the Japanese leadership is doing in its approach to Brazil. Citibank, for example, in the style of "Kremlinology," performs surveillance of changing Japanese plans and strategies by monitoring changes in key personnel and the shifting locus of power within major Japanese enterprises.[7]

## Role of the Japanese Government

### The Geopolitical View

In accordance with its national interests, Japan is perennially engaged in a search for "comprehensive economic security," a phrase attributed to Masayoshi Ohira. Since the end of World War II, however, the formulation of Japan's policies in pursuit of this objective has undergone considerable change. On the international plane, Japan's early postwar policies were formally expressed in terms of the support Japan could gain from trade and investment with other countries. In recent years, they have been expressed in terms of how other countries could gain from relations with Japan.

During the first postwar decades, the Japanese side of the complementarity equation was emphasized. Stability was sought by means of diversification of markets and sources of supply. As key actors in this effort, trading companies flourished. (They flourished also as heirs to the organizing role formerly performed by *zaibatsu* holding companies.) Later, trade was supplemented by investment: the stability of long-term contracts for raw materials supply was strengthened by ownership and control of foreign raw materials sources. This was known as the policy of *kaihatsu-yunyu* (develop and import). However, extrapolation of Japan's "miraculous" growth rate implied that it would become a disproportionately large consumer of the raw materials resources of the world. In view of the trend toward "resources nationalism" and emerging nationalistic development movements abroad, this was an ominous prospect. Accordingly, in 1971, MITI announced a new industrial policy, designed to reduce "pollution-prone" and "resource-consuming" activities in favor of "clean" and "knowledge-intensive" types with a higher degree of domestic value added per unit of imported raw material inputs.

By means of this shift in strategy, instead of appearing to frustrate the development ambitions of LDCs and condemning them to careers in extractive industries and primary production, Japan could appear to be their collaborator in import-substitution industrialization (ISI): a new type of complementarity was born. At the same time, instead of becoming the target of protectionist infant-industry policies abroad, Japan would be a beneficiary of them as an active supplier of capital for direct foreign investments. As a trader, Japan would benefit further as a supplier of plant, equipment, and technology to the newly industrializing nations. In this, as in other respects, Japan has a tendency to go from one extreme to another. When Prime Minister Kakuei Tanaka visited Brazil in 1974, he agreed to a list of projects that vastly overshadowed Japan's (unrealized) proposals for the development of Siberia. By 1983, for public inspection, Japan's foreign economic policy was formulated in entirely altruistic terms. As Saburo Okita expressed it, "Japan's role is to promote the development of the world economy."[8]

Politically, this posture pays dividends. It lends credibility to Japan's claim—as made known by Prime Minister Nakasone—to a larger role on the international stage. Apart from Japan's warranted qualifications for such a role, there is a bureaucratic propensity to seek it. As liberalization of the domestic economy curtails the turf of the bureaucracy at home, it seeks new worlds to conquer abroad. At the directors' level, government bureaucrats are in their mid-40s and have no personal knowledge of Japan's military defeat and occupation. On the contrary, as an elite group, they take personal success for granted and feel eager to abandon the "after you" policy Japan has pursued in relations with the United States. This "mood" (a favorite Japanese term) was reflected in a comment by Miyohei Shinohara. "Japan will have no failure for the next 20 years," he said. "But in the twenty-first century, who knows?"[9]

Shinohara is chairman of the Institute of Developing Economies, a MITI think tank. The institute employs Brazil specialists who coordinate their ideas with those of other Brazil specialists within MITI proper. Brazilianists are employed by four divisions of MITI, with four different constituencies and different interests. These are the Export Credit Insurance Division, the Economic Cooperation Division (which is in charge of the Institute of Developing Economies), the Foreign Exchange Division, and the America and Oceania Division (one of four regional market divisions). Although the ex post "consensus" at which these experts arrive is always presented as being in the national interest, the often opposing interests of the divisions have been resolved behind the scenes beforehand. Moreover, divisional rivalry is accompanied by interministerial conflict. MITI, for example, which represents the interests of Japan's principal exporters, defends the free-market principle in conflict with the protectionist Ministry of Posts and Telecommunications (MPT), whose constituency includes NEC. MPT is chiefly concerned to preserve its jurisdiction over software from MITI's encroachment. MITI and the Foreign Ministry advocate expansion of official development assistance (ODA), but the Ministry of Finance disagrees because of pressure on the budget. When funds are appropriated for ODA projects abroad, MITI wants construction orders to be awarded to Japanese suppliers, but the Foreign Ministry is unconcerned about this. Japan's increasing role in the world economy increases the roles of MITI and the Foreign Ministry, but it multiplies their conflicts as well. Fore example, the Foreign Ministry tells MITI to stay out of cultural affairs, but as Japan's external role expands, economic and cultural matters become increasingly mixed. JETRO, for example, which is exclusively supported by MITI, becomes unavoidably involved in "cultural" matters when it discusses Japanese management practices with foreign firms that deal with Japan. On the other hand, the Foreign Ministry threatens MITI's prerogatives when it argues that U.S.–Japan friction is a cultural as well as a trade matter.

MITI, however, together with the Ministry of Finance, is one of Japan's two most powerful and dynamic ministries. Its policies are determined in consultation with big business, with industrial associations, and with Keidanren (Japan Federation of Economic Organizations). Thus there is no doubt that in the future, as in the past, Japan's foreign economic policy will be dominated by MITI and its allies rather than by the Ministry of Foreign Affairs. In relations with Brazil, a scenario of that policy is suggested by the rationale discussed in Chapter 1. Schematically, it falls into three stages:

Stage I: Following World War II, Japan and Brazil were complementary in a direct bilateral sense. Japan imported raw materials and exported manufactured goods, while Brazil did the reverse. They shared a vertical division of labor.

Stage II: Brazil begins to expand and diversify its manufacturing production. Japan invests in Brazilian raw materials sources and in the production of final products. In some fields, a horizontal division of labor emerges. Competition from Brazilian raw materials reduces the price of primary products all over the world. This reduces the cost of Japan's imports of food and raw materials from sources *other* than Brazil. Complementarity emerges in a multilateral version. Japanese banks and trading companies in Brazil are instrumental in promoting it.

Stage III: Brazil becomes an important producer of intermediate goods. Japan exports its smokestack industries to Brazil. These include steel, petrochemicals, and aluminum. Japan's processing and fabricating plants in Brazil use the output of its own Brazilian raw materials sources. Japan becomes a headquarters country, concentrating on high technology at home and controlling a world network of primary and secondary types of production abroad.

Intertwined in the changing nature of Japan's complementarity with Brazil is a corresponding change in Japan's competitive-complementary balance with the United States. In stage I, Japan and the United States were complementary because the United States was supplying raw materials and food to Japan in exchange for manufactured goods. In stage II, the U.S.–Japan relationship is both complementary and competitive. In stage III, the relationship will be primarily competitive.[10] I described this scenario to Professor Kazushi Ohkawa at the International Development Center of Japan (IDCJ). His comment was, "Yes, we do think like that. But it will take 15 or 20 years."[11] The 15- to 20-year evolution of the three-stage scenario dovetails with Ohkawa's remark in the same interview concerning Japan's macroeconomic dilemma, which likewise, he believes, can be resolved only in a period of several decades. What is the dilemma? Externally, Japan tells the world that it is stimulating domestic consumption as a means of reducing its export surplus. At the same time, it promotes administrative reform at home in an effort to reduce consumption, especially in the public sector. In 1984, Japan's general government expenditures and interest payments amounted to 32.5 percent of the GNP, almost as high as the U.S. ratio of 34.4 percent.[12] In that year, Japan's GNP growth rate was 5.8 percent in real terms, of which export growth provided 3.6 percentage points, or two-thirds of the total. Typically, Japanese recessions have been overcome by means of export expansion. In the future, however, it is unlikely that its trade partners will continue to accept massive trade deficits as a normal feature of doing business with Japan.

It becomes imperative, therefore, for Japan to transform its portfolio assets into direct investment abroad. This may help to explain the persistently defensive and protectionist commercial policy the Japanese government has maintained despite the enormous pressures that have been applied against it by the United States and other nations. The threat of retaliatory protectionism on the part of Japan's trade partners is accelerating Japanese direct investment abroad. It would be rational for the Japanese government to welcome such threats in the interest of its own geopolitical strategy. Trade friction can serve the purposes of the Japanese government in hastening realization of the headquarters country concept. In an earlier postwar stage, the United States unconsciously performed a similar favor to Japan. U.S. protectionism against Japanese textiles and other low-technology products helped to push Japan into the high-technology field at a rate faster than would otherwise have occurred.

In its postwar beginnings, Japan's foreign direct investment was placed primarily in east and southeast Asia. What are the relative merits of Asia and Latin America for Japan's future investments? Is Japan *shifting* from the former to the latter, or is it *expanding* into Latin America? According to Professor Ohkawa, Japan is not abandoning its position in east and southeast Asia; it is expanding into Latin America. The dynamism of Asia is of great importance to Japan. But Japan's interests in Latin America will become complementary to its interests in east and southeast Asia. This constitutes still another dimension of the pyramid of complementarities that figures in Japan's external strategy.

Similar comments were made by Professor Shinohara. He observed that at present the Association of Southeast Asian Nations (ASEAN) is highly complementary with Japan: "Within ASEAN, however, there is little industrial diversification and interdependence. In the future this will change as the five members of ASEAN begin to specialize. At that point, they will achieve complementarity among themselves. As a group, they will become complementary to Latin America. The newly industrializing countries (Korea, Taiwan, Singapore, Hong Kong) are resource poor. Eventually, they too will be interested in the raw materials of Latin America."[13]

Saburo Okita observed that southeast Asia lacks the absorptive capacity of Brazil to receive the full measure of Japan's capital outflow. Thus in terms of my scenario, it will not replace Brazil or displace it in the scale of geopolitical priorities.[14] In the future, moreover, having already borrowed as much as it can, Brazil will be obliged to accept the inflow of Japanese direct investment.

In formulating its geopolitical views, the Japanese government collaborates with big business. In December of 1977, Masaki Nakajima, president of the Mitsubishi Research Institute, announced Mitsubishi's plan for a Global Infrastructure Fund (GIF). In 1981, a GIF Study Group was organized by Nakajima, including Toshio Doko, honorary chairman of Keidanren; Saburo Okita, former Foreign Affairs Minister; Eishiro Saito, chairman of Nippon Steel Corporation; and Shuzo Inaba, president of the Industrial Research Institute. These eminent figures authoritatively reflect establishment thinking. Ostensibly, the plan is designed to promote global economic development. Twelve superprojects, each designed to require 10 to 20 years for completion, have been proposed. They include construction of a massive hydropower complex in South America, greening of deserts, large-scale solar energy collection stations, construction of a Kra Isthmus canal, and others. Fulfillment of these projects would be highly compatible with the concept of Japan as a headquarters country, organizing, coordinating, and controlling its various interests around the world. According to the Japan Iron and Steel Federation, the project with highest priority and with highest probability for success is the construction of a second Panama Canal.[15] Associated therewith would be construction of an oversized port at Tubarao, Brazil and a huge relay port in southern Japan which would receive mammoth carrier ships from Brazil and transship their contents in smaller vessels to various destinations in Asia, including China and other NICs. These projects would greatly tighten the physical links between Japan and Brazil and magnify Japan's management role.

In the meantime, by means of commercial policy, industrial policy, financial policy, economic diplomacy, and foreign economic cooperation policy, the stages of Japan's evolution toward headquarters country status are clearly evident. The work is being done not by Japan alone, but also by other countries that collaborate with Japan in their own interest. In particular, the transformation of Japan's industrial structure is synchronized with a corresponding transformation in Latin America. Since 1976 there has been a dramatic decline in Japan's imports of raw materials and an increase in its imports of intermediate goods. There have been less imports of iron and steel scrap and more imports of steel, less imports of wood pulp and more imports of paper and paper products, less imports or rags and fiber for weaving and more imports of weaving yarns and textile products, less imports of nickel ore and more imports of nickel and nickel alloys, and less imports of aluminum scrap and bauxite and more imports of aluminum and aluminum alloys. Japan's raw materials-using industries are being progressively displaced by the processing and assembly industries, which consume intermediate goods. In Latin America, efforts to achieve import substitution are coordinated with efforts to reduce exports of raw materials and to increase the degree of value added per unit of exports. Thus there is a strong movement in favor of exporting intermediate products to Japan. This theme was emphasized in the keynote address of Manuel Ulloa Ellias, prime minister of Peru, at the Second Latin America/Japan Business Cooperation symposium held in Tokyo, September 28 to October 1, 1982.

### Economic Cooperation Policy

As mentioned earlier, among observers of Japan there are several schools of thought concerning the sources of its accomplishments. Within Japan itself, there are likewise partisans of each school whose interests are associated with one or another of the interpretations that presume to account for Japan's success. In the government, where interministerial rivalries are based on a hierarchy of power positions, a ministry's relative status may help determine its preference for more or less government control In the private sector, powerful economic groups may be in favor of a free-enterprise economy because they occupy commanding positions and feel confident of defeating any new competition that may arise. In addition to its competitive power in the marketplace, Japanese big business enjoys the security of a working relationship—in the "national interest"—with the seniors of the government bureaucracy. Nevertheless, at the lower end of the scale, there are enough degrees of freedom and enough prosperity in Japan to keep small and medium-sized businesses, reconciled to the system. But Japan's market mechanism is not a prototype for market systems elsewhere. There are many types of market mechanisms, just as there are many types of traditional economies and many types of centrally planned economies. In recommending the market mechanism for developing countries, however, Japanese policy-makers are often thinking of their own system. The same holds true with regard to institutional arrangements. Thus the confusion in thinking about the sources of Japan's economic accomplishments is reflected in thinking about types of economic cooperation that might contribute to development elsewhere.

From a Japanese point of view, however, in what rationale for economic cooperation does Japan's national interest lie? With reference to the stages scenario, regional and short-term versus long-term considerations are relevant. Regionally, Brazil could augment the international network over which Japan would preside as a headquarters country. Moreover, Brazil's enormous absorptive capacity for Japanese investment makes it a prime candidate among the various potential beneficiaries. Third, Brazil has been a relatively stable society. These are the chief characteristics of an eligible candidate for Japanese aid.[16] The criterion for Japanese economic cooperation can thus be expressed as "picking the winners."

Corresponding to the stages of Japan's development scenario, the candidates for its economic cooperation are evolving through stages of their own. Politically, it makes sense for Japan to formulate its aid proposals in terms of projects that would accelerate the progress of beneficiaries from lower to higher stages rather than in terms of projects that would contribute to Japan's own "comprehensive economic security."[17] In the case of Brazil, Japan's major projects clearly can be defined in terms of Brazilian progress through stages. Some Japanese authorities, moreover, argue that once the candidate country has been selected, a logical aid program would be one that minimizes palliatives for short-term exigencies in favor of maximizing long-term objectives.[18] In economic cooperation with Brazil, Japan's emphasis on construction of infrastructure is consistent with this concept. Another argument concerns the merits of the market mechanism versus government controls in the early stages of the development process. Some authorities assert that in early and even in later stages of development, the private sector does not function well.[19] Even in relatively advanced countries, the market may be ineffective or counterproductive, as for example in widening the gap between the modern and traditional sectors. Consequently, it is argued that the government, and thus the bureaucracy, should play a larger role. In the case of Brazil, Japanese proponents of this argument would have preferred an extension of the military regime to the advent of the democratic system that emerged in the *abertura* of 1985.

Japanese "economic cooperation" is not synonymous with "economic aid" as provided by the United States.[20] Officially, it is defined as comprising three categories: (1) official development assistance (ODA), which includes a grant element of more than 25 percent, (2) other official flows (OOF), and (3) private flows (PF).[21] ODA includes grant aid, yen loans,[22] technical cooperation, and contributions to international organizations. (Yen may be involved in Export-Import Bank arrangements, but the latter are not described as "yen loans" in Japanese government parlance.) OOF include financial resources provided by the Japan Export-Import Bank and other government agencies as export credits and direct investment. The Export-Import Bank is under the direction of the Ministry of Finance. It has considerable discretion, however, as to the extent of the concessionary content of its loans. PF include export credits, direct investment, and others, financed by the private sector. The technical cooperation component of ODA is administered by the Japan International Cooperation Agency (JICA) under the direction of the Ministry of Foreign Affairs. The JICA mostly makes loans, but it also invests. Official soft and "semisoft" loan assistance is administered by the Overseas Economic Cooperation Fund (OECF), subject to the direction of a four-agency coordination committee including the Ministry of Foreign Affairs, the Ministry of Finance, the Ministry of International Trade and Industry, and the Economic Planning Agency. OECF mostly invests (unprofitably), but it also makes loans. I asked Saburo Okita, "Which ministry is dominant in this committee?" He replied, "It is a matter of case by case. If serious differences arise among the four members of the controlling committee, the matter may go to the ministers of the agencies concerned, or eventually even to the prime minister. If agriculture, construction, or other sectoral interests are concerned, additional ministries may also become involved. Theoretically, it would be desirable to have a single Japanese government agency in control of economic cooperation; at present, there are delays in arriving at decisions. As a practical matter, it is not possible."[23]

In another conversation, I was told that "in the coordination committee, MITI is primarily concerned with the interests of Japanese business, the Gaimusho [Foreign Ministry] wants to spend more, the Okurasho [Ministry of Finance] wants to spend less, and the EPA is the 'scholar and gentleman' with no preconceived views."[24] The Ministry of Finance, which generally has the last word, seldom proposes policies or projects concerning foreign aid. Instead, it only examines line by line the proposals offered by other members of the committee and reacts in terms of the budget. MITI does make proposals, especially with reference to its industrial policy. The Foreign Ministry tries to reduce the trade element in the aid program, but this is contrary to the wishes of MITI. In attempting to separate aid from trade, the Foreign Ministry is chiefly concerned to reduce the role of MITI in the aid program.

In an interview with the director of the Economic Cooperation Division of MITI, I asked what are the weights attached by MITI to the economic, political, and security components of Japan's relations with aid recipients. He replied, "There are no fixed criteria as to the percentage. We look at the bilateral relationship and the whole spectrum of interests."[25] This was an "official" answer.

Next, I asked about the procedure for selection of project proposals. In each case it is known that the proposal takes the form of a "request" on the part of the beneficiary country. The Brazilian government, for example, may broach its request by approaching Japan through Keidanren, through the Japanese Foreign Ministry, through MITI, through a trading company, or through political contacts with the prime minister during state visits. "We don't make any suggestions as to what the request should be," said the director. This also was an "official" answer. In an interview with the director of the First Latin America and Caribbean Division of the Ministry of Foreign Affairs, who was a Brazil specialist, I asked the same question. "In looking out for the interests of Japanese business," he said, "MITI sometimes suggests desirable types of projects to the recipient country."[26]

As in many other aspects of Japan's institutional arrangements, its official financial cooperation facilities are segmented. Concessionary ODA loans are exclusively under the jurisdiction of OECF; hard loans are exclusively under the jurisdiction of the Export-Import Bank.[27] The terms of Export-Import Bank loans, however, are generally favorable to the borrower as compared with outright commercial loans. The Japan Export-Import Bank is the largest international financial cooperation agency in the world. Annually, it lends the equivalent of approximately US$5 billion. It is allowed considerable discretion by the Ministry of Finance to determine the terms of agreement with loan recipients. It has participated in many Japanese projects in Brazil, including the Usiminas project, Ishibras, Carajas, and others. The conditions for Export-Import Bank loans, however, are not public information. Moreover, the Export-Import Bank does not publish data concerning the amount of its loans to individual countries. The reason for this is that it does not want to provide information that could provoke invidious comparisons among its clients and give rise to unwelcome demands for further accommodation. It is interesting, however, that in accordance with the implications and rationale of the headquarters country scenario, the bank has reconstituted its operating structure. Formerly, its operations were directed by functionally organized loan departments; these have been reorganized along geographic lines. As perceived by the president of the Mitsubishi Corporation of Brazil, "When the Japanese government wants to help a foreign country, such as Brazil, they will allow the Export-Import Bank to finance the export of equipment provided that the foreign country buys the equipment from Japan."[28]

The broad issues of Japan's economic cooperation policy form a framework for its relations with Brazil. One issue concerns the contrast between Japan's "economic cooperation" and "economic aid" as extended by the United States. In commenting on this contrast, among other matters, Saburo Okita observed:

President Reagan has oriented U.S. aid to emphasize military assistance, especially in troubled areas. Japan has a broader approach. We do not wish to concentrate on troubled areas as much as the United States. In a sense, however, Japan has become more adversarial because it has shifted its diplomacy from an "all-direction diplomacy" ["friendship with all"] to a "Western-oriented diplomacy." As a global power, Japan's homogeneity is a weakness. The United States, as a multiracial nation, is more international in its orientation. Also, the United States is much bigger than Japan and has strong military capability. Therefore, it may adopt a more independent policy than Japan. The United States has increased its expectations of Japan. But Japan cannot respond so much. Japan must not frighten other Asian countries. Japan is on shaky ground; its economic success is shaky. Japan will never become a superpower. There is a present a consensus in Japan that we must strengthen our purely defensive military capability. Primarily, however, there should be a linkage between defense and development issues. To some extent, there could be joint U.S.–Japan foreign aid policy, as for example in population control and family planning. But joint planning is a matter of the "case by case" approach. In effect, there is a tradeoff between the burden Japan will carry in the form of providing soft loans to developing countries and the burden of nonnuclear self-defense. Other tradeoffs lie in the area of increasing involvement by Japan in global diplomacy.[29]

Professor Kazushi Ohkawa, however, takes strong exception to the tradeoff concept. "We cannot establish the precedent of a tradeoff," he said.[30] South Korea, for example, points out that much of its expenditure for military defense makes a direct contribution to Japan's welfare. It argues that Japan should either assist with military defense or provide an equivalent contribution in the form of economic aid. If the tradeoff principle is established, Japan might be obliged not only to increase its foreign aid expenditures, but also to increase them in areas where it may not prefer to do so. Many unwelcome demands would promptly be made for Japanese economic aid. Moreover, as a precedent, the tradeoff principle would be generalized from the military to other types of burden-sharing. Developing countries having an adverse trade balance with Japan might argue that they also were entitled to Japanese aid.

Apart from the issue of a tradeoff between defense and foreign aid, a policy issue in U.S.–Japan relations concerns the Japanese perception that President Reagan wants to reduce U.S. official aid and would like Japan to pick up the slack. At the same time, there are some possibilities for U.S.–Japan cooperation in the foreign aid field, such as the joint population-control effort proposed by Saburo Okita. Professor Ohkawa makes the point that uncoordinated aid activities of the United States and Japan may be less useful than a consortium approach, especially in the category of technical assistance.

In policy matters concerning Brazil, the issue of technical assistance has high visibility. One of Brazil's chief complaints against Japan is the inadequacy of its technical cooperation. There are several points to be made on this score. First, the nature of Japan's economic cooperation has evolved in accordance with the economic transition with Japan itself and the transition in the economies of aid recipients. Technology transfer is of increasing importance to Brazil as it advances in the production of intermediate goods by means of more sophisticated technology. A second point is that the share of technical assistance in Japan's ODA is below average in relation to that of other DAC member countries.[31] In the opinion of Professor Kazushi Ohkawa, it is important that the rate of increase in Japan's technical assistance programs should be greater than the rate of increase in loans in the 1981–1985 aid-doubling plan. If this were the case, he believes that more collaboration with the United States in the field of economic aid would be possible.[32] By 1984, Japan was second only to the United States in terms of its overall ODA contributions. In 1985, it ranked third after the United States and France (Table 4–1). The 5-year aid-doubling plan begun in FY1981 called for cumulative expenditure of US$21.4 billion by FY1985. In 1985, however, ODA disbursement amounted to US$3,797 million, a decline of 12.1 percent from the previous year. Future Japanese government assistance will concentrate on energy, food production, infrastructure, communications,

## Table 4–1
### Brazil: Net Inflow of Financial Resources from Japan, 1960–1985
(*millions of dollars*)

| Type of Flow | 1960–1980 | 1981 | 1982 | 1983 | 1984 | 1985 |
|---|---|---|---|---|---|---|
| Grand total | 6,002.4 | 542.1 | 611.1 | 223.0 | 1,040.4 | 123.2 |
| ODA (official development assistance) total: | 139.6 | 31.4 | 50.5 | 27.1 | 35.6 | 40.6 |
| ODA loans | 89.3 | 15.3 | 35.8 | 12.5 | 19.9 | N.A. |
| Total grants: | 50.3 | 16.1 | 14.6 | 14.6 | 15.8 | N.A. |
| Grant assistance | 2.0 | 0.0 | 0.0 | 0.0 | 0.0 | N.A. |
| Technical cooperation | 48.4 | 16.1 | 14.6 | 14.6 | 15.8 | N.A. |
| Other bilateral securities and claims[a] | 5,862.8 | 510.7 | 560.6 | 195.9 | 1,004.8 | 82.6 |
| Private direct investment and other private capital | N.A. | 480.2 | 580.8 | 213.0 | 1,004.5 | 58.4 |
| Other official flows | N.A. | 30.5 | − 20.2 | − 17.1 | 0.3 | 24.2 |

*Source:* Government of Japan, Ministry of Foreign Affairs.
[a] Includes export credits.

transportation and manpower training. A third point, incidentally, is that whatever its relative merits, during the period 1960–1980 Japan's technical assistance to Brazil has exceeded its technical assistance to any other Latin American country.[33] In general, however, economic cooperation has been a highly unpopular program in Japan.

Concerning Japanese subsidiaries abroad, it is a common complaint in host countries, including Brazil, that top positions are typically reserved for Japanese personnel. (The same is true of U.S. firms in Brazil.) Japanese methods of performing technology transfer may help to account for this practice, which differs from that of U.S. firms. According to Professor Ohkawa, in contrast to management methods in the United States, "In Japan, we keep to the traditional way. The Japanese produce no systematic manuals, as they do in the United States, and which anyone can read and apply. Japanese indoctrinate others by oral not by written means. Thus it is difficult to transfer know-how to the host country without the supervision of Japanese management." In the same vein, one of the important contributions Japan has to offer in the field of economic development is the transfer of management practices in small and medium-sized businesses. Knowledge of this sort is crucially needed in Brazil. The possibility for transfer of Japanese management methods, however, is greatly enhanced among countries with social organizations similar to that of Japan, in which small group cooperation and small group collectivism[34] are pronounced. In such cases, the transfer of management methods together with technology can be optimally accomplished. Moreover, even in large Japanese companies, quality control, for example, is performed in small groups.

A comment by a Brazilian-Japanese was of interest with reference to

Professor Ohkawa's anecdote. In the field of agricultural development, "Technology cannot be transferred from Japan to Brazil in a package," he said. "It must be implanted by Japanese *people*."[35]

Apart from technical assistance, what are Japan's outstanding economic aid issues with Brazil? According to the director of the Aid Policy Division in the Economic Cooperation Bureau of the Japanese Ministry of Foreign Affairs,

> Latin American countries are the most nationalistic of all the countries to which Japan gives aid. At the same time, they take pride in being "developed," not "underdeveloped." Brazil has a very nationalistic approach to receiving aid. It has various rules about giving advantage to Brazilian firms rather than to foreign companies that might gain a foothold. Brazil insists on 51 percent domestic equity participation in any project undertaken with Japan. They feel insecure. They refer to the "Japanese invasion." Japan has more programs in Brazil than in most other places, so we have more problems there. But the problems do not mean that our relations with Brazil are worse than elsewhere. The main issue concerns the sensitivity of the Brazilians. They demand, "Treat us as equals."[36]

As I was told in the same interview, in the opinion of the Foreign Ministry, Japan's economic cooperation policy, especially its ODA component, should be linked to Japan's foreign policy. However, whatever the ministry may think of the idea of international tradeoffs, domestically it is obliged to make tradeoffs with MITI, which regards economic cooperation as a hunting ground for Japanese firms. In the scenario of Japan as a headquarters country, there may be scope for more accommodation and less rivalry between the Ministry of Foreign Affairs and MITI. Partly this may come about through the increasing importance of foreign policy, which enhances the bargaining power of the Foreign Ministry in relation to its stronger adversary. In asserting a world leadership role, the Japanese government is increasingly preoccupied with external as opposed to internal policy. Formal evidence of this appears in the proposals for administrative reform, which in contrast to their general purpose of reducing the size of domestic expenditures of the Japanese government, contemplate augmented functions within the Foreign Ministry. In particular, administrative reform anticipates the strengthening of Japan's economic cooperation program.[37] Perhaps in anticipation of such a development, I was told by the director of the Economic Cooperation Division of the International Trade Policy Bureau of MITI, "There are no constants or absolutes in our aid policy. We are very flexible."[38]

## Administrative Guidance

At the government level, a characteristic shared by Japan and Brazil is the vague boundary between the formal and the informal. In both nations, the administrative is frequently more important than the statutory. In both nations, moreover—at the level of government—the very existence of administrative guidance is often denied.

In the Japanese case, "Administrative guidance occurs when administrators take action of no coercive legal effect that encourages regulated parties to act in a specific way in order to realize some administrative aim."[39] Administrative guidance (*gyosei shido*) is not a legal term; it appears in no Japanese statute. But as suggested in the matter of economic cooperation policy and elsewhere, it is clearly implicit in the typical Japanese government case-by-case and step-by-step modus operandi. The ostensibly sweet reasonableness of the motto, "We are flexible," moreover, relieves the administrator of the burden of producing his criteria for public inspection. The "flexibility" approach is not merely prudential; it is the judo tactic of using the strength of the opponent *against* him. It keeps the inquiring researcher in the dark and discourages his questions by foot-dragging. It keeps the regulated party in the dark as to the sanctions that noncompliance may invoke.

There are three modes of response concerning the question of administrative guidance. Some Japanese government officials will flatly deny its existence. Others will give a qualified answer. In the business community, few bones are made about it. The first mode was illustrated in an interview at MITI in which I was accompanied by the administrative assistant to a member of the House of Councillors. This undoubtedly prompted the MITI official to give "official" answers. (Interviews with Japanese government officials are most productive when no third person is present.) The MITI official declared, "As a free-market economy, the Japanese government cannot do anything with regard to influencing private activities. The relation between the Japanese government and private firms is the same as in any other free-market system."

The second mode of response was illustrated in an interview concerning Mexico with the deputy director of the Second Latin America and Caribbean Affairs Bureau of the Foreign Ministry. My question concerned areas of conflict between the United States and Japan in matters concerning Mexico. The deputy director replied, "We haven't come across any examples of strong conflict between the United States and Japan in Mexico. Therefore, we have prepared no guidelines for Japanese companies in competition with U.S. companies."[40] *Guidelines* may be understood as a euphemism. In an interview with the director of the First Latin America and Caribbean Division of the Foreign Ministry, I asked, "Does the Japanese government give administrative guidance to private firms in their relations with Brazil?" Without elaboration, he replied, "In a sense, yes."[41] I asked the same question of the director of the Aid Policy Division of the Economic Cooperation Bureau of the Foreign Ministry. "There is no guidance from the Foreign Ministry," he replied. "However, the private sector seeks advice from us in individual cases. Moreover, we have direct control over ODA, so administrative guidance is not necessary."[42]

At the private business level, there is less reticence on this subject. In Tokyo, in an interview with a member of a general trading company, I was told, "Nissho Iwai has informal meetings with MITI about once a month concerning economic cooperation projects and foreign trade. We also have meetings with the Foreign Ministry. They explain current trends and problems."[43] Farther from home, the veil was dropped with less ceremony. In an interview with the diretor vice-presidente of Mitsui Brasileira Imp. e Exp. Ltda., I pursued the matter of administrative guidance. "Does the Japanese government influence private investment in Brazil?" "Of course," he replied. "But it is secret, by means of *gyosei shido*. Mitsui cannot ignore MITI's wishes in the matter of foreign investment because MITI affects many other aspects of Mitsui's business activity and can retaliate."[44]

As mentioned earlier, Japan's economic cooperation activities include both government and private components, of which the latter are quantitatively predominant. By means of administrative guidance, the government plays a policy role both in projects in which it directly participates and in projects that nominally are wholly private. Instrumentally, Japan's private general trading companies (*sogo shosha*) play a strategic role in both types of projects. The trading company finds, organizes, and supervises the fulfillment of foreign projects. Its interaction with the government in the process of doing so was described to me by the general manager of the Research and Information Department of Nissho Iwai Corporation, one of the top six general trading companies in Japan:[45]

In many cases, economic cooperation is inaugurated in the first instance by the trading companies themselves. Our offices abroad observe that some project needs to be done. They notify the head office in Tokyo and send the particulars. The head office then notifies the companies that manufacture the needed products. The suppliers attempt to arrange financing. Our head office in Tokyo sends technicians, trainers, and other personnel to the host country abroad.

When the project is very large, the project partner in the host country needs the collaboration of its own government. So it sends a letter to its own government and to the banks in its own country. We make a feasibility study. We examine all the costs and implications of the project: what is the labor cost, the depreciation, the consumption of energy, the maintenance cost, expected profit, etc.? We send them an estimate of the cost of construction. Sometimes the host government will meet with me as representative of Nissho Iwai.

For reasons of foreign policy protocol, it is necessary that the idea of performing the project should appear to be the idea of the host country itself and should be broached by that country. I suggest that the minister of the host government contact the Japanese Embassy in the host country and ask it to request the Japanese government to extend economic cooperation. There is a discussion between the prospective host country and the Japanese government. The former makes its request by "exchange of notes." The Japanese government economic cooperation coordination committee considers the request. OECF may participate. This is ODA. If the desired loan is commercial, then the Export-Import Bank is included in the discussions.

In the meanwhile, on our part, we cannot take the whole risk. So we ask the Japanese government, "Can you help us?" As representative in the field, I write a letter to the headquarters of my company in Tokyo. I ask them to check the Japanese government budget to see whether there are available funds for the contemplated project in the potential host country. They also check the availability of funds from the Export-Import Bank, the OECF, MITI, and elsewhere. Export-Import Bank supports commercial projects. OECF supports social overhead, infrastructure, and other noncommercial projects where very low interest rates are required. The middle-sized projects will usually go ahead. The huge integrated projects are the most difficult to arrange.

The Japanese government asks us, "What is the economic nature of this project that you are proposing? What are its economic, political and military aspects and implications?" Sometimes MITI says, "We have no shopping list for this matter."

At the beginning stage, Nissho Iwai takes the technical steps. We then have to find good local partners in the host country. We submit the feasibility report to them and to the host government. About 40 percent of all projects are arranged in the above manner.

Sometimes we have to ask the IADB or the World Bank for their cooperation in making the survey. The World Bank may send technicians. These preliminary surveys are based on limited knowledge. After the provisional discussion, we ask the Japanese government to send a professional survey team, usually of about ten to twenty members.

Most projects are single-donor projects. Eighty to 90 percent of the projects are financed by a single source. Multinational finance is too complicated. Five years ago, most economic cooperation projects were based on tied loans. Recently, the trend has gone in favor of untied loans.

With regard to big projects, there are many ways of performing the project. Which is the best? The host government makes a judgment as to what is in its own best interest: the Russian method, the Japanese method, the American method, etc.

After the announcement of tender by the host government, bids are entertained. However, even the survey that a bidder needs to make before submitting his bid is very costly. Sometimes borings have to be made, engineering analysis, soil analysis, etc. It may take a year for bidders to make their appraisal and prepare their bids. Some prospective bidders will drop out. After a year or so, bidders gather together and submit their bids.

Now suppose that Japan makes the successful bid. The next question is, who will do the work? The work may be distributed to firms in more than one country. Sometimes the components of the job require inputs from countries other than that of the original bidder. In order to decide this question, it is necessary to calculate wage rates, the expected rate of inflation that will require wage increases, etc.

Suppose after 3 years, the project is finished: the ribbon is cut, the project is inaugurated! In most of these projects, the contractor is responsible contractually for the successful operation of the project. There is also moral responsibility. In any individual case, this is very complicated.

The "complications" were explained to me by Sumio Edamura, director general of Foreign Affairs in the Japanese Ministry of Foreign Affairs. Administrative guidance and other forms of government intervention are activated in the case of conflict between the contractor and the host government. "When the Brazilian government does not implement its promises to Japanese firms," for example, "the latter make a case to the Japanese government so as to induce it to put pressure on the Brazilian government."[46]

The more advanced or sophisticated the technology of the project, the more room there is for complications to arise between the contractor and the host country. Sophisticated projects, moreover, also may have other fallout with repercussions affecting the United States. First, of course, there may be competition between Japanese and U.S. firms for the contract award. Second, regardless of which receives the award, there may be cooperation in the execution of the contract. The reason for this is that in sophisticated projects the country of the prime contractor may not be able to supply all the components of the project. Thus in cases where a Japanese firm is awarded the contract, U.S. firms potentially might provide some of the inputs. Sophisticated projects also may generate upstream or downstream linkages that involve countries other than that of the prime contractor. The total impact of a project for U.S.–Japanese collaboration must be evaluated in terms of its linkages as well as in terms of the original project itself. Generally, sophisticated projects are undertaken by middle-advanced countries such as Brazil. Thus, theoretically, there is more scope for potential cooperation between the United States and Japan in Brazil than in less developed countries.

## Japanese Enterprise in Brazil

### Immigration from Japan

Although Japanese have a distinctively strong emotional attachment to their homeland, powerful motives led many to leave for Brazil after the Russo-Japanese War of 1904–1905. A push factor was the depression following the war, which was especially severe in the rural areas. Pull factors were the fascination of Brazil's physical immensity and the assurance of employn on the coffee plantations that were short-handed after the abolition of sla\ in 1888. The Brazilian government encouraged immigration from Japan well as from Italy and Portugal, because it regarded Brazil as be dangerously underpopulated. The first immigrant ship from Japan, *Kasato Maru,* carrying 781 passengers, arrived at the port of Santos on J 18, 1908. Most of the immigrants and those who followed quickly therea settled in the hinterland of Sao Paulo. Immigration from Japan was halted when Brazil broke off relations during World War II. It was resumed after the peace treaty of May 20, 1952. The accomplishments of the Japanese community in Brazil have been extraordinary. About 90 percent of the immigrants and their descendants live in the states of Sao Paulo and Parana. In Sao Paulo, where they constitute less than 10 percent of the agricultural work force, they account for about a third of total farm production. Japanese immigrants established the Cooperativa Agricola de Cotia (COTIA), which in 1983 had 11,000 members in eight states. It is the largest agricultural cooperative in Latin America. COTIA, incidentally, does not export anything to Japan. However, it does export fruits and vegetables to Europe, especially during November to March, competing with exports from Israel and Africa.[47]

In contrast to the prewar generation of settlers, which was employed mainly on coffee plantations, the postwar generation became farm owners. As of 1984, more than 75 percent of Brazilian-Japanese who worked in agriculture were owners of their own land.[48] They engage in diverse types of farming, such as sericulture, chicken raising, pomiculture, and cultivation of vegetables, rice, and cotton. They also predominate in the production of high-value, small-output specialty crops, such as tea, mint, black pepper, and silkworm cocoons. Moreover, the postwar Japanese community in Brazil, which constitutes less than 1 percent of the population, accounts for about 10 percent of the college student enrollment. The postwar generation is prominent in the clerical, service, management, and professional fields and government. Concerning immigration, "In the early years following World War II, a different type of Japanese came here. Japan was destroyed, and the types that came to Brazil were from the cities, but they disguised themselves as farmers because of Brazilian immigration policy."[49]

Among their other accomplishments, an observer commented on the striking success of Brazilian-Japanese in the financial field: "Even in a purely indigenous Brazilian national company, we often see that the comptroller is a nisei or even a Japanese. The Japanese are particularly good at finance, and they die with their secrets."[50] Another observation came from the U.S. commercial consul who had given a talk to the Brazilian Air Force, which is the only "technical" arm of the Brazilian armed forces. "I was stunned," he said, "by the number of Brazilian-Japanese who were in the ranks between major and brigadier general. This is the route for entry by Brazilian-Japanese into government enterprises and to attain high ranks in those companies."[51]

As of 1983, there were 850,000 Brazilian-Japanese in Brazil, of which 600,000 were in the Sao Paulo area. There were 4,000 Japanese from Japan, of which 1,500 were engaged in business and 2,500 were family members. In order to be a manager of a Japanese company in Brazil, a Japanese is required to hold a permanent visa. Among the colonies of immigrant descendants in Brazil, the Portuguese is the largest, followed by the Italian, the Spanish, and the Japanese.[52]

According to a member of the Ministry of Foreign Affairs in Tokyo, "Brazil insisted that we dismantle Japanese emigration companies. The reason was that the Japanese government was giving concessionary loans to Japanese emigrants and to descendants of Japanese in Brazil. They used to want immigrants, but they don't want them any more. They will still accept them, but they are not enthusiastic about it."[53]

As a community, "The Brazilian-Japanese have remained in a cultural mode that they brought with them at the time they emigrated from Japan to Brazil. They represent a type of Japanese culture that is no longer found in Japan. It is a kind of fossilized Japanism. In a sense, they are more Japanese than the Japanese. They are more traditional."[54] Having earned respect for their traditional Japanese virtues, the Brazilian-Japanese improved the auspices for Japan's trade and investment relations with Brazil. They also were recruited by Japanese enterprises in Brazil, which regarded them as more highly motivated and loyal than other Brazilians.

## Motives for Business Entry

As Japan's industrial structure and the structure of its foreign trade evolved in the postwar period, the strategy of its foreign investment evolved correspondingly. The evolution could be characterized in terms of offensive versus defensive investment. In the mid-1950s, Japanese general trading companies entered Brazil offensively for the purpose of marketing Japanese products, notably textiles. Very soon, however, Brazilian protectionism against "similars" for the purpose of promoting import-substitute industrialization (ISI) induced a defensive advance of Japanese manufacturers into Brazil. At the same time, Japanese enterprises searching for sources of raw materials and energy found dazzling prospects in Brazil. As markets and as sources of supply, both offensive and defensive investments were undertaken in advanced and developing countries, respectively. It is interesting that throughout the entire postwar period, Japan's direct foreign investment has been divided in approximately equal shares between advanced and developing countries.

In the 1950s, Japan's direct foreign investment was comprehensively controlled by the Japanese government. The objective of government policy was to reestablish Japan as an exporter of manufactured goods while securing stable foreign sources of raw materials, as in the prewar years. In taking the offensive, one of the classic strategies of Japanese foreign market penetration is to begin with distribution and then to proceed upstream to manufacturing. The textile industry, which undertook Japan's first postwar manufacturing efforts abroad, followed this strategy. In Brazil, Japanese spinning firms entered first, followed by synthetic textile and silk companies. This movement had logistic as well as "follow the leader" motivation. In the first place, as a large and rapidly growing economy, Brazil was a promising market for textile products. Second, for a 5-year period beginning in October of 1962, and thereafter renewed, exports from Japan to the United States, its principal market, were restricted by the Long-Term Arrangement Regarding International Trade in Cotton Textiles, negotiated for the purpose of controlling exports which "cause or threaten to cause 'disruption' of the market for cotton textiles." Brazil could serve as an export platform for Japanese exports to the United States, Europe, and elsewhere, especially nations where Brazil was regarded favorably. For example, as a mixed-race nation which has assimilated its black population, Brazil is highly esteemed in Africa, with which it is alleged to maintain a "special relation." Brazil is also popular in Iraq because when Geisel was president, he resisted efforts by the "Seven Sisters" (the world's leading oil companies) to persuade Brazil not to buy oil from that country. Together with black Africa, Iraq is a customer for heavy machinery products of Brazil, which it finds difficult to sell elsewhere.[55] Third, the textile industry was receiving favored treatment from the Brazilian government in accordance with its ISI program. Fourth, in the course of its high economic growth era (1955–1970), Japan found itself with a labor shortage, as well as a shortage of new plant sites. Fifth, the Japanese domestic market for textiles had matured and its possibilities for expansion at home were limited.

Complementarity between Japan and Brazil can be seen at three levels: in terms of physical endowment, in terms of public policy, and in terms of private business strategy. In the course of their postwar economic transition, there was a compatible evolution among these levels in relations between the two partners. This expressed itself in the changing nature of their trade and investment. In the mid-1970s, inauguration of Brazil's "market reserve" policy disrupted the symbiotic relationship between Japanese direct foreign investment and Brazilian ISI. At this point, Japan began to be willing to sell technology as such, not necessarily associated with sales of products. This helped the Brazilian government to maintain the market reserve policy. It also accelerated the shift in private Japanese strategy in favor of minority joint venture positions in Brazilian firms as opposed to exclusive Japanese ownership. U.S. firms did not want minority status because they feared this would mean loss of management control. Japanese strategy was more ingenious. Despite minority status, the Japanese often dominate management by their control of the firm's technology—its installation, operation, and maintenance. This was conspicuously the case in the electronics industry, where U.S. firms stayed out of the microcomputer field but Japanese firms flourished. Ultimately, however, both U.S. and Japanese firms have been blocked by the national security umbrella Brazil has placed over the electronics industry and its refusal even to spell out the extent of its restrictions under the "informatics" law.

The process of technology transfer is not a one-time operation. It requires a continuing flow of refinements, modifications, and improvements, which the Japanese conscientiously supply. They also dominate management by the control of credit and control of the international distribution networks of their general trading companies. The contrast between Japanese and U.S. equity preferences can be partly explained by differences in style and partly by differences in substance. In style, the Japanese does not prefer to be the front man. He doesn't mind remaining behind the scenes and having Brazilian nationals intercede with the government on his behalf. When the Japanese undertook the Albras aluminum joint venture, for example, they had to have an assured supply of electricity at a guaranteed price. They could not gamble on the price of electricity remaining constant while rampant inflation prevailed. So Rio Doce, their partner in Albras, went to the government and secured a long-term commitment for the price of electricity. In the aggregate, as a latecomer, Japan's position in Brazil is weaker than that of the United States. In particular areas, however, it is able to apply concerted pressure. By virtue of flexible strategies, including methods such as those mentioned earlier, Japanese firms may acquire the substance if not the form of leadership in joint ventures of which they are nominally minority stockholders.

Concerning technology transfer, Helson Braga of the Fundacao Centro de Estudos do Comercio Exterior maintains that as a strategy for market entry, Japanese firms have been more willing than U.S. firms to extend technological assistance to Brazil. According to Braga, Japan supplies a larger quantity of technology and makes it more readily available. He remarked that IBM, for example, contrary to Japanese practice, is more interested in developing its own products than in entering into relations with Brazilian firms for conveyance of technology to the latter.[56] Another contrast between Japanese and U.S. firms in Brazil concerns the time horizon they contemplate for the return on their investment. In planning, Japanese firms think of 5 years as short term and long term as more than 5 years. U.S. firms think of 5 years as long term.[57]

Even as minority stockholders, however, Japanese firms have had difficulty in entering oligopoly markets.[58] In the heavy equipment and chemical fields, so-called national projects have been undertaken, which are projects jointly sponsored by the Japanese and Brazilian governments, but in which the private sector participates. This is a means by which the Japanese government, in "running interference," has helped Japanese private firms to sidestep barriers to entry.[59] In important cases, however, it was the Brazilian government that approached Japan, rather than the reverse. Japanese participation was solicited by the Brazilian government in the Usiminas steel project, in the Ishibras shipbuilding project, and in the Cerrado. The same was true in the construction of Albras and Alunorte, where the Japanese government received a request for assistance in setting up an indigenous Brazilian aluminum complex as a competitor to the 100 percent foreign-owned company established by Alcoa and Alcan in the early 1970s.

One of the strategic questions for the Japanese direct investor in Brazil concerns whether the purpose of his investment is to produce chiefly for the Brazilian domestic market or chiefly for export. There may be conflicting motives. The Mitsubishi Corporation of Japan, for example, has twenty-four trade divisions. Each is an independent profit center with its own policies and its own products. However, the job of the Marketing and Coordination Department in Tokyo is to coordinate the various strategies of these divisions. "Suppose that Mitsubishi Japan wants to sell Japanese construction equipment to Brazil, but that Mitsubishi Brazil wants to sell its own similar equipment to the same customer. Or suppose that Mitsubishi Japan and Mitsubishi Brazil wish to sell similar equipment to the same buyer, but from competing suppliers. In such cases, the Coordination Department in Tokyo may tell Mitsubishi Brazil to hold back and not spoil the sale for Mitsubishi Japan. What determines whether or not the sale will be assigned to Japan? It depends on whether the particular sale is indispensable for future business. If it is merely a one-shot deal, the Coordination Department will not interfere with Mitsubishi Brazil."[60]

In the case of the Mitsubishi "group" (*keiretsu*), the preferred investments in Brazil in 1985 were those of the Tuberao or Albras type, namely, export-oriented projects using cheap raw materials, as in the production of ferromanganese, ferrosilicon, or pulp. For Mitsubishi Trading Company, as a member of the group, "third country trade" (exports from Brazil to countries other than Japan) is important and increasing. "This is the only way for a Japanese trading company to survive in Brazil." Other members of the group, such as Mitsubishi Heavy Industries of Brazil, may rely on the Brazilian government as their principal customer. According to an official at Citibank,

> The rationale for further loans by Japan to Brazil at the present time is to be able to sell more equipment to the state enterprises. Furthermore, that rationale takes account of the fact that restriction of imports due to the debt

crisis leads to more import substitution, which means an *increase* in the production of the state companies. In some cases, however, the budgets of the state companies are being cut back. The domestic market in general, in fact, is drying up. Thus it is necessary to export. But many of Japan's Brazilian subsidiaries were intended to produce only for the domestic market. In exporting, they compete with the exports of the parent companies in Japan, which is not at all welcome to the latter. So Japanese companies are now negotiating with their Tokyo headquarters concerning division of labor in some areas in which the parent company was supposed to have an export monopoly.[61]

This is an operational example of Japan as a headquarters country.

In accordance with Brazil's ISI ambitions, a good deal of Japanese investment is directed toward the domestic market. Yanmar do Brasil, S.A. (established in 1960), which makes agricultural machinery and diesel engines, is an example of a successful Japanese firm that relies exclusively on the Brazilian home market. However, the equity capital of 15 of the leading 250 exporting firms of Brazil is either wholly or substantially Japanese. Listed in order of their export performance during 1984, they are the following:[62]

Mineracoes Brasileiras Reunidas, S.A. (mining)

Samarco Mineracao, S.A. (mining)

Cia. Nipo-Brasileira de Pelotizacao—NIBRASCO (iron ore pellets)

Mineracao Rio do Norte, S.A. (mining)

Valesul Alumino (aluminum)

Celulose Nipo-Brasileira, S.A.—CENIBRA (wood pulp)

Cia. Florestal Monte Dourado (forestry)

Frigorifico Kaiowa, S.A. (frozen products)

S.A. Mineracao da Trinidade (mining)

Ajinomoto Interamericana Industria e Comercio Ltda. (pharmaceuticals, etc.)

Mitsubishi Corporation do Brasil, S.A. (trading company)

Companhia Siderurgica Tuberao (steel)

Nisshinbo do Brasil Industria Textil Ltda. (textiles)

Mitsui Brasileira Importacao e Exportacao Ltda. (trading company)

Industria Textil Tsuzuki Limitada (textiles)

As suggested in the Mitsubishi example, Japanese *keiretsu,* or group conglomerates, have certain advantages not available to their competitors. By means of their coordinating departments, to say nothing of their interlocking directorates, intragroup shareholding, common banking affiliations, "third Thursday" clubs for strategy meetings of group company presidents, and the like, Mitsubishi, Mitsui, Sumitomo, and other *keiretsu* are able to make long-term plans and long-term profits that are beyond the reach of lesser organizations. The tie between a bank and a trading company in a *keiretsu,* for example, makes it possible for a Japanese bank to extend a loan to a Brazilian firm at a lower rate of interest than a U.S. bank could offer because its trading company partner or some other member of the group is going to make a profit on the sale of products financed by the loan. Thus the group makes a profit regardless of the terms of the loan. Moreover, Japanese banks are more highly leveraged than U.S. banks. A Japanese bank can achieve the same return on equity as a U.S. bank even though it makes a lower return on assets employed. A Japanese group also can take a longer-term view than a single U.S. firm. If extending loans assists Brazil to accelerate its rate of development, it will become an increasingly better market in the long run. In the process of extending these loans, Japanese banks cultivate a cordial relationship with Brazilian borrowers that will bear fruit in the form of future sales by other members of their respective groups. Those sales might be made either by group members in Japan or by their subsidiaries in Brazil. Although a *keiretsu* is not integrated by means of a top holding company, as were the prewar *zaibatsu,* its collective interests provide powerful incentives for the linkage and coordination of its investment decisions in Brazil. In their coordination of physical production, services, and finance, the *keiretsu* constitute the embryo and nucleus of Japan's emergence as a headquarters nation.

The role of Japanese banking in the investment decision is taken a step further in the procedure known as "project finance." In this procedure, a bank provides funds for a development project from its inception at the stage of prospecting, surveying, and planning. Typical cases include the opening of mines, drilling for oil, and planning for pipelines. As their earnings from domestic business have begun to deteriorate, Japanese banks have become more entrepreneurial in terms of "making a profit," as distinguished from merely participating in the outcome of the entrepreneurship of others. In particular, project finance is being pursued on the international plane, notably in Brazil. A sharp increase in Japanese international project finance has been observed since 1981.

Leasing is another procedure that has recently emerged as a factor in Japan's investment relations with Brazil. It makes possible a maneuver by which the same equipment can be financed twice. In the first instance, a Japanese bank finances the purchase of equipment in Brazil. By leaseback arrangement, the same equipment may be financed again.

In a global context, Japanese project finance, *keiretsu* coordination of sources and markets, and long-term participation in Brazilian import-substitution programs may generate a "virtuous circle" effect that would rebound to the benefit of both Brazil and Japan. A key project, for example, would be the participation by Japan in Brazilian efforts to produce chemical fertilizer for development of the Cerrado, a vast area of 1,829,000 square kilometers, approximately 21 percent of the entire territory of Brazil, and about five times the area of Japan, of which about one-third is suitable for cultivation. The Cerrado is largely undeveloped and has enormous potential for agricultural and livestock production. In order to realize this potential, however, supplies of fertilizer must be greatly increased. With Japanese help, Brazil could expand its domestic production of chemical fertilizer, increase agricultural output, and increase its competitive power in world markets as a supplier of primary products. Such a project would be good for Japan in assisting the transfer of its heavy and chemical industries abroad and in reducing the world price of food products. It would be good for Brazil by promoting the expansion and sophistication of both its primary and secondary industries and contributing to the improvement of its balance of payments. I proposed this idea to Ren Usami, diretor financeiro, CAMPO (an agricultural development company), in charge of pioneering the development of the Cerrado. He was very much in accord with it.[63]

While development of the Cerrado may be good for Brazil and Japan, it may not be welcome to other suppliers of primary products to Japan. World commodity prices, including those of mineral products, were already greatly depressed in the early 1980s, which in combination with Japan's conservation and retrenchment policies have already increased its bargaining power as a buyer of primary products. Brazil has already begun to displace Australia as a supplier of iron ore to Japan. Having spent most of the 1960s and 1970s building up its ore imports from Australia, Japan's geopolitical strategy now calls for promoting competition between Australia and other suppliers as a means of reducing prices. In 1985, Japan was Brazil's leading customer for iron ore, accounting for sales in the amount of US$457.8 million. At the same time, Japan continues to make large direct and indirect (portfolio) investments in Australia to develop its role as a supplier of primary and middle-technology products not merely to Japan, but to the world market at large. In the period July 1984 to June 1985, Japan became the principal source of foreign investment in Australia, outranking both the United States and the United Kingdom. Thus Japan's strategy in Australia is parallel to its strategy in Brazil. In both cases, its roles as a consumer and as an investor are calculated to increase the world supply of primary products and middle-technology intermediate goods. In the course of time, its role as an international investor and manager may transcend its role as a customer with regard to these products. Japan's domestic resources will be reallocated into high-technology industries. This evolution is central in the strategy of Japan's challenge to the United States. The United States unconsciously collaborates with this strategy by becoming increasingly protectionist not only in the primary-product sector, but also in the declining industry sector that is being phased out of Japan's domestic economy.

In the meantime, however, at the micro level, Japan itself is not immune from repercussions—described by Professor Miyohei Shinohara as the "boomerang" effect—of Brazilian advance in the heavy and chemical industry sector. It is Japan's declining industries in that sector that are most sensitive to the present transition, which is of central concern in MITI's industrial policy. The steel and shipbuilding industries, for example, are especially troubled by the loss of markets attributable to the transfer of their technology to developing countries. The computer and electronics industries are further ahead and are less vulnerable. Since 1981, Japan has imported from Brazil increasing amounts of ferroalloys (a major subsidiary material used in iron making), produced in Japan at high cost, mainly in electric furnaces. The cost of electricity is much lower in Brazil. Some ferroalloy makers in Japan have been forced to terminate production there earlier than they had planned. Thus as an exception to the collapse of Japanese direct investment in Brazil in 1984 (discussed below), Kawasaki Steel Company was investing in new Brazilian ferrosilicon facilities.

An interesting example of Japanese investment symbiosis with Brazilian ISI ambitions is found in Manaus, capital of Amazonia in the heart of the northern jungle, an area unsuited for agriculture or livestock production. At the turn of the century, it was a minor town producing a single product, namely, rubber. The military authorities, however, decided that the population of the Amazon should be increased in order to better control illegal entry into Brazil. Accordingly, like Brasilia, in 1967, Manaus was more or less made to order as a major city. The device in this case was the designation of Manaus as a free port for a period of 30 years; its special status is due to expire in 1997. In the meanwhile, it is under the jurisdiction of the Manaus Free Trade Zone Superintendency (SUFRAMA), which determines the eligibility of firms for fiscal "incentives." Besides exemption from import duties, these include income tax exemptions and exemptions from excise and value-added taxes. By 1985, Manaus had approximately 650,000 inhabitants and about 250 industrial firms, among which Japanese and Brazilian–Japanese firms were the most prominent. In addition to fiscal subsidies, the principal attraction of Manaus as a free port is its location on the upper Amazon River, about 1,000 miles from the Atlantic Ocean, and its accessibility to ocean-going vessels. Indeed, its port provides the most efficient container loading and offloading facilities in Brazil. The ease of importing components for assembly in Manaus has made it Brazil's principal center for the electronics and motorbike industries. Firms such as Sharp, Sanyo,

Toshiba, Honda, and Mitsubishi are well established there. Philco is the principal American firm in Manaus. Final output produced in Manaus may either be exported or shipped to domestic destinations in Brazil. Brazilians go to Manaus as though it were a foreign country, passing through customs on entry and departure. There is a quota on the amount of goods they can take home. Manaus has been criticized as being a parasitical and sterile anomaly that produces virtually no indigenous inputs—it imports even chickens and eggs. (Economists, of course, would quarrel with this criticism.) Its imports consistently exceed its exports. Moreover, it has figured prominently in smuggling scandals. For such reasons, Delfim Netto was no admirer of Manaus. In 1973, he said to one of my respondents, "Manaus is the cesspool of Brazil."[64]

The procedure of Japanese firms in implementing their investment strategy has been observed by Robert Blocker, president of Blocker Assessoria de Investimentos e Participacoes, S.A. According to Blocker, "Japanese do 70 percent of their investigation before they undertake a project; they do 30 percent after initiating the project. With Americans, it is the other way around." As an exception to this generalization, however, "In the early 1970s, up to 1976, the Japanese made errors by jumping into Brazil too precipitously. There were a number of conspicuous losers. Japanese do not understand the Brazilians. They think Brazilians are like Americans. But the Brazilians are weak in planning, organization, and ethics. In summary, therefore, Japanese have not invariably been more effective than Americans in preparing a project."[65]

Whether the projects were well judged or not, there is Japanese government reinforcement behind the major joint ventures that have been undertaken by Japanese firms with the Brazilian government's state enterprises. When the Japanese government was approached by the Brazilian government for collaboration in these projects, the former responded by recruiting firms in the Japanese private sector. Since MITI and the Ministry of Finance asked Japanese firms to participate in these joint ventures, they incurred an implicit obligation—Japanese style—to support the companies that did so. In the case of Tuberao, for example, the Japanese government continued to put money into the project, but the Brazilian government did not.

Quite apart from such obligations, Japanese firms can depend on support from institutions and organizations that have no counterpart in the United States or Brazil. The "intimate relation" that Japanese banks have with their clients, for example, is not found in the United States or Brazil. Besides loans, Japanese banks provide information, advice, and management expertise to their clients. "In Brazil, the bank says, 'Have you come to me with a request?' In Japan, the bank says, 'How can I help you?' "[66] Assistance to prospective overseas investors is provided by MITI by means of expert investment survey missions which it sends to evaluate proposed projects. The Overseas Trade

Association (*Kaigai Boeki Kyokai*) makes feasibility and financial studies for small and medium-sized firms that wish to invest abroad. In Japan, moreover, government financial institutions play a larger role in promoting private foreign investment than is correspondingly the case in the United States.

The Japan Overseas Enterprise Association (JOEA) is another source of support for foreign investors. It was established in July of 1974 after Prime Minister Tanaka's ill-fated trip to southeast Asia, where he got a hostile reception. The organization was designed to monitor the situation abroad and to take countermeasures in advance of anticipated difficulties. "After our members have invested abroad, we help them to be accepted by the host country." Recently, JOEA also has become a pressure group to influence the Japanese government in ways conducive to the benefit of its members.[67]

## Notes

1. Statistics from Saburo Kawai, president, International Development Center of Japan (IDCJ), in Tokyo, July 11, 1983.
2. Interview with Yoichi Yabu, senior division officer, Corporate Planning Division, C. Itoh & Co., Ltd., in Tokyo, July 14, 1983.
3. Interview with Akira Urabe, director, First Latin America and Caribbean Division, Ministry of Foreign Affairs, in Tokyo, July 6, 1983.
4. Interview with David Shapiro, Mitsubishi International Corporation, in New York, June 15, 1983.
5. Interview with Consul General Tadatsuna Yabu, Japanese Consulate, in Sao Paulo, July 13, 1983.
6. Interview in Sao Paulo, July 4, 1984.
7. Interview with Hiroshi F. Katayama, vice president, Citibank, N.A., in Sao Paulo, July 3, 1984.
8. Interview in Tokyo, July 18, 1983.
9. Interview in Tokyo, July 6, 1983.
10. When I described this scenario to Kazuo Nukazawa, director of the Financial Affairs Department of Keidanren, he remarked that at present the United States and Japan are approximately in stage 1½. Interview in Tokyo, July 7, 1983.
11. Interview in Tokyo, July 7, 1983. Professor Ohkawa is emeritus at Hitotsubashi University. At present he is research and training director at the IDCJ.
12. Bank for International Settlements, *Annual Report, 1985*
13. Interview in Tokyo, July 6, 1983.
14. Interview in Tokyo, July 18, 1983.
15. *Japan Steel Bulletin,* Vol. 7, No. 2, June, 1983, p. 2.
16. At a meeting I attended in Tokyo on February 16, 1972, Shinkichi Eto, professor of international relations at Tokyo University, stated that "the *real* principles of Japanese foreign aid are (1) enthusiasm of the recipient for economic development, (2) efficiency of capital, and (3) Japanese national security." He also remarked that "Japan will be disliked by her foreign aid beneficiaries in southeast

Asia, just as the United States is disliked by U.S. foreign aid beneficiaries. Tension between Japan and southeast Asia will arise in the 1980s."

17. Foreign aid was associated with Japan's "comprehensive economic security" in a report commissioned by former Prime Minister Ohira in the summer of 1980. In its beginnings, Japan's foreign aid was concerned primarily with export promotion.

18. According to this way of thinking, problems of social equity or problems of redistribution of income and wealth have lower priority than economic growth.

19. Professor Kazushi Ohkawa remarked, "I was not happy to learn that President Reagan wants to replace government with private enterprise everywhere." Interview in Tokyo, July 7, 1982.

20. The principal difference is that in the United States, the government (AID) is the exclusive actor. In Japan, the private sector plays a very important role in everything from discovery of the project to its final implementation. Moreover, flows of private-sector resources are statistically included among the categories of economic cooperation. The latter are predominant in Japan's economic cooperation with Brazil.

21. Association for the Promotion of International Cooperation, *A Guide to Japan's Aid* (Tokyo, April 1982), p. 5.

22. A yen loan is a concessionary ("soft") loan, with an interest rate of less than 5 percent, a long grace period, and a long period for reimbursement. Yen credits are not necessarily tied to procurement from Japan. There are two types of untied aid: (a) the recipient can use the proceeds of the loan anywhere and (b) the recipient is free to use the proceeds of the loan either in Japan or in any developing country. Eligibility for yen credits is based on per capita GNP. By World Bank standards, Brazil no longer qualifies. However, when Prime Minister Suzuki visited Brazil in 1982, he promised untied aid of Y10 billion for the purchase of an irrigation system. When Prime Minister Tanaka visited Brazil, he presented a yen credit equivalent to US$100 million for the improvement of Brazil's ports. The United States does not provide ODA to Brazil because it classifies it as an NIC rather than an LCD.

23. Interview in Tokyo, June 29, 1982.

24. Interview with Koichiro Matsuura, director of the Aid Policy Divison, Economic Cooperation Bureau, Ministry of Foreign Affairs, in Tokyo July 19, 1982. Although formally, EPA is in charge of OECF, it does not have a strong voice in matters concerning economic aid. This administrative anomaly arose because of interministerial rivalry in the mid-1960s when MITI and the Ministry of Finance were jointly in charge of OECF and each contended it should have exclusive authority over that agency. As a solution to the controversy, EPA was placed in charge of OECF. Otherwise, EPA would never have become involved in economic cooperation affairs.

25. Interview with Masao Teruyama, director, Economic Coooperation Division, International Trade Policy Bureau, MITI, in Tokyo, July 20, 1982.

26. Interview with Chihiro Tsukada, director, First Latin America and Caribbean Division, Ministry of Foreign Affairs, in Tokyo, July 27, 1982.

27. This division of labor, dating from July of 1975, was arranged by Saburo Okita when he was in charge of OECF. Prior thereto, the Export-Import Bank had shared ODA responsibilities with OECF.

28. Interview with Toshio Oda, diretor presidente, Mitsubishi Corporation do Brasil, S.A. in Sao Paulo, August 1, 1983.

29. Interview with Saburo Okita, in Tokyo, June 29, 1982. The tradeoff theme also was emphasized ino Okita's address to the National Press Club in Washington,

D.C. on May 19, 1982. In describing the occasion to me, Okita remarked that his address was warmly endorsed by U.S. Secretary of State Geroge Shultz.

30. Interview with Kazushi Ohkawa, research and training director, International Development Center of Japan (IDCJ), in Tokyo, July 7, 1982.

31. DAC is the Development Assistance Committee of OECD.

32. Interview with Kazushi Ohkawa, research and training director, International Development Center of Japan (IDCJ), in Tokyo, July 7, 1982.

33. Among other forms of cooperation, the Japan Society for the Promotion of Science, a semiprivate organization, cooperates with the Brazilian Council for the Development of Science and Technology (CNPQ).

34. Because of its Marxist connotations, however, "collectivism" is not a satisfactory translation of the Japanese term *shudan shugi*.

35. Interview with Isidoro Yamanaka, assessor, Coordenadoria de Assuntos Economicos, Ministerio da Agricultura, Cabinete do Ministro, in Brasilia, on August 10, 1983.

36. Interview with Koichiro Matsuura, director, Aid Policy Divison, Economic Cooperation Bureau, Ministry of Foreign Affairs, in Tokyo, July 19, 1982.

37. See Liberal Democratic Party, Diplomatic Investigative Department, Committee for Intensifying Diplomacy, *A Declaration Relating to Strengthening of our Diplomatic System* [in Japanese], June 17, 1982.

38. Interview with Masao Teruyama, director, Economic Cooperation Division, International Trade Policy Bureau, MITI, in Tokyo, July 20, 1982.

39. Michael K. Young, "Judicial Review of Administrative Guidance: Governmentally Encouraged Consensual Dispute Resolution in Japan," *Columbia Law Review*, Vol. 84, No. 4, May 1984, p. 923. See also Mitsuo Matsushita, "Administrative Guidance and Economic Regulation in Japan," *The Japan Business Law Journal*, Vol. 1, December 1980.

40. Interview with Shisei Kaku, deputy director, Second Latin America and Caribbean Division, Latin American and Caribbean Affairs Bureau, Ministry of Foreign Affairs, in Tokyo, July 27, 1982.

41. Interview with Chihiro Tsukada, director, First Latin America and Caribbean Division, Ministry of Foreign Affairs, in Tokyo, July 27, 1982.

42. Interview with Koichiro Matsuura, director, Aid Policy Divison, Economic Cooperation Bureau, Ministry of Foreign Affairs, in Tokyo, July 19, 1982.

43. Interview with Masami Wakasugi, general manager, Research and Information Department, Nissho Iwai Corporation, in Tokyo, July 22, 1982.

44. Interview with Masayuki Ikeda, director vice-presidente, Mitsui Brasileira Imp. e Exp. Ltda., in Rio de Janeiro, July 17, 1984.

45. Interview with Masami Wakasugi, general manager, Research and Information Department, Nissho Iwai Corporation, in Tokyo, July 22, 1982.

46. Interview in Tokyo, July 13, 1983.

47. Interview with Americo Utumi, diretor Financeiro, Cooperativa Agricola de Cotia, in Sao Paulo, August 5, 1983. Other important agricultural cooperatives founded by Brazilian-Japanese include the Cooperativa Sul Brasil and the Cooperativa de Sao Paulo.

48. *Brazil Trade and Industry*, May 1984.

49. Interview with Trajano Pupo Netto, executive vice president, Banco Noroeste do Estado de Sao Paulo, S.A., in Sao Paulo, August 1, 1983.

50. Interview with Jean Bernet, president, Guia Interinvest, in Rio de Janeiro, August 16, 1983.

51. Interview with Kelly Joyce, commercial consul, United States Consulate General, in Rio de Janeiro, July 16, 1984.

52. Interview with Tadatsuna Yabu, consul geneal of Japan, in Sao Paulo, August 2, 1983.

53. Interview with Koichiro Matsuura, director, Aid Policy Division, Economic Cooperation Bureau, Minstry of Foreign Afairs, in Tokyo, July 19, 1982.

54. Interview with David Shapiro, Mitsubishi International Corporation, New York, June 15, 1983.

55. In 1980–1981, Iraq entertained bids for a US$1.4 billion railroad construction job. Interbras, which entered a bid, was in third place at the start of the bidding. When the contract was awarded, however, with the help of the Brazilian government, it was obtained by Interbras.

56. Interview in Rio de Janeiro, August 16, 1983.

57. Interview with Shigeo Uno, vice president, Japan Trade Center, in Sao Paulo, August 3, 1983.

58. Interview with Brian Michael F. Neele, head, Trade Information Division, Ministry of External Relations, in Brasilia, July 11, 1984.

59. Interview with Rikuzo Koto, counsellor, Japan-Brazil Businessmen's Economic Committee, Keidanren, in Tokyo, July 14, 1983.

60. Interview with Yoshiyuki Suga, manager, The Americas and Oceania Team, Marketing and Coordination Department, Mitsubishi Corporation, in Tokyo, July 8, 1983.

61. Interview with Hiroshi F. Katayama, vice president, Citibanks, N.A., in Sao Paulo, August 4, 1983.

62. Source: CACEX (Foreign Trade Department of the Bank of Brazil).

63. Interview in Brasilia, July 11, 1984.

64. Interview with Dr. Felippe Arno, president, Arno Corporation, in Sao Paulo, August 4, 1983.

65. Interview in Sao Paulo, August 2, 1983.

66. Interview with Makoto Tanaka, executive director, Banco Bradesco de Investimento, S.A., in Sao Paulo, August 4, 1983.

67. Interview with Keiichiro Sawada, senior executive director, Japan Overseas Enterprise Association, in Tokyo, July 12, 1983.

# 5
# The Japanese Experience in Brazil

nough has been said to make it clear that there is nothing spontaneous about Japanese "consensus" and that interests, strategies, and rationales at the macro and micro levels may be in conflict. An obvious question arises at this point concerning the extent of the discrepancy between Japanese views of Brazil at the micro level and the macro anticipations of Brazil as contemplated in the scenario of Japan as a headquarters country. How are Brazilians seen by the Japanese business community? What are their affinities? What are the Japanese difficulties and complaints?

## Affinities and Successes

The affinities of Japan for Brazil were expressed in pristine form during the Brazil "boom" of the early 1970s. Translation of a summary of the proceedings of a conference in 1974 of managers of Japanese trading companies in Brazil is as follows:[1]

> The chairman observed that Brazil has a stable government and inflation has been controlled.
> In the opinion of Mitsui Company, which started in Brazil earlier than others, the role of trading companies in Brazil is to develop its potentialities and to contribute by offering technology and capital. "It takes at least 10 years to develop anything, so we must do long-term business which will be completed in the nineties or in the next century."
> In the opinion of C. Itoh Company, Brazil has been trying to follow Japan, which completed a miraculous economic development. Brazil has tried to do whatever Japan did, and in this way the friendly relationship between the two countries has been getting stronger. "Brazil is a desirable country with which Japan can cooperate. It has a large potential market and plenty of natural resources. Also, there is no problem of ideology. There is a little problem of the cost of freight. However, we have a lot of possibilities

for cooperation with Brazil. We must be careful not to make the same error of *überfremdung* [overforeignization] we made in southeast Asia."

In the opinion of Marubeni Company, the Brazilians are generally pro-Japanese. "Among Latin peoples, the Portuguese are more peaceful than the Italians or the Spanish. And generally, they are good workers. On this point, they are similar to the Japanese. But I am sorry to say that their educational level is not so high as ours. Another characteristic is their strong nationalism. They like to feel conscious of doing something for the sake of Brazil. But the Latin people are not so unselfish as the Japanese; they can't work only for the sake of the nation; that is, we can't tell what would happen in case of a terrible lack of food, clothing, or housing."

In the opinion of C. Itoh, a remarkable point about Brazil is the enthusiasm of the people. "They are full of confidence and believe that they can do anything. We Japanese also had such a time, didn't we?"

As seen by Mitsui, the good relation of the Brazilian-Japanese has made it easier for Japanese to start businesses in Brazil. It is also helpful that in Brazil there is no racial prejudice. "But we must be very careful. If we do business with a mind to holding down Brazilian enterprises by force, that kind of competition will certainly cause friction between us."

The president of Marubeni observed that the Brazilian-Japanese contributed to Brazil's welfare in agriculture, especially in the improvement of fruit and vegetables. "It is owing to them that the Brazilians learned to eat vegetables, whereas formerly they ate only meat and beans."

The chairman asked, "Is it true that Japanese enterprises have been spoken ill of by Brazilian-Japanese since last year?" The president of Marubeni replied, "This is a very delicate question. Sometimes they misunderstand what we say, or they don't accept what we think and do. In my opinion, there is a difference in the way of thinking. The Japan Chamber of Commerce and Industry of Sao Paulo includes both Japanese and Brazilian-Japanese, and it was ill-managed formerly. We were always in discord, and we thought this was due to a lack of conversation. We have tried to have more opportunities to understand each other. Recently, we began to get along much better."

According to the manager of C. Itoh Company, "The minimum salary here is fixed by law, and in addition we must increase wages regularly. So in recent years the salaries have increased too much. This is a serious problem for trading companies where wages occupy the greater part of cost."

The president of Mitsubishi observed that in Japan, the salary of a manager of a factory is only eight times the minimum salary. "But in Brazil it is thirty or fifty times! "

The manager of C. Itoh remarked that "in Japan, everybody has loyalty because of the system of lifetime employment. But I wonder whether we can expect it here." The president of Marubeni replied, "I dare not say that they have no loyalty at all, but I think we had better not expect it." The chairman commented, "In spite of that, you must employ people and pay a lot of salary because demand exceeds supply. We are in a seller's market."

The chairman mentioned that when Mr. Uemura was president of

Keidanren, he was interviewed by a Brazilian reporter to whom he said that Brazil has developed so much that it is time to increase the proportion of profit that we can send back to Japan. These words caused trouble. Was it a matter of the translation? The president of Mitsubishi replied, "I think Mr. Uemura misunderstood something about the situation. If the interpreter had been more adept, he would have given Mr. Uemura some advice, such as "It's a little strange. I think you had better not say that."

The manager of C. Itoh commented that two-thirds of Brazil was still undeveloped. "We must aim at the twenty-first or twenty-second century. I think Brazil has the possibility of becoming a second U.S.A."

The chairman remarked, "By the way, none of the Japanese ministers went to the inauguration of President Geisel, although the Brazilian ministers had come to Japan twice a year. Didn't this cause a bad relationship between Japan and Brazil?" The president of Marubeni replied, "In my opinion, it didn't. But generally speaking, Japan has little understanding of Brazil. Except for the businessmen who are in charge here, nobody in Japan has any idea about Brazil. It was only a few months ago that the first resident Japanese correspondent was appointed here, by the Nihon Keizai Shimbun. We must now look at Brazil from a wider angle.

Evidently, even during the "boom" there was some ambivalence in Japanese thinking about Brazil. In general, however, the mood was ebullient. In 1973, a gem of Japanese reporting about Brazil was as follows:

> Once I was amazed at the lackadaisical attitude of people in Brazil, but now they have become very industrious." With these words, the Mitsubishi Corporation president, Chujiro Fujino, left Haneda Airport for Brazil in late January.[2]

In 1984, the president of a Japanese *sogo shosha* in Sao Paulo remarked, "I like it here better than in New York. It's an easier life. You can walk slow. Moreover, my children are going to college here. They are 'Brazilian.' If they had to go back to Japan, they could not possibly compete with Tokyo University graduates."[3]

Until recently, Brazil missed out on its vocation of specializing in middle-technology goods. Now that course is being pursued. Japanese *sogo shosha* will help them export these products. In doing so, the *sogo shosha*, despite their various internal and external problems, conform well to the following criteria for survival in the Brazil of the 1980s:

1. Do business that requires relatively little capital.

2. Do business with your own money. If you have to borrow in Brazil, it is difficult to make profits because of high interest payments.

3. Do business of a kind in which at least a part of the output can be exported.

For success, it is also desirable to be engaged in business that attracts relatively little government intervention. Unfortunately, this condition is not fulfilled in activities by foreigners. In any event, *sogo shosha* profits, which are characteristically low even in Japan, are low in Brazil as well. Profits may be low, however, partly because of having been shifted elsewhere through transfer pricing.

In recognition of the role of Japanese enterprises in Brazil, it is noteworthy that the major banks have all created Japanese departments to deal with them. An indicator of the extent to which those enterprises have become solidly established can be seen in the declining degree of their reliance on the Brazilian-Japanese community. The distancing of the Japanese from the Brazilian-Japanese can be noticed from the fact that the banks usually hire a native Japanese to head their Japanese departments rather than a Brazilian-Japanese. "Japanese companies in Brazil are not happy about banking with Brazilian-Japanese. Perhaps it is because the nisei have become more Brazilian than Japanese."[4]

Entry of Japanese business into Brazil has been welcomed as a means of reducing Brazil's dependence on the United States. In serving their own purposes, however, the Japanese as latecomers still have much to learn from the United States. In this sense, there is scope for cooperation between the two nations. As yet, apart from participation in Usiminas, Ishibras, Albras, and the Cerrado, few Japanese firms have attained national influence in Brazil. In the future, as the economy matures and the "vacant industrial spaces" become more fully occupied, there will be more competition among all parties, and attitudes may change. At present, major Japanese firms in Brazil are mostly engaged in large projects of different types, and so they have not competed greatly either with each other or with indigenous enterprises. In some cases, however, competition is becoming more intense. Already, as seen by an American observer,

> Japan controls the electronics industry in Brazil, including radio, television, and stereo equipment. There is not one company in this field that is not related to a Japanese firm either through a partnership or a license agreement. Most of the components of the Brazilian electronics industry come from Japan. There used to be a large components industry in Brazil that was indigenous, but it was destroyed because of Manaus and the superior quality of Japanese components. If the present trend continues, there is not much doubt that the Japanese will control the Brazilian economy. The way they will do it is to bring down the profitability of other competitive operations. I would like to add that there are huge illegal imports by Japan into Brazil. Make a note of that.[5]

According to the U.S. consul for economic affairs in Sao Paulo, television, videocassettes, and motorcycles are the only sectors actually dominated by the Japanese. According to the U.S. Embassy in Brasilia, textile firms have been among the most successful of Japanese firms in Brazil. Toyobo and Kanebo, for example, began a decade ago to produce yarns of a quality that had never been seen in Brazil before.

## Difficulties and Complaints

Brazilian complaints against Japan were described earlier. From a Japanese point of view, difficulties arise in Brazil at the policy and practical levels, as well as in the public and private sectors.

"As a result of their recent experience of rapid economic growth, the Brazilians are forming a new identity that is more nationalistic. This forms a framework for other difficulties that have been encountered by Japanese enterprises in Brazil."[6] (Japan's economic "miracle" was likewise marked by a revival of nationalism.) The nationalistic milieu compounds some other characteristics of Brazil's business environment that trouble the Japanese. The list includes economic, political, and financial uncertainty; excessive government interventionism and changes of policy that are both erratic and frequent; balance of payments difficulties that make business life difficult; and the relatively low level of education of the Brazilians and their 'manana' complex.

At the policy level, the Brazilian government is notorious for changing the ground rules. As acknowledged by an establishment insider, "It is common to change the rules of the game when the other side is winning."[7] As seen by a Japanese, "The Brazilian government wanted Japanese companies to establish subsidiaries to produce goods necessary for the economy. The government gave the Japanese subsidies in order to help them. But after a few years, they cut the subsidies. This is a frequent occurrence in Brazil. Another case concerns communications equipment. The government invited NEC to help establish its communications system. But now the government says that new orders will be given only to Brazilian national companies and not to foreign companies."[8] According to another observer, "Frequent changes in government policy are perhaps the most important difficulty that Japanese companies face in Brazil. To anticipate these changes, we use the 'amigo' system as channel into the Brazilian government. There is a contrast between Mexico and Brazil on this point. In Mexico, they change their minds frequently about the commitments they have made. In Brazil, they simply fail in the execution of their commitments."[9]

Among the changes in Brazilian government policy is the change in visa policy:

> During the Brazilian economic miracle, we were welcome. Now it is difficult even to get a visa to enter Brazil—it takes about 2 months. In the Carajas

project, the Brazilians want Japanese money and Japanese technology, but they do not want Japanese personnel. With regard to land and mineral resources, the Brazilians are very sensitive about the presence of Japanese. The federal ministries say that they want Japanese technology. But the state governments and the politicians of the opposition parties oppose the entry of Japanese technicians. In the Cerrado project, which was undertaken by Japan at the request of the Brazilian government, there is Japanese ownership of only 50,000 hectares. But the Brazilian newspapers and politicians say, "We should not sell our land to the Japanese."[10]

"Brazilianization" is one of the aspects of nationalism. Beginning with President Geisel, laws and administrative regulations quite independent of the laws became severe with regard to foreign enterprise in Brazil. Having been longer and better established in Brazil than Japanese firms, U.S. firms were better able to cope with Brazilianization. Domestic content rules are a principal component of Brazilianization. "Japanese firms must use approximately 50 percent of domestically produced components in any manufacturing or assembly that they do in Brazil. When they make international tenders in Brazil, they must reserve 10 to 20 percent of the work for indigenous Brazilian firms."[11]

After the first oil crisis, Brazilianization was intensified in favor of national firms. "Ishibras is always complaining that the Brazilian government favors indigenous companies. The president of Ishibras has often visited Brasilia to appeal for special financing, but with no luck."[12] However, despite the restrictions against providing cheap finance to foreign companies, "there is no discrimination against Japan as compared with other foreign countries."[13] Moreover, in the case of textile manufacturing, there is apparently no discrimination at all against small and medium-sized foreign firms. According to C. Itoh Company's textile manager, "I felt no discrimination when I was in Brazil. We had the full right to receive special government financing. We still have no problem up to the present time." In this discussion, however, there was no mention of export obligations on the part of the textile firms.[14]

To improve competitive power, it is Brazilian policy to seek technological transfers from abroad. "No direct foreign investment can be made in Brazil without a transfer of desired foreign technology along with the investment. In 1976, there was a Brazilian mission to Japan that requested the transfer of technological information without payment of royalties. Koji Kobayashi, the president of NEC, became angry at this request. Technology is not free! "[15]

At the policy level, Japanese complaints are directed at both the public- and private-sector bureaucracies. According to one observer of the Brazilian government, "As technocrats, they are OK. But they are not experienced in business. Still, they are better than the Argentinian or Mexican bureaucrats. In the exercise of influence, the school tie is less important than in Japan.

However, as in Japan, influence depends on personal connections. Whom you know is very important."[16] According to another observer, "The top bureaucrats are good. But the top layer is thin. It does all the work and makes all the decisions. At the lower levels, the bureaucracy is of poor quality. There is poor coordination in the Brazilian bureaucracy; in this respect, it is not like Japan. Therefore, if you want a quick answer, it is difficult to get it. You have to go around to the various ministries and provide the coordination yourself, as it were."[17] A Japanese tactic is employed by the Brazilian bureaucracy in dealing with matters of which they disapprove. For example, concerning a request for an import or export license it is disinclined to authorize, CACEX may not say no, but it may simply hold up the application in channels.

In the Brazilian government, there are parallel power centers. They may or may not be coordinated. Is export promotion connected with economic planning? "In theory, yes; in practice, no."[18] Does the Brazilian government deliver on its promises? The government was in excessive haste to make economic progress; this sometimes led it to make commitments it could not fulfill. Moreover, conditions may change rapidly in Brazil, making it difficult to fulfill commitments. Japanese complain about the fact that after have been cordially invited by the Brazilian government to participate in the development program, the government then says, "You are now a Brazilian company. You cannot repatriate profits to Japan." An important example of Japanese complaints against unfulfilled promises occurs in the case of the Usiminas steel project, the largest of Japan's joint ventures with the Brazilian government. Usiminas has been a technological success but a financial disaster for both the Brazilian and Japanese partners. According to a former director general of Latin American affairs in Japan's Ministry of Foreign Affairs, "This is the most unfortunate example of our participation in a government project in Brazil. The Brazilians make promises and then do not deliver. Partly, this is at the instigation of the indigenous national companies."[19]

In the private sector, "Management is generally poor in Brazil, quite apart from the quality—which may be excellent—of the basic plant."[20] As in the government sector, Japanese say that Brazilians make decisions too quickly and then run into difficulties at the implementation stage. This tendency arises from the structural fact that Brazilian negotiators are usually company presidents fully authorized to enter into contractual relations. Japanese negotiators are usually in middle management and have to refer their recommendations to higher authority, a process that takes time. The Brazilians complain that the Japanese are too slow in decision making.

Besides a tendency to act quickly, Japanese feel that Brazilian decision makers, like the Americans, take an excessively short-term point of view. Concerning policy-making in the private sector, I was interested in the response to the president of the Arno Corporation to my question about how they are positioning themselves for the 1990s? "I don't know," he said, "I will be retired. It's not my problem."[21]

In Tokyo, in a conversation with the Bank of Tokyo's senior official for Latin America, I asked a question concerning the lessons of Japan's experience with the Brazilian policy-making bureaucracy. "It is difficult to establish *our* policy in Brazil," he said. "It is difficult to get the Brazilians to be cautious and to make appropriate plans consistent with their ability to perform."[22]

At the practical level, "the Japanese are very thorough in the preparation of their projects. The Brazilians are very good at presenting projects and looking good on paper. But they don't necessarily plan to follow through." This remark was made by an American observer, the executive vice president of the American Chamber of Commerce in Sao Paulo.[23] "A practical problem," he added, "is that a Brazilian can't communicate well with a Japanese." According to another American, "Japanese do not complain publicly about their difficulties in Brazil. Only in private."[24] Similarly, "the Brazilian-Japanese are very quiet, especially concerning politics."[25]

Outside of Brazil, however, Japanese that have had experience there are perhaps less reticent. "In 1972–1973, we were taken in by the fascinating Brazilian proposals, but the reality was not so sweet. The dream was about Brazilian resources plus Japanese technology. This was the dream of Japanese manufacturers and traders. But now we know Brazil: poor productivity, poor synchronization of execution. Major projects that were supposed to be completed already are still not functioning."[26] Another observer in Tokyo said in reply to my question concerning the quality of Brazilian output,

> In the case of raw materials, they are of standard quality specifications and they are competitive in world markets. In the case of manufactured goods, Brazilian products are of second-class quality. Manufacturers of general merchandise observe no standard specifications in production or in the quality of production. There is poor delivery service and poor after-sales servicing. Deadlines are not kept. Suppliers receive many large claims from buyers, but settlement takes a long time and often the Brazilian government may not allow reimbursement for claims. These products make their way in world markets by means of subsidies.[27]

"The basic Brazilian problem is inefficiency. It causes prices to be uncompetitively high. Therefore, Brazil can survive only by means of government subsidies and government interference."[28] This is central to the Brazilian predicament. In order to compete, Brazil must subsidize, but to subsidize means that government bureaucracy and graft also increase, which in turn renders Brazil *less* competitive. And if the government raises taxes, the underground economy will increase correspondingly in order to evade them.

In the case of heavy machinery and other high-value-added products, government export subsidies may take the form of generous supplier's credit or tax refunds to the manufacturer. Tax refunds to trading companies, however, are provided only to "national" trading companies, meaning that the company is "Brazilian controlled." But the law does not define the meaning of *control*. This is administratively determined.

Critical remarks concerning Brazilian competitive power were made by another Brazil specialist in Tokyo. "Brazil can produce any kind of electrical machinery. However, it is of poor quality. Moreover, Brazil cannot produce stainless steel. The basic materials industries are very weak. The manpower used in the assembling industries is poor. The quality of Brazilian works is about one-quarter or one-third that of Japanese workers. But they are not paid proportionately less. We have tried many times to export machinery from Brazil, but without subsidies it is not competitive with machinery exported from Japan."[29] In assessing Brazil's steel-making projects, the same expert observed that "except for Usiminas, in which Japanese participation was important at the outset, the projects are poor. Products of the machinery industry are second-class. Machinery exports consist largely of cars and small military tanks. The Brazilian cost of production is not competitive internationally, and Brazil does not deliver on time. The domestic market for heavy equipment is shrinking to about 50 percent of what it was 5 years ago, and there is a huge volume of excess capacity in both national and foreign firms."

Qualified pessimism was expressed by Rikuzo Koto, counsellor of the Japan–Brazil Businessmen's Economic Committee of Keidanren:

> All of the projects in which Japanese are engaged are good projects and reasonably practical. However, they are not going on schedule. As a result of inflation, the original calculations no longer make sense. The Brazilian government wants to slow down these projects for financial reasons. Another problem is that once you have constructed a fine mill or factory, the Brazilian government wants to use it for development purposes. So they keep the price too low and allow insufficient depreciation. Usiminas is a good mill and produces quality products. It has been operating for 10 years but has paid no dividends. It cannot pay dividends because of the government's low price policy for steel. Therefore, shareholders will not put in more capital for expansion of the plant. We are requesting the Brazilian government to allow us to raise the price of steel.[30]

Lack of knowledge as to how to cope with a high rate of inflation was one of the reasons for some of the errors made by Japanese investors in Brazil. A period of several years is required in planning for large projects. By the time implementation of the project begins, costs have risen. Characteristically, moreover, there are delays in the Brazilian process of project implementation. This further raises the cost of a project. At the inception of the Usiminas project, inflation was 30 percent annually; by 1983, it had risen to 127 percent. The difficulty of making long-term plans in the midst of high inflation is an especial deterrent to the Japanese inasmuch as their investment projects are typically of a long-term nature.

According to the general price index (GPI), the annual rate of inflation of May of 1985 was 225.6 percent. Inflationary conditions of this degree promoted a black market, speculation, and corruption that jeopardized legitimate business activity. The black market—euphemistically known as the "parallel market"—was so well established that its price statistics were openly published in the press. According to a Japanese trading company president,

> I estimate that 30 to 35 percent of the economy is underground. The government says it is 8 to 9 percent. Besides the usual government red tape that adds to the cost of doing business, moreover, it is necessary to pay bribes in order to set up a company, even an export company. Half of the startup capital of an enterprise in Brazil goes to bribes and payoffs to officials. You have to pay under the table every time you want to do anything. Government inspectors come to your company and they try to get money too. Yet bad as it is, Brazil still is better than other Latin American countries in this respect.[31]

A typical black market operation concerns the import of prohibited merchandise. Obtaining the currency for such a transaction is no problem: dollars are readily available at the black market rate. The problem consists in satisfying government auditors that the cash assets of the company were expended in a legal fashion. Therefore, the company buys in the black market receipts that were created in accordance with legitimate dollar transactions. It presents these to the auditors as evidence that its cash was spent legally.

On the export side, if a Brazilian coffee grower sells his crop to the government marketing board, he receives cruzeiros at the overvalued legal rate of exchange with regard to the dollar value of the coffee. However, if he smuggles the coffee to Paraguay, he receives dollars directly for the full value of the coffee. He can take those dollars to the Brazilian black market and exchange them for cruzeiros (now cruzados) at a premium over the legal rate of exchange.

Even for registered foreign investors it is difficult to repatriate dividends to their head offices abroad. Interest, but not principal or royalties, can be remitted. In 1984, Brazilian national trading companies were eligible to receive low-cost finance and VAT refunds on their export sales, and Brazilian manufacturers who did their own exporting were likewise eligible, but Japanese trading companies were not eligible. As a result, major Brazilian manufacturers would not sell to Japanese trading companies because to do so would deprive them of the export subsidy.

As compared with U.S. companies in Brazil, Japanese firms tend to be more pessimistic in the face of difficulties. As latecomers, they are more adversely affected by import restrictions and other government controls than firms that have been long established. Among other than major Japanese firms, these difficulties are a barrier to the expansion of Japanese investment in Brazil. Moreover, despite their vaunted "intelligence network," the Japanese have made many mistakes in Brazil. In banking, for example, they overcommitted themselves.[32] In other cases, they were fleeced by their Brazilian partners.

Although in Brazil, as in Japan, personal networks and contacts are of great importance, the Japanese are not known to mix actively with Brazilians. A complaint of the Japanese Embassy staff in Brasilia is that they do not meet Brazilian businesspeople. Perhaps this is accounted for by constraints of protocol. Americans do not mix much more, but for cultural reasons this may be less noticeable. Because of their deeper roots in Brazil and their wider acquaintance with Brazilians it also may be less important. "Brazilians say, 'Japanese businessmen come to Brazil only to talk business.' Japanese say, 'Brazilians are pleasant personally, but not so easy to do business with.' Moreover, at the Embassy level, the daily difficulties of dealing with Brazil are increasing. In case a Brazilian trainee in Japan gets hurt, they want the Japanese government to assume responsibility. Furthermore, they demand 'reciprocity' in Japanese economic cooperation. They want 'horizontal relations.' They don't want 'vertical relations' with Japan on top."[33]

On the factory floor, there is a problem concerning status or class that annoys Japanese management. "Brazilian university-trained engineers consider themselves to be white-collar workers. They don't want to touch the machine. Only low-class workers are willing to touch the machine. For this reason, IHI [Ishibras] in Rio has a policy of not employing as engineers any university graduates. They train their own engineers from the common labor work force."[34]

There is a general agreement in the Japanese business community and elsewhere that good Brazilian partners are hard to find. "Small Brazilian companies, of course, want to join up with Mitsubishi, but they are too weak for Mitsubishi to consider it."[35] From an American perspective, "sure, there is a shortage of good Brazilian partners, especially those with capital. If they are good, they don't want partnership with a foreigner."[36]

## The *Sogo Shosha* Transition

The Brazilian trading company law provides that if a company is registered in accordance with the provisions of the law, it becomes eligible for tax benefits and export incentives. To be eligible for registration, however, among other administrative requirements, majority ownership of the company must be in the hands of Brazilian nationals. In 1983, about eighty Brazilian companies were registered as trading companies in accordance with the law. Of these, only twenty were "active." At that time, no Japanese *sogo shosha* were registered as national trading companies in accordance with the law.

According to the executive vice president of Mitsui Brasileira Imp. e Exp. Ltda., "Except for Interbras, Kobek, and Cotia Trading Company [no relation to the COTIA agricultural cooperative], the Brazilian trading companies are fake."[37] (Mitsui Import and Export itself was a wholly owned affiliate of Mitsui in Tokyo, but incorporated as a Brazilian company.) The president of Mitsubishi Corporation described Brazilian trading companies as having well-developed domestic distribution channels within Brazil, but lacking distribution channels abroad.[38] He added that if Mitsubishi Corporation could become a national company in accordance with the law, Brazil's exports would substantially increase. This would require relinquishment of 51 percent of the company's stock ownership to a Brazilian partner. Assuming it were willing to do so, it would be difficult to find a reliable Brazilian partner for that purpose. "Even Interbras cannot compete with Mitsubishi's well-educated and experienced organization. It cannot duplicate Mitsubishi channels." According to information from C. Itoh & Company, "Sixty percent of the business of Interbras comes from business generated by the Brazilian government which is simply assigned to them." However, "Interbras is a real *sogo shosha*. It is not a mere trading company. And it is successful. In contrast with the integrated, conglomerate type of *sogo shosha* organization, some trading companies in Brazil that specialize in some particular commodity may do a good job, but they are not as good as Interbras."[39]

Lacking export capability and foreign distribution channels of their own, many national Brazilian trading companies assign transactions to Japanese *sogo shosha*, which perform the transactions on a commission basis. It is estimated that including such assignments, Japanese *sogo shosha* perform about 10 percent of Brazil's total export transactions.[40] The limited scope and initiative of indigenous Brazilian national trading companies are indicated by the fact that while there are more than thirty Japanese trading companies in Brazil, not a single Brazilian trading company has opened an office in Tokyo. This despite the fact that during the first 10 months of 1985, Japan was Brazil's third leading market (after the United States and the Netherlands), with exports amounting to US$1,150 million.[41]

In June of 1984, subject to compliance with specified conditions, foreign trading companies at last became eligible for national treatment under the trading company law of Brazil. Despite its previous disclaimer of interest, Mitsubishi was the first to comply with the conditions and to qualify for national treatment. The conditions include the requirement that the company become a corporation controlled by stockholders.

As a conglomerate organization combining many activities and functions, *sogo shosha* business strategy is one that approximates the balance of payments strategy of a nation. Finance is one of the key strategic components, and in providing finance (directly or indirectly through the group bank), the *sogo shosha* participate in the most profitable form of economic activity in Brazil today. The strategy is to kill three or four birds with one stone. First, a loan is extended. Interest is received on the loan. Second, by means of the loan, equipment is sold to Brazil from a *sogo shosha* supplier. Third, management control is acquired by means of the technology transfer that accompanies sale of the equipment. Fourth, by proliferation of management control in Brazil and elsewhere, internationalization of the Japanese economy is promoted.

In the past, Japanese manufacturers and the *sogo shosha* advanced hand in hand into Brazil. The *sogo shosha* possessed language resources and were in close contact with the Brazilian government. They controlled channels through which to sell products in third countries. In the initial stage of Japan's advance into Brazil, it was usual for the Japanese manufacturer to provide 90 percent of the equity and the *sogo shosha* to provide 10 percent. At the outset, the *sogo shosha* arranged for the procurement of machinery in Japan and for the construction of the plant in Brazil. Then it would procure the raw materials for production. In shipping the final product, the *sogo shosha* would prepare the documentation and obtain the licenses.

In Brazil, the *sogo shosha* also created trading opportunities by means of establishing manufacturing subsidiaries; the earliest of these were in textiles and ceramics. The *sogo shosha* would serve the requirements of the subsidiaries for imported materials and equipment and would export the output they produced. The *sogo shosha* also attempted to establish companies that could secure the Brazilian government as a principal customer. In establishing operating companies, they attempted to benefit from Brazil's import-substitution program.

Now all this is changing. Japanese manufacturers are accustomed to doing business in foreign countries. If they act without assistance, they save the "margin" that used to go to the *sogo shosha*. Long ago, in fact, some companies such as Kanebo, one of the first textile companies to come to Brazil, came on its own without *sogo shosha* affiliation.

Moreover, in the course of Japan's postwar economic expansion, its industrial structure became more sophisticated; its export products are increasingly of a technical type, as in the electronics field, or require extensive after-sales servicing, as in the case of automobiles. The type of business in which the *sogo shosha* formerly specialized, namely, huge shipments of bulk commodities, gave way to new products with which they were not operationally familiar. The *sogo shosha* began to lose touch with some of Japan's leading manufacturers.

Another transitional problem—one that is shared in common with

American multinational firms—is the "matrix" problem. Traditionally, *sogo shosha* have been organized in terms of commodity departments—the textile department, the iron and steel department, etc. But now that their interests are so diversified and deeply extended, a new managerial layer—the country managers—has come into existence. This creates a double set of bosses for the subsidiary in the field, an unwieldy state of affairs. In order to overcome the problem of having to satisfy both a product manager and a country manager, there has been a trend in *sogo shosha* headquarters thinking to give greater independence to the subsidiaries outside Japan. That is, there is a tendency for the *sogo shosha* form of organization to become more transnational and less multinational.

In Rio, I asked about the extent of control the Mitsui headquarters in Tokyo exercises over Mitsui in Brazil. "There is discipline from Tokyo in personnel matters," was the reply, "but in economic activities the president here is very independent." At Toyomenka in Sao Paulo, I asked the same question. I was told, "the president here can give credit up to US$500,000 without clearing with Tokyo. Beyond that, he must apply to the head office."

An observer of the matrix system in U.S. multinational operations remarked that the results are increasingly unsatisfactory. In the U.S. version, there is frequent turnover of local managers in Brazil in addition to turnover in head office managers. This results in policy shifts and repeated learning periods. "European companies keep their managers here for 10 to 20 years. U.S. companies rotate their managers every 2 or 3 years."[42]

For the *sogo shosha*, the trend away from traditional products is not unconditional. At Toyomenka, I was told, "So far, we deal mainly in traditional products. But in the future, we will deal in new products and we will find new ways of doing business. At present, we do triangular trade with east Europe, excluding the USSR. We open letters of credit for Brazil in trade with Japan and east Europe." I asked about their relations with American firms in Brazil. "In banking, we deal primarily with Citibank. New York has a closer eye to Brazil than Tokyo. Therefore, Citibank information is of better quality. They forecast what is going to happen in Brazil, including the inflation rate. The Citibank information service is of high quality. That's how they keep their customers. Also, when the New York Philharmonic came here, they invited us to attend. U.S. companies do this sort of thing more than Japanese companies. With Japanese bankers, we play golf."[43]

The transition in the life of the Japanese *sogo shosha* intersects the transition in the Brazilian economy, with resultant interaction effects. One of these effects is the compounding of *sogo shosha* efforts to expand their third-country trade. All the *sogo shosha* have done this. Brazilian inflation has a relatively greater depressing effect on trade-oriented than on non-trade-oriented investment because direct exports from Brazil are hampered by the effect of inflation in undermining Brazil's international competitive power.

On the other hand, while the *sogo shosha* complain that they are making no profit in Brazil, it may be observed that they made very little profit even in Japan during the period of the economic "miracle." There is more to this phenomenon than meets the eye.

In its Brazilian context, then, how will the *sogo shosha* transition proceed? In accordance with the scenario of Japan as a headquarters country, the *sogo shosha* can act as implementing agents. They can provide coordination, consultation, and communication facilities in Brazil and elsewhere. They can provide backup services for pioneering efforts in new fields of enterprise, in the leading sectors of the Brazilian as well as the Japanese economies. As a technical example of the services they can provide, the *sogo shosha* can assume the risk of foreign exchange fluctuations in international transactions, thus relieving both large and small manufacturing enterprises of that burden. In a world of floating exchange rates, foreign exchange risk is one of the principal impediments to trade. Another impediment is the trend toward protectionism in the world economy. The *sogo shosha* are ideally positioned to provide switch and countertrade types of facilities to manufacturing firms. The *sogo shosha* innovate in ways of conducting business as well as in the types of products they handle. As a headquarters country, Japan will instruct other countries in the manufacture of new products, with the use of Japanese technology and know-how. The *sogo shosha* will manage the technology transfer and will sell the products in world markets.

In order to pursue this mission, the *sogo shosha* want political stability in Brazil. Before the presidential election that was to terminate the military government in March of 1985, I asked the president of a *sogo shosha*, "Whom do you favor for president?" He replied, "We want stability. Whoever can provide it is the person we favor."

Although the *sogo shosha* are flexible in strategy and technique, they are rather inflexible in their bureaucratic constraints. For example, they cannot readily discharge redundant personnel. As his principal assignment at the time I interviewed him in Tokyo, Mr. Yoichi Yabu of C. Itoh & Company was working out a "rolling strategy" for the company. He was seeking new locations for C. Itoh branches abroad and better ways to utilize its personnel.

In view of their Brazilian difficulties, as well as the cartel implications of economic concentration, Japanese government administrative guidance, and other factors, I was prompted to inquire about the extent to which major Japanese firms compete among themselves, as distinguished from the extent to which they compete with others. The Japanese ambassador to Brazil pointed out that in the early 1970s, Mitsubishi had developed a fertilizer industry in Iraq (his previous post), while Mitsui established its fertilizer plant in Iran. "The Middle East territory was thus divided between the majors."[44]

How about the trading companies? "Do the *sogo shosha* compete with each other in Brazil?" I asked the chief executive of C. Itoh in Sao Paulo.

"Yes, but they are specialized," he replied. "C. Itoh specializes in textiles, pulp, paper, iron, and steel. Mitsui specializes in iron and chemicals. Mitsubishi specializes in coffee and foodstuffs. Sumitomo specializes in shoes—they started the export of Brazilian shoes to the United States. Marubeni is not so strong in Brazil."[45] I asked the same question at the headquarters of C. Itoh in Tokyo. "They engage in 'friendly' competition," was the answer.[46]

## Notes

1. The conference was reported in *Kokusai Keizai* (*International Economics*), Tokyo, June 1974. Participants were Shigeki Suzuki, president of Mitsui Brasileira Ltda.; Kiyoshi Matsuyoshi, general manager for Latin America of C. Itoh do Brasil. S.A.; Kazuo Seko, president of Mitsubishi Corporation do Brasil, S.A.; and Fujio Gunji, president of Marubeni, S.A.

2. JETRO (Japan External Trade Organization), "Japan into the Multinationalization Era," 1973.

3. Interview with Takashi Oka, diretor presidente, Toyomenka do Brasil Import e Export, Ltda., in Sao Paulo, July 6, 1984.

4. Inteview with Mark S. Abrams, gerencia de credito, Banco de Boston, in Sao Paulo, July 5, 1984.

5. Interview with Frederick Leroy Sherman, adviser, Philco Company, in Sao Paulo, August 6, 1983.

6. Comment in interview with Rikuzo Koto, counsellor, Japan–Brazil Businessmen's Economic Committee, Keidanren, in Tokyo, July 14, 1983.

7. Interview with Ricardo R. de Araujo Cintra, chefe, Departamento de Economia, FIESP (Federation das Industrias do Estado de Sao Paulo), in Sao Paulo, July 4, 1984.

8. Interview with Toshiro Kobayashi, general manager, Bank of Tokyo, Hibiya Office, in Tokyo, July 15, 1983.

9. Interview with senior divison officer, Corporate Planning Division, C. Itoh & Company, Ltd., in Tokyo, July 14, 1983.

10. Interview with Akira Urabe, director, First Latin America and Caribbean Division, Ministry of Foreign Affairs, in Tokyo, July 6, 1983.

11. Interview with Koichiro Matsuura, director, Aid Policy Division, Economic Cooperation Bureau, Ministry of Foreign Affairs, in Tokyo, July 19, 1982.

12. Interview with Yoichi Yabu, senior division officer, Corporate Planning Division, C. Itoh & Company, Ltd., in Tokyo, July 14, 1983.

13. Interview with Junji Takaoka, senior regional manager, Latin America Division, Bank of Tokyo, Ltd., in Tokyo, July 15, 1983.

14. Interview with Yoshiyuki Asada, deputy manager, Subsidiaries and Affiliates Department, C. Itoh & Company, Ltd., in Tokyo, July 14, 1983.

15. Interview with Shigeo Uno, vice president, Japan Trade Center, in Sao Paulo, August 3, 1983.

16. Interview with Rikuzo Koto, counsellor, Japan–Brazil Businessmen's Economic Committee, Keidanren, in Tokyo, July 14, 1983.

17. Interview with Jun Kawashima, minister, Embassy of Japan, in Brasilia, August 10, 1983.

18. Interview with Brian Michael F. Neele, head, Trade Information Division, Ministry of External Relations, in Brasilia, July 11, 1984.

19. Interview with Sumio Edamura, director general of foreign affairs (formerly director general of Latin American affairs), Ministry of Foreign Affairs, in Tokyo, July 13, 1983.

20. Interview with Rikuzo Koto, counsellor, Japan–Brazil businessmen's Economic Committee, Keidanren, in Tokyo, July 14, 1983.

21. Interview with Dr. Felippe Arno, president, Arno Corporation, in Sao Paulo, August 4, 1983.

22. Interview with Junji Takaoka, senior regional manager, Latin America Division, Bank of Tokyo, Ltd., in Tokyo, July 15, 1983.

23. Interview with Ercole A. Carpentieri, Jr., executive vice president, American Chamber of Commerce for Brazil, in Sao Paulo, August 3, 1983.

24. Interview with Hilton Lee Graham, economic consul, American Consulate General, in Sao Paulo, July 2, 1984.

25. Interview with Takashi Oka, president, Toyomenka do Brasil, in Sao Paulo, July 6, 1984.

26. Interview with Yoichi Yabu, senior divison officer, Corporate Planning Division, C. Itoh & Company, Ltd., in Tokyo, July 14, 1983.

27. Interview with Yoshiyuki Suga, manager, The Americas and Oceania Team, Marketing and Coordination Department, Mitsubishi Corporation, in Tokyo, July 8, 1983. During the early 1980s, Brazil also lost international competitive power because the acceleration of inflation exceeded the rate of devaluation of the cruzeiro. To some extent, subsidies were necessary as a substitute for an appropriate rate of devaluation.

28. Interview with Takashi Oka, president, Toyomenka do Brasil, in Sao Paulo, July 6, 1984.

29. Interview with Jose H. Kojima, manager, General Machinery Department, Machinery Headquarters, Mitsubishi Heavy Industries, Ltd. inTokyo, July 12, 1983.

30. Interview in Tokyo, July 14, 1983.

31. Interview with Takashi Oka, president, Toyomenka do Brasil, in Sao Paulo, July 6, 1984.

32. Interview with Richard Huber, senior vice president, Citibank, N.A., in New York City, June 13, 1983.

33. Interview with Jun Kawashima, minister, Embassy of Japan, in Brasilia, August 8, 1983.

34. Interview with Shigeo Uno, vice president, Japan Trade Center, in Sao Paulo, August 3, 1983.

35. Interview with Toshi Oda, diretor presidente, Mitsubishi Corporation do Brasil, S.A., in Sao Paulo, August 1, 1983.

36. Interview with Robert H. Blocker, president, Blocker Assessoria de Investimentos e Participacoes, S.A., in Sao Paulo, August 3, 1983.

37. Interview with Masayuki Ideda, diretor vice-presidente, Mitsui Brasileira Imp. e Exp. Ltda., in Rio de Janeiro, July 17, 1984.

38. Interview with Toshi Oda, diretor presidente, Mitsuibishi Corporation do Brasil, S.A., in Sao Paulo, August 1, 1983.

39. Interview with Yoichi Yabu, senior division officer, Corporate Planning Division, C. Itoh & Company, Ltd., in Tokyo, July 14, 1983.

40. Interview with Kazuo Uesugi, president, Japan Trade Center, in Sao Paulo, July 14, 1984.

41. Data from CACEX.

42. Interview with Robert H. Blocker, president, Blocker Assessoria de Investimentos e Participacoes, S.A., in Sao Paulo, August 3, 1983.

43. Interview with Takashi Oka, president, Toyomenka do Brasil, in Sao Paulo, July 6, 1984.

44. Interview with Ambassador Kuniyoshi Date, Embassy of Japan, in Brasilia, July 9, 1984.

45. Interview with Shigeki Tsutsui, diretor-superintendente, C. Itoh do Brasil, S.A., in Sao Paulo, August 5, 1983.

46. Interview with Yoichi Yabu, senior division officer, Corporate Planning Division, C. Itoh & Company, Ltd., in Tokyo, July 14, 1983.

# 6
# Challenge of the Debt Crisis

B razil's external debt is the key problem in the present U.S.–Brazil relationship and central to the nature and effectiveness of any U.S. response to Japan's leadership challenge. Because of its impact on trade, growth, and development, the debt issue ramifies through the Brazilian economy and threatens the Brazilian people in the most alarming way: it makes them feel that their fate is "in the hands of others." This strikes at the sorest point of Brazilian nationalism. Thus external debt has been the most politicized of all Brazil's international economic issues. The way in which the United States manages this issue will affect its relations with Brazil and its stature in Latin America for years to come. However, the power of initiative that the debt issue places in the hands of the United States is a wasting asset. As reflected in the IMF accommodation with Mexico in July of 1986, a shift is taking place in the bargaining position of debtors and creditors in the world economy. IMF "flexibility" in yielding to some of Mexico's demands will constitute a precedent in other cases as well.

In caricature, as Brazil's principal creditor, the United States is cast in the role of villain. As Brazil's third leading creditor, Japan is seen as having "lent a helping hand." In mid-1986, when Mexico again took center stage as a financial emergency case, when Brazilian currency reform seemed to have good counterinflationary results, and as U.S. interests rates declined and the OPEC cartel was in a state of relapse, the issue of Brazilian debt seemed to dwindle in the U.S. foreign policy agenda. Similarly, 2 years earlier, the United States had become complacent about the Mexican debt. In contrast with Japan, the United States tends to wait until crises arise and then apply policy as an emergency device. As an official of the USTR remarked to me, "We are a firefighting brigade." Thus by deferring to the United States in its management of the debt issue, Japan provides another example of judo tactics: using the strength of the adversary *against* him.

This chapter will not attempt to propose long-term policy or spell out the mechanics of how the United States should avail itself of the breathing space afforded by the anti-inflationary cruzado reform of February of 1986. The fate of that reform depends partly on the outcome of the further radical economic proposals presented by President Sarney in July of 1986. Instead, this chapter will offer some perspective on the debate from a Brazilian point of view. This may help point to the direction in which the United States may mobilize its present policy opportunities.

As Brazil's chief creditor and as the most influential member of the IMF—with which Brazil's relations are distinctly adversarial—the United States is politically embarrassed in Brazil. "The Brazilian government, however, knows that in the dark days of 1982–1983, the United States was of more help than any other country. Germany and Switzerland were negative. Japan was waffling. Consequently, at the highest level, the United States gained clout in Brazil, but not at the popular level. The present dilemma is this: the American government would have trouble with U.S. domestic public opinion if it didn't hold Brazil to the fire. The dilemma is one of balancing U.S. foreign policy with U.S. domestic policy. Should the government attempt to support the U.S. banks? Or should it attempt to placate Brazilian public opinion?"[1]

## Statistical Ambiguities

Prior to the demise of the Brazilian military regime on March 15, 1985, opposition economists maintained that the public accounts had been manipulated and the figures "cooked." They were rightly skeptical of the government's claim that it had managed to balance public expenditure and revenue on an operational basis. The IMF and Brazilian authorities were sharply divided on how the public-sector deficit should be defined; thus they were divided on what items should be cut.

In the external sector, even for official insiders, "Data on loans and investments are confusing and hard to obtain."[2] Breakdowns of loans by country of origin and by sector are not generally available in Brazil. One reason for this is the procedure by which foreign loans are often arranged. For example, should a loan from the Bank of Tokyo in London be attributed to England or to Japan? The balance of payments statistics are ambiguous on this point. Syndicated loans from an assortment of national sources that are routed through Panama or other transfer points present similar difficulties. Another problem arises in distinguishing foreign loans from foreign investments. Because the rules for repatriation of interest are more lenient than those for repatriation of dividends, many foreigners prefer to lend money to Brazil rather than to invest. Therefore, many real investments in Brazil are disguised as loans.

Brazil's external debt crisis began in September of 1982, after the Mexican default of a month earlier. A series of unrealistic IMF programs was formulated for Brazil following its first acknowledged approach to the IMF in November of 1982. Partly, the IMF programs were inadequate because of the weak statistical foundations on which they were based. There was even ambiguity as to the extent of Brazil's short-term as compared with long-term debt. Partly, the programs were inadequate due to wishful thinking on the part of all parties concerned. This was reflected in the debate among Brazil's commercial creditors and the IMF as to whether its financial difficulties should be described as a "liquidity problem" or a "solvency problem." Describing it as a liquidity problem served the purposes of those in Brazil who were opposed to fundamental reforms, it served the purposes of creditors who declined to assume any responsibility for sharing the cost of extricating Brazil from its problem, and it served the purposes of the IMF, which presented its standard deflationary prescription to the debtor.

At the end of 1982, according to the World Bank, Brazil's outstanding external public debt amounted to US$62.7 billion.[3] According to the Inter-American Development Bank, it amounted to US$64.2 billion.[4] According to the Central Bank of Brazil, it amounted to US$70.2 billion as of that date. At the end of June of 1983, the IMF calculated that Brazil's external indebtedness was US$73 billion, while the Bank for International Settlements (BIS) estimated that it was only US$57 billion. Similar discrepancies can be found in comparisons of various sources concerning the ratio of external debt to exports, the ratio of external debt to GNP, and the ratio of service payments on external debt to exports.[5]

Developing country debt-service problems typically emerge when the ratio of external debt to exports of goods and services rises above the 200 percent level.[6] In Brazil, that ratio was 339 percent in 1982, rising to 368 percent in 1985. Brazil's scheduled interest payments on foreign debt declined from 54 percent of exports of goods and services in 1982 to 41 percent in 1985. The annual average net inflow of foreign direct investment into Brazil declined from US$1,834 million during 1977–1980 to US$1,250 million during 1985.[7] Statistics concerning the structure of the outstanding external public debt show a progressive shift toward shorter maturities between 1970 and 1984. In 1970, 39.6 percent of the debt had a maturity of 5 years or less; by 1984, the figure had risen to 67.4 percent. In 1970, 39.3 percent of the debt had a maturity of more than 10 years; by 1984, the figure had declined to 3.8 percent. By December of 1984, according to the Central Bank of Brazil, the registered medium- and long-term external debt amounted to US$91.09 billion. On the same date, unregistered external debt amounted to US$10.9 billion. By 1986, the total external debt had risen to US$106 billion (see Tables 6–1 and 6–2). Brazil's charm for foreign lenders was not enhanced by the mammoth amount of its obligations scheduled to mature during 1987–1989. In August of 1986, the Morgan Guaranty Trust Company observed, "By any reasonable standard, the present maturity schedule cannot be met."[8]

Table 6–1
**Brazil: Registered Medium- and Long-Term External Debt, by Type of Creditor, 1977–1986**
(*billions of U.S. dollars, end of period*)

| | 1977 | 1978 | 1979 | 1980 | 1981 | 1982 | 1983 | 1984 | 1985 | June 1986 |
|---|---|---|---|---|---|---|---|---|---|---|
| Total | 32.04 | 43.51 | 49.90 | 53.85 | 61.41 | 70.20 | 81.32 | 91.09 | 95.86 | 99.62 |
| Multilateral lenders: | 2.36 | 2.89 | 3.21 | 3.48 | 3.58 | 3.85 | 4.32 | 5.71 | 7.41 | 7.98 |
| IBRD | 1.54 | 1.98 | 2.18 | 2.24 | 2.26 | 2.34 | 2.59 | 3.90 | 5.06 | 5.39 |
| IFC | 0.19 | 0.18 | 0.16 | 0.19 | 0.25 | 0.30 | 0.30 | 0.29 | 0.28 | 0.25 |
| IDB | 0.63 | 0.73 | 0.87 | 1.05 | 1.07 | 1.21 | 1.37 | 1.39 | 1.92 | 2.06 |
| Other | — | — | — | — | — | — | 0.06 | 0.13 | 0.15 | 0.28 |
| Bilateral lenders: | 2.94 | 3.20 | 3.24 | 3.48 | 3.89 | 4.16 | 4.85 | 6.60 | 8.20 | 9.89 |
| West Germany | 0.37 | 0.44 | 0.51 | 0.50 | 0.62 | 0.61 | 0.72 | 0.64 | 0.80 | 0.93 |
| Japan | 0.18 | 0.34 | 0.40 | 0.49 | 0.51 | 0.48 | 0.50 | 0.39 | 0.35 | 0.49 |
| United States | 2.16 | 2.15 | 2.10 | 2.05 | 2.03 | 1.98 | 1.99 | 1.72 | 1.59 | 1.52 |
| Other | 0.23 | 0.27 | 0.23 | 0.44 | 0.73 | 1.09 | 1.64 | 3.85 | 5.46 | 6.95 |
| IMF | — | — | — | — | — | 0.54 | 2.65 | 3.97 | 4.61 | 4.75 |
| Supplier's credits | 3.77 | 5.34 | 5.67 | 5.65 | 5.89 | 5.98 | 7.51 | 6.49 | 7.43 | 7.77 |
| Bonds | 1.22 | 2.38 | 2.96 | 3.24 | 2.90 | 2.61 | 2.23 | 1.74 | 1.92 | 1.91 |
| Financial loans: | 21.53 | 29.50 | 34.63 | 37.82 | 44.99 | 52.92 | 59.64 | 66.47 | 66.20 | 67.23 |
| Resolution 63 | 5.24 | 7.27 | 7.73 | 9.92 | 13.46 | 16.15 | 15.12 | 13.63 | 11.38 | 10.11 |
| Law 4131 | 16.26 | 22.20 | 26.88 | 27.89 | 31.52 | 36.76 | 44.51 | 52.83 | 54.81 | 57.11 |
| Other | 0.03 | 0.03 | 0.02 | 0.01 | 0.01 | 0.01 | 0.01 | 0.01 | 0.01 | 0.01 |
| Other | 0.22 | 0.20 | 0.19 | 0.18 | 0.16 | 0.14 | 0.12 | 0.11 | 0.09 | 0.09 |

*Source:* Central Bank of Brazil.

**Table 6–2**

**Brazil: Registered Medium- and Long-Term External Debt, by Type of Debtor, 1977–1986**

*(billions of U.S. dollars, end of period)*

| | 1977 | 1978 | 1979 | 1980 | 1981 | 1982 | 1983 | 1984 | 1985 | June 1986 |
|---|---|---|---|---|---|---|---|---|---|---|
| Total | 32.04 | 43.51 | 49.90 | 53.85 | 61.41 | 70.20 | 81.32 | 91.09 | 95.86 | 99.62 |
| *By legal debtor:* | | | | | | | | | | |
| Central government: | 11.78 | 17.54 | 23.40 | 25.54 | 28.23 | 31.76 | 41.83 | 58.86 | 66.40 | 72.20 |
| Direct | 3.55 | 4.09 | 5.47 | 5.70 | 5.45 | 5.51 | 9.01 | 13.47 | 16.80 | 19.13 |
| Guaranteed | 8.23 | 13.45 | 17.93 | 19.84 | 22.78 | 26.25 | 32.82 | 45.39 | 49.60 | 53.07 |
| States and municipalities: | 0.91 | 0.72 | 0.52 | 0.43 | 0.38 | 0.44 | 0.46 | 0.41 | 0.33 | 0.31 |
| Direct | 0.71 | 0.55 | 0.37 | 0.29 | 0.26 | 0.35 | 0.41 | 0.36 | 0.30 | 0.26 |
| Guaranteed | 0.20 | 0.17 | 0.15 | 0.14 | 0.12 | 0.09 | 0.05 | 0.05 | 0.03 | 0.05 |
| State enterprises: | 6.62 | 9.30 | 10.11 | 11.30 | 13.18 | 14.65 | 18.00 | 12.49 | 11.95 | 10.86 |
| Direct | 5.02 | 6.62 | 7.46 | 9.04 | 11.03 | 12.17 | 15.83 | 10.55 | 9.92 | 8.97 |
| Guaranteed | 1.60 | 2.68 | 2.65 | 2.26 | 2.15 | 2.48 | 2.17 | 1.94 | 2.05 | 1.89 |
| Private sector | 12.73 | 15.95 | 15.87 | 16.58 | 19.62 | 23.35 | 21.03 | 19.33 | 17.18 | 16.25 |
| *By economic debtor:* | | | | | | | | | | |
| Central government | — | 4.09 | 5.47 | 5.70 | 5.45 | 5.51 | 9.01 | 13.47 | 16.80 | 19.13 |
| States and municipalities | — | 1.51 | 1.78 | 2.29 | 2.68 | 3.06 | 3.21 | 3.79 | 5.15 | 5.41 |
| State enterprises: | — | 19.51 | 25.10 | 27.64 | 32.45 | 36.93 | 46.75 | 53.31 | 55.50 | 57.74 |
| Binational entities and public enterprises | — | 2.47 | 3.45 | 3.89 | 5.22 | 5.75 | 5.96 | 6.90 | 8.08 | 7.68 |
| Mixed enterprises | — | 11.92 | 14.27 | 16.21 | 18.94 | 23.08 | 24.12 | 26.14 | 28.75 | 28.90 |
| Other[a] | — | 5.12 | 7.38 | 7.54 | 8.29 | 8.10 | 16.67 | 20.27 | 18.67 | 21.16 |
| Private sector[b] | — | 18.40 | 17.55 | 18.22 | 20.83 | 24.70 | 22.35 | 20.52 | 18.41 | 17.34 |

*Source:* Central Bank of Brazil.

[a] Includes autonomous bodies, public foundations, and enterprises with majority public-sector participation.

[b] Includes enterprises with minority public-sector participation.

## Evolution of the Debt Crisis

In a phrase often used by Paul A. Volcker warning of dire prospects for the U.S. economy, the origins of the Brazilian debt crisis were rooted in "unsustainable trends." At year end 1972, Brazil's registered foreign debt amounted to US$9.5 billion; by the end of 1978, it amounted to US$43.5 billion (according to the Central Bank of Brazil). As a result of the first oil price shock of 1973–1974, Brazilian terms of trade received a devastating blow. Instead of retrenching, however, Brazil's policymakers attempted to maintain a high rate of economic growth. In the absence of a robust domestic capital market, the government was obliged to turn to foreign lenders.

Borrowing from international banks seemed a highly propitious option following 1973–1974. As a result of OECD inflation, by early 1974, real interest rates (the difference between nominal interest rates and anticipated inflation) had become negative. Lenders appeared to be subsidizing borrowers; thus it would have been foolish not to borrow. On the supply side, international banks in the first half of the 1970s, awash with recycled petrodollars, were eager to lend. By giving Brazil the goods and the money too, advanced countries seemed to be doing themselves a favor: they were selling capital goods that provided employment for their labor force as well as employment for the funds of the banks. By 1983, Brazil's medium- and long-term external debt amounted to US$81.3 billion, 8.5 times larger than at the end of 1972. After 1976, interest on the debt exceeded the trade deficit as the major component of the current account deficit. Moreover, after 1978, nominal interest rates rose drastically and real interest rates became increasingly positive.

After 1973, along with increased borrowing, the government had made a major effort to impose its import-substitution policies. For this purpose, it multiplied both import restrictions and export subsidies. Targeted for special government support were the intermediate goods and capital goods industries, and enormous expenditures were made for the completion of infrastructure projects. The lengthy gestation period for these projects made Brazil highly vulnerable to the second oil shock that occurred in 1979. World recession and rising interest rates compounded the balance of payments effect of the fall in commodity prices that began in 1980–1981. Rising interest rates, incidentally, were partly due to the financial deregulation that followed the first oil shock, when it became convenient for governments and central banks to give commercial banks more flexibility in recycling the financial surpluses of OPEC.

Prior to the first oil shock, Brazil's foreign borrowing was primarily for the purpose of installing infrastructure. Unfortunately, although the social rate of return on such projects may be high, the financial rate of return is low.

Moreover, return on the investment may not be realized by the time the loan matures. Between the first and second oil shocks, some of the foreign borrowing was used for consumption as well as for productive purposes. Statistically, Brazil's economic growth was "successfully" maintained between the first and second oil shocks. However, widespread subsidies and buoyant demand, as well as series of poor harvests, contributed to a rising rate of inflation. In their impact on both the cost of production and the availability of consumer goods, import restrictions during 1974–1978 were a further inflationary factor. In the United States, after the second oil shock, deflationary policies relied almost exclusively on monetary restraint, while fiscal policy remained expansionary. This accelerated the increase in interest rates that was already under way and together with the shortening of the maturity structure of outstanding foreign loans compounded Brazil's difficulties in servicing the debt.

For the retirement of their external debt, developing countries require export markets in the advanced countries. Much of Brazil's development program, however, was designed to expand output for the domestic rather than the external market. Onset of the world recession in 1980–1981, moreover, reduced both the volume and the foreign currency price of Brazil's basic commodity exports. Domestically, by 1980 inflation was running at a rate in excess of 100 percent annually. In that year, the balance of payments deficit on current account amounted to US$12.8 billion.

A further complicating factor for the creditors was the collapse in the inflow of funds to the international banks from OPEC. The world recession induced by the second oil shock reduced the demand for oil and reduced OPEC's revenues. Consequently, while in 1980 OPEC had contributed about $42 billion to the loanable funds of banks reporting to the Bank for International Settlements (BIS), recycling declined to $3.2 billion in 1981.[9]

After the Mexican default of August of 1982, the international banks became apprehensive about Brazil. Their first response was to restrict its access to medium- and long-term credits and to provide only short-term loans (Table 6–3). In order to induce them to advance new loans, it became necessary for Brazil to pay high fees and large spreads above the London interbank offered rate (LIBOR, which is the price of dollars borrowed outside the United States). Thus new loans were both a help and an additional burden to Brazil (see Tables 6–4 and 6–5). In addition to the external debt, the government had the problem of rolling over the domestic debt. In doing so, it crowded out domestic private investment. This had further counterproductive effects, for in restricting private investment, the government was restricting export production as well. By 1982–1983, as a result of the growth of subsidies and investment in state-owned enterprises, the public-sector deficit constituted approximately 15 percent of the GDP.

Table 6–3
Brazil: Structure of External Public Debt Outstanding, by Maturities,
1970, 1975, 1981, 1983, 1984, and 1985
*(percent, on basis of total balance outstanding at year end)*

| Year | Up to 5 Years | More than 5 and up to 10 Years | Over 10 years |
|------|------|------|------|
| 1970 | 39.6 | 21.1 | 39.3 |
| 1975 | 39.0 | 31.4 | 29.6 |
| 1981 | 50.1 | 41.4 | 8.5 |
| 1983 | 63.1 | 32.1 | 4.8 |
| 1984 | 67.4 | 28.8 | 3.8 |
| 1985 | 62.6 | 31.0 | 6.4 |

*Source:* Inter-American Development Bank, based on official statistics from IBRD and the member countries, as presented in IDB, *External Public Debt of the Latin American Countries,* July 1985, p. 20. Data for 1984 and 1985 from International Economic Section, IDB.

ª Debt contracted by public agencies or by private institutions with government guarantee, payable in foreign currency and with maturities of more than 1 year.

Table 6–4
Brazil: Service Payments on External Public Debt, 1973–1985
*(millions of dollars)*

| Year | Total | Amortization Payments | Interest Payments |
|------|------|------|------|
| 1973 | 944 | 555 | 389 |
| 1974 | 1,224 | 634 | 590 |
| 1975 | 1,781 | 925 | 856 |
| 1976 | 2,047 | 1,086 | 961 |
| 1977 | 2,873 | 1,680 | 1,193 |
| 1978 | 4,484 | 2,638 | 1,845 |
| 1979 | 6,520 | 3,601 | 2,919 |
| 1980 | 8,039 | 3,850 | 4,189 |
| 1981 | 9,071 | 3,923 | 5,148 |
| 1982 | 10,099 | 4,158 | 5,941 |
| 1983 | 6,793 | 1,789 | 5,004 |
| 1984 | 8,037 | 1,601 | 6,436 |
| 1985 | 7,776 | 1,497 | 6,279 |

*Source:* Inter-American Development Bank, official documents from IBRD and the member countries, as presented in IDB, *External Public Debt of the Latin American Countries,* July 1985, Tables 54, 55, and 56. Data for 1983 and 1984 from International Economic Section, IDB.

Table 6–5
Brazil: External Public Debt[a] 1961, 1965, and 1968–1985
(*millions of dollars*)

| Year | External Debt |
|------|---------------|
| 1961 | 2,200 |
| 1965 | 2,983 |
| 1968 | 3,839 |
| 1969 | 3,278 |
| 1970 | 4,706 |
| 1971 | 5,939 |
| 1972 | 8,078 |
| 1973 | 10,206 |
| 1974 | 14,085 |
| 1975 | 17,897 |
| 1976 | 23,430 |
| 1977 | 29,018 |
| 1978 | 38,903 |
| 1979 | 46,127 |
| 1980 | 50,922 |
| 1981 | 57,476 |
| 1982 | 64,233 |
| 1983 | 67,433 |
| 1984 | 75,711 |
| 1985 | 85,847 |

*Source:* Inter-American Development Bank, official documents from IBRD and member countries, as presented in IDB, *External Public Debt of the Latin American Countries,* July 1985, Table 1. Revised data for 1983 and 1984 from International Economic Section, IDB.

*Note:* Data for a more comprehensive concept, namely, Brazil's total external debt (including guaranteed and nonguaranteed debt) are as follows (in billions of U.S. dollars):

| | |
|------|-------|
| 1982 | 90.5 |
| 1983 | 92.9 |
| 1984 | 100.2 |
| 1985 | 102.7 |

[a] Includes disbursed and undisbursed portions.

## Incriminations and Recriminations: Brazil and the United States

If there were flaws in the rationale of borrowing, were there flaws in the rationale of lending as well? Did the lenders act in an irresponsible manner? Can there be overborrowing without overlending?

From a macroeconomic point of view, the recycling of OPEC petrodollars in the late 1970s, combined with recessionary conditions in the major industrial nations, made developing countries appear to be a natural target for lending by the Western banks. The funds loaned to developing nations at that time were then recycled again in the form of purchases of industrial products, including capital goods, from the lending nations. In the case of Japanese banks that are affiliated with Japanese trading companies, the linkage is direct: by providing loans to Brazil that result in business for the trading company, the Japanese *keiretsu* (group) gets its money back with profit as well as interest. At the macro level, the banking systems of the West were not supervised with regard to the sustainability of the expansion of their balance sheets. Central banks have been accused of being derelict in failing to supply such supervision.

At the micro level, in competing with American banks in the 1970s, Japanese banks were aggressive in entering the Brazilian market. As latecomers, they went in with low spreads to increase their market share, just as they had done a bit earlier in western Europe. American banks, however, were the principal channel for recycling of petrodollars. As of June of 1982, 37.4 percent of all external bank claims on Brazil were attributable to lending by U.S. banks.[10] According to an American banker, "Foreign banks pushed money down Brazil's throat, but not only Brazil's. It is the *job* of banks to push money. Those who leverage most either gain most or lose most. Moreover, Brazil, chose to make itself vulnerable."[11]

In a conversation with a banker in New York, I raised the question of the economic impact of U.S. bank lending to Brazil. In particular, I wanted to estimate the real (nonfinancial) effect of U.S. lending as compared with Japanese lending. I asked, "What is the Brazilian export performance resulting from your loans?" "I have never inquired," he replied. At Citibank in New York, I asked the same question of a member of the steering committee for U.S. banks that were organizing the "rescue" of Brazil in June of 1983. "You are talking to me like an economist," he said. "I'm not familiar with figures like that." Citibank's lending philosophy was explained by Citicorp Vice Chairman Thomas Theobald in an interview with *Business Week*. "If there's an opportunity," he said, "take advantage. Don't analyze it to death."[12]

On the Brazilian side, opportunism likewise prevailed. Borrowing was preferred to an inflow of equity capital in order to prevent foreigners from "dominating our economy" or "usurping our land." It was fashionable and "progressive" to despise multinationals, especially American multinationals. As described by *The Economist* (London), this was an expensive mistake. "Instead of cash that had to make a profit before any dividends were sent abroad, poor countries took bank loans that carried a front-end fee and then 6-monthly interest charges which were set by the vagaries of American monetary policy and the exchange rate of the dollar. The foreign exchange cost of servicing multinational investment was about 4 percent a year in 1978–1980, whereas bank loans cost 13 percent a year. Direct investment by multinational companies would have come with know-how. Loans from international banks have come with reams of legal bumph."[13]

Not only was foreign "domination" by means of equity capital precluded, but gigantic new federal enterprises were inaugurated with borrowed money. "From 1974 to 1981, investments in capital goods, steel, nonferrous metals, petrochemicals, fertilizers, paper, and cellulose totaled approximately US$32 billion, at 1981 prices." Daring projects, "particularly those under the responsibility of Eletrobras, Siderbras, Nuclebras, and Sunamam, together with the construction of the so-called Steel Railroad and two subway systems, had a certain destabilizing impact on the Brazilian economy, by the fact that they were, to a great extent, carried out with foreign resources."[14] As of March of 1984, according to the Central Bank of Brazil, federal enterprises accounted for approximately US$65 billion of the total Brazilian foreign debt of about US$100 billion. In the debt-rescheduling process, moreover, some funds that were obtained on behalf of the private sector have been assumed as a responsibility of the Central Bank. The domestic debt, which in 1983 amounted to approximately 15 trillion cruzeiros, likewise arose primarily from the operations of the public sector. Financing difficulties were increased by the fact that during 1974–1982, approximately one-eighth of the net funds borrowed from abroad disappeared from Brazil in the form of capital flight.[15]

These facts suggest that Brazil has been more successful in the procurement of foreign loans than in the use of them. From a Japanese point of view, a similar distinction has been made concerning the merit of Brazilian planning as compared with Brazilian execution of physical projects:

> In the private sector, Brazilian planning is confident. But Brazilian execution is not synchronized. For example, the foundation may be finished, but the machinery has not yet been ordered. When the machinery arrives, it is poorly installed. This was evident in the case of Cenibra, the project for manufacture of wood chips. They forgot to arrange for a constant lumber supply. The rainy season was not taken account of. They had only 1 month's supply, then only 1 week, then only 2 days. But the Brazilians don't worry. They are constantly optimistic about a bright future. It was this same thinking that got them into trouble with IMF. They didn't worry about the bills coming due. In the execution stage, they improve only slowly, and over the long run.[16]

From a Brazilian point of view, in the context of IMF affairs, the United States is the culpable party. The United States became the world's largest debtor in 1985, and its enormous credit demands have raised the cost of credit worldwide. The United States competes with the LDCs for the world's savings. However, instead of being disciplined by the IMF, it is the latter that appears to Brazilians to be the bill collector that will maintain the solvency of American banks at Brazil's expense. As seen by Brazilians, their external debt is purely an artifact of inappropriate and inconsistent U.S. monetary and fiscal policies. It was created in large part not by an original contractual agreement, but merely by the extraneous and arbitrary effect of U.S. tight money which raised U.S. interest rates and thus the cost to Brazil of rolling over the debt. In 1984, Professor Maria da Conceicao Tavares maintained that

> No textbook approves of a tight money policy combined with a loose fiscal policy. Tight monetary control combined with financial deregulation is another inconsistency of U.S. economic policy. I could understand U.S. policy if it contributed some benefit even to the United States. But it does not. It is not an economic policy; it is not an imperialist policy; it is simply a stupid policy that benefits nobody. We can adjust to the oil shock by conservation and by alcohol substitution. But we cannot adjust to the financial problem because it is not our problem. It is your problem. The Treasury, the Fed, and the banks all blame each other. This is nonsense. They should get together and design a rational policy. Moreover, there should be two rates of interest—a domestic rate and an international transfer rate. For purposes of rollover of the debt, the international transfer rate of interest should be equal to the rate of growth of trade. Therefore, it cannot be greater than 7 percent. For purposes of amortizing the debt, the rate of interest should be *less* than the rate of growth of trade, for example, 5 percent.[17]

In mid-1984, Ernane Galveas, minister of finance, estimated that no less than US$64 billion of Brazil's foreign debt had been created by the oil sheikhs who raised oil prices and the international bankers who raised interest rates.[18] New loans were required merely to keep the economy running. As a result of the rise in U.S. interest rates, not only was Brazil's debt service multiplied, but its major development projects, which might have been viable at the lower rates prevailing at their inception, became viable no longer. Professor Rudiger Dornbusch of MIT put the matter as follows: was it right, he asked, that resources should continue to be transferred from the poor of Latin America just because the United States had "crazy macroeconomic policies?"[19] According to an estimate of a congressional investigating committee in Brazil, the effect of increased interest rates exceeded the effect of increased oil prices in raising the level of Brazil's external debt. The committee's report, dated September of 1984, was prepared under the direction of Professor Cristovam Buarque, a former economic adviser to the late Tancredo Neves. The report attributed at least US$40 billion of Brazil's debt to the rise in U.S. interest rates. It maintained that this portion of the debt rests on unilateral decisions by the U.S. government aimed at pushing up interest rates to cover

U.S. government deficits. To the extent that this is the case, the report questioned the legality of the debt.[20]

The impact on Brazil's debt of rising U.S. interest rates increased over the course of time. In August of 1983, it was estimated that a 1 percent increase would result in raising the debt by US$500 million during the period of a year. "This has nothing to do with whether Brazilian economic management is good or bad."[21] In April of 1984, the rule of thumb employed by Brazilian ministers attributed an increase in the debt of US$600 million per year to each 1 percent rise in the U.S. interest rate.[22] In May of 1984, *The Economist* estimated that an additional percentage point in the rates would cost Brazil US$650 million, if maintained for a year.[23] In July of 1984, it was estimated that if the U.S. prime rate went up 1 percent, Brazil's debt-service obligation would rise by US$700 million.[24] According to a spokesman of the Central Bank of Brazil, only about 25 percent of Brazil's total international debt is contracted for at fixed interest rates (9 percent annually).[25] In a paper prepared by Professor Mario Henrique Simonsen for purposes of discussion at a Citibank meeting in Sao Paulo, the application of floating interest rates to Brazil's foreign debt was described as the practice of "colonialism with modern economic weapons."[26]

Until the decline in U.S. interest rates in mid-1985, Brazil was locked into a vicious circle of "borrowing to repay and repaying to borrow." With regard to the polemics of the matter, however—polemics that have profound international political implications—there is an argument on the American side that denies the usual explanation concerning the origin of those high interest rates. The usual explanation attributes high U.S. interest rates to the gargantuan U.S. budget deficit, a deficit which is therefore construed to be "irresponsible" for international as well as for domestic U.S. reasons. Some writers, however, differ with the usual interpretation. Milton Friedman maintains that "extensive empirical studies by respected economists . . . have found no historical relation between deficits and interest rates."[27] If these studies are valid, the U.S. government is absolved of maintaining an irresponsible fiscal policy that has direct adverse repercussions on Brazil and other Latin American debtors.

U.S.–Brazil creditor-debtor relations are, of course, strongly conditioned by their relations in a broader economic, political, and security context. From a Brazilian point of view, U.S. cognizance of Brazil's obsession with economic growth and development has never been translated into commensurate financial assistance. In trade relations, there has been a good deal of friction over Brazilian export subsidies. Brazil is presumed to have graduated from its status as a developing nation eligible for trade benefits in accordance with the program known as the generalized system of preferences (GSP). In trade relations, the Brazilian government also was antagonized by the U.S. concept of reciprocity. In accordance with its predilection for bilateral rather than multilateral diplomacy, the Reagan administration sought to embrace Brazil in a "special relationship" of a strategic type. However, Brazil does not share the U.S. geopolitical perspective in security affairs. Indeed, during 1982–1984, in the midst of the debt crisis, Washington's total preoccupation in Latin American affairs with insurgency in the Caribbean was taken as something of an affront by Brazilians. I asked a Brazilian official, "Why is Brazil less concerned than the United States about Russian imperialism?"

"Because we know how to count," he replied. "How many times has the Soviet Union intervened in Latin America as compared with how many times the United States has done so?"[28]

As a debtor, Brazil blamed the United States for the fact that during 1980–1982, the inflow of foreign funds declined at the same time that the U.S. recession reduced Brazil's ability to export and thus to earn enough to service the debt. During the U.S. recovery of 1982–1984, Brazil blamed the United States for its protectionist threats with regard to imports of shoes and steel. "Suddenly we are going to be punished for making this fantastic effort that everyone told us to do," bitterly complained President Jose Sarney. "It's a real contradiction."[29] When Brazil's merchandise exports to the United States rose to unprecedented heights in 1983 and 1984, there were incriminations about the export of capital from a poor country to a rich country. It was asserted that large net outflows of capital from Latin America were helping to sustain the overvaluation of the U.S. dollar. These outflows resulted from the fact that none of the region's debtors were able to borrow enough from abroad to meet their interest obligations. When the price of oil declined in 1983, Brazilians complained that there was no benefit because oil had to be paid for in increasingly expensive dollars. Quoting the late President-elect Tancredo Neves, President Sarney declared, "This debt cannot be paid with the hunger of the Brazilian people."[30] When the Federal Reserve discount rate rose a half point in April of 1984, Finance Minister Ernane Galveas protested, "The United States is playing with fire. International interest rates, which are the direct outcome of the U.S. inability to reduce its budget deficit, are doing more damage than the whole oil crisis. If Brazil can negotiate an agreement with the International Monetary Fund to wipe out its public-sector deficit, why can't the United States make the same effort?"[31]

From a Brazilian point of view, it is also anomalous that the role of U.S. economic policy should be so disproportionately large in relation to the declining importance of U.S. trade and output in the world economy. In opposite disproportion, Brazil feels slighted and underrepresented. For example, as the eighth largest market economy in the world, Brazil feels unfairly excluded from the annual economic summit meetings of the seven major industrial nations. If membership in that group were determined by economic impact, Brazil and Mexico would be included before Canada and Italy. Sensitivity on this point is indicated by the fact that the term *NIC* (newly industrialized country) is taboo in Brazil.

## Financing versus Adjusting the Deficit

Brazilians believe the IMF to be dominated by the United States, which can exercise control by means of its veto power. Thus IMF policies and practices, which they generally regard as adversarial to Brazil, have implications for the tenor of U.S.–Brazil relations. With U.S. approval, IMF policies have changed drastically during the past decade, often in ambiguous and inconsistent ways. As originally conceived in the Bretton Woods version following World War II, the IMF was intended to provide short-term revolving loans for temporary balance of payments problems in order to stabilize foreign exchange rates. It was never intended as a channel for development. A member was entitled to call upon the IMF to finance temporary balance of payments disequilibrium within the limits of its quota. In other words, the IMF was truly a fund, not a bank: a member could take out only what it had put it, plus an increment in some circumstances. The IMF was restricted to providing assistance for stabilization in the external sector; it was not authorized to finance long-term deficits caused by large-scale domestic development programs.

Typically, balance of payments deficits that are regarded as temporary or self-correcting are those which are financed. Financing a balance of payments deficit may be done by means of liquidating foreign exchange reserves, including gold, convertible foreign currencies, Special Drawing Rights (SDRs), and reserve positions in the IMF. A deficit that is structural, however, cannot be financed; it must be adjusted. Adjustment usually occurs by means of restrictive monetary and fiscal policy, that is, by reducing the level of economic activity. It also may be attempted by means of incomes policies, import restrictions, and devaluation of the currency or by a combination of these measures. When the system of fixed foreign exchange rates established by the Bretton Woods regime was abandoned in March of 1973, the era of floating rates was inaugurated. Ostensibly, the advent of floating rates destroyed the raison d'être of the IMF. At that time, it was assumed that the new system would always cause exchange rates to settle at a point that would clear the market and that consequently no balance of payments deficit could occur. Instead, however, foreign exchange rates became extremely volatile and disorderly, and balance of payments disequilibrium among the major industrial nations as well as among LDCs became pronounced and persistent. The reasons for this disequilibrium were structural and institutional, as well as financial. Thus a new role for the IMF emerged. In its new role, the IMF assumed responsibility for a vastly greater task than the short-term financing of transitory balance of payments deviations. It became involved in the long-term structural adjustment of national economies and a party to their economic development programs. In effect, the IMF became an international development bank. In 1974, for example, it established a long-term "extended facility . . . to support comprehensive economic programs designed to restore sustainable financial balance to the economy. It included policies of the scope and character required to correct structural imbalances in production, trade, and prices. Particular attention was paid to policy measures intended to mobilize domestic and foreign resources, to improve their utilization, and to reduce reliance on restrictions on international transactions."[32] The resources of the extended facility were made available "subject to relevant policies on conditionality, phasing, and performance criteria." By its policies of conditionality and surveillance, the IMF has been perceived in Mexico and Brazil as practicing "imperialist intervention" in their economies.

Although the IMF has shifted the central focus of its activities from financing to adjusting, however, the although its discipline, conditionality, and surveillance of the domestic economies of its clients have become more detailed, comprehensive, and intense, its professed rationale remains what it always has been, namely, that of external balance of payments management. This is one of the ambiguities of the new regime. From a Brazilian point of view, it appears that the IMF imposes its deflationary bias on the economy as a whole in the name of equilibrium in the external sector. It appears that the tail is wagging the dog. In the case of Brazil, which is one of the most "closed" of the major nations, this disparity is particularly acute. During the 1970s, its exports of goods and nonfactor services were less than 7 percent of GDP; in the 1980s, they have been approximately 8 percent. The anomaly of the "new" IMF abiding by the textbook criteria of the "old" may have something to do with its persona as a "bill collector for foreign banks," as the Brazilians say. Among various indicators of progress on the part of its clients, the IMF continues to place primary emphasis on the achievement of a balance of trade surplus. (In the case of Brazil, it has been inconsistently "flexible" about inflation.) It is this surplus that chiefly determines the level of foreign exchange reserves in the hands of the central bank of the debtor country, which in turn determine whether or not it can pay the interest on its debt.

A rising proportion of the IMF's resources has been disbursed subject to conditionality and performance criteria.[33] "Conditionality, which ties the availability of resources to satisfactory economic programs, has become the distinctive feature of the Fund's financial activities. The use of resources is no longer undertaken in defense of a par value system but to promote effective and durable adjustment and restoration of the conditions for *balanced and sustained economic growth* [emphasis added]."[34] By definition, however, "balanced and sustained economic growth" is a development matter and lies in a long-term context. Yet the IMF continues to use the language and instruments of a short-term approach. There are two points to be raised here. First, in principle, the IMF's programs are designed to achieve sharp correction of balance of payments disequilibrium by requiring its clients to "live within their means." But the short-term horizon of the IMF, which looks for equilibrium in 1 to 3 years, is clearly insufficient for the problems facing Brazil. The deflationary "shock therapy" that was prescribed by the IMF mission that visited Brazil in June of 1985 is an example of its short-term approach. Second, in the development context, is "balanced" growth necessarily preferable to "unbalanced" growth? Can balanced growth be imposed on Brazil in the short term? Moreover, in espousing balanced growth, is the IMF confining its policies to macroeconomic affairs, as it professes to do? Or is it inadvertently intervening in the determination of how the burden of adjustment will be distributed among the various segments of the economy?

In the language they use, the IMF and even the World Bank continue to speak of Brazil's difficulty as one of liquidity (a short-term concept) rather than solvency (a long-term concept). Mr. A. W. Clausen, president of the World Bank, maintained that "the success of the developing countries, especially the middle-income countries, in coping with the stresses of the seventies is strong evidence that their present payment problems are liquidity, not solvency, problems."[35]

One of the factors leading to the breakdown of the Bretton Woods version of the IMF was the disproportionate pressures it placed on debtors as opposed to creditors in the resolution of balance of payments deficits. In accordance with its traditional bias, does the IMF still place the burden of adjustment of a deficit principally on the debtor rather than symmetrically on debtor and creditor alike? At present, it is the LDC debtors that appear to be bearing the brunt of demands for adjustment rather than the United States, which is the greatest debtor of all. In its role as a debtor, until 1986 the United States did not conform with the standard IMF prescription of currency devaluation for debtors. In its role as a creditor, the United States did not relieve LDC debtors carrying dollar-denominated debt of the consequences of its inappropriate macroeconomic policies that had maintained the dollar in an overvalued state. In Brazil, the IMF has been accused of representing the interests of the affluent and imposing deflationary programs that require contraction of demand and reduction of living standards in poor countries rather than on reforms that may be achieved through accelerated growth. According to the assessment of a World Bank officer, "Official disclaimers notwithstanding, the IMF-sanctioned austerity program in Brazil is likely provoke a deepening of the 1981–1982 recession, with a concomitant increase in unemployment. Should this occur, per capita income growth would be negative for the third consecutive year."[36] Central Bank data show that Brazil's per capita real GDP growth rate was in fact negative during 1981, 1982, and 1983. It turned positive in 1984 and 1985. In discussing the IMF's objectives with regard to the "problem countries" that have sought its assistance, the managing director pointed out the IMF emphasis on the balance of payments as a "common element" of its prescriptions in every case. He also pointed out the short-term orientation of the IMF approach. In every case, he said, the IMF programs "have one objective in common: that is, to restore a viable external payments position within a few years."[37]

In contrast, the Japanese take a long-term view. According to the president of the Bank of Tokyo, "It seems to me that many discussions of the debt crisis are overly concerned with the short-term viewpoint and that a longer-range historical perspective is often lacking." Moreover, in accounting for the severity of the crisis, he all but explicitly placed the blame on the United States. "As the world entered the 1980s, the exacerbation of the debt crisis basically came about because real interest rates moved to a high plateau, this being a consequence of the stringent and long-lasting tight-money policies adopted by the advanced nations."[38]

The 1985 annual reports of the IMF and the Inter-American Development Bank (IDB), were noteworthy for the different directions in which their aspersions were respectively cast. The IMF report denounced U.S. economic policies, with special reference to the fiscal deficit, trade deficit, high interest rates, and overvalued dollar.[39] In calling for greater international coordination of economic policy-making, it implicitly expressed disapproval of Reagan administration policies that had consistently rejected such coordination. The IDB annual report, especially in a chapter by Professor Albert Fishlow, denounced the IMF for its short-term palliatives in Latin America that exacerbated inflationary pressures and undermined long-term growth prospects. The IMF was criticized for its stress on sharply restrictive monetary and fiscal policies designed to generate short-term trade surpluses and the means of servicing foreign debts. The report stated that this approach deprives debtors of the option of laying adequate foundations for the long-term growth they would need in order to service their debts in the future. Three years of economic "adjustment" in Latin American had left the region starved of private-sector investment, as meagre savings were diverted to interest payments to foreigners. Professor Fishlow pointed out that the main Latin American debtors faced a debt-servicing burden that was more than double the level of reparations that Germany found intolerable in the 1920s. "There are valid reasons to resist," he wrote.

Neither report referred to the erratic shifts in U.S. official policy with regard to the roles of the IMF and the World Bank in coping with the debt crisis. At its inception, the Reagan administration had little enthusiasm for international institutions, multilateral development banks, or international economic cooperation. The World Bank, in particular, was regarded as using U.S. financial resources for the support of unfriendly communist regimes. At a debt conference convened in Caracas by the Organization of American States in September of 1983, the United States opposed a proposal to expand the IMF's compensatory financing facility to cover increased debt-service payments caused by higher international interest rates. (As constituted, that facility grants funds to countries whose exports have been adversely affected by falling world commodity prices.) Before the Mexican default of August of 1982, the United States opposed any increase at all in the lending capacity of the IMF. When President Reagan changed his mind about this, the administration still had to wage an enormous struggle with the Congress in order to obtain its approval for a 50 percent increase (involving a $8.4 billion U.S. contribution). The legislation was passed in November of 1983. In December of 1983, the United States stood firm on a decision to reduce its contribution to the International Development Association (IDA), the concessional lending arm of the World Bank. Until September of 1985, the Reagan administration had remained consistently opposed to any international coordination of monetary, fiscal, exchange rate, or economic development policies.[40] In October of 1985, at the IMF–World Bank annual meeting, U.S. Treasury Secretary James Baker proposed that the World Bank and IDB should assume a wider role, reinforcing the resources of the IMF and providing guarantees for more cofinancing of loans by the World Bank and commercial lenders. The proposal was a radical departure from the Treasury's former critical attitude toward the World Bank and a departure from its former unwillingness to assume an activist role in coping with the debt crisis. As a separate matter, in October of 1985, the United States agreed in principle that IDA funding also should be increased.

In Brazil as well, there have been differences of opinion and changes of attitude toward the IMF. In 1959, to great popular acclaim, President Juscelino Kubitschek broke off negotiations with the IMF. Thereafter, to receive an IMF loan would have been regarded as a national humiliation. In November of 1982, however, the Brazilian government confirmed that negotiations with the IMF were being resumed. In an article concerning those negotiations published in January of 1983, Professor Mario Henrique Simonsen, a former minister of planning and former minister of finance, wrote that "the requirements of the IMF were relatively mild. . . . The Fund left the Brazilian authorities plenty of leeway."[41] A year later, in an article in *Conjuntura Economica,* however, Simonsen called for a revision by the IMF of its stringent adjustment criteria. Simonsen attacked the IMF program as being limited to the correction of "transitory external imbalances." Not only did they "prevent economic growth," but they were "socially destabilizing" by crushing the middle class.[42] In August of 1983, support for the IMF program was expressed by the head of the Economics Department of the Central Bank of Brazil. "I agree with the IMF austerity prescription. We must overcome inflation and the uncertainty of expectations. The banks think likewise, but they do not say so. They are in favor of a restrictive policy in order to overcome inflation and to forestall nationalization of the banking system. On the balance sheet, inflation produces profit, but this does not augur well for the future of the banks."[43]

Shigeaki Ueki, president of Petrobras, was strongly opposed to the IMF prescription. "We cannot shrink our employment and production to pay the debt. The deflationary approach is wrong. Even in terms of the balance of payments, IMF policy is wrong. Any policy that reduces output reduces exports. We can expand output and increase exports with a small amount of additional financial resources. In the Planning Ministry, however, there are many divergent opinions—some favor and some oppose the IMF."[44] In September of 1983, Carlos Langoni, governor of the Central Bank resigned his post. In leaving, he asserted that the IMF program was unrealistic. The IMF insisted that inflation should be brought down from 160 percent in 1983 to 55 percent in 1984. (Actually, the general price index rose 223.8 percent in 1984 and 235.1 percent in 1985.) Langoni was succeeded by Alfonso Pastore, a close associate of Planning Minister Antonio Delfim Netto.

The administration inherited by President Jose Sarney included two conservatives, Francisco Dornelles, nephew of Tancredo Neves, who was elected president but who died before assuming office, and Antonio Carlos Lemgruber. Dornelles was minister of finance, and Lemgruber was governor of the Central Bank. Their authority rapidly deteriorated in the Sarney administration. In August of 1985, Dornelles was quoted as saying that "there are two schools of thought in this government. One wants an agreement now, and the other wants to break with the International Monetary Fund."[45] At the end of August of 1985, Dornelles and Lemgruber resigned their positions. Brazilian negotiations with the IMF thereby became increasingly adversarial.

By that time, it was generally believed in Brazil that the IMF cure was worse than the disease. One part of the cure was the imposition of a controversial wage-suppression law (Decree Law No. 2065) in November of 1983. Jacques de Larosiere had personally singled out the wage law as the keystone of IMF's prescription for economic stabilization in Brazil. In the public sector, which employs about one-third of all workers, the law was designed to limit pay increases to about 85 percent of the inflation rate; in the private sector, it allowed a little more. Unemployment increased sharply as a result of the austerity measures that were imposed beginning in late 1980. In 1984 there were 6 to 8 million unemployed in the industrial sector. However, Brazil provided no unemployment insurance or social security safety net. The result was a massive growth of the underground economy, which alone generated employment. According to an official in the Ministry of Finance, "The IMF is seeking a low-level type of adjustment."[46] It was seen to be demanding a financial adjustment without providing for a social cure. In so doing, the IMF was accused of compounding the nonfinancial problems and making their eventual solution more difficult. Moreover, in working essentially with macroeconomic data, the IMF fails to perform sectoral analysis. The IMF program, therefore, even if financially "sound" from an international point of view, was not considered to be politically viable domestically.

Domestically, the program was accused of not even being sound financially because it would indiscriminately raise the interest rate burden of efficient and inefficient companies alike and increase their demands for credit even further. Firms that were unable to borrow more would be forced into bankruptcy whether or not they were efficient.

Another criticism of the IMF program referred to the fact that the improvement in Brazil's current account in 1983 and 1984 was attributable in substantial degree to restriction of imports rather than expansions of exports. Import restrictions were applied to capital goods as well as to consumer goods, including imports from both the United States and Japan. By 1985, however, the lack of imports of capital equipment was becoming critical to the maintenance of output because domestic substitutes were unavailable or too costly to produce. Conceptually, the IMF was inconsistent in taking credit for the improvement in Brazil's current account while expressing disapproval of import restrictions, which was one of the means by which that improvement was accomplished.

Conceptually also, as well as in practical effect, there was a further major flaw in the IMF austerity program for Brazil. The flaw lay in the fact that austerity programs also were prescribed for Argentina, Mexico, and other debtor nations, including some of Brazil's principal trade partners. However sound or successful on an individual country basis, contractionary policies can be counterproductive when applied multilaterally. Simultaneous efforts by major debtors to restrain imports and expand exports will generate a regional recession. Thus the value of austerity programs in hastening the repayment of a country's debt may be less than the IMF supposed.

What was the reply of the IMF to these charges and allegations? The reply was denial or self-justification in every particular. Moreover, from the point of view of the Reagan administration as perceived in Brazil, the IMF program for the rescue of Brazil was welcomed as a recipe for the rescue of American banks.

Playing the devil's advocate, an initial argument offered by the IMF is that it must indeed appear to be rigid and inhumane so that governments of debtor countries can deflect the blame for necessary but unpopular actions to an external enemy. Besides making it easier for debtor governments to adopt necessary policies, the IMF must furthermore maintain its credibility among creditors. (Its credibility had already been battered by the failure of its first program for Brazil in May of 1983.) If the terms of its conditionality and surveillance are seen to be relatively weak, further borrowing or restructuring of the debt would be that much more difficult to arrange. For Brazil's sake, as well as for its own, the IMF could not afford to be accused of leniency.

In a pamphlet entitled "Does the Fund Impose Austerity?" Managing Director J. de Larosiere presented a detailed reply to critics of the IMF.[47] First, he observed that adjustment is inescapable. No country can permanently live beyond its means. If a country attempts to continue borrowing indefinitely, adjustment will occur anyway, but without outside assistance and in a disorderly manner. Second, adjustment as sought by the IMF is not synonymous with restricted growth or economic retrogression. The decline in Latin American growth began before the IMF intervened in any of the debtor countries. IMF programs aim not at recession, but rather at a more rational combination of economic policies to achieve balance of payments equilibrium and thus to achieve more vigorous and lasting growth. Third, IMF programs do entail sacrifices. But these sacrifices must be compared with the alternatives. The sacrifices caused by IMF discipline over national budgets and credit must be compared with those which would result in the absence of IMF support and the absence of the private financing for which it serves as a catalyst. Fourth, concerning the social costs of IMF adjustment programs, it is inescapable that *any* action to restore balance of payments equilibrium involves costs, namely, the cost of reducing the amount of absorption of external resources. This cost would be incurred whether adjustment occurred in response to IMF programs or not. The way these costs are distributed within the society is not a matter for the IMF to decide, but a question of political choice to be made by the debtor governments themselves. Fifth, it is argued that the impact of foreign exchange adjustments that are a condition of IMF support imposes a burden on the poor. However, this is not universally the case. There is no standard model. If an agricultural country has an overvalued exchange rate, exchange depreciation would help the farmers to sell more farm products abroad. Sixth, the IMF is an organization that works with revolving credit for financing short- to medium-term imbalances. The IMF's adjustment programs must be supplemented by long-term structural support that can come partly from the World Bank. In summary, debtor countries have little hope of achieving higher employment and long-term growth if they seek to avoid or postpone needed adjustment.

At the annual IMF–World Bank meeting held in Seoul in October of 1985, de Larosiere, in a significant shift of policy emphasis, declared that "today, with the necessity in so many countries for major structural adjustments and sectoral reforms, the role of the World Bank has never been more important." In endorsing a greater role for the World Bank, the managing director echoed the statement of U.S. Treasury Secretary James Baker at the same meeting, who similarly revealed a significant shift in U.S. policy with regard to the World Bank. In describing the task awaiting both institutions, Mr. Baker said, "It will be particularly important for the Fund to work closely with the World Bank in this effort."

Although the Reagan administration was explicit in encouraging private American banks to increase their lending to developing countries, the lending of the World Bank to those countries declined 4.9 percent in fiscal year 1985 as compared with 1984. Brazil is the World Bank's leading borrower. In

1984, there were ten World Bank loans to Brazil amounting to US $1,604.3 million; in 1985, there were nine World Bank loans to Brazil amounting to US $1,523.0 million.[48] Traditionally, the World Bank focused on long-term project loans; recently, however, it has shifted about 11 percent of its portfolio to structural adjustment or policy-based loans. This shift has contributed to the need for more cooperation between the World Bank and the IMF.

In the past, a source of friction between the IMF and the World Bank has arisen from the dominant role that short-term policies of the IMF could impose on long-run policies of the World Bank. In the future, although IMF officials resist the idea of becoming a long-term lender, their different time perspectives may cause less friction. Debtor countries dread that increased future collaboration between the IMF and the World Bank may give rise to cross-conditionality requirements, in which the restrictiveness of lending terms would be compounded. Although Brazilians perceive the United States as the dominant force in determining policies of both the World Bank and the IMF, they prefer the policies of the World Bank to those of the IMF.

## The United States and the Debt Crisis

If the "seal of approval" conveyed by an IMF loan does indeed have a multiplier effect in generating further loans from private financial institutions, the size of the multiplier is a matter of great interest. According to the managing director of the IMF, during 1983 and 1984, the IMF "unlocked about seven dollars of new loans and refinancing from commercial banks and governments" for every dollar lent to Brazil by the IMF.[49] The multiplier effect did not occur spontaneously, however. In the Brazilian case, "the IMF adopted a new approach of historical significance. Contrary to previous practice, whereby the IMF merely hoped that an adoption of a standby lending program would act as a seal of approval to encourage the return of foreign private lending, the IMF now explicitly told the private banks that if they did not provide new lending themselves, there would be no new IMF funds whatsoever."[50] From the outset of the debt crisis, it was chiefly U.S. banks that were mobilized by this pressure. In November of 1982, Brazilian Central Bank Governor Carlos Langoni emphasized the importance of spreading the risk of the financial rescue operation among the half-dozen main countries that were already committed. In the world banking community, however, Latin America was generally regarded as "an American problem." U.S. banks already had the largest exposure. They were faced with the technical difficulty of the potential conflict with banking regulatory authorities who might disapprove of further commitments to particular borrowers. On this point they received the personal encouragement of

Federal Reserve Board Chairman Paul Volcker, who gave specific assurance that bank supervisors would be "understanding."[51] In officially associating itself with the financial rescue effort in December of 1982, for the first time since 1977, the Reagan administration utilized an obscure Treasury resource, the Exchange Stabilization Fund, to provide short-term loans to Brazil. In addition to other motives, the U.S. government "at the highest political level" had decided to sponsor the rescue effort in an attempt to conciliate Latin American resentment against U.S. help to Britain during the Falklands war.[52]

Negotiations concerning the Brazilian debt were discussed in terms of an elastic vocabulary. In ascending order of severity, the term *refinancing* was used to describe a situation in which the borrower paid off one loan with the proceeds of another. *Restructuring* referred to lengthening the maturity of the debt, possibly by issuing securities to retire bank loans. *Rescheduling* referred to postponing repayment of the principal of the debt, while interest payments continued. A fee and a higher margin were usually imposed by the lender for this arrangement. *Default* referred to failure of the borrower to fulfill the terms of the loan, as defined by the lender. *Moratorium* was a declaration by the borrower that he would make no further payments for a certain interval. *Repudiation* was a declaration by the borrower that he did not intend either to service or repay the debt. By 1985, interest on Brazil's external debt amounted to US$12 billion annually. The extent of the burden of servicing the debt may be judged from the fact that between 1983 and 1992, in order to meet its interest payments without further borrowing, Brazil's trade surplus would have to average 4 percent of GNP. In comparison, Japan's unprecedented trade surplus in 1984 was less than 3 percent of GNP.

According to an IMF official, "Foreign banks were happy when Mexico defaulted, because every one of the foreign banks was thus locked in. When Brazil did not default, some banks have backed out."[53] As reported in the press, for example, in November of 1983 the number of Brazilian bank creditors was 830.[54] By October of 1985, it had declined to approximately 700.[55] Ironically, however, the very fact that the banks were reducing their exposure reduced their bargaining power with Brazil. In general, if Latin American debtors were to become convinced that no further financial inflows were forthcoming, they would have little incentive or ability to abide by their existing loan agreements.

In a cable to the U.S. State Department dated September 21, 1982, U.S. Ambassador to Brazil Langhorne Motley wrote, "Japanese banks are out of the market, European banks are scared, regional U.S. banks don't want to hear about Brazil, and major U.S. banks are proceeding with extreme caution." In November of 1982, following discussions between Morgan Guaranty Trust Company and Citibank, a four-part plan emerged for the financial rescue of Brazil by its international creditors. Project 1 proposed a "new money" loan facility amounting to US$4.4 billion. Project 2 proposed a rollover of loans amounting to US$4.4 billion falling due in 1983. Project 3 proposed maintenance of credit lines of US$10.3 billion for the finance of merchandise trade. Project 4 proposed restoration of an interbank facility with a target of US$10.5 billion in deposits by creditors in branches of Brazilian banks abroad. Morgan Guaranty was put in charge of project 1, Citibank was in charge of project 2, Chase Manhattan Bank was in charge of project 3, and Bankers Trust Company was in charge of project 4. Other banks joined separate committees for each of the projects respectively. Projects 1 and 4, new money and the interbank facility, were the most difficult projects of the rescue proposal. Project 3, short-term trade credits, was heavily oversubscribed. One reason for the generosity of the international bankers in subscribing to project 3 was their belief that declining imports into Brazil made it unlikely all these funds would ever be used. Moreover, trade finance is backed by physical collateral. Collectively, the four projects were known as "phase one"; in 1984 they were succeeded by four corresponding projects in "phase two."

One of the difficulties in fulfilling the targets of phase one was the attitude of some governments that this was "an American baby." Foreign bankers also were angered by what they regarded as a plan unilaterally imposed by the Americans. There was considerable haggling over the respective responsibilities of the various parties in sharing quotas and criticism of the "high handed" way in which the Morgan Guaranty Trust Company and Citibank had assumed leadership of the rescue effort. With regard to the interbank deposit project, there was an additional technical difficulty. The interbank market exists primarily for the purpose of enabling banks to temporarily dispose of excess liquidity by placing funds on very short term deposit with other banks or, conversely, to overcome very short term needs for additional funds. Interbank deposits are placed or borrowed for a period from overnight to a maximum of 1 year. Branches of Brazilian banks in New York, however, were bidding heavily in the interbank market for the purpose of providing medium-term funding to their head offices in Brazil; by this route; interbank loans became transformed into balance of payments loans. The risk of such loans was no longer determined by the credit standing of the borrowing institution, but rather by the credit worthiness of its parent country. In accordance with standard operating procedure, money-center banks need to be able to control the distribution of their exposure to troubled borrowers. But misuse of the interbank market, principally by Brazil, among others, made it impossible for them to do this. In the Brazilian case, interbank lines had to be regarded as part of Brazil's national debt.[56]

Japanese banks were generally perceived as followers rather than leaders in the renegotiation process. "They did not disagree with the fourteen members of the Advisory Committee. But they did not want to be up front.

Moreover, if one Japanese bank took a position, they all did the same, en bloc."[57] As observed by a Japanese diplomat, "When foreign debts are rescheduled, there are no dropouts among Japanese banks." This is an example of the headquarters country strategy in action. In one important case, moreover, the Japanese did more than merely go along with the majority. In mid-January of 1983, when efforts to implement project 1 were at an impasse, the Japanese banks broke the deadlock by coming forward as a group with a commitment of US$727 million in new money. In the case of project 4, almost half of the 455 banks that previously had placed significant interbank deposits in Brazilian banks refused to cooperate with the request to restore those deposits. Interbank lending is the easiest form of lending to curtail. Among the least cooperative were U.S. regional banks, as well as West German and Swiss banks. Again, the Japanese were blameless. There were two reasons for this. First, Japanese regional banks had relatively little international exposure; for them, fortunately, internationalization had come too late. The fact that minor regional banks were not involved in the renegotiation process placed the burden squarely on the shoulders of the Japanese city banks, which acted as a group. Ironically, this group behavior made it easier for Japan to appear to be cooperative in the rescue effort. Second, however, it should be added that their group action was instigated and coordinated by "guidance" from the Japanese Ministry of Finance. My informant added, "However, if the debtor is not performing according to the conditionality requirements of the IMF, then no Japanese bank will be authorized to grant one yen of additional loans."[58]

Japanese banks, it might be noted, were not enthusiastic about the policy of the Ministry of Finance. They wondered why they should be asked to increase their exposure to Latin America when U.S. regional banks were not doing so. Clearly, the U.S. stake in performing the Brazilian rescue was greater and more direct than that of Japan. Why should Japanese banks be dragged into it? It is significant that, all other things being equal, the conservative Ministry of Finance would be the first to acknowledge the pertinence of these questions. However, all other things were not equal. Japan was in the process of establishing its leadership position on the international stage. It was shifting from low posture to high posture. The Ministry of Finance was helping to pave the way for Japan's emergence as a headquarters nation. The development of Japan's financial role in Latin America was an essential complement to its projected industrial and management role in the region. In "flexibly" interpreting the rule that overseas lending could not exceed 20 percent of the net worth of any individual bank, the Ministry of Finance had not suddenly become frivolous. There was, moreover, a bureaucratic principle at stake. In accordance with their own role in the implicit headquarters country scenario, it was essential for the bureaucrats to remind the private bankers as to who was boss.

At the end of 1984, the United States was Brazil's principal bilateral creditor, accounting for 26.1 percent of its external medium- and long-term debt. Japan accounted for 5.9 percent.[59] Among the multilateral creditors, outstanding claims of the IMF amounted to US$4.25 billion.[60] Between December of 1977 and June of 1982, claims on Brazil alone by the nine largest U.S. banks amounted to approximately 40 percent of their capital assets.[61] Thus the banks had their own "solvency" crisis, being enormously vulnerable to delinquency or writeoffs of their loans to Brazil. At the same time, the profitability of these loans was correspondingly enormous. As compared with Japanese banks in Brazil, "U.S. banks are much more profitable. Japanese banks are more hesitant than U.S. banks."[62] For example, Brazil has long been the most profitable overseas operation for Citicorp. In 1982, Brazil produced over a fifth of Citicorp's profits, although it accounted for only 5 percent of the bank's total assets. In 1983, Brazil again accounted for 19.5 percent of Citibank's total profits, which was almost four times its overall return on assets.

From the creditor's point of view, these profits were commensurate with the risk of lending to a distressed borrower. From the Brazilian point of view, they were exploitative. It also was observed that "ultimately, the cost of bailout funds supplied by the IMF or by governments will be borne by Western taxpayers. If it is to give more credits, either direct or through such agencies as the IMF, the U.S. government must require at least that American banks limit their interest rates and fees from these loans and deposit the income in loan-loss reserves rather than pay it out in dividends."[63] Another remark, attributed to Barton Biggs, managing director of the Morgan Stanley investment banking firm, was as follows: "Somehow the conventional wisdom of 200 million South Americans sweating away in the hot sun for the next decade to earn the interest on their debt so Citicorp can raise its dividend twice a year does not square with my image of political reality."[64]

In January of 1983, Brazil was offering "sweeteners" in the form of commitment fees and higher interest rates to foreign banks that would agree to extend interbank lending and restore credit lines to the Brazilian government and private borrowers. Most reschedulings were made at "crisis" rates of 2 percent or more above the cost of funds to the lending institutions. In October of 1983, for the first time, creditor banks agreed to more lenient terms by reducing loan margins one-eighth of a percent and extending maturities by a year. U.S. bankers acknowledged privately that concessions of this sort were motivated by an attempt to drive a wedge between debtor countries and forestall the formation of a debtors' cartel.[65]

On the other hand, I was told by a nisei Brazilian at the Central Bank that "some politicians in Brazil do not want the debt to be renegotiated because in that even they would lose their cut of foreign bank profits. All the foreign banks make payoffs. The U.S. banks pay off more than Japan. They are also more efficient. The Americans come direct to the point: they make one big payoff. The Japanese are more polite and roundabout. They make many small gifts. Payoffs are not so dangerous in Brazil. If a person is rich, he is allowed to do anything."[66]

On June 27, 1936, speaking of his own generation, Franklin D. Roosevelt made a dramatic pledge in accepting the nomination for his second term as president. "Of this generation," he said, "much is expected. This generation of Americans has a rendezvous with destiny." Although times have changed, much is still expected from the United States, especially by developing countries. In international affairs, whereas formerly the United States suppressed its short-term interests in favor of its long-term interests, in recent times it has sacrificed the latter in favor of the former. This is the opposite of Japanese strategy. Moreover, it has generated a conflict of interests between the United States and other countries, including Brazil.

Brazilians are sensitive to intimations of conflict between their own national interests and those of the United States. A looming area of conflict concerns plans for development of the Cerrado, a vast area about five times the size of Japan, strategically located in central and western Brazil. The Cerrado has immense importance as a prospective source of agricultural, livestock, and forestry products. It is highly suitable for merchanized, large-scale farming and will enable Brazil to match the United States as a granary for the world. Together with Brazilian plans for alternative energy resources and other types of import substitution, moreover, it plays a key role in terms of the export-promotion policy for overcoming the debt crisis and achieving sustained economic growth. In view of the importance of this matter, a speech delivered in Rio de Janeiro on August 11, 1983 by John R. Block, U.S. secretary of agriculture, was remarkably inopportune. Mr. Block said that he had just visited the Cerrado and was extremely impressed. "However," he said, "I have to admit the visit also left me worried. World markets are already being swamped by overproduction. . . . The world is on the verge of technological breakthroughs that will push agricultural output up more than anything yet seen. . . . I am concerned about the effect these tremendous increases will have on the international marketing system in the future. . . . The U.S. poultry and soybean industries are even now being affected by unfair competition from Brazil and other countries."

The implied as well as the overt hostility of Mr. Block's anti-Cerrado speech did more than offend Brazilian sensibilities. It also struck at a vital area of Japanese collaboration with Brazil and at a taproot of what was described earlier as a scenario for Japan's emergence as a headquarters country. By means of cooperation between the Brazilian and Japanese governments, Japan has been a pioneer in the development of the Cerrado. The two governments signed an agreement whereby the Japan International Cooperation Agency (JICA) was charged with commissioning an assessment of the potential of the Cerrado region. The study was performed by the International Development Center of Japan (IDJC) and issued in July of 1979. Subsequently, the Japan–Brazil Cooperation Program for Agricultural Development of the Cerrado (PRODECER) provided the means for establishment of CAMPO, a Cerrado management company, in which the Brazilian Agrindustrial Participation Company (BRASAGRO) acquired 51 percent of the shares and the Japan–Brazil Agricultural Development Cooperation (JADECO) acquired 49 percent of the shares. For Japan, the Cerrado project is the core of the Asian port concept which proposes a linkage between a southwest Atlantic port in Brazil and a port to be constructed in southwest Japan, the latter to have multiple functions of storage, handling, and processing of raw materials. These superports are to be serviced by mammoth supertankers carrying ore and grain. From Japan, the products are to be transshiped to destinations in Asia. The significant point is that the Asian port concept is itself a component of the Global Infrastructure Fund (GIF) proposal discussed earlier. In conception and pending implementation, the GIF proposal is central to the headquarters country scenario. Mr. Block's anti-Cerrado speech implicitly attacked that scenario.

As summarized by Albert Fishlow, the attitude of the Reagan administration toward Brazil was "informed more by the principles underlying our foreign policy as a whole" than by consideration for the particular circumstances of Brazil. "First, the dominant concern of the United States is its strategic capability vis-à-vis the Soviet Union. Second, North-South issues have their solution in free trade and free flows of capital, both of which are to be exclusively determined by marked forces. Third, political stability in Latin America not only contributes to faster economic growth by attracting private resources but is also necessary in order to deflect a new potential wave of Soviet and Cuban-inspired subversion. Fourth, diplomacy is to concentrate on matters of bilateral concern, with only nominal support for multilateral procedures and even less for the substance of global issues like nuclear proliferation, the law of the sea, and the international economy. From these axioms the specific corollaries of the Reagan administration's policy toward Brazil can be deduced."[67]

An episode that illustrated Fishlow's argument occurred in February of 1984 when during a visit to Brazil by U.S. Secretary of State George Shultz, a memorandum of understanding on military-industrial cooperation between the Brazilian and U.S. governments was signed. The memorandum provided for the transfer of sophisticated U.S. military technology to Brazil, but in doing so, it brought Brazil under the purview of the U.S. Export Administration Act and the Arms Export Control Act, which on a global basis regulate the export and re-export of U.S. military equipment as well as goods and technologies subject to "dual use" (civilian or military). Any U.S. arms exported to Brazil or armaments produced in Brazil with components or technology of U.S. origin are subject to controls under these laws. The Shultz memorandum, accordingly, was construed in Brazil as imposing, for the first time, restrictions on Brazil's export of arms, a source of income amounting to about US$2 billion a year. The agreement caused an uproar of protest from the Brazilian arms industry. In addition to the military-industrial memorandum, a nuclear pact also was signed releasing Brazil from its previous obligation to purchase nuclear fuel only from the United States for its first nuclear reactor, Angra-1. (Brazil has not signed the Nuclear Non-Proliferation Treaty.) However, Mr. Shultz was not successful in attempting to persuade the Brazilians to relax their strict restraints on foreign investment in retail banking and computers. His argument that Brazil should rely more on foreign investment and less on foreign loans annoyed the Brazilians, who responded with complaints about U.S. import protectionism.

In the trade field, Brazil has many grievances against the United States. By increasing the necessity for augmenting its export income, the debt crisis has accelerated the appearance of Brazil in world markets as a U.S. competitor. The famous "chicken war" is an example. Brazil has been an important international supplier of frozen poultry only since 1980. However, by 1982, it had become the world's second largest supplier, behind France and ahead of the United States. In June of 1984, Brazilian authorities complained that supported by the extension of very favorable credits to Egypt, the United States was threatening Brazil's sales of poultry to that country. In the case of tobacco, having exported none a decade earlier, the value of Brazilian exports in 1983 was US$0.5 billion, as compared with sales of US$1.5 billion by the United States. This incursion into the U.S. export market has been regarded with hostility by American growers. In consequence, the U.S. import duty on Brazilian tobacco was doubled to 36 cents a pound in 1983. The situation is complicated by the fact that thirteen of the nineteen tobacco companies buying in Brazil are U.S. companies.[68]

Part of the Brazilian predicament in expanding exports in accordance with the exigencies of the debt crisis is the fact that the more excellent its export performance, the more export earnings expand the money supply, which is inflationary. Another element of the same predicament is that the nation has been impelled to increase the trade surplus not only by expanding exports, but also by restricting imports. In 1983, for example, imports of fertilizer were restricted. In consequence, smaller subsequent harvests required Brazil to import more food. Food shortages and inflated food prices have been a leading cause of social unrest.

The dominance of U.S. bankers in negotiating the terms of loan renewals and debt restructuring has, in effect, cast them in the role of agents of U.S. foreign economic policy. The question arises whether at this juncture, U.S. private interests are consistent with the public interest in the policies being imposed on debtor countries. In analyses of LDC country risk, for example, bankers are prone to lend to the borrower they consider to be most secure, namely, the government. If they lend to the private sector, they demand a government guarantee. But it is embarrassing for the government to guarantee the payment of scarce foreign currency to foreign bankers when it is restricting imports of the essentials of national existence. In order to preclude such embarrassment, there exists a predisposition on the part of LDC governments to nationalize weak private-sector firms in order to justify providing them with foreign currency. Thus contrary to established U.S. foreign policy, private banks promote public rather than private enterprise abroad. In the context of the debt crisis, the argument that banking is too important to be left in the hands of private bankers is explicit in the demand by President Jose Sarney for a "political solution" to the crisis "beyond the influence of market forces."[69]

## Remedies for the Debt Crisis

Among the creditors, debtors, and outside observers of Brazil's debt crisis, both optimists and pessimists are to be found. When he was presiding as minister of planning Antonio Delfim Netto demurred that while the Bank of Brazil "is facing difficulties, it is not *in* difficulties."[70] In a somber reflection on country risk, George Soros, a New York fund manager, observed, "Sovereign nations cannot go bankrupt, but as history has amply demonstrated, they may fail to pay."

Early in 1983, Brazil signed a 3-year agreement with the IMF, placing itself under the IMF's tutelage for the implementation of an adjustment program. However, it repeatedly failed to meet the targets it proposed to achieve. Wishful thinking was evident in the successive and rapid revisions of its letters of intent. The third letter of intent, issued only 8 months following the agreement, was so unrealistic that it prompted the resignation of Carlos Langoni, governor of the Central Bank. Midway through the 3-year agreement scheduled to run through February of 1986, Brazil had doubled its annual inflation rate and increased both its monetary expansion rate and its nominal public deficit. In January of 1985, the seventh letter of intent was delivered in Washington; at the time of delivery, however, the Brazilian authorities knew that they had already breached its requirements in the preceding month. The managing director of the IMF notified Brazil's creditor banks that "the nature and size of these deviations are not consistent with the agreed program." Negotiations with the creditors were thereupon suspended.

Nevertheless, the IMF itself was prone to wishful thinking. Speaking of Brazil with reporters at the conclusion of the IMF annual meeting in Washington in September of 1983, Jacques de Larosiere declared, "Economic policy decisions that have been taken since June in the areas of prices, subsidies, taxation, public spending, and monetary policy are extremely impressive." And the improvement in Brazil's trade balance—based largely on import restrictions—was "remarkable, not to say spectacular."[71] The IMF was satisfied, moreover, with its own policies. In an address before the International Monetary Conference on June 4, 1984, "The managing director stressed that . . . the problems are manageable. The strategy that has served so well in the past will continue to be used in the future."[72] That strategy, however, as was abundantly clear then and increasingly so in the course of time, was largely ad hoc and lacking in long-term rationale.

Wishful thinking at the IMF was evident from the fact that its technicians had made wholly inadequate and politically unrealistic calculations from the outset of the 3-year agreement with Brazil until its rejection of the seventh letter of intent. Perhaps the IMF had been persuaded to be "flexible" on the assumption that American banks had too much at stake for them to allow a financial collapse to occur. It was wishful thinking that prompted the IMF to repeatedly extend emergency loans to Brazil prior to reaching a firm and viable agreement on the adjustment program. It was wishful thinking on the part of the banks to which the proceeds of these loans were recycled in the form of interest payments to then regard their loans to Brazil as still sound. It was wishful thinking on the part of their accountants to report these loans as highly profitable, although they were backed up by inadequate loss reserves.

New York bankers, notably those represented on the fourteen-bank creditors' advisory committee, were most vulnerable and thus most prone to wishful thinking. In November of 1984, William R. Rhodes, a senior vice president of Citibank and chairman of the committee, announced, "The worst is probably behind us." The same sentiment was expressed by a Citibank official in Brazil. "The period of maximum stress is over," he declared.[73] There were no similar comments from the Japanese.

From the bankers' point of view, in the search for solutions, the idea of capitalizing Brazil's interest obligations was regarded as radical. In the first place, in order to arrange the conversion, American banking regulations required the loans to be classified as "nonperforming." Japanese and European banks were not subject to this requirement. Second, however, for Japanese and American banks alike, capitalization of interest would tend to puncture the illusion that the principal of the loans would eventually be repaid.

The spectrum of proposed remedies for the debt crisis is wide. American, Japanese, and Brazilian views are overlapping, however, with sharp differences of emphasis. In general, the U.S. approach favors a market solution, while the Japanese and Brazilian approaches are predisposed in favor of nonmarket solutions. In the area of overlap, the extent to which government intervention is consistent with a market solution is something the economists enjoy arguing about.

The U.S. proposal for a solution to the Latin American debt crisis presented by Treasury Secretary James W. Baker at the IMF–World Bank annual meeting in Seoul on October 8, 1985 was in accord with the official American preference for a market approach. Baker emphasized that the Latin American nations should reduce the role of the state in their economies and promote private enterprise; they should allow foreign exchange rates to be settled by market forces; they should adopt tax policies conducive to private investment; and they should encourage direct investment by foreigners. From the Japanese point of view, an authoritative statement was made by Tomoo Miyazaki, senior managing director of the Bank of Tokyo. "Markets tend to react without long-term perspective," he said. For example, with regard to the widespread use of the secondary market for bank loans, "It is not advisable to leave the assessment of loan values to market mechanisms." More generally, with regard to market control over bank policies, "It is important to disclose necessary information as regards bank credit engagements and exposure in problem countries, but to leave the banks' business policies to market control through such disclosure is not practical." Identifying areas of agreement concerning the debt renegotiations, Mr. Miyazaki specified rescheduling of the debt principal, debtor country adjustment within IMF programs, and the need for new finance from the IMF and the creditor banks. He added, however, "Though this scheme of renegotiation has been successful so far, the present debt crisis management scheme has a shortcoming in that adjustment programs tend to force the debtor countries to achieve the performance criteria in a short-term period at the cost of potential better economic performance in the long run. Fundamental approaches to the debt problem should be determined in a longer-term perspective with the aim of securing social, political, and financial viability as a whole. We must try to find a way to harmonize debtor countries' long-term needs with IMF's short-term goals."[74]

At a conference on the international debt crisis in October of 1983, Professor Carlos Langoni, who had resigned a month earlier as governor of the Central Bank of Brazil, was highly critical of the workings of the international market place. He described as irrational the sudden reversal in the banks' concept of risk, which he charged with precipitating Brazil's financial crisis.[75] One of Brazil's leading economists, Celso Furtado, argued for a total break with the IMF and a 25-year moratorium on foreign debt payments.[76] Trade and Industry Minister Joao Camilo Penna called for renegotiation of both principal and interest. Without it, he said, Brazil's GNP would have to grow 4 percent annually just to meet interest payments.[77] Among the more whimsical proposals, considering its source, was that of Senator Roberto Campos, who asserted that Brazil should pay its debts in cruzeiros rather than in dollars.[78]

As mentioned earlier, a "political solution" was the nonmarket remedy demanded by President Jose Sarney. From a Brazilian point of view, it was political decisions in the White House that made the United States far more culpable than Brazil for the outbreak of the debt crisis. Accordingly, the crisis must be cured at the political level. Brazilian officials have not specified in detail what they mean by a political solution. As a purely statistical matter, regardless of any other relief Brazil might be granted, the industrialized countries could not realistically expect repayment unless they are prepared to accept trade deficits with Brazil for decades to come. In the meantime, as explained by Finance Minister Ernane Galveas, "We're not going to pay our debt at all. The bankers know that, official financial institutions know that, and governments know that, too. What we are going to do is keep up our interest payments, within our possibilities. When we can't pay the interest, they [the banks] lend us the money and we pay it."[79] President Sarney's rhetoric assumed an increasingly uncompromising tone as well. In August of 1985, he declared, "We cannot accept intolerance from international financial organizations to impose on the country an unnecessary recessive policy."[80] Shortly thereafter, he described the IMF as "an auditing firm that imposes terms Brazil can't live with."[81] In terms of the way the austerity program was implemented, there was a further change to be noted. During the 1983–1984 fiscal year, the federal companies most severely affected by budget cuts were those engaged in research, teaching, health services, and regional development. Their budgets were cut 12 percent, while those of federal companies engaged in directly productive activities were cut only 5 percent. In a television address to the nation in July of 1985, however, President Sarney declared that "our major option is social. No cuts will be made in official education, health, housing, or food supply programs."

At the political level, incidentally, decisions may not necessarily redound to Brazil's advantage. In October of 1983, Prime Minister Margaret Thatcher and Finance Minister Nigel Lason insisted that Britain would not subscribe to a US$2.5 billion multigovernment loan for Brazil. British bankers confided that this was to "teach Brazil a lesson" for its denial during the war with Argentina of landing rights to British airplanes en route to the Falklands.[82] The Brazilian government's wish for a political solution has not induced it to endorse the idea of a "debtors' cartel." Apart from other considerations, the diverse circumstances of Latin American debtors would preclude the formation of a common bargaining position.

From a Brazilian point of view, as expressed by President Sarney, the correct operational approach would be to abandon efforts to manage the debt problem as a crisis issue and to resolve it instead in the context of economic growth. Rhetorically, the United States and the IMF have come to agree with Brazil on this point. However, their views conflict with those of Brazil on how economic growth is to be achieved. Typically, debtors seeking the IMF's assistance have been required to accept its standard prescription, including deflationary monetary and fiscal policies, currency devaluation, and trade liberalization, all within a short-term timetable. In July of 1986, however, in rescheduling the terms of Mexico's US$97.6 billion foreign debt, there was a perceptible softening of the IMF's conditionality rules. The emphasis on austerity was reduced. This reflected a shift in the balance of power between debtor and creditors in favor of the former. According to a Mexican government economist, "The threat to suspend payments was the key to the success of the negotiations."[83]

In the accord with Mexico, the IMF agreed to a "cautiously expansionary" policy within a medium-term rather than a short-term period of adjustment. It provided for continuing large budget deficits. Moreover, a commitment was made to provide Mexico with further financing if its domestic growth should fail to recover or if oil prices should fall below $9 a barrel. IMF flexibility in the accord with Mexico reflected its concern for social and political stability in that country. This no doubt establishes a precedent for its future relations with other debtor nations. However, the IMF did not wholly abandon its standard prescription. Mexico remained subject to IMF surveillance. There was no forgiveness of debt or debt service: if Mexico became poorer, it would simply be allowed to owe more. Moreover, Mexico agreed to carry out sweeping structural changes in its economy. In these respects, IMF conditionality was similar to the conditionality of the Baker plan, which called for "fundamental reforms," including greater reliance on the private sector, trade liberalization, encouragement of direct foreign investment, and market-oriented exchange rates.

The Brazilians were very interested in the Mexican accord. However, Finance Minister Dilson Funaro asserted that so far as IMF monitoring was concerned, "never again" would an IMF mission set foot on Brazilian soil.[84] Furthermore, in July of 1986, Mr. Funaro staked out his negotiating position by serving notice that in 1987 Brazil would seek to restrict its foreign debt service to 2.5 percent of GDP. In 1988, it intended to rescue the ratio to 2 percent of GDP. In 1985, the cost of financing Brazil's total foreign debt of US$104 was 5.1 percent of GDP; it was expected to decline to about 4.6 percent in 1986.

In July of 1986, an interim agreement was signed between Brazil and foreign creditor banks, without IMF supervision. It postponed US$15.5 billion in principal payments due in 1985 and 1986 and maintained US$15.5 billion in trade credits and interbank facilities on behalf of Brazil. Foreign creditor banks and their governments, however, continued to insist that as a condition for long-term rescheduling of its debts, Brazil would have to submit to IMF surveillance of its economic policies.

It is interesting that in assuming responsibility for implementation of the Baker plan, the U.S. government escalated the commitments and the dialogue between Brazil and its creditors from the private to the official level. This conforms with and emphasizes the trend toward bureaucratization of international economic relations that is a key feature of Japan's geopolitical scenario. In their own approach to the debt issue, the Japanese have produced no "Baker plan." Moreover, they are not necessarily enamoured of the classroom free-market ideology that it urges on Brazil. At the same time, they are not averse to taking advantage of any market-opening measures that the United States, in the assertion of its leadership role, might succeed in imposing on Brazil. Of their own accord, however, the Japanese do not address the debt issue ideologically. They are anxious to see Brazil achieve economic and political stability. Whether it does so by means of economic planning or the free market, by means of democracy or dictatorship, is a matter of indifference to them. In further contrast to the United States, the Japanese have no axe to grind with the Brazilians concerning military security matters. In this respect, as well as in their mutual desire to reduce the degree of their dependence on the United States, Japan and Brazil have a relatively benign environment in which to discuss the debt issue. Moreover, inasmuch as the proportion of Japanese government loans and government-guaranteed loans constitutes a higher proportion of total Japanese lending to Brazil than correspondingly holds true of the United States, Japan's long-term national interests predominate in its encounter with Brazil, as contrasted with the short-term sectional interests that predominate on the American side.

## Notes

1. Interview with Lawrence B. Smith, senior vice president, Citibank, N.A., in Sao Paulo, July 5, 1984.

2. Interview with Ricardo R. de Araujo Cintra, chefe, Deparamento de Economia, Federacao das Industrias do Estado de Sao Paulo (FIESP), in Sao Paulo, July 4, 1984. Principal sources of statistics in Brazil include CACEX (Foreign Trade Department of Bank of Brazil), SEST (a department of SEPLAN, the Planning Secretariat), IBGE (Brazilian Institute of Geography and Statistics), and FIRCE (Departamento de Fiscalizacao e Registro de Capitais Estrangeiros, Banco Central do Brasil).

3. World Bank, *Annual Reports, 1984*, p. 155.

4. Inter-American Development Bank, *External Public Debt of the Latin American Countries*, July 1985, Table 1.

5. Reasons for statistical discrepancies include nonuniformity of sources from which data were collected, differences in coverage (registered versus unregistered debt, government-guaranteed versus nonguaranteed debt, disbursed versus undisbursed funds, etc.), and differences in timing among the data sources.

6. During the first half of the 1980s, the foreign debts of the ten major LDC debtors continued to increase. On average, their debt-to-export ratios increased from 257 percent in 1982 to 308 percent in 1985. Data from Morgan Guaranty Trust Company.

7. Data from Morgan Guaranty Trust Company.

8. Morgan Guaranty Trust Company, *World Financial Markets*, August 1986.

9. In 1982, OPEC actually reversed the flow of funds by withdrawing about $18 billion of its deposits from international banks.

10. Paul A. Volcker, chairman, Board of Governors of theFederal Reserve System, in statement before the Committee on Banking, Finance and Urban Affairs, U.S. House of Representatives, Table III, February 2, 1983.

11. Interview with Lawrence G. Smith, senior vice president, Citibank, N.A., in Sao Paulo, July 5, 1984.

12. *Business Week,* May 16, 1983, p. 124.

13. *The Economist,* February 18, 1984, p. 16.

14. Ernane Galveas, minister of finance, *The Economic-Financial Policy of Brazil* (Brasilia: Central Bank of Brazil, 1982), p. 15.

15. Michael Dooley, William Helkie, Ralph Tryon, and John Underwood, *An Analysis of External Debt Positions of Eight Developing Countries through 1990* (Washington, D.C.: Federal Reserve Board, International Finance Discussion Papers, No. 227, August 1983).

16. Interview with Yoichi Yabu, senior divison officer, Corporate Planning Division, C. Itoh & Company, Ltd., in Tokyo, July 14, 1983.

17. Interview in Rio de Janeiro, July 23, 1984. Professor Tavares is an influential economist and a close adviser of Ulysses Guimaraes, president of the Partido Movimento Democratico Brasileiro (PMDB), the senior party in the ruling Democratic Alliance of the Sarney administration.

18. *The Economist,* July 7, 1984, p. 30.

19. *Financial Times,* June 7, 1984.

20. *Journal of Commerce,* September 12, 1984.

21. Interview with Jose Botafogo Goncalves, secretario de cooperacao economica e tecnica internacional, Secretaria de Planejamento, in Brasilia, August 8, 1983.

22. *Gazeta Mercantil,* April 9, 1984.

23. *The Economist,* May 5, 1984, p. 19.

24. Interview with J. A. de Macedo-Soares, chief, Commercial Divison, Ministry of External Relations, in Brasilia, July 12, 1984.

25. *Journal of Commerce,* June 28, 1984.

26. Unpublished manuscript, dated July of 1984.

27. *The Wall Street Journal,* April 26, 1984.

28. Interview with J. A. de Macedo-Soares, chief, Commercial Division, Ministry of External Relations, in Brasilia, July 12, 1984.

29. *The Wall Street Journal,* August 7, 1985.

30. *The Journal of Commerce,* May 8, 1985.

31. *Gazeta Mercantil,* April 9, 1984.

32. Manual Guitian, Exchange and Trade Relations Department, International Monetary Fund, *Conditionality* (Washington, D.C.: International Monetary Fund, 1981), p. 8.

33. See graph in International Monetary Fund, *Annual Report, 1985* (Washington, D.C.: International Monetary Fund, 1985), p. 68.

34. International Monetary Fund, *IMF Survey,* August 26, 1985, p. 261.

35. A. W. Clausen, "Third World Debt and Global Recovery," The 1983 Jodidi Lecture at the Center for International Affairs, Harvard University, February 24, 1983.

36. Interview in Washington, D.C., June 10, 1983.

37. Address by J. de Larosiere, managing director of the International Monetary Fund, before the International Monetary Conference, in Philadelphia, June 4, 1984.

38. Yasushi Watanabe, "The Debt Crisis in Historical Perspective," *Tokyo Financial Review*, Vol. 10, No. 1, January 1985.

39. International Monetary Fund, *Annual Report, 1985*, pp. 25–26, 31–33.

40. In September of 1985, the Reagan administration arranged a meeting of the "Group of Five" leading industrial countries for the purpose of coordinating foreign exchange intervention against the overvalued dollar.

41. Mario Henrique Simonsen, "Critical Factors of the Government Program," *Brazilian Index*, January 1983.

42. Article quoted in *Latin America Regional Reports: Brazil*, April 20, 1984.

43. Interview with Alberto Sozin Furuguem, head, Economics Department, Banco Central do Brasil, in Brasilia, August 11, 1983.

44. Interview with Shigeaki Ueki, president of Petrobras, in Rio de Janeiro, August 15, 1983.

45. *Financial Times*, August 12, 1985.

46. Interview with Carlos Alberto Amorim, Jr., coordenador adjunto, Ministerio da Fazenda, Coordenadoria de Assuntos Internacionais, in Brasilia, August 10, 1983.

47. J. de Larosiere, managing director, International Monetary Fund, *Does the Fund Impose Austerity?* (Washington, D.C.: International Monetary Fund, June 1984).

48. World Bank, *Annual Report, 1984*, p. 140; and World Bank, *Annual Report, 1985*, p. 146.

49. Remarks by J. de Larosiere, managing director of the International Monetary Fund, before a symposium organized by the Federation of Swedish Industries, in Stockholm, February 6, 1985.

50. William R. Cline, *International Debt: Systematic Risk and Policy Response* (Washington, D.C.: Institute for International Economics, 1984).

51. *Financial Times*, October 13, 1983.

52. *Financial Times*, November 25, 1982.

53. Interview with J. Horst Struckmeyer, director, Atlantic Division, Western Hemisphere Department, International Monetary Fund, in Washington, June 6, 1983.

54. *Journal of Commerce*, November 10, 1983.

55. *Financial Times*, October 4, 1985.

56. The interbank market, which includes most of the Euromarket, is a pool of funds amounting to about US$1 trillion. In 1981, a Bank of England study found that Japanese banks in London were raising three-quarters of their funds in the interbank market.

57. Interview with Lawrence G. Smith, senior vice president, Citibank, N.A., in Sao Paulo, July 5, 1984.

58. Interview with Motomichi Ikawa, assistant director, Short Term Capital Division, International Finance Bureau, Ministry of Finance, in Tokyo, July 18, 1983. It is the International Finance Section of the Ministry of Finance that is in charge of Japanese renegotiation of the Brazilian debt. The Bank of Japan enters only tangentially and makes no policy in this matter. Thus in their perennial sparring for position, the debt crisis may have enhanced the role of the Ministry of Finance in relation to that of the Bank of Japan.

59. Data from Central Bank of Brazil.

60. Data from Morgan Guaranty Trust Company, *World Financial Markets,* September-October 1985.

61. Statement by Paul A. Volcker, chairman, Board of Governors of the Federal Reserve System, before the Committee on Banking, Finance and Urban Affairs, U.S. House of Representatives, February 2, 1983.

62. Interview with Yasuharu Mizutani, diretor executivo, Banco de Tokyo S.A., in Rio de Janeiro, July 17, 1984.

63. *Business week,* June 6, 1983.

64. Darrell Delamaide, *Debt Shock: The Inside Story of the Crisis that Threatens the World's Banks and Stock Markets* (Garden City, N.J.: Doubleday, 1984).

65. *Financial Times,* June 8, 1984.

66. Interview with Yoji Yoshihara, coordenador, Departamento de Fiscalizacao e Registro de Capitais Estrangeiros (FIRCE), Banco Central do Brasil, in Brasilia, July 10, 1984.

67. Albert Fishlow, "The United States and Brazil: The Case of the Missing Relationship," *Foreign Affairs,* Spring 1982, p. 918.

68. *Financial Times,* August 9, 1984.

69. Address by President Jose Sarney to the Council on Foreign Relations, in New York, September 24, 1985.

70. *Journal of Commerce,* December 16, 1982.

71. *Gazeta Mercantil,* October 3, 1983.

72. International Monetary Fund, *IMF Survey,* June 18, 1984.

73. Interview with Lawrence G. Smith, senior vice prsident, Citibank, N.A., in Sao Paulo, July 5, 1984.

74. Tomoo Miyazaki, "Bank Lending to Developing Countries and a Possible Solution to the Debt Problems," *Tokyo Financial Review,* Vol. 10, No. 2, February 1985.

75. *Journal of Commerce,* October 6, 1983.

76. *Financial Times,* September 29, 1983.

77. *Journal of Commerce,* December 1, 1983.

78. *Gazeta Mercantil,* September 24, 1984.

79. *Gazeta Mercantil,* July 30, 1984.

80. *Journal of Commerce,* August 12, 1985.

81. *Business Week,* September 9, 1985.

82. *The Wall Street Journal,* October 19, 1983.

83. *Journal of Commerce,* August 5, 1986.

84. *Gazeta Mercantil,* April 7, 1986.

# 7
# Comparative Positions: The United States and Japan in Brazil

I n the past, it has been common for countries in Latin America to seek a "special relationship" with some major industrial nation outside the region. Argentina, for example, once tied itself to the United Kingdom and then later to the United States. In the case of the United States and Brazil, a special relationship has been conspicuous by its absence. Presumably, such a relationship should be based on common or complementary objectives. On that score, however, "economic development remains the prime Brazilian objective, and there we are insensitive and even in active opposition." Not only do priorities of the Reagan administration "resurrect U.S. security concerns of the cold war at the expense of traditional Brazilian economic development objectives, it is also seemingly blind to the profound internal transition Brazil is undergoing."[1] From a Brazilian point of view, however, a "correct" attitude on the part of the United States might not be a sufficient condition. "By virtue of events since World War II, the United States is no longer the dominant world actor. Indeed, no single nation can any longer presume to play such a role. Therefore, Brazil should not associate itself exclusively with any one superpower. We associate with all of them and dilute the predominance of any one of them. We should benefit from their conflict."[2] As seen by an interested observer in General Motors Corporation, the Brazilians have indeed been following that policy: "For the past 15 years or so, the Brazilians have been consciously and deliberately playing off the United States against Japan, as well as against Germany and other Europeans."[3]

## Foreign Investment in Brazil: The United States and Japan

In terms of its giant dimensions and enormous natural endowment, Brazil ranks as a major country in the world economy. It still has far to go, however, along the path of economic development. It feels itself to be an innocent victim of some of the difficulties it has encountered along the path. Moreover, while wishing to be regarded as the peer of other major nations, it also feels entitled to the immunities and exemptions conceded to developing nations. These schizoid feelings are reflected in the inconsistencies of its trade and foreign investment policies. The United States, having difficulties of its own, has put Brazil on the defensive with regard to these inconsistencies and has brought the issues into the open, while Japan has refrained from doing so. Moreover, U.S. defensive policies concerning its declining industries conflict with Brazil's defensive policies concerning its emerging industries. As defined by a Brazilian, the rationale of Brazil's development policy contemplates a negotiated division of labor between advanced and developing countries. "Advanced countries must leave certain activities for the LDCs," he said.[4] From a Japanese point of view, this accords perfectly with MITI's concept of an evolving division of labor in the world economy in which the headquarters role would be assigned to Japan. It also accords with the possibility that in the event of progressively increasing restrictions on U.S. imports from Japan, the latter could retaliate by shifting its procurement of primary products in favor of Brazil.

Brazilian development objectives are codified in the statement of purposes of its National Economic and Social Development Bank (BNDES): "The BNDES system has three basic objectives: to continue the country's economic and social development process, lessen the regional and social imbalances in income, and strengthen the Brazilian-controlled private company. . . . In its field of activity, the BNDES contributes also to the decentralization policy of the country's industrial growth."[5] The aim of BNDES to "strengthen the Brazilian-controlled private company" is not exactly identical with the intention of Article 2 of Law No. 4131, which states that "foreign capital invested in the country will receive identical judicial treatment as that given to national capital, under equal conditions, and any discrimination not specifically provided for in this law is forbidden."

The two basic laws governing foreign capital in Brazil are Law No. 4131 of September of 1962 and Law No. 4390 of August 29, 1964, both of which are subject to regulations specified in Decree Law No. 55,762 of 1965. Foreign investment is prohibited in the following activities:[6]

Exploration and mining of ore deposits and other mineral reserves and the development of electric and atomic power

Exploration and production of petroleum, except by means of risk contract

Coastal trade and shipping of merchandise

Ownership and management of newspapers and magazines, etc. and of television of radio

Ownership of property in rural areas and of businesses near the national borders

Securities market

Fishing industry

Post office and telegraph

Airlines with concessions for domestic flights

Financial institutions (except for minority holdings)

Aerospace industry

For various reasons—such as the difference in the volume, distribution, and later vintage of their investments in Brazil—the Japanese complain less (or at least less openly) than the Americans about the nature of these restrictions and the administrative procedures that apply to such investment as is permitted. In principle, such as, for example, in Article 2 of Law No. 4131, the Brazilian government looks with favor or direct foreign investment. In practice, many of its administrative procedures have been hostile to it. A great deal of discretion lies in the hands of the Central Bank, which exercises it restrictively in interpreting the investment laws. Unregistered direct investment cannot be repatriated, nor can dividends on such investment be remitted. The Central Bank generally permits registration only of machinery and equipment, not of intangible assets. Sometimes permission for remittance of interest payments on loans has been suspended. Such suspension is doubly hostile to foreign capital inasmuch as Central Bank regulations are conducive to the inflow of capital in the form of loans rather than of equity funds. Profits on equity capital may be remitted free of tax up to a limit of 12 percent of the average amount of invested capital registered during a prior 3-year period. A tax of 40 percent applies to remittance of profit in the 12 to 15 percent range, 50 percent tax applies in the 15 to 25 percent range, and 60 percent tax applies to remittance of profit amounting to more than 25 percent of the value of direct foreign investment. This "confiscatory" schedule has generally induced companies to remit to their foreign parent profit amounting to no more than 12 percent of the value of invested capital. It also has induced foreign parents to supply their subsidiaries in Brazil with loans rather than with equity capital on the assumption that repatriation of interest would be unrestricted. When remittance of interest is suspended, the Central Bank compounds the restriction of capital outflow that it has contrived by constraining the growth of the equity capital base. Moreover, although the Brazilian government professes to welcome foreign equity capital, restricts its entry not only by means of exorbitant progressive taxation, but also by arbitrarily classifying intracompany capital transfers as loans rather than as investments.

One of the ways in which American complaints about Brazilian government foreign investment policies has been publicized is by means of the U.S.–Brazil joint study groups, five of which were formed by the two governments following the visit of President Ronald Reagan to Brazil in 1982. In October of 1983, the Trade and Finance Study Group reported that a leading obstacle to foreign investment was the rupture of the link between foreign exchange transactions and the monetary correction of domestic investment values. Multinational firms were thereby penalized in the conversion of their cruzeiro balances into dollars. The report also emphasized the unfavorable effects of industrial price controls, recentralization of foreign exchange transactions in the Central Bank, legal discrimination against foreign capital, and frequent and unpredictable changes in Brasilia's economic regulations.

Another clearing house for criticism of Brazilian policies concerning foreign investment is the American Chamber of Commerce for Brazil, with branches in Sao Paulo and Rio de Janeiro. At a Chamber of Commerce meeting in Sao Paulo in May of 1984, Robert M. Gerrity, president of Ford Brasil, S.A., described Brazil's prospects in both optimistic and pessimistic terms. Potentially, he said, Brazil could become "a new automotive Japan," exporting up to a million vehicles annually. In order to export vehicles valued at US$1 billion annually, a further investment of US$4 billion would be required. Entry into Brazil of the foreign capital that would make this possible, however, was blocked by six major obstacles. First, he mentioned price controls that precluded profits in the domestic Brazilian market, "where most of our production is sold." (Ford's export sales from Brazil, however, were very profitable.) Second, he observed that taxes constitute 45 percent of the price of a domestically sold vehicle. "With lower taxes, we could sell more and achieve economies of scale." Third, high port charges and inefficiency in Brazilian maritime transport account for about 4 percent of the cost of each automobile exported. Fourth, Mr. Gerrity criticized the restricted access of foreign firms to certain domestic sources of capital supply. Eligible firms include only those which are at least 51 percent (and in many categories 100 percent) domestically owned. Ford, however, is opposed to "mixed capital" companies: "it disapproves of joint ventures in principle."[7] He also criticized excessive remittance taxes and barriers against foreign investment in reserved areas such as advanced electronics. Fifth, he criticized the regulation that requires at least 51 percent of the capital of trading companies to be of domestic origin. "I don't know one capable of handling our exports. It's like choosing your worst salesman to sell your best product." Sixth, Mr. Gerrity criticized restrictions on Brazil's trade with other Latin American countries.

In September of 1985, at a Partners in Progress seminar in Rio do Janeiro sponsored by the Association of Foreign Chambers of Commerce, Mr. Ronaldo Camargo Veirano, president of the American Chamber of Commerce for Brazil in Rio de Janeiro, charged that growing economic nationalism and exclusion of foreign companies from Brazil's development process constitute a matter of "great preoccupation" to the excluded companies and a threat to the success of the development process itself. He declared that although "the structural problems of the Brazilian economy cannot be resolved without outside help," its government has displayed visible reluctance to attract new foreign investment in recent years. He stated that foreign investors fear that existing restrictions against them in the microelectronics field may be extended to other high-technology fields such as fine chemicals and biotechnology. The Brazilian government's growth target of 6.5 percent annually requires investment of approximately 30 percent of GNP, but domestic saving is reported to be only 17 percent of GNP. (Savings statistics in Brazil, however, are not reliable.) Mr. Veirano noted that although the law allows repatriation of profit up to a maximum of 12 percent without tax, during the previous 5 years remittances averaged only 3.6 percent of foreign invested capital. He criticized as unjust the requirement that commercial banks limit multinational corporations to no more than 30 percent of their total lending.

American complaints against Brazilian foreign investment policy have been chronic in the field of informatics. (As used in Brazil, the term refers to data processing, including computer hardware, software, and services.) Restriction of foreign entry into the informatics field is implemented by means of the "market reserve" principle, which is an extension of the "law of similars." In accordance with this principle, the manufacture, import, or sale of products within designated high-technology categories is reserved exclusively to narrowly defined indigenous Brazilian firms.[8] As of 1984, moreover, measures for the legal protection of foreign software property rights were virtually nonexistent. Although Brazil is a signatory to the two international copyright agreements (the Berne Universal Copyright Convention and the World Intellectual Property Organization), it is subject to no adjudicatory or enforcement supervision, and its laws concerning the protection of software have not been tested in the courts. In particular, the issue of whether the Berne Convention on copyright is applicable to computer programs has not been settled. Thus software in Brazil receives neither copyright nor patent protection. Formal completion of the required registration of patents and trademarks, moreover, is sometimes subject to acceptance by the foreigner of a very low schedule of royalty or other payments. U.S. firms are reluctant to send their best technology to Brazil because the formulas and designs, which must be registered with the patent authorities, are then pirated by Brazilian firms. "Technology in pharmaceuticals, pesticides, and chemicals, as well as informatics, is copied by the Brazilians, and they do not pay royalties."[9] The office of the U.S. Trade Representative (USTR) has formulated a list of "talking points" for use in its negotiations with Brazil on these matters. In attempting to persuade the government to liberalize its informatics policy, the USTR argues mainly that the present policy is unfair to the United States and—in the case of restrictions on licensing of electronic components imported under World Bank contracts—in violation of the principles of international competitive bidding. To some extent it also joins forces with those domestic Brazilian critics of the informatics program who argue that it is counterproductive from a Brazilian point of view. In rebuttal, the Brazilian government takes the position that the market reserve policy is warranted for the protection of infant industry. It also observes that its market reserve policy is identical with the market reserve policy of the Japanese, which was used with pronounced success in generating Japan's economic "miracle." Moreover, at a meeting of the Brazil–U.S. trade subgroup in Rio de Janeiro in March of 1984, a senior official of SEI, the federal agency in charge of regulating the computer industry, remarked that the profits of IBM do Brasil were relatively larger than those of the parent company in the United States.[10]

Foreign investors and would-be investors in other industries have similar complaints against the Brazilian government. Restrictions on the entry of foreign banks in the investment and commercial banking fields have been an issue for more than a decade. Most non-Brazilian banks have been limited to local representative offices. Some have held minority partnerships in Brazilian investment banks. A very small minority—including Citibank, Bank of Boston, Chase Manhattan Bank, and Lloyds Bank International—have engaged in commercial banking by virtue of having entered Brazil before restrictions on foreign banks were imposed. In the throes of the debt crisis, American bankers who have been under pressure to provide further loans to Brazil regard these restrictions as particularly unfair.

In the pharmaceutical industry, foreign investment in Brazil is unprofitable and highly vexed. As in the case of informatics, there is no patent protection in the pharmaceutical industry. Some companies do better by investing their cash reserves than by productive operations. According to my informant, "Brazil gives you 5 percent of your profits and 60 percent of your problems." He anticipated that "U.S. firms will bail out of Brazil." As pharmaceutical producers, the Japanese have established virtually no presence in Brazil. With regard to market reserve, when any indigenous firm tells the government that it can supply a given product, CACEX will then "close the border" to imports. Often, after the borders have been closed, the domestic firm proves unable to supply the product. Even when the borders are open, a foreign supplier must convince the pharmaceutical bureaucrats that the proposed import would be desirable. One way of convincing them is by means of payoffs, provided chiefly by the Germans and the Swiss.[11]

From an American point of view, there are thus alternative merits and demerits for strategies of producing in Brazil for the domestic market, producing in Brazil for the foreign market, or not producing in Brazil at all. Arguments for attempting export-oriented production in Brazil refer to export-promoting factors such as the availability of raw materials, abundant labor supply,[12] and export incentives (subsidies) provided by the government; alternatively, production for the domestic market is inhibited, among other factors, by price controls and business difficulties due to the debt crisis. Accordingly, the Ford Motor Company has shifted its strategy from domestic-oriented production to production for export. The cheap labor appeal of producing in Brazil, however, must compete with the alternative of producing with highly automated facilities in the United States. Those facilities can be operated 24 hours a day, without absenteeism, strikes, illness, or quality control problems. Many industries, including steel, automobiles, textiles, glass, and various consumer durables, are candidates for automation. In the United States, moreover, there is no problem concerning political instability, exchange controls, or repatriation of profits. From the point of view of managers of American subsidiaries in Brazil, many of which are highly leveraged with a debt-equity ratio of as much as 4:1, the expectations of their head offices in the United States for a hard currency profit seem almost unreasonable.

With head offices in the United States being preoccupied by the possibilities for high-technology investment at home, they may be less able or inclined to provide investment funds for their subsidiaries in Brazil. The latter, therefore, in many cases may have to generate their own investment capital. To do this by means of exporting may be difficult because of the rising tide of protectionism in the world economy and the depressed level of export commodity prices, which reduces the import capacity of many of Brazil's trade partners. Moreover, with the exception of primary products and relatively few manufactured goods, Brazil is not an efficient export producer. These considerations prompt the alternative strategy of producing primarily for the domestic market. The attractiveness of this alternative is enhanced by the continuing emphasis of the Brazilian government on import substitution. The importance of the domestic market will therefore survive the debt crisis, while prospects in the export market remain problematic. Foreign firms that produce for the Brazilian domestic market, furthermore, are beneficiaries along with purely indigenous firms of the import barriers that, in this case at least, are imposed without discrimination against foreigners.

Practical obstruction to the contrary notwithstanding, in principle, the Brazilian government welcomes foreign direct investment. According to the then Minister of Industry and Commerce Joao Camilo Penna in 1982, "Four fields that are replete with opportunities for foreign investors are the development of agriculture and agroindustry, increased exports, oil substitution and energy production, and the large-scale industrial production of consumer goods."[13] Along these lines, the Brazilian government provides an investment incentive program administered by the Council for Industrial Development (CDI). Under certain conditions, CDI can provide fiscal and financial benefits. According to the U.S. Department of Commerce, factors that may induce CDI to take a favorable view of a foreign investment proposal are the following:[14]

1. Involvement of a Brazilian company in the project as a joint venture partner

2. Bringing in a form of technology which can be transferred to the local market

3. Employing as high a number of Brazilians as possible, especially in management or supervisory positions

4. Future plans (if not commitments) to export

5. Willingness to bring in foreign capital (as opposed to borrowing funds in Brazil or using technology as a contribution in a joint venture

6. Location of the project outside the main industrial areas of Sao Paulo, Rio de Janeiro, and Minas Gerais

Differences of opinion regarding the progress of the Brazilian economy may reflect contrasts in the statistics of capital inflow and capital outflow. During the 4-year period from January 1, 1979 to December 31, 1982, the Central Bank of Brazil reported that the total of foreign direct and portfolio investment entering Brazil amounted to US$7.44 billion. According to a World Bank estimate, the total amount of capital flight from Brazil during the same period amounted to US$3.5 billion.[15] At the end of 1984, the Central Bank of Brazil reported that the total of foreign direct and portfolio investment, including reinvested profits, amounted to US$22.84 billion (see Table 7–1). Of this amount, the United States accounted for US$7.70 billion, or 33.7 percent of the total. Japan accounted for US$2.10 billion, or 9.2 percent of the total. The United States was the leading foreign investor in Brazil, West Germany was second (with US$2.79 billion, or 12.2 percent of the total), and Japan was third. Since 1979, the U.S. share has been steadily growing (see Table 7–2). The statistics as compiled by the Central Bank of Brazil, incidentally, are decidedly smaller for the United States and Japan than those compiled by the reporting agencies of those countries respectively. According to the U.S. Department of Commerce, the cumulative U.S. direct investment position in Brazil in 1984 amounted to US$9.38 billion. According to the Japanese Ministry of Finance, Japan's direct foreign investment in Brazil in 1984 amounted to US$4.27 billion. In the case of the United States,

**Table 7–1**
**Foreign Direct and Portfolio Investment in Brazil, 1977–1986**
*(billions of U.S. dollars, end of period)*

| | 1977 | 1978 | 1979 | 1980 | 1981 | 1982 | 1983 | 1984 | 1985 | June 1986 |
|---|---|---|---|---|---|---|---|---|---|---|
| Total | 11.23 | 13.74 | 15.96 | 17.48 | 19.25 | 21.18 | 22.30 | 22.84 | 25.66 | 27.05 |
| Initial investment | 7.54 | 8.90 | 10.59 | 11.99 | 13.53 | 14.64 | 15.55 | 16.34 | 17.92 | 18.67 |
| Reinvested profits | 3.69 | 4.84 | 5.37 | 5.49 | 5.72 | 6.54 | 6.75 | 6.50 | 7.74 | 8.38 |
| By sector: | | | | | | | | | | |
| Manufacturing | 8.59 | 10.59 | 12.06 | 13.01 | 14.25 | 15.49 | 16.38 | 17.13 | 19.18 | 20.30 |
| Food, beverages, and tobacco | 0.73 | 0.88 | 0.96 | 1.00 | 1.14 | 1.22 | 1.39 | 1.44 | 1.65 | 1.75 |
| Textiles and clothing | 0.34 | 0.11 | 0.44 | 0.47 | 0.47 | 0.53 | 0.54 | 0.53 | 0.62 | 0.66 |
| Paper and rubber | 0.59 | 0.70 | 0.74 | 0.76 | 0.94 | 0.98 | 1.00 | 1.02 | 1.20 | 1.27 |
| Chemicals and pharmaceuticals | 2.04 | 2.56 | 2.98 | 3.16 | 3.49 | 3.78 | 3.96 | 4.19 | 4.70 | 4.98 |
| Metallurgy | 0.95 | 1.17 | 1.32 | 1.39 | 1.38 | 1.51 | 1.65 | 1.74 | 1.93 | 2.10 |
| Machinery | 0.92 | 1.18 | 1.48 | 1.70 | 1.82 | 2.03 | 2.11 | 2.22 | 2.36 | 2.42 |
| Electrical products | 0.97 | 1.19 | 1.34 | 1.39 | 1.48 | 1.54 | 1.65 | 1.76 | 1.97 | 2.05 |
| Transport equipment | 1.54 | 1.91 | 2.06 | 2.34 | 2.59 | 2.85 | 2.97 | 3.13 | 3.54 | 3.81 |
| Other | 0.51 | 0.59 | 0.74 | 0.80 | 0.94 | 1.05 | 1.11 | 1.10 | 1.21 | 1.26 |
| Public utilities | 0.23 | 0.24 | 0.04 | 0.04 | 0.05 | 0.05 | 0.05 | 0.04 | 0.05 | 0.05 |
| Financial services | 0.40 | 0.50 | 0.57 | 0.57 | 0.75 | 0.85 | 0.89 | 0.93 | 1.06 | 1.16 |
| Other services | 1.49 | 1.81 | 2.45 | 2.85 | 3.12 | 3.56 | 3.72 | 3.41 | 3.87 | 4.03 |
| Other | 0.52 | 0.60 | 0.84 | 1.01 | 1.08 | 1.23 | 1.26 | 1.33 | 1.50 | 1.51 |
| By country of origin: | | | | | | | | | | |
| United States | 3.42 | 3.82 | 4.37 | 5.01 | 5.77 | 6.60 | 7.20 | 7.70 | 8.06 | 8.16 |
| Federal Republic of Germany | 1.53 | 2.10 | 2.46 | 2.45 | 2.63 | 2.93 | 2.85 | 2.79 | 3.55 | 4.00 |
| Switzerland and Liechtenstein | 1.30 | 1.76 | 2.06 | 1.90 | 2.09 | 2.14 | 2.08 | 1.87 | 2.23 | 2.47 |
| Japan | 1.20 | 1.40 | 1.52 | 1.72 | 1.81 | 1.95 | 2.04 | 2.10 | 2.38 | 2.52 |
| United Kingdom | 0.55 | 0.74 | 0.94 | 1.11 | 1.02 | 1.09 | 1.13 | 1.13 | 1.43 | 1.54 |
| Canada | 0.52 | 0.70 | 0.63 | 0.64 | 0.90 | 0.98 | 1.02 | 1.07 | 1.25 | 1.38 |
| Netherlands and Netherlands Antilles | 0.53 | 0.54 | 0.73 | 0.74 | 0.78 | 0.92 | 0.89 | 0.83 | 0.75 | 0.80 |
| France | 0.43 | 0.58 | 0.66 | 0.70 | 0.68 | 0.73 | 0.70 | 0.70 | 0.93 | 0.99 |
| Panama | 0.35 | 0.38 | 0.41 | 0.50 | 0.65 | 0.70 | 0.84 | 1.10 | 1.17 | 1.15 |
| Belgium–Luxembourg | 0.43 | 0.51 | 0.61 | 0.65 | 0.62 | 0.64 | 0.70 | 0.66 | 0.74 | 0.77 |
| Italy | 0.11 | 0.21 | 0.22 | 0.48 | 0.50 | 0.59 | 0.89 | 0.92 | 0.96 | 1.02 |
| Liberia | 0.05 | 0.05 | 0.20 | 0.22 | 0.43 | 0.47 | 0.48 | 0.48 | 0.48 | 0.48 |
| Sweden | 0.23 | 0.34 | 0.38 | 0.41 | 0.38 | 0.35 | 0.39 | 0.39 | 0.41 | 0.42 |
| Other | 0.58 | 0.61 | 0.77 | 0.95 | 0.99 | 1.09 | 1.09 | 1.10 | 1.32 | 1.35 |

*Source:* Central Bank of Brazil.

Table 7–2

U.S. Direct Investment Position in Brazil by Industry, 1982–1985

(*millions of dollars*)

|  | 1982[a] | 1983[a] | 1984[a] | 1985[a] |
|---|---|---|---|---|
| All industries | 9,290 | 9,068 | 9,377 | 9,480 |
| Petroleum | 436 | 358 | 302 | 286 |
| Total manufacturing | 6,474 | 6,451 | 6,764 | 7,078 |
| Food products | 660 | 673 | 710 | 671 |
| Chemicals | 1,384 | 1,276 | 1,275 | 1,274 |
| Primary and fabricated metals | 676 | 697 | 762 | 756 |
| Nonelectrical machinery | 1,215 | 1,127 | 1,097 | 1,161 |
| Electric and electronic equipment | 479 | 457 | 446 | 558 |
| Transportation equipment | 497 | 734 | 899 | 999 |
| Other manufacturing | 1,564 | 1,488 | 1,576 | 1,659 |
| Wholesale trade | 392 | 394 | 410 | 429 |
| Banking | 400 | 379 | 474 | 285 |
| Finance (except banking, insurance, and real estate) | 1,231 | 1,141 | 1,113 | 1,085 |
| Services | [b] | 133 | 135 | 135 |
| Other industries | [b] | 212 | 178 | 182 |

*Source:* U.S. Department of Commerce, Bureau of Economic Analysis, *Survey of Current Business*, August 1986.

[a] Revised data reflect the results of *U.S. Direct Investment Abroad: 1982 Benchmark Survey Data*, December 1985.

[b] Suppressed to avoid disclosure of data of individual companies.

the discrepancy (amounting to about 20 percent) arises chiefly from the fact that contrary to standard balance of payments accounting principles, the Brazilian government regards an investment by a multinational parent company in its Brazilian subsidiary as a loan. A second reason is that there may be a time lag between the reporting of capital outflow from the United States and capital inflow into Brazil. A further distortion in the statistics of national origin lies in the fact that a U.S. multinational may invest in Brazil by way of its subsidiary in a third country. For example, the Gillette Company of Boston, Massachusetts, owns Braun A.G. of Frankfurt, West Germany; the latter has invested in Braun do Brasil & Cia. in Sao Paulo. In the case of Japan, the statistics are compiled on the basis of investments "notified to and approved by" the Ministry of Finance; some of those proposed investments, however, may never be performed.

In terms of Brazilian balance of payments statistics, the data concerning loans by country source are not good because Brazil does not borrow from "countries," it borrows from "markets," such as the capital markets of Panama, Bahamas, Singapore, London, Paris, or New York. The Central Bank does not know the identity of the country of origin of the capital that moves through these markets. Citibank, for example, may extend a jumbo loan to Brazil that combines capital from various national sources. Only Citibank, as creditor, knows what the national sources are. According to an estimate from an informed source, however, as of July of 1984, the exposure of U.S. banks in Brazil was approximately US$18 billion. The exposure of Japanese banks was approximately one-third that of the U.S. banks.[16]

The ratio of new equity capital entering Brazil to new medium- and long-term external debt has declined sharply in recent years. According to the Central Bank of Brazil, the ratio declined from 23.5 percent in 1977 to 17.9 percent in 1984. During 1984, the Central Bank reports that 28 percent of total direct foreign investment in Brazil was attributable to reinvested profits. In part, this reinvestment may have been involuntary due to the difficulty of repatriating profits from Brazil to parent companies abroad. According to the U.S. Department of Commerce (USDC), during the 6-year period 1977–1982, the total return (interest, dividends, branch profits, fees, and royalties from affiliates) on U.S. direct investment in Brazil amounted to $3.8 billion. During the same period, the amount of reinvested earnings amounted to $2.0 billion. In 1982, the USDC figures show an average return of 10.0 percent of U.S. direct investment in Brazil.

In FY1984, according to the Japanese Ministry of Finance, the Brazilian share of total Japanese direct foreign investment was 6.0 percent. This was the third most important area for Japanese direct foreign investment following the United States (27.9 percent) and Indonesia (11.2 percent). In calendar year 1984, according to the Bureau of Economic Analysis, U.S. Department of Commerce, Brazil accounted for 3.7 percent of total U.S. direct foreign investment. This was the sixth most important area for U.S. direct foreign investment, following Canada (19.6 percent), the United Kingdom (12.5 percent), Switzerland (6.2 percent), West Germany (5.9 percent), and Bermuda (4.6 percent).

By sector, the distribution of foreign direct investment in Brazil is heavily concentrated in manufacturing (see Table 7–3). U.S. direct investment in Brazil, which is the principal component of the total, is similarly distributed. According to figures of the Central Bank, as of September 30, 1983, manufacturing accounted for 74.5 percent of U.S. direct investment, services accounted for 18.8 percent, mining accounted for 4.8 percent, and agriculture 0.1 percent. Within manufacturing, the chemical industry was the leading area of U.S. direct investment, accounting for 13.2 percent of total U.S. direct investment. Machinery industries were second, accounting for 11.7 percent of the total. Vehicles and car parts accounted for 9.0 percent of the total. Electrical and communication products accounted for 8.7 percent.

It is interesting that in terms of major categories, the distribution of Japanese direct investment in Brazil is almost identical with that of the United States. As of September 30, 1983, manufacturing industries accounted for 73.4 percent of Japan's direct investment, services accounted for 18.6 percent, mining accounted for 1.8 percent, and livestock accounted for 1.2 percent. Within the manufacturing sector, however, the distribution of

**Table 7–3**
**Sectoral Distribution of the Stock of Foreign Direct Investment in Brazil, First Quarter of 1983**
*(percent)*

| | United States | Japan | West Germany | Switzerland | United Kingdom | France |
|---|---|---|---|---|---|---|
| Agriculture (including cattle-ranching, fishing, etc.) | 0.76 | 1.94 | 0.12 | 0.92 | 0.49 | 1.27 |
| Mining | 5.08 | 1.80 | 1.77 | 0.14 | 2.45 | 0.47 |
| Manufacturing | 73.74 | 73.23 | 89.99 | 79.28 | 56.95 | 55.37 |
| Steel | 0.26 | 11.49 | 0.65 | 0.30 | 0.20 | 0.43 |
| Metal products | 3.55 | 6.49 | 9.42 | 1.26 | 4.04 | 5.01 |
| Machinery and capital equipment | 12.22 | 8.31 | 16.30 | 5.18 | 3.74 | 5.14 |
| Electrical and communication equipment and products | 8.03 | 12.52 | 5.66 | 8.98 | 1.65 | 2.79 |
| Transportation equipment (excluding parts) | 6.48 | 3.08 | 27.19 | 15.74 | — | 0.42 |
| Parts and equipment for automobile sector | 1.89 | 0.72 | 9.58 | 4.96 | 0.76 | 0.44 |
| Chemicals (excluding oil chemicals) | 13.33 | 1.68 | 6.82 | 2.03 | 11.55 | 13.87 |
| Oil derivates (including petrochemicals) | 2.09 | 1.21 | 0.06 | 0.09 | 25.27 | — |
| Pharmaceutical industry | 5.10 | 0.09 | 4.36 | 3.98 | 1.49 | 3.61 |
| Textiles | 0.72 | 8.14 | 0.15 | 2.37 | 4.02 | 0.46 |
| Food products | 4.45 | 1.90 | 0.54 | 13.73 | 0.29 | 2.57 |
| Tobacco | 2.11 | 0.07 | 0.04 | 0.11 | 0.36 | 0.12 |
| Miscellaneous and other | 13.46 | 17.53 | 9.22 | 20.56 | 3.58 | 20.51 |
| Public utilities (transportation and other services) | 0.15 | 0.01 | 0.21 | 0.16 | 0.12 | 0.20 |
| Services sector | 19.07 | 18.77 | 7.51 | 18.10 | 37.96 | 41.28 |
| Banking | 2.89 | 6.77 | 1.61 | 0.55 | 4.88 | 11.82 |
| Holdings and representation offices | 9.88 | 3.29 | 2.36 | 13.76 | 26.63 | 19.88 |
| Other services | 6.30 | 8.71 | 3.54 | 3.79 | 6.45 | 9.58 |
| Other sectors | 1.20 | 4.25 | 0.4 | 1.40 | 2.03 | 1.41 |
| Total | 100.00 | 100.00 | 100.00 | 100.00 | 100.00 | 100.00 |

*Source:* FIRCE-DIVAP, Central Bank of Brazil.

Japanese and U.S. direct investment was highly incongruent. In the case of the United States, the chief form of manufacturing investment was in basic chemical products (13.2 percent of its total investment), followed by machinery industries (11.7 percent). In the case of Japan, the chief form of manufacturing investment was in electrical and communications equipment (12.6 percent), followed by investment in the steel industry (11.8 percent). Japan is also the major foreign investor in textiles, in which the United States is virtually not represented. For purposes of further comparison, it may be noted that in basic chemical products, the United States accounted for 42.0 percent of total foreign direct investment in Brazil, while Japan accounted for 1.5 percent. In machinery industries, the United States accounted for 39.8 percent of total foreign direct investment in Brazil, while Japan accounted for 7.9 percent. On the other hand, while the electrical and communications equipment industry accounted for the largest share of Japan's direct investment, its share of total foreign investment in the industry was 15.6 percent, while that of the United States, which ranked third among its manufacturing investments, was relatively much more important, contributing 38.1 percent of total direct foreign investment in the industry. This result, of course, arises from the fact that in absolute terms, the total direct investment of the United States in Brazil was 3.5 times as large as that of Japan. It should be observed, moreover, that within the major categories, U.S. direct investment in Brazil was considerably more diversified than that of Japan, especially in consumer products, and that U.S. enterprises were not substantially in competition or conflict with those of Japan.

During 1978 to 1982, although the rate of increase was slow, there were increases in almost every category of U.S. direct investment in Brazil (An exception was electrical machinery, in which the direction of change was negative during 1979–1981.) Investment preferences, however, shifted drastically as a result of the collapse of the domestic market in 1981 and the 3-year recession that ensued. Despite barriers to foreigners in commercial and investment banking, there was a notable expansion in the U.S. position in the banking sector. Citibank is the leading private bank in Brazil in terms of loans, and Chase Manhattan (formerly Banco Lar Brasileiro, which in July of 1986 changed its name to Banco Chase Manhattan S.A.) and Bank of Boston have been gaining ground. In January of 1984, First National Bank of Chicago purchased a minority share in a Brazilian investment bank, the Banco Denasa de Investimento. Corresponding to the relatively high profits they earn as compared with manufacturing firms is the relatively high influence the banks wield in the Brazilian economy. U.S. banks exercise much more influence in Brazil than Japanese banks, and those which have already been established in Brazil benefit greatly from barriers to the entry of new banking competitors from the United States and elsewhere. As the leading private bank, Citibank has twelve branches in Brazil and has attempted to expand its loans to the public sector. "Fifty percent of Citibank profit in Brazil is derived from the public sector."[17]

After 1983, it was mostly foreign-owned banks that still had access to dollar credits. This was a principal source of their profitability. They would convert the dollars into cruzeiros, which they would then either lend to Brazilian borrowers at enormous rates of interest, invest in the money market, or use to buy indexed government bonds. The return on such lending greatly exceeded the cost of forward cover for the repatriation of the dollars they had received from abroad. In 1983, Citibank earned an operating profit of 101 percent of net worth, the Bank of Boston earned 128 percent of net worth, and Lar Brasileiro (Chase) earned 20 percent of net worth. There are only three Japanese banks of importance in Brazil. Other Japanese banks are representative offices, of which there are about twenty, or minority partners in other banking institutions. The majors include the Bank of Tokyo, which in 1983 earned 148 percent of net worth; Sumitomo Bank, which earned 143 percent of net worth; and Mitsubishi Bank, which earned 89 percent of net worth.[18] It should be noted, however, that because of the restrictions imposed by the Brazilian government on the growth of foreign banks, they are all undercapitalized as compared with Brazilian banks.

Citibank has achieved its remarkable profit record despite a number of difficulties. Although lending to the public sector is profitable, the public sector is also the area in which the greatest amount of nonperformance occurs. Internally, the bank has a productivity problem. When an employee makes a mistake, the bank does not fire him. Instead, it appoints another person to take charge of him. As a result of this policy, Citibank's organization in Brazil is becoming overloaded.[19] Its income statement has not been adversely affected because Citibank has been very innovative in the field of financial services and consumer business, including insurance, securities transactions, interest swapping, hedging and investment banking (performing brokerage services in the purchase and sale of operating companies).

Analysis of the profitability of Japanese enterprise is more complex than in the American case. Japanese banks and their clients often own equity in each other, especially in Japan, as U.S. banks do not. This makes for a quite different business relationship. In its Brazilian activities, moreover, a major Japanese bank does not stand alone: each of the principal Japanese city banks is formally and informally affiliated with a diversified set of firms collectively known as a *keiretsu* (group), including members representing primary, secondary, and tertiary sectors of the Japanese economy. A Japanese bank may extend an ostensibly profitless loan for the sake of financing a profitable sale of equipment by a manufacturer that is a member of its group. Profit also would accrue to the group trading company (*sogo shosha*) that arranges and fulfills the transaction. Insurance, warehousing, shipping, and other services provided by the *keiretsu* membership generate collateral profits. Direct profitability, moreover, is not the whole story. Japanese management control of the Brazilian customer may be acquired by means of the technology transfer that accompanies sale of the equipment. Apart from Japanese control by means of formal management contracts, control arises from the repair, servicing, and replacement role of the supplier. If the Brazilian customer is engaged in export production, the Japanese trading company may impose further controls in the process of providing the services of its worldwide distribution network. As a consequence of the debt crisis, Brazil's increasingly urgent need to expand its exports is a structural factor conducive to augmentation of the influence of Japanese trading companies. These various means of exercising influence and control are precisely the instruments by which the scenario of Japan as a headquarters country may be implemented. Thus, whereas the United States is seeking a negotiated structural *adjustment* of its relations with Brazil through reduction of barriers to trade and investment, the Japanese are seeking a structural *evolution* conducive to the emergence of Japan as a headquarters nation. Apart from any negotiated advantage it may acquire, Japan is systematically evolving a structural advantage in various dimensions of its relationship with Brazil.

In comparing the position of Japan with that of the United States in Brazil, the idiosyncrasies of Japanese profit-taking, compounded by the idiosyncrasies of Japanese methods of imposing control, help account for the willingness of Japanese firms—in contrast to the attitude of U.S. firms—to accept a minority equity share in their joint ventures. The willingness of Japanese firms to occupy minority ownership positions makes it easier for Brazil to accept the Japanese style of control than the U.S. style of control. A Japanese minority equity position in a Brazilian firm, moreover, may be sufficient to provide the means of preventing the firm from becoming involved with U.S. or other foreign firms. A still further form of Japanese control, which may be imposed without any equity ownership whatever, is by means of Japanese monopsony buying of the output of Brazilian raw materials suppliers. Except where they have been forced to relinquish majority ownership because of "national security" or similar Brazilian government rules, U.S. companies usually insist on maintaining a majority position of 100 percent ownership. This is a special priority in high-technology fields, pharmaceuticals, and chemicals, where the security of patents and formulas is of great concern. The top-management positions in U.S. joint ventures, although not necessarily all executive positions, are usually occupied by Americans. In view of this American operating style, the virtual absence of U.S. equity investment in Brazilian state enterprises may be more than a coincidence. That absence also may be all to the good as a means of forestalling further nationalist apprehensions about U.S. domination of the Brazilian economy. By the same token, however, the participation of Japanese firms in Brazilian state enterprises—many of which are qualitatively different from those in the private sector—presents a further analytical difficulty in comparing the relative positions of the United States and Japan in the Brazilian economy.

Within the private sector, however, some comparisons can be made of the role of Japanese as compared with U.S. firms in Brazil. Measured in terms of 1981 sales, the 100 largest Brazilian firms included 40 U.S. affiliates; these performed 45.6 percent of the total sales of the group. In the group of 100, Ishibras was the only Japanese firm included.[20] According to an estimate by the Japan External Trade Organization (JETRO), as of October of 1981, there were 421 Japanese enterprises in Brazil. At about the same time, the U.S. State Department estimated that approximately 600 U.S. firms had direct investments in Brazil.

An irony in the U.S.–Brazil controversy about the proper conduct of trade and investment affairs is that each side appeals to good principles and good policies, but these principles and policies may be inconsistent. In the American context, principle refers to the right of individuals to receive nondiscriminatory treatment and to have access to a multilateral, free-trading system in the world economy. Brazilian policy emphasizes practices that redound to the greatest good of Brazilian society as a whole. With regard to investment, the United States argues that Americans should have the right of "national" treatment in Brazil, that is, the same rights as Brazilians. In theory, but not in practice, the Brazilian government agrees. In practice also, the United States violates its own principles by various types of protectionist measures. Brazilian policy is dedicated to practices for the promotion of economic growth and limitation of the proprietary role of foreigners in the Brazilian economy. Consequently, it provides trade and investment protection and subsidies for its infant industries, contrary to American principles. Apart from the question of whose principles and policies are appropriate for whom and to what extent they are observed by those who espouse them, as a practical matter, it is clear that the debt crisis has given the creditor countries, chiefly the United States, an enhanced degree of leverage in putting pressure on Brazil for the liberalization of its economy. The debtor-creditor confrontation has repercussions on the trade and investment relationship.

The U.S. confrontation with Brazil concerning economic liberalization is ironic also inasmuch as it recapitulates the controversy between the United States and Japan that commenced almost immediately after the Occupation. The U.S. demand that Japan liberalize the international flow of investment, commodities, and finance has continued in one form or another up to the present day. The Japanese industrial policy prescription for economic development provided the Brazilians with a textbook example of the uses of nationalism and protectionism. It is ironic further that Brazil's political liberalization (*abertura*) has dampened the prospects for economic liberalization. Brazil's protectionism, of course, now presents a barrier to Japan as well as to the United States. In classic fashion, however, while the United States attempts to breach the barrier by a head-on confrontation (football style), the Japanese respond by attempting to go around it (judo style) and to utilize it in the fulfillment of their own scenario.

Prior to World War II, there was very little direct Japanese investment in Brazil. After the war, the Japanese government encouraged the trading companies to establish branches abroad for the purpose of finding markets for Japanese exports and sources of raw materials supply. The trading companies in turn established many subsidiaries of their own, such as, for example, in textiles. The latter created both import and export transactions from which the trading companies could profit. The trading companies also attempted to set up subsidiaries that would seek the Brazilian government as a principal customer. Thus Japan's direct investment strategy in Brazil achieved a linkage between industrial policy in the public sector and economic planning in the private sector that was far more sophisticated than anything practiced by the Americans. Offices in Brazil were established by the Marubeni Company and the Mitsubishi Company in 1955, C. Itoh & Company in 1957, and Mitsui Company in 1960. The foreign exchange constraint on imports of raw materials into Japan induced some Japanese textile producers to establish plants in Brazil, where an indigenous supply of raw cotton was available. Textile manufacturers among others were anxious to invest in Brazil in order to defend their markets in the midst of Brazil's import-substitution protectionism. Reciprocally, from a Brazilian point of view, Japanese investment was welcomed for the purpose of promoting its import-substitution policies. The import-substitution process began with nondurable consumer goods and progressed rapidly to durable consumer goods, intermediate goods, and finally, capital goods. Japanese investments made during the 1950s were mainly of modest size by present standards. However, the first wave also included Yanmar Diesel (1957), Usiminas (1957), and Ishibras (1959). During the "welcome" period of the first wave of Japanese investment, head offices in Japan either held majority equity positions or were sole owners of the subsidiaries. Investment in Brazil leveled off in the late 1960s. A second boom ensued during the period 1972–1974. It was in the second period that major projects were undertaken, especially those in collaboration with the Brazilian government. In these joint ventures, Japanese firms assumed minority equity positions. Most of the major projects were designed for natural resource and basic materials development; here again, Japanese and Brazilian interests coincided in terms of Brazil's second 5-year plan during 1975–1979. Projects of the 1970s included Tubarao steel (1976), Cenibra cellulose and pulp (1977), and Alunorte alumina and Albras aluminum smelting (1978).

As Brazil's second 5-year plan moved forward, the government's attitude toward foreign direct investment became more restrictive. It became more selective in terms of the types of investment that were welcome and more emphatic in its support of domestic capital as opposed to foreign capital in joint venture enterprises. As a countermeasure to the two oil shocks, import restrictions were tightened, which reduced the access of foreign firms to components and replacement parts from their home offices. This forced the pace of the import-substitution process within Brazil. The impact on machinery firms was particularly adverse. Japanese firms engaged in joint ventures with the Brazilian government were in some respects less disadvantaged than those wholly in the private sector; however, they also were subject to the hazard of frequent policy changes on the part of the government.

The priority assigned by the government to strengthening domestic capital as opposed to foreign capital in Brazil was implemented by means of privileges and subsidies conferred on indigenous firms. In the Japanese investment boom of the 1970s, this provided an additional reason for joint venture and for the acceptance of minority equity positions on the part of Japanese firms. Majority control by indigenous capital was required, for example, as a condition of eligibility for subsidies in the Industrial Development Council (CDI) program and in the Manaus Free Trade Zone. Success was heavily dependent on the quality of the Brazilian joint venture partner.

A good example of a successful joint venture is that of Sharp do Brasil.[21] It combined resources from Nippon Sharp (25 percent) and Sharp S.A. (75 percent), a domestic Brazilian enterprise. The success of the enterprise is based on technology contributed by Japan and sales competence contributed by the Brazilian partner. With a 25 percent share of the Brazilian market, this company is now a leader in the color television field.

In some cases, Japanese firms have been obliged to accept a minority equity position in place of a majority position in order to qualify for subsidized government finance, such as that the Special Agency for Industrial Financing (FINAME). Fiscal incentives in the Manaus Free Trade Zone likewise are subject to a combination of Japanese capital and indigenous Brazilian capital. Sony, Sanyo, Honda, Sharp, Toshiba, Yamaha, Mitsui, Matsushita, and Mitsubishi are among the famous Japanese names represented in Manaus. Recently, however, the Brazilian government has reduced its emphasis on fiscal incentives for import substitution, such as remission of ICM (state value-added tax) and IPI (federal industrial product tax), in favor of incentives for expansion of exports. These include subsidies from the Special Program of Fiscal Incentives for Exporters (BEFIEX) and a drawback policy for duties on parts and raw materials for the purpose of re-export. Imports were restricted by severe rationing of foreign exchange; in August of 1982, all foreign currency payments were centralized and controlled by the Central Bank of Brazil. The domestic recession in Brazil associated with the debt crisis was a further reason for the shift in support for production for the domestic market in favor of production for the foreign market. Besides the push to export, there were various pull factors. In the United States, for example, the overvalued dollar was an enormous magnet for exports from Brazil. In the U.S. iron and steel industry, there was a movement toward importing Brazilian intermediate iron products in lieu of building expensive new blast furnaces.

During the Brazilian boom years of 1968–1974, Japanese companies invested in Brazil in follow-the-leader fashion. The precedent for this had been established during the economic "miracle" in Japan, when firms plunged into new activities in which they had little or no experience and everything had turned out well. In Brazil, circumstances were less auspicious for firms that were poorly prepared. By 1977, some Japanese firms began to pull out of Brazil. By the time of the second oil crisis, there were not many weak Japanese firms left in Brazil. There was retrenchment among the strong firms that remained, but they had no intention of abandoning their long-term commitment to a bright Brazilian future. Indeed, in 1979, there was a substantial increase in the value of Japan's direct investments in Brazil, attributable to a few major corporations.

In terms of volume, about 20 percent of Japan's direct investment in Brazil was placed before 1970; about 80 percent was placed thereafter. Although the domestic market shrank following the debt crisis, Japan's relative market share increased.[22] At the micro level, the rationale of Japanese direct investment in Brazil is consistent with the rationale of Japan's foreign economic policy described in Chapter 1 and with the scenario of Japan's emergence as a headquarters country. The major projects, all joint ventures, are of several types. One type, the "national project," is based on an understanding between the Japanese government and the Brazilian government, as in the case of Usiminas. On the Japanese side, some projects, such as the Program de Cooperation Nipo-Brasileira para o Desenvolvimento dos Cerrados (PRODECER), are chiefly Japanese government arrangements with a small symbolic private component. In other cases, the arrangement is essentially private, with a minor or symbolic Japanese government component. In the latter type, the risk inherent in a major project is spread by the formation of a consortium of twenty or thirty private Japanese firms in establishing company A, to which they collectively contribute, say, 60 percent of the equity. The Japanese government would provide 40 percent of the equity. Company A then invests in company B, a Brazilian company. Schematically, Japan's major projects in Brazil began with industrial enterprises (shipbuilding and steel); these were followed by mining and metallurgy projects; the latest phase includes agricultural, scientific, and technical projects. To a large extent, this evolution can be accounted for by Japanese association with the federally owned Companhia Vale do Rio Doce (CVRD), of which the guiding genius has been its former president, Eliezer Batista. Excluding loans, CVRD projects in which Japan participates and the extent of Japan's ownership in each as of August of 1984 were as follows:[23] Albras

(49.0 percent), Alunorte (39.2 percent), Cenibra (49.38 percent), Nibrasco (48.21 percent), and Minas da Serra Geral (49.0 percent).

In Brazil's mineral sector, as of June of 1983, the United States was the leading foreign investor in mining (US$339.7 million as compared with US$35.3 million for Japan) and equal to West Germany as leader in foreign investment in metallurgy (US$260.6 million as compared with US$128.5 million for Japan). In steel, Japan was the leading foreign investor (US$237.6 million as compared with US$18.1 million for the United States).[24] In terms of mineral exports, however, Japan is the leading destination. In 1982, Brazil's mineral exports to Japan were valued at US$681.1 million, as compared with only US$50.0 million for exports to the United States.[25]

On the Japanese side, there is synergistic interaction between Japanese loans and Japanese investments, especially in the large infrastructure and basic materials projects. The interaction provides benefits to Japan entrepreneurially as a source of control of Brazilian economic strategy, as well as a source of business profits through the sale of plant, equipment, and services required for the projects. Technical assistance and engineering services alone, supplemented perhaps by suppliers' credit, has generated large orders for Japanese plant and equipment. Japan also exerts strategic control as a purchaser and exporter of the output. Economic cooperation provides a role for both direct and indirect contacts between the Japanese government and the Brazilian government in the planning of development strategy. Within Japan, by means of coordination of the investment and lending activities of Japanese government agencies (JICA, OECF, Export-Import Bank) and private banks and trading companies, the strategy of Japanese ministries concerning the role of Japan as a headquarters country can be implemented.

In the case of the state-owned Companhia Siderurgica Nacional (CSN), established by the government of Getulio Vargas, Japan provided no direct investment, but only technical assistance in the design, construction, and operation of the plant. The same was true in the case of the Companhia Siderurgica Paulista (COSIPA), the second in the "big three" triumverate of steel enterprises under the aegis of the federally owned holding company Siderbras. Japanese direct investments have been made in only two projects of the Siderbras group, the first being Usiminas (in which Nippon Usiminas holds 19 percent of the shares), the second being the Tuberao Steel Company (CST) (in which Kawasaki and others hold 24.5 percent of the shares). In the case of CSN, Tuberao, and Itaipu, Japanese firms provided inputs not only from Japan, but also from their production facilities within Brazil itself. Thus the benefit to Japan of participation in major projects accrued not only to major Japanese firms acting as principals, but also to small and medium-sized Japanese subcontractors. Among the important advantages of Japanese involvement in Brazilian major projects was the worldwide dissemination of information concerning the excellence of Japanese technology. Regardless of the size of Japan's equity share, the utilization of Japanese technology in the Brazilian steel industry created market demand for that technology elsewhere. Prior to the Usiminas project, the extent of Japan's technological advance in steel was not widely appreciated. Thereafter, following the "Brazilian connection," demand for Japanese steel-making equipment opened up in Europe and the United States. By the 1970s, it became widely known that Japan had surpassed the United States in steel-making technology.

Although technically excellent, Brazilian public-sector steel has been described as a financial "disaster." According to the senior vice president of Citibank in Sao Paulo, Brazilian steel is financed by $9 of debt for every dollar of equity, a ratio much more extreme even than in Japan. The United States steel industry is financed by $1 of debt for every dollar of equity.[26]

The Usiminas case is interesting as an example of how Japanese influence may not be directly related to the degree of Japanese equity participation. Originally, Usiminas started as an American project. U.S. interests dropped out and it became Japanese when President Juscelino Kubitschek invited the participation of the Japanese government. The latter, through OECF, joined forces with a private consortium led by Yawata Steel, which designed and installed the equipment.[27] At the outset, a Japanese consortium held 40 percent of the equity. Although technically perhaps Brazil's finest mill, it has been disadvantaged from the investors' point of view by the fact that the Brazilian government imposed a stringently low price policy on Usiminas for anti-inflationary and economic-development purposes. As a result, its depreciation allowances were insufficient and its profits were low. Thus it has been unable to pay dividends. As the project expanded, Japanese investors have been unwilling to contribute more capital. By 1983, the Japanese equity share had been diluted to 11 percent. In summary, Usiminas is a clear case of how the direct results must be distinguished from the indirect results of Japanese direct investment in Brazil.

The comparison of U.S. and Japanese accomplishments in Brazil is not so much a contrast between success and failure, but rather a comparison of relative degrees of success in alternative types of effort. U.S. financial influence in Brazil is much greater than that of Japan. It is also very strong in chemicals, automobiles, and the electronics field, as represented by IBM. Japan is strong in iron and steel, textiles, general machinery, pulp and paper, and consumer electronics. Thus with the exception of electronics, telecommunications, and computers, where future conflict between the United States and Japan may accelerate, the configuration of interests is largely complementary rather than competitive. The basic point concerning U.S.–Japan competition in matters concerning Brazil is that it may be indirect rather than direct, and at present it is more potential than actual. It may not refer to confrontation between the United States and Japan within Brazil itself. Instead, it refers to the development support provided by Japan to Brazil's primary and intermediate goods industries, which increasingly compete with their declining counterparts in the United States. Japan will be a beneficiary of this competition. By the same token, the export drive that is now being mounted by General Motors and Ford in the Brazilian automobile industry may adversely affect Japan in third markets.

As compared with the U.S. comparative advantage in finance, automobiles, and chemicals, Japan's comparative advantage in Brazil lies in the field of development planning, information transfer, technology transfer, and the organizational and operational services of its trading companies. "In steel and in petrochemicals, the Japanese now win hands down in the supply of technology and equipment to Brazil."[28] The way they sold the equipment was to sell the technology first. They also became partners, and the technology was part of their capital contribution.

As mentioned earlier, Japan's direct investment activities in Brazil are much less diversified than those of the United States. One of the reasons for Japan's success in Brazil is directly analogous to a reason for its success in market entry as an exporter to the United States. In both cases, Japanese entrepreneurs have concentrated their efforts in a limited number of industries, which they have penetrated in depth. (In Brazil, this strategy was adopted following the failure of the initial shotgun approach of indiscriminate investment in the early postwar period.) An apparent defect of this approach, of course, is that it makes Japan highly vulnerable to discriminatory or protectionist measures that may be adopted by the host country. On the other hand, as already observed, the web of Japanese involvement is not only vertical, but also horizontal by means of its *keiretsu* network.

Other reasons for the success of Japan's direct investment in Brazil include the community of interest between the Japanese government and the Brazilian government in creating a "special relationship" as an offset to the "missing relationship" between Brazil and the United States. Brazil's plan for the development of its infant industries is complementary to Japan's industrial policy for the liquidation of its declining industries. Import substitution in Brazil has served the purposes of both Brazil and Japan, while it has served to create friction between Brazil and the United States. Brazilian export promotion has likewise been largely competitive with the United States, while it has been largely, but not completely complementary from a Japanese point of view. The Japanese and Brazilian governments have signed economic cooperation agreements that opened the door to Japanese multinationals at the operating level. Brazil also has entered into a tax treaty with Japan, but not with the United States. In accordance with its provisions, Japanese companies are able to deduct their Brazilian tax payments from their Japanese tax obligations. (In accordance with U.S. law, however, U.S. companies can deduct their Brazilian tax payments from their U.S. tax obligations even in the absence of a U.S.–Brazil tax treaty.) Earnings of

Japanese company employees in Brazil are not subject to Japanese income tax. As investors, Japanese firms also took advantage of BEFIEX incentives and of the benefits of producing in the Manaus Free Trade Zone. In the case of the United States, the bilateral agreement concerning scientific and technical cooperation signed during President Reagan's visit to Brazil in December of 1982 will be an advantage to U.S. investment in the high-technology field. In agriculture, moreover, the experience of the United States in large-scale, mechanized agribusiness, as contrasted with Japan's experience with small-scale farming, provides potential—as yet underutilized—for U.S. participation in agricultural development projects in Brazil. In the Cerrado, for example, it is Japan rather than the United States that has taken the initiative.

Another way of evaluating the relative success of Japanese and U.S. firms in Brazil is in terms of their failure rate and the extent to which Brazilian and Japanese firms respectively have withdrawn during the period of the debt crisis. As mentioned earlier, the statistics on this matter are imprecise and ambiguous. An informed opinion, however, is that of Jean Bernet, president of Guia Interinvest and publisher of *Interinvest Guide,* concerning the status of foreign enterprises in Brazil. In the summer of 1983, he stated that "more U.S. firms are quitting Brazil than Japanese firms."[29] Apart from their relative competence at the production level, one of the common problems of both U.S. and Japanese firms was the difficulty of doing business in an environment of high inflation, with which neither U.S. nor Japanese firms had had recent experience. In 1984, three of the top five losers among private-sector foreign firms were American. Alcoa was the leading loser (US$409.8 million); General Motors was second (US$223.5 million); fourth in the list was Ford Brasil (US$193.7 million).[30] In 1983, General Motors sustained the greatest loss among all private-sector foreign firms in Brazil (US$298.4 million), and Ford Brasil was second (US$260.2 million).[31] Esso was the only U.S. firm included in the list of the top five most profitable private-sector foreign firms in 1983 (US$127.8 million) and 1984 (US$118.7 million). No Japanese firm appeared in either list in either year.

## Foreign Trade with Brazil: The United States and Japan

From a Brazilian point of view, the United States has committed many errors, some of which have had adverse repercussions for Brazil, whereas the Japanese have "done things right." (Brazilians may acknowledge their own errors as well, but they profess them to be errors of naiveté rather than errors of misconduct.) Some U.S. errors have been attributed to intellectual confusion, others to confusion of policy. At the intellectual level, in the course of a single decade, U.S. government economic thinkers progressed from "we are all Keynesians now" to "money matters" to "monetarism is dead." At the policy level, one of the most intractable arguments between the United States and Brazil has concerned the latter's "fiscal subsidies" to exports, in the form tax remission at the micro level. At the macro level, however, it is U.S. fiscal policy on which Brazil blames much of its dilemma in the debt crisis.

It is of interest that although the United States has been a comparatively strong market for Brazilian manufactured goods in the first half of the 1980s and Japan has not, it is the United States that is perceived in Brazil as protectionist, while Japan has largely escaped criticism. From a Brazilian point of view, the apparent inconsistency may be explained by the perception that the defense of U.S. declining industries has crippling implications for Brazil's development, while Japanese industrial policy has dynamic implications for Brazil's development. In commodity trade, for example, the sorest conflict between the United States and Brazil concerns the emergence of Brazilian steel as a competitive force in the U.S. market. The source of Brazil's competitive power in steel, however, lies in technology transfer from Japan. Thus the United States is seen as resisting an advance that Brazilians associate with help from Japan. In adopting a case-by-case policy approach (an approach, incidentally, that is one of the most notorious weapons in the Japanese policy arsenal), the United States is seen as attempting to nip Brazilian competitive power in the bud wherever such buds appear, in steel, informatics, or elsewhere. The U.S. case-by-case application of pressure to Brazil, moreover, is a further instance of bilateralism, while in theory the United States espouses a multilateral approach. Japanese bilateralism, on the other hand, is seen as innocuous or benevolent.

From a U.S. point of view, there is an inconsistency in the Brazilian attitude. For purposes of trade and investment, Brazil wishes to be considered a developing nation. But for geopolitical purposes, it wishes to be considered an advanced nation. The difference in Brazil's relative stature in various dimensions is indeed one aspect of its transition and of its present predicament. Recently, the United States began to describe Brazil as an "advanced developing nation." This semantic distinction has the policy purpose of putting pressure on Brazil to liberalize its economy. As an ordinary developing nation, however, Brazil feels entitled to provide infant industry protection to its manufacturing sector as a means of generating economies of large-scale production. Possibly one of the reasons for the violent reaction of the United States against some of the devices of Brazilian protectionism is that for the most part they are faithful copies of Japanese originals, to which the United States has already become allergic. Meanwhile, the United States practices protectionism of the opposite sort in the form of measures in defense of its declining industries. U.S. protectionism is a response to the fact that while exports have increased as a component of U.S. GNP, the U.S. share of world markets has declined and its competitive power has come increasingly into question. To an increasing degree, the trade barriers that have been devised in the United States, Japan, and Brazil are either in violation of GATT or an evasion of its principles.

In the foreign-trade sector, these circumstances suggest the environment surrounding conflict, competition, and cooperation among the United States, Japan, and Brazil. Description of their multilateral interactions in the trade sector may begin with some comments on the statistical dimensions of performance by the parties respectively.

*Foreign Trade Performance*

In former times, Brazil's imports of industrial goods were made possible by earnings from a series of primary-product exports; successively, sugar, cotton, and coffee were of principal importance. Following World War II, Brazil engaged in import-substituting industrialization, implemented by means of import restrictions and other subsidies to industry. Since protection of producers of import substitutes makes them profitable, they draw economic resources away from unprotected activities. This has an adverse effect on exports. Exports, however, are required in order to pay for imports. The import-substitution industrialization process, therefore, had an antitrade bias that made Brazil one of the world's most closed economies.[32] Excluding imports of crude oil and refined petroleum products, the ratio of its imports to GNP is only about 3 percent. In the 1970s, export receipts averaged about 7 percent of GNP.(In 1985, U.S. exports were only about 5 percent of GNP.) The export imperative resulting from the debt crisis of the early 1980s raised the export ratio to about 8 percent. Export subsidies only partially offset the superior profits that manufacturers can obtain in the domestic market as opposed to selling abroad; the removal of these subsidies in response to pressures from the United States would depress manufactured goods export prospects further. It should be recalled, moreover, that many of the exports statistically included in the manufactured goods category are only slightly processed agricultural commodities such as orange juice, soybean oil, or soluble coffee—not far from the basic export commodities on which Brazil has traditionally relied. If shoes and textiles are also classified as being of agricultural origin, than half of Brazil's exports in 1984 were still of agricultural origin (see Table 7–4).

Starting from a low base, the takeoff in Brazilian exports began in the 1970s. In 1960, Brazil's exports of goods and services (FOB in 1982 dollars) amounted to US$3,661 million. In 1970, they amounted to US$6,504 million. By 1984, due to recession in Brazil's domestic market, import restriction, and export expansion largely attributable to U.S. growth and to the overvalued dollar, they amounted to approximately US$27,000 million

Table 7–4
Brazil's Foreign Trade: Total Exports and Imports, by Calendar Year,
1979–1986
(*millions of U.S. dollars, FOB basis*)

| Year | Exports from Brazil | Imports into Brazil | Balance |
|------|------|------|------|
| 1979 | 15.244 | 18,083 | −2,839 |
| 1980 | 20,132 | 22,955 | −2,823 |
| 1981 | 23,293 | 22,091 | 1,202 |
| 1982 | 20,175 | 19,395 | 780 |
| 1983 | 21,899 | 15,429 | 6,470 |
| 1984 | 27,005 | 13,916 | 13,090 |
| 1985 | 25,639 | 13,168 | 12,471 |
| 1986 | 22,393 | 14,044 | 8,349 |

*Source:* Central Bank of Brazil.

(in 1982 dollars). Although Brazil is approximately the eighth largest market economy in the world, in 1983 it provided only 1.32 percent of world exports. Despite the high rate of growth in production of manufactures, by 1984 the ratio of exports to output in manufacturing remained less than 9 percent. In 1984, moreover, despite the diversification and multiplication of its export activities, the largest 200 exporters from Brazil accounted for as much as 80 percent of its total exports.

Thus Brazilian external-sector statistics may be observed from either an optimistic or a pessimistic point of view. In 1984, for example, the peak year for exports, the trade account showed a surplus of US$13.1 billion, having improved from a deficit of US$4.7 billion in 1974. But this surplus was virtually exhausted by external debt service obligations; the current account, accordingly, showed a surplus of only US$0.2 billion. Brazil's cumulative current account deficit for the period 1983–1985 amounted to −US$8.0 billion.

It is ironic that although Brazil's trade relations with Japan are much more amicable than those with the United States, it is the latter that figures much more prominently in the benefit ratio. The United States is Brazil's largest export market. During the period 1976–1984, Brazil's average annual exports to the United States were three times as large as its exports to Japan (see Table 7–5). In terms of the cumulative trade balance for the period as a whole, Brazil had a favorable balance of US$503 million in trade with the United States and a favorable balance of US$355 million in trade with Japan. Between 1980 and 1984, however, the trend of improvement in Brazil's trade balance with the United States has been progressive and spectacular. According to the Central Bank of Brazil, the bilateral deficit of US$638 million in trade with the United States during 1980 was transformed into a surplus of US$5,413 million during 1984. This constituted 39.2 percent of the unprec-

Table 7–5
Brazil's Bilateral Trade with the United States and Japan, by Calendar
Year, 1979–1985
(*millions of U.S. dollars, FOB basis*)

| Year | Brazil's Trade with the United States | | | Brazil's Trade with Japan | | |
|---|---|---|---|---|---|---|
| | Exports from Brazil | Imports into Brazil | Balance | Exports from Brazil | Imports into Brazil | Balance |
| 1979 | 2,900 | 3,216 | −316 | 887 | 1,085 | −198 |
| 1980 | 3,440 | 4,078 | −638 | 1,232 | 1,066 | 166 |
| 1981 | 4,040 | 3,480 | 560 | 1,220 | 1,240 | −20 |
| 1982 | 3,980 | 2,837 | 1,143 | 1,294 | 881 | 414 |
| 1983 | 4,990 | 2,400 | 2,590 | 1,433 | 561 | 872 |
| 1984 | 7,710 | 2,297 | 5,413 | 1,515 | 553 | 962 |
| 1985[a] | 6,162 | 1,826 | 4,336 | 1,150 | 441 | 709 |

*Source:* Central Bank of Brazil.

[a] First 10 months.

edented total trade surplus of US$13.09 billion achieved in that year, which
was more than twice the size of the total surplus in the preceding year.
Exports to the United States constituted 28.6 percent of Brazil's total exports
in 1984. Imports from the United States declined from US$4,078 million in
1980 to US$2,297 million in 1984. Thus import dependency on the United
States declined, while export dependency increased. Brazil's ambivalence
toward the United States is rooted in these qualitatively different types of
dependence, compounded, of course, by its enormously increased dependence
in the financial sector. Brazil's export surplus in trade with the United States,
for example, has been largely attributed to U.S. growth and to the overvalued
dollar, but both of these factors were associated with U.S. monetary and fiscal
policies that raised interest rates and thus the cost of debt service to Brazil.
The surplus in Brazil's trade with Japan during 1984, amounting to US$962
million, was uncomplicated by these inconsistent results of policy. Thus
Brazil has less reason to be ambivalent toward Japan.

Trade conflict between Brazil and the United States is implicit in the
evolution of the commodity structure of Brazil's foreign trade, in the policies
by which Brazil has accelerated that evolution, and in the policies by which
the United States has resisted it. As a result of the import-substitution
program, a considerable degree of industrialization and diversification was
achieved by Brazil in the 1970s. This was reflected in the structure of bilateral
trade with the United States. The share of agricultural and agroindustrial
products (including raw sugar, cocoa, and coffee beans) in Brazil's exports to
the United States declined from 76.4 percent of the total in 1971 to 32.2
percent of the total in 1983. During the same period, the share of industrial
products (including footwear and steel products) rose from 18.0 to 54.0

percent of total exports to the United States. On the import side, Brazilian purchases of U.S. industrial products declined from 80.9 percent of total imports from the United States in 1971 to 69.7 percent in 1982.[33] In the course of this transition, conflicts have arisen concerning entry of Brazilian products into the United States, as have conflicts concerning competition with Brazil in third markets. By 1982, the list of such products included the following, all of which were subject to U.S. countervailing duty proceedings (discussed below): nonrubber footwear, leather handbags, castor oil and castor oil products, scissors and shears, cotton yarn, leather wearing apparel for men and boys, certain textile articles, pig iron, weapons, ferrochromium, carbon steel plate, certain carbon steel products (including wire rod), welded carbon steel pipe and tube, certain stainless steel products, tool steel, frozen concentrated orange juice, and commuter airplanes (see Tables 7–6 and 7–7).

Even within the U.S. government, sympathy has been expressed for Brazil concerning U.S. restrictions against its exports. The quota limit on Brazil's

**Table 7–6**
**Exports from Brazil, by Major Product, 1984 and 1985**
*(millions of U.S. dollars and percent)*

| | 1984 | | 1985 | |
|---|---|---|---|---|
| *Product* | *FOB Value* | *Share* | *FOB Value* | *Share* |
| Total | 27,005 | 100.0 | 25,639 | 100.0 |
| Primary products | 8,755 | 32.4 | 8,533 | 33.3 |
| Coffee in beans | 2,564 | 9.5 | 2,338 | 9.1 |
| Iron ore | 1,605 | 5.9 | 1,666 | 6.5 |
| Tobacco in leaf | 449 | 1.7 | 438 | 1.7 |
| Cocoa beans | 249 | 0.9 | 360 | 1.4 |
| Soybeans | 454 | 1.7 | 764 | 3.0 |
| Soybran | 1,460 | 5.4 | 1,177 | 4.6 |
| Beef | 214 | 0.8 | 264 | 1.0 |
| Industrialized products | 17,955 | 66.5 | 16,822 | 65.6 |
| Semimanufactured | 2,824 | 10.5 | 2,760 | 10.8 |
| Chemical wood paste | 393 | 1.5 | 276 | 1.1 |
| Unrefined soy oil | 557 | 2.1 | 332 | 1.3 |
| Pig iron | 266 | 1.0 | 268 | 1.0 |
| Cocoa butter | 168 | 0.6 | 203 | 0.8 |
| Iron alloys, raw | 235 | 0.9 | 227 | 0.9 |
| Manufactured | 15,131 | 56.0 | 14,062 | 54.8 |
| Orange juice | 1,415 | 5.2 | 753 | 2.9 |
| Footwear | 1,702 | 4.0 | 969 | 3.8 |
| Transport material | 1,354 | 5.0 | 1,688 | 6.6 |
| Boilers, mechanical instruments | 1,396 | 5.2 | 1,574 | 6.1 |
| Petroleum fuel oils | 605 | 2.2 | 412 | 1.6 |
| Steel products | 1,548 | 5.7 | 1,362 | 5.3 |
| Organic chemical products | 638 | 2.4 | 646 | 2.5 |
| Machines, electrical apparatus | 591 | 2.2 | 580 | 2.3 |
| Special transactions | 295 | 1.1 | 284 | 1.1 |

*Source:* CACEX (Foreign Trade Department, Central Bank of Brazil).

**Table 7–7**

**Imports into Brazil, by Major Product, 1984 and 1985**

(millions of U.S. dollars and percent)

| Product | 1984 | | 1985 | |
|---|---|---|---|---|
| | FOB Value | Share | FOB Value | Share |
| Total | 13,916 | 100.0 | 13,168 | 100.0 |
| Machinery and equipment | 2,151 | 15.4 | 2,494 | 18.9 |
| Fuels and lubricants | 7,345 | 52.8 | 6,176 | 46.9 |
| Crude oil | 6,735 | 48.4 | 5,418 | 41.1 |
| Derivatives | 131 | 0.9 | 276 | 2.1 |
| Grains | 835 | 6.0 | 731 | 5.6 |
| Wheat | 755 | 5.4 | 591 | 4.5 |
| Other | 80 | 0.6 | 140 | 1.1 |
| Organic chemical products | 662 | 4.8 | 718 | 5.5 |
| Inorganic chemical products | 208 | 1.5 | 157 | 1.2 |
| Fertilizers | 246 | 1.8 | 231 | 1.7 |
| Artificial plastic materials | 155 | 1.1 | 170 | 1.3 |
| Natural or synthetic rubber | 152 | 1.1 | 161 | 1.2 |
| Cast iron and steel | 159 | 1.1 | 174 | 1.3 |
| Other | 2,003 | 14.4 | 2,156 | 16.4 |

Source: CIEF (Economic and Financial Information Center, Ministry of Finance).

exports of sugar to the United States was reduced in the farm bill that was passed in December of 1985. In signing the bill into law, President Reagan described its provisions concerning U.S. sugar imports as "highly objection-able" and "inconsistent" with U.S. foreign policy goals.[34] Conversion of Brazilian sugar into ethyl alcohol for export to the United States is likewise discouraged by the inordinately high duty of U.S. imports of that product.

## Trade Policy

Policies of the Brazilian government that have contributed to U.S.–Brazil trade conflict include those whose purpose has been to change the structure of Brazil's foreign trade in accordance with the evolution of its domestic industrial structure. From a U.S. point of view, many of these policies, including policies for import restriction and export promotion, are considered inappropriate for an "advanced developing country." Policies for import restriction have included multiple exchange rates, tariff protection, quotas, and application of the "law of national similars" (a nonstatutory "law"). Some import restrictions were imposed by Brazil in accordance with an effort to cope with its debt crisis by improving its balance of payments performance. Some of the import restrictions imposed for this purpose were actually injurious to its industrial development program. The import content of output plays a role in a dilemma that constitutes one aspect of the Brazilian predicament. If for balance of payments purposes essential imports are restricted, output is restricted and growth is restricted. If growth is restricted, Brazil cannot pay its debts. But if imports are unrestricted, the balance of payments falls into arrears before growth can occur, and again debt service becomes more difficult. Resolution of this dilemma calls for walking a narrow line between short-term and long-term objectives.

Polices for export promotion have been more diverse. As summarized by the Morgan Guaranty Trust Company,

> To promote exports of manufactures ... exemptions were granted from many indirect taxes; corporate income taxation was reduced by the share of exports in total sales; a drawback system was established to waive import duties; nontariff barriers were lifted for companies committing to specific long-term export targets; and an export tax credit [subsequently eliminated] was introduced. Besides tax incentives, exporting companies were given access to concessional credit. Other measures favored processed agricultural exports, such as soybean and cocoa products, and yarn and cloth. Most important, exchange rate policy was supportive: starting in 1968, the currency was devalued frequently in line with domestic inflation. Nevertheless, there was no steady, generalized reduction in tariff and nontariff barriers, nor in the overall antiexport bias facing industry. Incentives for import substitution remained virtually intact.[35]

An anomaly in the conflict about fiscal subsidies concern the Special Program of Fiscal Incentives for Exporters (BEFIEX). The program was inaugurated in 1972; its benefits are negotiated by the Brazilian government with individual firms that make a commitment to reach agreed export targets over a period (generally) of 10 years. Fiscal incentives have aroused strong objections in Washington on the ground that they oblige private U.S. enterprises to compete with a foreign government in U.S. home market. BEFIEX has also been opposed by the U.S. government as a violation of GATT. U.S. policy concerning BEFIEX, however, is inconsistent. While the office of the USTR has threatened retaliation, the U.S. Department of Commerce draws attention to the program and urges U.S. firms to take advantage of it.[36] General Motors and Ford are prominent among those which heavily rely upon it.

Policies of the U.S. government that play a role in trade conflict with Brazil include those which ostensibly are designed to provide traffic rules for a multilateral free-trade system in the world economy as well as others, such as the Multifiber Arrangement (MFA) and "voluntary restraint agreements" that clearly are an abridgement of it. Tariff protection is the first policy usually cited. Although, on average, tariffs have been greatly reduced since World War II by a series of multilateral trade negotiations (Dillon, Kennedy, and Tokyo rounds), the general structure of the U.S. tariff system remains unchanged; its incidence with regard to raw materials is low, with higher rates on intermediate products, and highest rates on manufactured goods. Although tariffs charged on imports from Brazil are generally low, they are high in the case of some commodities of special importance to Brazil, such as orange juice, tobacco, and particular textile and apparel items. Sugar is subject to severe import quota restrictions. Brazil has been especially concerned about the level of U.S. tariffs on imports of fuel alcohol (ethanol), which was increased from 10 cents a gallon in the early 1980s to 60 cents a gallon by July of 1985. In the United States, ethanol is produced from corn rather than from sugar. Thus U.S. corn producers join hands with U.S. sugar producers in making it more difficult for Brazil to earn the foreign currency with which to pay its external debt.[37]

In the other direction, in its demand for greater access to the Brazilian market, U.S. criticism of Brazil is tempered by the obvious fact that Brazil must achieve a balance of trade surplus in order to pay its debts. In the event that the debt crisis subsides, it will no longer exercise a moderating influence on U.S. demands. On the optimistic assumption that the debt crisis will subside, an ironic statement appears in an official Brazilian government document. It concludes that "a reasonably safe prediction, therefore, is that U.S. complaints about Brazilian commercial policies—and industrial and investment policies as they affect trade—will grow in intensity over time."[38]

Because of the fact that tariffs remain high on types of manufactured products of importance to Brazil, it is clear that the effective rate of tariff protection in the United States is higher than the nominal rate so far as Brazil is concerned.[39] Accordingly, tariff preferences to Brazil assume a greater importance than would be apparent merely from the reduction of average overall tariff rates in accordance with multilateral trade negotiations.

Countervailing duties (CVD) have been applied on U.S. imports from Brazil since 1974. Countervailing duties are imposed when the U.S. International Trade Commission (ITC) determines that subsidized imports "cause or threaten to cause" material injury to a domestic producer. The amount of the countervailing duty is equal to the net amount of subsidy as calculated by the U.S. Department of Commerce. The number of CVD orders issued against Brazil increased sharply in 1981. By September of 1982, at least sixteen products exported by Brazil to the United States were subject either to CVD orders in the United States to export taxes imposed by Brazil to forestall such orders. The majority of countervailing duty cases have been resolved by means of "suspension" agreements, whereby Brazil undertakes to impose an offsetting export tax equivalent to what the countervailing duty would be. One of the subjects of controversy between the United States and Brazil concerns the question, when is an incentive a subsidy? In arguing about definitions, pressure may be applied by the United States for changes in Brazilian policy.

Antidumping duties are another controversial instrument of U.S. commercial policy. *Dumping* is defined as exports priced at "less than fair value." This concept is even more difficult to evaluate than subsidies; consequently, fewer antidumping than countervailing duty actions have been filed. Since 1982, however, the number of antidumping cases against Brazil has increased. These mainly involve Brazilian exports of steel, and for the purposes of this discussion, it is interesting that in most cases the exporters have been such producers as CSN, Cosipa, and Usiminas—enterprises with which Japanese interests have been prominently associated. Another U.S. policy instrument is the escape clause (GATT Article 19 and Sections 201–203 of the Trade Act of 1974). This is employed for the purpose of providing import relief to U.S. industries that suffer injury because of rapidly increasing imports, regardless of subsidization or dumping. Further, under Section 301 of the Trade Act of 1974, the President of the United States is "required to take all appropriate action, including retaliation, to obtain the removal of any act, policy or practice of a foreign government which violates an international agreement or is unjustifiable, unreasonable, or discriminatory and burdens or restricts U.S. commerce." In accordance with this provision, the USTR has conducted investigations concerning Brazilian exports of poultry and soybean derivatives to ascertain whether, by means of subsidies, Brazil has obtained a more than equitable share of world exports. Section 22 of the Agricultural Act of 1933, as amended, provides for quotas or fees to prevent imports from interfering with U.S. price-support programs. Among other effects, due to quotas imposed in May of 1982, Brazil's exports of raw sugar to the United States declined from 797,170 tons in 1980 to 286,806 tons in 1983. Brazil is also subject to quotas in accordance with the Multifiber Arrangement (MFA); since 1982, it has reached the maximum permitted volume of exports of cotton yarn, the most important category for its textile exporters.

In addition to sugar and cotton textiles and apparel quotas, specialty steels also have been subject to U.S. nontariff barriers in the form of quantitative import restrictions. In 1984, Brazil signed a "voluntary" 5-year agreement for restraint of its exports of steel to the United States. As a new entrant to the market, Brazil was handicapped in the assignment of quotas. I was informed that "quotas for the import of steel into the United States were assigned in November of 1983 on the basis of the average exports of each country to the United States during the previous 5 years. But in two of those years, Brazil had exported no steel to the United States. So again, the new entrant was handicapped. This problem is very severe for Brazil because we are attempting to enter the market with new products that have no base period performance record. Moreover, one-half of Brazil's actually performed exports of manufactured goods to the United States are under some kind of restraint or investigation."[40] My informant, Sr. Macedo-Soares, continued, "The investigations concerning Brazilian exports to the United States are harmful even when no unfavorable verdict is rendered. A North Dakota importer who reads that the ITC is investigating imports from Brazil may decide not to order the goods under investigation because he fears they may never be delivered. U.S. protectionism instigated by complaints from the private sector is more pernicious than protectionism of the government itself."

The merits of the case seem to shift drastically depending on which statistics are cited. On the steel issue, William Brock, U.S. trade representative, rejected the argument that the United States was being protectionist. He pointed out that the level of import penetration in the U.S. steel market was double that of the EEC and three times of that of Japan.[41] In 1984, Americans took the position that the United States, with its 1984 merchandise trade deficit of $123.3 billion, could not be considered protectionist. On the contrary, they argued it was Brazil, with its US$5.1 billion surplus in trade with the United States, as well as its many barriers against imports, that should be considered the protectionist offender.

On the whole, however, the results of trade negotiations depend as much on political bargaining as on the merit of economic arguments. The more highly politicized the bargaining becomes, the wider is the area of the tradeoffs. In a memorandum of understanding (MOU) following President Reagan's visit to Brazil in November of 1982, for example, Brazil accepted restrictions on its exports of armaments in return for access to U.S. defense high technology.[42] As the leading arms exporter in the developing world, this was a major decision for Brazil.

In the case of steel, political bargaining in 1984 took the form of an agreement that Brazil would voluntarily accept an annual quota limit of 500,000 tons in return for termination of the threat of antidumping proceedings against Brazilian steel. This agreement reveals that the disposition of such proceedings may or may not have any relevance to the formal criteria for a favorable or unfavorable verdict. In a broader context, the Brazilians insist that the nature of the international division of labor is essentially a political rather than an economic issue. The classical theory— that specialization takes place in accordance with comparative advantage based on the structure of factor endowments—is no longer persuasive. As Macedo-Soares observed, "Comparative advantage can be created—by means of biotechnology, new materials, and even by new methods of organization. Division of labor depends on how things are produced, and on relative priorities, as well as by natural endowments." In another interview at the Foreign Ministry, I was told, as I had been told before, "Some kinds of industries have to be left to the developing countries."[43] In this context, it was not contended that Brazil was an "advanced country."

As argued in the Brazilian Foreign Ministry, the idea that specialization and division of labor in the world economy are subject to negotiation rather than being given as an act of God is complementary with a new concept of reciprocity in international trade as advanced by the United States. Both are also a source of friction and conflict between vested interests in the two countries. Traditionally, *reciprocity* has meant that in aggregate terms, trading partners should offer each other equivalent concessions in multilateral negotiations on trade liberalization, all products being considered. As recently formulated by the United States, however, reciprocity has been interpreted to mean that each nation should have equal access to the market of its bilateral trade partner in specified commodity categories. This concept of reciprocity replaces the concept of "free trade" with the concept of "fair trade" and promotes bilateralism at the expense of multilateralism. In relations with Brazil, the United States has focused the new reciprocity concept on sectors where the United States is internationally competitive, especially high technology and services. In its impact on Japan, the concept has had the effect of accelerating decisions by exporters to establish manufacturing plants in the United States. In a sense, the "new reciprocity" is the concept of the "law of similars" turned inside out. As reformulated, it is also the basis for a U.S. demand that rules concerning international trade in services be placed within the jurisdiction of GATT, which at present is limited to trade in physical commodities only. (This is discussed further later.) In its traditional version, developing countries were not expected to comply with the requirements of reciprocity. In accordance with the new version, the United States expects compliance.

The argument in defense of noncompliance by Brazil has been stated by William R. Cline:

> Brazil and Mexico are countries that probably would be high on the list of targets of application for reciprocity pressure. Both have high protection and both actively affect the pattern of international trade through local content and export requirements in their agreements with multinational corporations.
>
> The cases of Mexico, Brazil, and other developing countries are complicated, however. Their "reciprocity" tends to be automatic at the aggregate level, because their need for foreign exchange is so great that they tend to spend whatever amounts of it they can earn. They are not accumulating large idle reserves; indeed, they have rapidly built up sizable foreign debts. Their tariff and quota protection and investment requirements distort the composition of imports, but the level of their imports is essentially determined by their export earnings (and capital inflows). To force compositional changes in their industrial structure would benefit some U.S. exporters but hurt others because, if Brazil (for example) imported more automobiles, it would have less foreign exchange left to import wide-bodied aircraft.
>
> Moreover, Brazil, Mexico, and some other newly industrialized countries (NICs) can legitimately point to the argument of infant industries to justify some of their protection, considering that their domestic markets are

large enough for potential economies of scale and that they have an increasingly sophisticated base of skilled labor. Over the longer run, better rules of the game will have to be worked out for trade with newly industrialized countries. However, now is hardly the time to impose additional pressure on exports from Mexico and Brazil, considering their high external debt (much of it held by American banks) and their already severe balance of payments problems.[44]

In addition to pressure for compliance with the new version of the reciprocity concept, Brazil has been subject to other pressures from the United States as well. As a signatory to the GATT subsidy code (Article 14:45 of Part III of the Tokyo round agreement), Brazil accepted the commitment to phase out its export credit premium by June of 1983 (later extended to April of 1985). As a "country under the agreement," as it then was designated, Brazil became subject to Title VII of the Tariff Act of 1930, as amended by the Trade Agreements Act of 1979, with regard to subsidized imports. In accordance with provisions of the latter, Brazil became subject to countervailing duties if its subsidized exports "cause or threaten to cause" material injury to a U.S. domestic producer. In April of 1985, however, Brazil failed to meet the deadline for removal of its export credit premium. On the grounds that Brazil had not honored its commitment, several U.S. senators urged the U.S. Trade Representative's office to impose countervailing duties without according Brazil the benefit of the injury test.[45]

Conflict between the United States and Brazil has mounted rather than subsided in the informatics area. In 1985, the office of the USTR was preparing a case against Brazil in accordance with the provisions of Section 301 of the Trade Act of 1974. In so doing, the U.S. approach was precisely opposite to that of the Japanese in dealing with the same difficulty. According to my informant in the office, "The United States is backing Brazil into a corner by making a public issue of this. We are attacking the problem head-on. The Japanese do the opposite. They play it the Brazilian way. Perhaps they are more accommodating because they have imposed similar restrictions of their own on access of outsiders to the Japanese market."[46] From a Brazilian point of view, protection of the informatics sector, including computers, is wholly consistent with GATT principles concerning the development of an infant industry. Moreover, Brazil classifies the industry as strategic, thus further justifying protection on "national security" grounds. Protective and restrictive devices imposed by the Brazilian government's informatics policy include the following: performance requirements for investors, discretionary and duplicative import licensing procedures, market reserve policy, restrictive government procurement policy, compulsory registration of software, mandatory use of a central gateway for transborder data flows, and high tariffs. An important argument in the informatics field concerns the U.S. proposal that the information component of computer software should not form part of the dutiable value of imports and that only the carrier medium should be taxed. Brazil and India are the principal opponents of this proposal.

## The Services Controversy

International trade in services, which constitutes approximately one-third of world trade, includes transactions in such fields as banking, insurance, telecommunications, data processing, shipping, aviation, construction and engineering. As an economic-development issue, the proposal to place these transactions within the purview of GATT is pregnant with controversy between Brazil on one side and the United States and Japan on the other. In July of 1986, after 4 years of procedural debate, the United States, with the support of Japan, persuaded the GATT membership to hold a ministerial meeting to negotiate an agenda for broadening the jurisdiction of GATT to include services, intellectual property, trade-related investment, and other matters. The meeting, held in September of 1986 at Punta del Este, Uruguay, was presented with three alternative texts as a basis for negotiation. Brazil, together with India as leaders of a group of countries including Egypt, Yugoslavia, and Argentina, took strong exception to the idea of discussing both goods and services in common under GATT auspices. They feared that under the guise of liberalization, the advanced countries sought to perpetuate their existing competitive advantage in high-technology services by preempting the market for such services in developing countries and stifling the development of their indigenous capability. Inasmuch as there are enormous economies of scale in the high-technology services industries, these fears were well-founded. The construction sector is perhaps the principal area in which some LDCs have a comparative advantage in services.

Both fear and suspicion lay beneath Brazil's resistance to a GATT round of negotiations on both goods and services. Fear of linkage between concessions concerning the flow of goods and concessions concerning the flow of services was of foremost concern. In particular, it was feared that Brazil would be expected to offer market-opening concessions in services in exchange for access to the U.S. goods market that previously had been promised but never delivered. It was argued that the United States should implement market-opening commitments already made before a new GATT round undertook to negotiate further commitments. In 1982, for example, a GATT ministerial meeting agreed on a work program providing for rollback of barriers to trade that contravened GATT rules and of restrictions on textiles and clothing, as well as liberalization of trade in agricultural products. By November of 1985, little progress had been made in any of these areas. The United States was accused of being inconsistent in attempting to open up markets for its bankers, insurance companies, and purveyors of other services while at the same time resisting imports from developing countries that were attempting to earn the revenue to service their debts. It was asked how there could be a new GATT round when there was no credibility of commitment to the previous (Tokyo) round. Inconsistency on the part of the United States also was seen in its demand for a multilateral agreement about services while it was steadily pursuing bilateral agreements in commodity trade, including steel and other products. Cynicism concerning GATT was not alleviated by the fact that the Multifiber Arrangement (MFA), although contrary to GATT principles, was negotiated under GATT auspices. (This arrangement, covering about half of world trade in clothing and textiles, was renewed in August of 1986 in a form more restrictive than its predecessors.) In its bilateral agreements, the United States was attempting to protect its technologically obsolete industries while demanding a multilateral agreement in services under the pretext that such an agreement would not perpetuate the existing U.S. competitive advantage in that category of trade.

It was charged furthermore that the U.S. preference for bilateral agreements concerning its technologically backward industries was indirectly reducing economic opportunities for developing countries. If a double standard is admissible, surely it is appropriate for use by developing countries, whose economies are typically dualistic, rather than by the United States. For these reasons, Brazil argued that negotiations about services, if undertaken at all, should be conducted in a parallel forum, such as UNCTAD, outside the jurisdiction of GATT.

Alternatively, in association with India, Brazil demanded preconditions for an agreement to negotiate both services and trade in a new GATT round. First would be the precondition of "standstill": all GATT members would have to guarantee that they would adopt no new import restrictions inconsistent with GATT rules. Second would be "rollback": all GATT members would be required to make a commitment to phase out within a specified period (perhaps within 3 years) all existing restrictions on imports from LDCs that are inconsistent with GATT rules or based on waivers from GATT obligations. Third would be "safeguards": these are protective devices authorized by GATT for the protection of industries subject to "unforeseen developments." The formula has been abused, especially by the use of bilateral "voluntary" export restraints. Brazil demanded that a comprehensive agreement on safeguards should be concluded before any other business in the proposed GATT round in order to prevent the United States from using safeguards as a bargaining chip with which to obtain concessions concerning services transactions. Fourth would be "preferential treatment": Brazil wanted assurance that the United States would not attempt to gain concessions in the services field by means of threatening to withdraw preferential treatment in favor of LDCs to which it had previously been committed.

Besides its suspicion of GATT and the uses made of it by advanced countries, including the failure of those countries to live up to the 1979 Tokyo round accord, the Brazilian government feared the domestic political repercussions of any new liberalizing agreement they might accept. Entry of new foreign competition in the Brazilian domestic market would require the government to make difficult political decisions that it would rather avoid. The Brazilian brief included a further argument that the United States itself preferred to avoid, namely, the need for international monetary reform. It was pointed out, for example, that after lengthy negotiations resulting in concessions to Brazil concerning subsidy policy, a shift in the value of the dollar could wipe out its results overnight.

From an "objective" point of view, the United States and Japan took the position that to exclude services from the purview of GATT would be to restrict its jurisdiction to a relatively diminishing category of world trade. Besides constituting about a third of world trade, in 1985, services accounted for 74 percent of U.S. employment. In Japan during 1985, services accounted for 61 percent of GDP and 57 percent of total employment. The United States and Japan argued that it was not fair that they should import from Brazil under the reasonably free trade regime subject to oversight by GATT while products of the most important sector of their own economies were subject to systematic trade barriers abroad.

Underlying this argument were issues concerning both Brazilian policy and issues concerning U.S.–Japan competition in matters concerning Brazil. Among the former were complaints by U.S. firms about counterfeiting, copyright and patent infringement, and nontariff barriers to trade. According to a memorandum prepared by the U.S. Trade Representative, the United States was primarily concerned with four objectives: (1) national treatment of foreign firms (foreign and domestic firms should receive identical treatment), (2) transparency of discriminatory laws and regulations, (3) public enterprises should be subject to foreign competition, and (4) consultation and dispute settlement procedures should be available to "provide enforcement teeth to the understanding."[47] Above all, the United States placed priority on liberalization of data-processing rules and reduction of barriers to the international transmission of data.

At its deepest level, however, the controversy concerning the role of GATT in relation to international services transactions is merely the shadow of a greater battle to come. Impending is a struggle for world supremacy in the high-technology services field. The U.S. strategic defense initiative ("star wars"), whose military applications are far more remote than its industrial spinoffs, can be construed in practical terms as a strategic initiative in the emerging high-technology struggle with Japan. For the United States, the stakes are so high that it has been willing to grievously antagonize Brazil and other nations by its aggressive tactics to secure consensus concerning the proposed GATT round. For Japan, there is no alternative to supporting the

U.S. proposal, although it has been very quiet in doing so. Japan's competitive advantage in the low- and middle-technology fields has vanished. It must survive by means of sophisticated high technology and international financial services. This is a central part of the rationale for the headquarters country scenario.

Many Brazilians, notably including Roberto Campos, maintain that it is in Brazil's interest to abandon the effort of developing a wholly indigenous capability in the high-technology information field. They argue that it cannot succeed and that Brazil will become a stagnant backwater in high technology. In contrast, Brazil could bargain for unrestricted access to the U.S. market for its primary and middle-technology secondary products as well as access to the Japanese market for textiles and food in return for a willingness to accept the jurisdiction of GATT in services.

Aside from its economic implications, the services controversy carries a political implication as well. According to Robert Fendt, "Brazil no longer considers itself to be 'leader of the third world.' This concept is out of date. Our Foreign Ministry may talk this way, but in practice we don't want to be considered 'third world.' We want to be regarded as an advanced country."[48] However, in assuming the role of principal lobbyist against the U.S. proposal for expanding the jurisdiction of GATT, Brazil has enlarged its image as a leader of third world nations.

## Competition and Cooperation

In foreign trade, conflict between the United States and Japan has generated cooperation between Japan and Brazil. A dramatic example is the soybean case, arising from the third of the "Nixon shocks" received by Japan. (The first shock was President Nixon's trip to China in February of 1971; the second was the new economic policy of August of 1971; and the third was the soybean embargo in the summer of 1973, which was imposed even on contracts that had already been concluded.) In the early 1970s, there was a great deal of pessimism about prospects for world food supply in relation to the population explosion. As the world's foremost food supplier, this seemed to place the United States in a strong position. Food became an economic and political weapon, which the Nixon administration decided to use in relations with Japan. In a tour sponsored by the U.S. State Department, a Nixon economic adviser, Pierre Rinfret, explained to the Tokyo Foreign Correspondents Club that the soybean embargo had been employed "strictly with malice. . . . We wanted to show something to the people who thought our economic strength was low," he said, "and frankly, the Japanese have been increasingly cooperative since then."[49]

At that time, the United States occupied almost a monopoly position in the world production and export of soybeans. Brazil produced virtually none.

Its potential output, however, was enormous. When Prime Minister Kakuei Tanaka visited Brazil in September of 1974, one of his main purposes was to arrange a project for Japanese agricultural cooperation with Brazil. Tanaka's agreement with President Geisel included the plan for development of the Cerrado. Instigated by the U.S. embargo, Brazil's output of soybeans rose from about 20,000 bushels a year in the mid-1960s to over 400 million bushels in 1976, more than one-quarter of the U.S. soybean crop. By the beginning of the 1980s, soybeans had displaced coffee as Brazil's leading cash crop and its leading export product. Brazil became the world's second largest supplier to the world market, after the United States. Japanese maintain that U.S. soybeans are of poorer quality and more expensive than those from Brazil. By 1984, Brazil had embarked on competition with the United States for the entire Asian soybean market.

This new competition has been accompanied by incriminations and recriminations. In July of 1983, the U.S. National Soybean Processors Association filed a complaint against Brazil under Section 301 of the Trade Act of 1974. The association alleged that Brazil used export subsidies on soyoil and soymeal products, with a depressing effect on world market prices. In November of 1983, President Martino de Faria of the Brazilian Vegetable Oils Industry Association (ABIOVE) charged that the United States subsidized its soy exports to a much greater extent than Brazil.[50] The shadowy ramifications of conflict and cooperation in U.S.–Brazil soybean competition are suggested by the fact that a "cartel of ten multinational grain companies" (American, French, Swiss, and West German), including Cargill, the Cargill subsidiary Tradax, and Continental Grain of the United States, purchase and export substantially all Brazil's soy products. ABIOVE has complained that the cartel has been guilty of spreading unfounded rumors and manipulating the market.[51]

In 1983, Brazil exported about 50,000 tons of soybeans to Japan. "It could export ten times as much."[52] The cost of transportation for exports from Brazil to Japan is about US$8 per ton more than for exports from the United States to Japan. Plans have been studied for the construction of huge vessels, twice as large as those with 60,000-ton capacities presently in service, that would reduce the shipping costs from Brazil. They would have separate compartments for minerals and agricultural products. Japanese assistance in the expansion of Brazil's output of agricultural and mineral products, however, is not necessarily directed toward increasing Brazil's exports to Japan. The main purpose is to increase the world supply of those products and thus to reduce the cost of Japan's agricultural and mineral imports from the United States and elsewhere, as well as from Brazil.

As in the case of soybeans, Brazil has emerged within a period of a few years as a leading exporter of poultry. In 1976, Brazil exported no poultry at all; by 1983, it was the world's third largest exporter (after the United States and France). Protests by the U.S. Department of Agriculture (USDA) against alleged Brazilian subsidies for poultry exports have been rejected by the Brazilian Poultry Union, which declares that exemption from value-added tax, which is allowed by GATT, is the only official aid extended. Brazilians assert that the real reason for the USDA protest is Brazil's success in selling to Japan, an established U.S. market. In a similar case, mentioned earlier, antidumping charges were filed by the Archer Daniels Midland (ADM) Company against Brazilian exporters of ethanol. In March of 1985, Brazilian defense lawyers complained to the U.S. International Trade Commission that the real reason for the charges was that Petrobras had refused to grant ADM's request to be named exclusive distributor of Brazilian ethanol in the United States.

In competition with the United States, orange juice concentrate is another lightly processed primary product in which Brazil's export position has advanced sharply in recent years. Brazil's earnings from citrus exports increased from US$281 million in 1979 to US$1,200 million in 1984. In citrus, however, Brazil is vulnerable in being excessively dependent on the United States as its principal market. Indeed, much of its export expansion in recent years has been made possible only by blights in the orange groves of Florida. In the event that the United States succeeds in persuading the Japanese to reduce their barriers against citrus imports, it is anticipated that Brazil rather than the United States will be the principal beneficiary.

On the U.S. side, it may be surprising that its principal individual product market in Brazil is the market for wheat, which in 1984 accounted for 15.0 percent of total U.S. exports to Brazil. Brazilian wheat imports are encouraged partly by its wheat consumption subsidy program and partly by special U.S. export financing. As development of the Cerrado proceeds, however, the Brazilian market for wheat is a wasting asset for the United States. Prospectively, with the assistance of Japan, the Cerrado will place Brazil in the same league as the United States as a food supplier to the world. U.S. competition with Brazil as an agricultural supplier will be the complement of U.S. competition with Japan in the world market for high-technology information and financial services.

In the meantime, the long-term prospect in these major matters is obscured by the vicissitudes of U.S.–Brazil conflict concerning poultry, apples and pears, nonrubber footwear, and the like, as well as issues in the middle-technology field concerning steel, aircraft, and ethanol, that dominate the attention of the U.S. Trade Representative. In interviews at the USTR, incidentally, as well as in interviews at the IMF with officials in charge of negotiations with Brazil, I was struck by the fact that none with whom I spoke had any notion at all about the contribution of U.S. or Japanese loans or investments in Brazil to Brazilian export production. That contribution is critical for an evaluation of Brazil's future role in the world economy, to say nothing of prospects for resolution of the debt crisis.

Besides seeking competitive power as a supplier of primary and middle-technology manufactured goods, Brazil has followed in Japan's footsteps in the administration of trade, including government control through licensing of transactions and pricing of commodities. Brasilia intervenes directly in commercial agreements and also exerts leverage on trade by means of Interbras, the trading company arm of Petrobras. Having a monopoly on the foreign trade transactions of its parent company, Interbras is the largest trading company in Brazil. In association with its transactions for Petrobras, Interbras is able to negotiate huge reciprocal purchase agreements on a government-to-government basis for products having nothing to do with petroleum. In October of 1984, for example, Interbras arranged the sale to Iraq of 145,000 tons of frozen chickens; this was the largest contract ever negotiated in the international poultry trade. The practice of establishing a central "channel" for imports or exports of bulk commodities is a typical Japanese procedure. The Japanese practice, which has served as a model for Brazil, was described to me by Shigeaki Ueki, president of Petrobras:

> For major basic agricultural and mineral commodities, Japan creates a single—or at least a restricted—import channel. China, for example, can sell oil to Japan only through a single designated Japanese importing firm—I forget its name. All iron ore imported by Japan from Brazil is sold to Nippon Steel. Australia can sell iron ore to Japan only through Nippon Kokkan. This is cartelization. In coffee and cotton, quotas are assigned to the various *sogo shosha* [general trading companies]. MITI doesn't like *sogo shosha* to compete in basic imports. Concentration of purchases promotes economies of scale: Japan buys large amounts and pays a low price.[53]

Its institutional arrangements for dealing through channels provide one of the means by which Japan will emerge as a headquarters country. Channels facilitate the collaboration of Japanese business and government in preparing projects of major importance with other nations. In the case of Brazil, Roberto Fendt observed, "It is easy for Japan to work with the Comphania Vale do Rio Doce (CVRD) because it is a government-controlled enterprise."[54] Relations at the government level are very convenient for both Japan and Brazil. Long-term contracts of huge dimensions are convenient for both because Brazil needs the assurance of stable markets for development projects that will mature slowly and Japan needs long-term stability of supply at low prices. From a Japanese point of view, channels also provide the means of applying pressure on Brazil. I asked Senator Severo Gomes whether Japan had done so or whether any of Brazil's creditors had taken advantage of the debt crisis to apply pressure in favor of their own national interests. "The

U.S. has not taken advantage of the debt crisis to gain benefits for particular enterprises," he said; "they have applied pressure only in terms of broad economic questions. Japan and Germany, however, have applied pressure. They have attempted to persuade Brazil of its 'opportunities.' "[55]

As in the case of Interbras and Petrobras, CVRD likewise serves as a focal point, or channel, for the negotiation of deals that have nothing to do with its principal business, namely, mining. In general, the channels afforded by Brazilian federal enterprises are of great benefit to Japan, sometimes at the expense of policies officially pursued by the Brazilian government. It has been shown, for example, that Brazilian companies prefer Japanese capital equipment to that of any other country.[56] Ordinary private enterprises are subject to the government's rule that capital equipment should be procured domestically. Federal enterprises have been more independent. In May of 1974, it was "recommended" to the state enterprises that for the sake of the import-substitution program, they should make "a special effort" to increase their procurement of domestic capital equipment.[57] The recommendation was largely ignored. In the absence of indigenous design capacity and the consequent lack of experience in the manufacture of capital goods, domestic Brazilian producers have not been considered reliable by major users, especially state enterprises. (Indeed, the lack of indigenous experience in the design, manufacture, and maintenance of capital goods was in itself a barrier to the transfer of technology to Brazil from abroad. Without minimal competence in the design and manufacture of capital goods, foreign blueprints and know-how are not of much help.) It is estimated that the federal enterprises have been responsible for 50 percent of Brazil's total demand for capital goods and for an even higher percentage of the demand for complex, custom-built equipment.[58] Besides their privileged access to foreign exchange facilities within Brazil and prerogatives in the way foreign exchange is used, the federal enterprises have been the chief beneficiaries of World Bank and IDB loans to Brazil, which confer freedom on the borrower in choosing sources of supply. World Bank loans, moreover, imply some bias against Brazilian suppliers of capital goods because of their emphasis on the qualifications of suppliers in terms of previous experience. Brazilian federal enterprises share this bias, to the benefit of Japan. "The United States is not successfully competing with Japan in selling capital equipment. It is able to do so only in a few specialty items."[59] U.S. suppliers, did, however, succeed in providing a minor amount of equipment for the Usiminas project. To some extent, U.S. companies have themselves purchased Japanese capital equipment. Ford bought Japanese presses and welding robots for production of its Escort car in Brazil.

According to an official of the U.S. Export-Import Bank, price and after-sales service are among Japan's heaviest weapons in selling capital equipment. "In bidding, their price is as much as one-third less than that of

U.S. companies. And when something goes wrong with Japanese equipment, they come over in platoons to fix it. They come instantly, at the first moment trouble arises. Even the Japanese, however, are undercut by the French in providing cheap credit. But the Japanese offer more cooperation than the French because they see the long-term implications. The French are not willing to cooperate."[60] By 1983, however, under the impact of the debt crisis, the Brazilian government reduced imports of foreign capital equipment virtually to zero.

In its role as an export base, Brazil serves as a means by which U.S. firms can cooperate with Brazil, compete with Japan, and compete in the U.S. home market as well. In performing exports, U.S. firms "cooperate" with Brazil in the most welcome way. In 1984, exports of the members of the American Chamber of Commerce for Brazil constituted 19.3 percent of Brazil's total exports. In 1984, as in 1983, 155 members of the Chamber of Commerce each achieved exports valued at more than US$1 million. Being more diversified than Japanese firms in Brazil, U.S. firms have been more affected by the adverse general conditions of the early 1980s; consequently, they have been subject to more pressure to export to compensate for the loss of domestic sales. In the opinion of a Brazilian government authority with reference to the performance of direct investment, the ratio of exports to output is far greater in U.S. firms than in Japanese firms in Brazil.[61] As a class, foreign firms are more export-oriented than indigenous Brazilian firms. Moreover, "in the United States, Brazil has a market for manufactured and semimanufactured goods. In Japan, we have no market for those products. Yet the United States is getting all the criticism."[62] Taking all foreign companies in the aggregate, Helson Braga found that in 1978 a dollar of subsidy to a multinational corporation resulted in more exports than a dollar of subsidy to an indigenous national company. It should be noted, incidentally, that the contribution of U.S. firms to Brazilian exports is not directly comparable to that of Japanese firms because, to a substantial extent, Brazilian exports are performed by Japanese trading companies that have no U.S. counterpart. The volume of Japanese trading company export transactions from Brazil is not public information. It has been estimated, however, that including exports they perform for Brazilian "window" trading companies, Japanese *sogo shosha* account for as much as 10 percent of total exports from Brazil.[63]

Although Ford Industria e Comercio Ltda. lost US$193.7 million in its Brazilian operations during 1984, it was the leading U.S. exporter from Brazil during that year, with export sales of US$477.5 million. In June of 1983, as a recipient of BEFIEX export subsidies, it was announced that Ford was committed to generate exports in the amount of US$3 billion by 1989.[64] Without BEFIEX export subsidies, Ford cars would not be competitive with Japanese cars in the European market, where both are currently being sold.

As summarized by the U.S. Department of Commerce, subject to the fulfillment of mandatory export quotas, export subsidies provided by BE-FIEX (Commission for the Concession of Fiscal Benefits and Special Export Programs) are the following:[65]

A 70 to 90 percent reduction of import duties and exemption from the tax on industrialized products (IPI) on imported machinery and equipment.

A 50 percent import duty reduction and tax reduction on imported raw materials, components, and intermediate parts

Complete income tax exemption on profits attributable to exports of manufactured products.

With an investment in Brazil comparable to that of Ford, General Motors do Brasil attempted to launch a new truck that would recover its share of the Middle East truck market lost to Japan. In announcing its plans for this venture, Peter House, marketing director for General Motors, stressed its "free market" aspect: "This is not like the Iraqi deals, where the Brazilian government and the Iraqi government get together and arrange the sale of 50,000 (Brazilian-made) Volkswagens."[66] In conforming to Brazilian practice for export expansion, General Motors do Brasil also has undertaken a countertrade program, initially within Latin America.[67] Brazil is among the leading countries in the world in the promotion of countertrade. At the end of 1985, as a means of overcoming its comparative disadvantage, the Brazilian government was planning to provide incentives for the inclusion of capital goods in its countertrade program.

Brazil figures prominently in competition and prospective competition between the United States and Japan in the world market for aluminum. The aluminum industry has been afflicted by the rise in the price of oil (mitigated by its decline in 1986) and by the pressure of substitute products, such as plastics. In the United States, prior to 1986, it also has been depressed by the overvaluation of the dollar. Almost all aluminum smelters in Japan, many in the United States, and most in Europe, even though modern and efficient, are no longer competitive at current prices. Thus both the United States and Japan have invested heavily in aluminum facilities in Brazil, where extensive bauxite deposits have recently been found and where hydroelectric energy rather than thermoelectric energy (produced from fuel oil) is used in the production process.

Accordingly, with no Brazilian participation, in one of the largest single private investments ever made in Brazil, a partnership between Alcoa (60 percent) and Shell (40 percent) undertook the Alumar alumina refining and aluminum smelting project, whose completed cost is estimated to be US$1.5

billion. The complex was inaugurated in 1984. According to the terms of its BEFIEX subsidy, Alumar is committed to export aluminum ingots and products during the next 15 years in the amount of US$2.7 billion. Among others, Alumar plans marketing offensives in Japan. In the United States, however, in October of 1985, Alcoa was planning to file an unfair trade practice case against Japan, charging that Japanese aluminum sheet product exports were subsidized. As of June of 1986, the case had not yet been filed pending the outcome of negotiations between the USTR and the Japanese government.

In Brazil, joint ventures Japanese style are with a Brazilian partner. In accordance with an Economic Cooperation Agreement between the governments of Japan and Brazil, signed on the occasion of President Geisel's visit to Tokyo in September of 1976, the Albras-Alunorte project was undertaken in the northeast, in the same region as the Alumar project. As of October of 1985, the projected cost of completion was estimated at US$2.5 billion. Alunorte is an alumina refinery; Albras is an aluminum smelter. On the Japanese side, thirty-three associates of NAAC (Nippon Amazon Aluminum Company) participate in holding 49 percent of the share capital of Albras and 39.2 percent of the share capital of Alunorte. The leading shareholder in the consortium is the Japanese government agency called the Overseas Economic Cooperation Fund (OECF). Others include five aluminum producers, ten trading companies, sixteen consumer finance companies, and a private bank. On the Brazilian side, CVRD, the Brazilian state company, holds 51 percent of the share capital of Albras and 60.8 percent of the share capital of Alunorte. Albras, which is Brazil's largest aluminum project, was inaugurated on an experimental basis in July of 1985. Alunorte is scheduled to be completed in 1988. Its technology is being supplied by the Nippon Light Metal Company. Technology for Albras has been supplied by Mitsui Aluminum Company. The resources contributed by the shareholders are partly in the form of venture capital and partly in the form of loans and credits. On the Japanese side, the loans are being made by a pool of twenty-three private banks headed by the Export-Import Bank of Japan; on the Brazilian side, they are provided by the National Bank for Economic and Social Development (BNDES). These details may suffice to describe a classic instance of what the Japanese refer to as a "national project," alluded to earlier, which officially is undefined.

The aggregate productive potential of Alumar, Albras and Alunorte, and other aluminum producers in Brazil is vastly greater than the absorptive capacity of the Brazilian domestic market. They must export to justify their existence. But in 1985, the price of aluminum was falling, and prospects in the external market were poor. Considering the investments at stake, there is a good possibility that U.S.–Japanese competition in exporting aluminum from Brazil may become more vicious than anything seen heretofore.

As mentioned earlier, in its role as an export platform, Brazil serves as a means by which U.S. firms can cooperate with Brazil or compete with Japan or with others in the U.S. home market. First, subsidiaries of U.S. firms in Brazil can serve both their own and Brazilian interests by exporting to countries with which the United States does not have amicable relations. Caterpillar Tractor Company, for example, has exported to Mozambique from Brazil. U.S. firms also can benefit from exports to countries in the Middle East and Africa with which Brazil has a "special relationship." Second, U.S. firms can serve Brazilian interests by exporting to the United States. In so doing, they also may serve the interests of their head offices by effectively competing either with other American suppliers, with U.S. imports from Japan, or with imports from other sources. Third, they can serve their own and Brazilian interests by exporting to other destinations in Latin America or to other regions outside the United States. In this case, they might be competing either with their own U.S. headquarters, with other U.S. firms, or with non-U.S. firms, including Japanese firms. A corresponding set of options is encountered by Japanese firms that export from Brazil.

These export options interact with foreign investment options for both the United States and Japan. In appraising the U.S. choice of options, Brazilians have been critical of overall U.S. strategy. Thus in the opinion of Shigeaki Ueki, "The U.S. is not investing in Brazilian agriculture because this would create competition for U.S. agricultural exports. Japan, however, is investing in Brazilian agriculture because Brazilian exports would be complementary with those of the Japanese economy. Japan has also invested in fertilizer production in Brazil, which would promote the agricultural development of Brazil and hence its agricultural exports. Japan has also invested in forestry and mining for the same purpose. But the United States has invested in none of these."[68]

A similar comment was made by the chairman of the Brazilian–American Chamber of Commerce in New York: "U.S. firms are reluctant to export from Brazil to the United States because they do not want to upset the markets for their domestic U.S. plants. The Japanese, however, attempt to export from Brazil to all parts of the world. Therefore, Japan is more helpful to Brazil than the United States."[69]

The merits of these comments should be statistically tested. Data with which to do so are not readily available. It may be noted, however, that Dow, Monsanto, and other U.S. companies produce agricultural chemicals, including insecticides and herbicides, for use in Brazil. The perception that U.S. firms in Brazil are reluctant to export to the United State also must be qualified by the fact that many U.S. firms have sister companies elsewhere in Latin America. The decision as to which of these will export to the United States depends on the respective comparative advantage of each. In some cases, moreover, such as Ford's "world car," the Escort, plans have been openly announced for prospective exports from Brazil to the United States.[70] However, Brazil would have to compete with Mexico as a source for the Escort. Brazilian automobile parts, especially unsophisticated cast parts, many of which are made in Ford plants, and car radio receivers made by Ford's Philco subsidiary are found everywhere in the United States. These compete with auto parts from Japan. Similarly, Komatsu has sent tractor parts and IBM has sent labor-intensive computer components from Brazil to Japan. Another example is that of Goodyear Tire and Rubber Company, which in 1983 began importing tires from its Brazilian subsidiary to the United States in order to compete with low-priced tires from Japan, South Korea, and East Germany that were reducing the market share of its U.S. plants. U.S. shoe and apparel makers have made similar moves. In the middle-technology range of products, some U.S. companies have closed their U.S. plants and rely wholly on Brazilian subsidiaries to supply their customers worldwide. As example is Cummins Brasil, whose plant in the Sao Paulo area is its sole producer of 230- to 535-horsepower six-cylinder motors for use in generators, locomotives, and boats.

In the case of Japan, where in 1984 the yen was undervalued and productive efficiency was high, it was a wrenching decision for head offices to allow their Brazilian subsidiaries to bid for export orders from third countries that otherwise they themselves would fill. For the sake of long-term strategy, however, it became increasingly necessary to do so, especially because the domestic Brazilian market was seriously depressed. Indeed, in some fields indigenous Brazilian firms collapsed, leaving Japanese firms as the main survivors. It was in the interest of Japanese head offices in Tokyo to ensure the continued survival of their subsidiaries by allowing them to compete for export sales.

With regard to trade promotion, during 1983–1985, U.S. profligacy was the chief contribution of the United States to Brazil. In terms of the debt crisis, excessively high interest rates were the most damaging. Likewise confusing the issue, cross-purposes and ambiguity damage other aspects of U.S. foreign trade relations with Brazil. Among various examples is the generalized system of preferences (GSP), which grants Brazil, as well as other LDCs, duty-free access to U.S. markets in specified commodities. The U.S. system of GSP tariff exemptions is more generous than that of Japan, which merely offers reduced tariffs on commodities that satisfy its criteria. Japan also applies quotas or ceilings on goods that may be imported under GSP. The tariff preference policy is a concession on the part of industrial countries to offset the bias against LDCs in their tariff rate structure. Typically, they impose higher rates on processed than on unprocessed goods. This hampers the industrialization of LDCs by impeding their exports of high value-added products. As of 1985, the GSP program of the United States granted duty-free treatment to approximately 3,000 tariff items, mainly manufactured and semimanufactured goods. Some items of importance to Brazil, such as textiles, apparel, footwear, and steel products, which constituted one-quarter of Brazil's exports to the United States in 1983, were not eligible for GSP preferences. A GSP beneficiary must demonstrate continuing "competitive need" for each commodity eligible for duty-free treatment. Competitive need is extinguished if (1) U.S. imports of a product from a specific country equal 50 percent or more of total U.S. imports of the given product, or (2) the value of U.S. imports of a product from a specific country exceeds a value limit that is adjusted annually in relation to U.S. GNP. In 1985, Brazil was the third largest beneficiary of the U.S. GSP program. In that year, imports from Brazil valued at US$1,278 million (16 percent of total U.S. imports from Brazil) were accorded GSP treatment.

In concept, the benevolent aspect of GSP is that it is "nonreciprocal": officially, no obligations inhere on the Brazilian side. In practice, however, as an "advanced developing nation," Brazil is subject both to "graduation" and "reciprocity." Based on a country's level of economic development, its balance of payments position, or the general economic interests of the United States, the President may graduate a country from eligibility for GSP benefits for any of its export products that become "competitive." In effect, graduation may depend on how much protectionist political pressure the President receives. As for reciprocity, the President may withdraw GSP privileges for any country that engages in "unreasonable export practices" or maintains "inappropriate" barriers to trade in services. Implicitly, there is a quid pro quo.

The United States and Japan both cooperate with Brazil and compete with each other by providing credits for Brazilian imports. The rationale for these credits is ambiguous. U.S. government appropriations on behalf of IMF assistance to Brazil are predicated on the assumption that Brazil will comply with an adjustment program that requires it to import less. But appropriations for the U.S. Export-Import Bank provide credits to Brazil that induce it to import more. For purposes of competing with Japan, among others, a further inconsistency lies in providing subsidized credit for exports to Brazil while penalizing subsidized Brazilian exports to the United States.

In August of 1983, competition for export sales to Brazil was braced by the establishment of a U.S. Export-Import Bank credit facility of US$1.5 billion on its behalf. This was at a time when, owing to the debt crisis, other sources of credit to Brazil were scarce. Indeed, in December of 1983, MITI suspended Brazil from eligibility for export credit insurance coverage; the suspension was lifted in May of 1984. However, when the U.S. credit facility of US$1.5 billion expired in March of 1985, it had been virtually unused because in the meantime, Japan, West Germany, and France had offered Brazil more attractive official financing terms.

In assessing the growth of Brazil's international competitive power, shifts in the GSP status of its exports to the United States may serve as an indicator. In 1985, the leading U.S. import products from Brazil that were eligible for GSP preference included the following: chemical mixtures, pneumatic tires, parts of engines, leather shoe parts, refrigeration and air-conditioning compressors, paper-making machinery, wood and glass-making machinery, and switchboard panels. Products that were graduated from GSP eligibility in 1985 included the following: methanol, piston-type engines, hardboard, ferosilicon, and ferrosilicon manganese.[71] It may be noted that in 1984, Japan's direct foreign investments in ferrosilicon production facilities were among its principal direct investments in Brazil.

## Notes

1. Albert Fishlow, "The United States and Brazil: The Case of the Missing Relationship," *Foreign Affairs,* Spring 1982.

2. Interview with Roberto Fendt, Jr., director of studies and research, Fundacao Centro de Estudos do Comercio Exterior (FUNCEX), in Rio de Janeiro, July 20, 1984.

3. Interview with Marie Welling, Brazil specialist, General Motors Corporation, in New York, June 30, 1983.

4. Interview with Edgardo Amorim Rego, senior manager, International Division, Banco do Brasil, S.A., in Rio de Janeiro, July 19, 1984.

5. *Brazil Trade and Industry,* December 1984.

6. Price Waterhouse, *Foreign Capital in Brazil,* February 1984.

7. Interview with Frederick Leroy Sherman, adviser, Philco Company, in Sao Paulo, August 6, 1983.

8. In 1984, IBM was engaged in a publicity campaign for its personal computers even though it was restricted from selling them in Brazil. Besides attempting to prompt the government to liberalize its policy, IBM also sought tie-ups with indigenous Brazilian producers in order to circumvent restrictions against foreign companies.

9. Interview with Hilton Lee Graham, economic consul, American Consulate General, in Sao Paulo, July 2, 1984.

10. *Gazeta Mercantil,* March 19, 1984.

11. Interview with Frank E. Downing, vice president, Atlantic Arena, SmithKline Chemicals, in Rio de Janeiro, July 1, 1984.

12. In manufacturing industries, according to the U.S. Bureau of Labor Statistics, the hourly pay of Brazilian labor was 9 percent of U.S. average during 1984. In Japan, it was 50 percent of the U.S. average.

13. Quoted in Banco do Brasil, S.A., *Monthly Letter,* October 1982.

14. U.S. Department of Commerce, International Trade Administration, *Investment Climate Statement: Brazil,* November 1984.

15. The World Bank, *World Development Report, 1985,* p. 64.

16. Interview with Wataru Aoki, chief representative, Export-Import Bank of Japan, in Rio de Janeiro, July 16, 1984.

17. Interview with Lawrence G. Smith, senior vice president, Citibank, in Sao

Paulo, July 5, 1984. The Bank of Tokyo has only five branches in Brazil, the maximum the government has so far permitted.

18. *Gazeta Mercantil,* April 2, 1984.

19. Interview with Hiroshi F. Katayama, vice president, Citibank, in Sao Paulo, July 3, 1984.

20. Data from *Balanco Annual, 1982.*

21. See Hajime Mizuno, *Burazil Nikkei Kigyo no Kenkyū (Research on Japanese Enterprises in Brazil)* (Tokyo: Sophia University, March 1984).

22. Interview with Tasuku Nagata, secretario geral, Camara de Comercio e Industria Japonesa do Brasil, in Sao Paulo, August 3, 1983.

23. Letter dated August 14, 1984 from Euclides Penedo L. Borges, chief manager of finance, International Division, Companhia Vale do Rio Doce (CVRD).

24. Airgram "CERP 429, Brazil's Mineral Sector, 1984," from American consulate general, Rio de Janeiro, to U.S. Department of State, May 22, 1984, Appendix 12.

25. *Ibid.,* p. 18.

26. Interview with Lawrence G. Smith, senior vice president, Citibank, N.A., in Sao Paulo, July 5, 1984. It should be mentioned that in calculating the competitive power of a steel plant, the main question concerns the way in which charges are assessed for the cpaital equipment installed. In the iron and steel industry, the capital investment is so great that this factor may overwhelm the comparative advantage arising from the cost of the raw materials. Thus a plant might be competitive if the terms of the loan by which it is financed are 10 rather than 14 percent, regardless of the quality or the cost of the coal and iron ore that are used as inputs.

27. Yawata Steel and Fuji Steel merged in 1970 to form Nippon Steel.

28. Interview with Professor Fabio Stefano Erber, Institute of Industrial Economics, Federal University, in Rio de Janeiro, July 19, 1984.

29. Interview with Jean Bernet, president, Guia Interinvest, in Rio de Janeiro, August 16, 1983.

30. *Gazeta Mercantil,* August 19, 1985.

31. *Gazeta Mercantil,* October 15, 1984.

32. Among the very few countries more closed than Brazil are India, Turkey, and Uganda.

33. Data from CACEX Leading items in U.S. exports to Brazil are wheat, coal, and chemicals. Leading U.S. imports from Brazil are footwear, coffee, and mineral products.

34. *Journal of Commerce,* January 2, 1986.

35. Morgan Guaranty Trust Company, *World Financial Markets,* May 1985, pp. 5–6.

36. See International Trade Administration, U.S. Department of Commerce, *Investment Climate Statement: Brazil,* November 1984.

37. In 1985, fifteen U.S. corn producers, led by Archer Daniels Midland Company, filed an antidumping action with the International Trade Commission as well as an appeal to the U.S. Commerce Department for countervailing duties against Brazilian ethanol.

38. Institute for Economic and Social Planning (IPEA), *Trade Relations Between Brazil and the United States* (Brasilia, 1985), p. 130.

39. The extent of effective tariff protection received in the United States is

measured by comparing the amount of domestic value added in a finished product under the existing tariff structure as compared with the amount of domestic value added that would be competitively practicable under a free-trade regime. The ratio of the difference between these two amounts is defined as the *effective rate of protection* to the finished product.

40. Interview with J.A. de Macedo-Soares, chief, Commercial Division, Ministry of External Relations, in Brasilia, July 12, 1984.

41. *Financial Times,* December 6, 1984.

42. The MOU was signed in February of 1984. In effect, it reaffirmed the close military link between the United States and Brazil that had been unilaterally abrogated by Brazil in 1977 in protest against President Jimmy Carter's human rights and nuclear nonproliferation policies. It should be noted that, in general, the USTR has a low opinion of the effectiveness of MOUs.

43. Interview with Embaixador Rubens Ricupero, Departamento das Americas, Ministerio das Relacoes Exteriores, in Brasilia, July 11, 1984.

44. William R. Cline, " 'Reciprocity': A new Approach?" in William R. Cline (Ed.), *Trade Policy in the 1980s* (Washington, D.C.: Institute for International Economics, 1983), p. 130.

45. *Financial Times,* May 29, 1985.

46. Interview with an official in the office of the U.S. trade representative, November 20, 1985.

47. *Journal of Commerce,* November 22, 1985.

48. Interview with Roberto Fendt, Jr., director of studies and research, Fundacao Centro de Estudos do Comercio Exterior (FUNCEX), in Rio de Janeiro, July 20, 1984.

49. *Journal of Commerce,* October 18, 1973.

50. *Journal of Commerce,* July 1, 1983 and November 10, 1983.

51. *Financial Times,* February 13, 1984.

52. Interview with Isidoro Yamanaka, assessor (advisor to the minister), Ministry of Agriculture, in Brasilia, August 10, 1983.

53. Interview with Shigeaki Ueki, president of Petrobras, in Rio de Janeiro, July 20, 1984.

54. Interview with Roberto Fendt, Jr., director of studies and research, Fundacao Centro de Estudos do Comercio Exterior (FUNCEX), in Rio de Janeiro, July 20, 1984.

55. Interview with Senator Severo Gomes, Federal Senate of Brazil, in Brasilia, August 10, 1983.

56. A clear preference on the part of Brazilian firms for Japanese capital equipment has been shown in a study by Charles H. Smith, III, *Japanese Technology Transfer to Brazil* (Ann Arbor, Mich.: UMI Research Press, 1981), p. 92.

57. CDI (Industrial Development Council) Resolution of May 23, 1974.

58. Fabio S. Erber, "Technological Development and State Intervention: A Study of the Brazilian Capital Goods Industry." Ph.D. thesis, University of Sussex, September 1977, p. 291.

59. Interview with Richard Huber, senior vice president, Citibank N.A., in New York, June 13, 1983.

60. Interview with Richard Crafton, vice president, Latin America Division, Export-Import Bank of the United States, in Washington, D.C., June 7, 1983.

61. Interview with Jose Botafogo Goncalves, secretario de cooperacao economica e tecnica internacional, Secretaria de Planejamento, in Brasilia, August 8, 1983.

62. Interview with Carlos Eduardo de Freitas, chief of department, International Operations Department, Central Bank of Brazil, in Brasilia, July 12, 1984.

63. Interivew with Kazuo Uesugi, president, Japan Trade Center, in Sao Paulo, July 4, 1984.

64. *Journal of Commerce,* June 28, 1983.

65. Office of Trade and Investment Analysis, U.S. Department of Commerce, March 23, 1984.

66. *Journal of Commerce,* February 3, 1983.

67. *Financial Times,* January 15, 1985.

68. Interview with Shigeaki Ueki, president of Petrobras, in Rio de Janeiro, August 15, 1983.

69. Interview with Vicente J. Bonnard, chairman of the Executive Committee, Brazilian–American Chamber of Commerce, in New York, June 13, 1983.

70. *Gazeta Mercantil,* January 30, 1984.

71. See U.S. Department of Commerce, Bureau of Economic Analysis, Working Paper, "Brazil: Trade and Investment Actions and Policy Issues," April 22, 1986.

# 8
# Brazil's Economic Transition

In the context of its implications for the United States and Japan, what progress has Brazil been making? U.S.–Japan rivalry is indirect as well as direct. From a Japanese point of view, progress may include exacerbation of Brazil's relations with the United States and an increase in their agricultural and industrial competition. It also may include a decline in the credibility of U.S. leadership as it attempts to cope with the issue of Brazil's external debt. The nonfinancial as well as financial effects of the debt crisis are of vast importance to both the United States and Japan. Among these, the foremost is *abertura,* the democratic opening that terminated the military regime in March of 1985. In its first year, after a weak start, the Sarney administration achieved astonishing progress and reforms. By 1987, the Sarney administration had lost its credibility. It proved incapable of overcoming the economic and social dualism that was augmented by the debt crisis. Likewise, it seemed incapable of forestalling the political polarization of the nation. Brazil is not alone in its economic transition: the United States and Japan have a stake in the outcome. Where is the relationship among the parties headed? A summary of some points mentioned in previous chapters and a selective survey of recent developments may provide a sense of direction.

## Nonfinancial Effects of the Debt Crisis

"Brazil Potencia" (Brazil, great power) was the concept to which Brazilian authorities appealed as a legitimating device for their policies during the economic "miracle" of 1968–1973. In the decade that followed, their attempt to sustain the "miracle" by means of foreign borrowing was justified in the name of the same slogan and in response to the popular demand for growth. The consequent debt crisis of the 1980s, which had real (nonfinancial) effects for debtor and creditor alike, was an open crisis for Brazil and part of a latent crisis for its creditors in the advanced industrial nations.

Brazil's enormous potential was trapped between its own predicament and the predicament of the world at large. Dim prospects for growth of the world economy in the second half of the 1980s provided a poor environment for growth within Brazil itself. A growth recession began in the United States in mid-1984.[1] In 1985, according to GATT, "World trade growth showed signs of slowing down." Trade also was becoming increasingly managed. In 1985, it appeared unlikely that future growth in world trade would suffice to generate enough demand for Brazil's exports to enable it to readily service its external debt.

Nevertheless, an inexorable real effect of the debt crisis was that Brazil can no longer remain isolated: its future is inescapably associated with external trade. A decade ago, there was talk of self-sufficiency. That idea is dead. The debt crisis opened Brazil to its international era, with totally congenial implications for Japan's geopolitical strategy.

Like traditional China, Brazil's outlook in the 1970s was that of a huge nation that presumed to be self-sufficient. When borrowing from abroad made Brazil's dependence on the world economy manifest, various aspects of its predicament became apparent. The debt crisis focused attention exclusively on short-term considerations. In the closing days of the military regime, "Nobody want[ed] to talk about fundamental reforms in financial institutions, taxation, or foreign exchange."[2] In the short term, Brazil was obliged to curtail its imports, but this reduced the rate of growth and increased unemployment. Import restrictions reduced export capacity. With disuse and lack of maintenance, much of the capital goods industry deteriorated into useless scrap. Major federal enterprises were largely capital-intensive; thus they generated relatively little employment. Even so, it was difficult to abolish, diminish, or denationalize federal companies because this would increase unemployment. Prior to the debt crisis, Brazil had achieved growth in its modern sector while regional poverty and stagnation persisted. With the debt crisis of the 1980s, when the modern sector itself miscarried, the economy as a whole fell into an impasse. It appeared that regional development, especially in the impoverished northeast, where one-fourth of the population resides, would become a casualty of the debt crisis. Agricultural productivity declined because of the reduction of subsidies for fertilizer.

During the first half of the 1980s, in an attempt to forestall a social explosion, the government financed its expenditures by inflationary means, either by issuance of treasury bills or outright printing of money. Government borrowing created a crowding-out effect in the money market, which further raised the cost and reduced the availability of working capital for the private sector. Bankruptcies ensued as the economy became decapitalized. Speculation superseded physical production as a profitable activity. The middle class, which in good times constituted only about 10 percent of the population, became progressively impoverished because salaries were indexed at less than the rate of inflation. With the exception of 1980, 1983, and 1986, when housing loans were indexed at less than the rate of inflation, interest on housing loans was fully indexed; this put a squeeze on members of the middle class who had mortgage obligations. Indexing itself, by stimulating inflationary expectations, contributed to the vicious circle of inflation. The regressive effect of these factors reinforced the dualistic character of the Brazilian economy.

In focusing attention exclusively on short-term expedients for paying the bills and closing the gaps, the debt crisis had major nonmonetary effects. It destroyed the priorities of structural readjustment; thus the eventual cost of adjustment was increased. In the meantime, resources were misallocated, and unemployment and underemployment mounted. In the midst of the world predicament, Brazil was attempting to shift the composition and distribution of its trade. In so doing, it became less complementary with the advanced nations and more complementary with the LDCs. Frequent and drastic shifts in policy on the part of the managers of Brazil's transition led to confusion and uncertainty in the private sector. "The government says one thing and does something different 2 weeks later." This also reduced Brazil's credibility in negotiations with foreign lenders. Government controls proliferated but were openly evaded in the "parallel" market economy that was beyond the reach of the tax collector.

In terms of the structure of industry, a real effect of the debt crisis was renewed emphasis on import substitution. The policy issue concerned whether this would be done efficiently by means of foreign exchange depreciation or inefficiently by means of protectionism. In the event, the principal approach was protectionist. The balance of decision making in these matters was determined less by economic logic than by the preference of influential ministers. (In Brazil, the personality of a minister may determine the power of the ministry he leads. Delfim was dominant regardless of the post he happened to occupy.) Import substitution was hampered, however, by the restrictions on imports of capital goods. Cotton fiber manufacturers, for example, were in trouble because they could not import the machinery they needed to expand production. The same was true in electronics; many computer services companies collapsed. Even federal companies were placed on a leash. Import restrictions also imposed a constraint on capacity for export production. Exports expanded, however, partly because of the domestic recession and partly because of the overvalued dollar. The combination of various incentives and constraints was more effective in inducing exports on the part of foreign firms than indigenous Brazilian firms.

In the process of change in industrial structure implied by import substitution, a significant tendency was a shift in favor of labor-intensive rather than capital-intensive products. This was a further effect of the debt crisis which intensified the capital shortage and raised interest rates. Domestically, it was very expensive to borrow, and foreign sources of credit had dwindled. Foreign sources of direct investment had dried up as well. Among other reasons for the decline in foreign investment was Brazil's restriction on royalty payments. This restriction was an important example of policy inconsistency arising from the structural economic predicament. In theory, Brazil was trying to augment technology transfer. It was essential to do so inasmuch as domestic funds for research and development were sparse and basic science had been neglected. In practice, the inflow of new technology was inhibited because of conflicting balance of payments constraints.

Thus both policy and structural factors contributed to the decapitalization of the Brazilian economy. In these circumstances, the types of enterprise that were most readily financible were those with low capital-output ratios. The latter yield output of a shorter-lived and "softer" type than the long-lived hard goods of the heavy industries that are at the frontier of Brazil's development effort. If it continues, this shift in the degree of capital-intensiveness of Brazilian industry has implications for both the commodity composition of output and the geographic distribution of Brazil's foreign trade.

Compounding the real effect of decapitalization was the pronounced trend toward economic concentration in Brazil as a result of the debt crisis. In the context of the present discussion, the importance of economic concentration is its implications for future U.S. and Japanese relations with Brazil. While the amount of capital in the economy declined, it was held in fewer hands. The causes are various. According to Senator Severo Gomes, "Our legislation is conducive to economic concentration. It is a perverse process."[3] Bankruptcies, among large as well as among small and medium-sized firms, increased steadily from 1981 to 1985. Consolidations increased simultaneously, with weaker firms being absorbed by stronger ones. In many cases, the survivors were subsidiaries of foreign firms. "Despite the decline in the absolute size of the domestic market, the market share of Japanese firms is rising. Some U.S. firms, such as General Electric, are increasing their market share as well."[4] According to another observer, "Japanese are now buying heavily of undercapitalized Brazilian firms."[5] Excruciating as this process may be for the firms that are swallowed up, some Brazilians regard it as simply one means of achieving economies of scale and therefore compatible with the rationale of economic development. According to a professional economist, "We have spread ourselves too thin. So some economic concentration, by means of bankruptcy, may be desirable in the private sector."[6] Concerning concentration in exports, according to the estimate of a private statistical agency, 75 percent of total Brazilian exports are performed by the 250 largest companies.[7]

In terms of official statistics, "There are no data concerning economic concentration. Also, there are no data concerning cartels."[8] However, the trend toward increasing concentration is apparent from circumstantial evidence. Even those who are skeptical about the steepness of that trend will grant that one reason it may be difficult to see is that a high degree of concentration existed even before the debt crisis. It may be argued that since many sectors were "born" with a restricted number of units, their concentration cannot be "increasing." "The Brazilian government tries to prevent competition by granting only a few licenses for production in each major sphere of activity. Thus cartels are implicit in this form of industrial regulation. The consumer has little choice."[9] The anticompetitive model conforms, moreover, with the "empty space" policy of federal enterprise in Brazil: in order to prevent MNCs from preempting any new vacant sector, the government typically establishes a state company with monopoly privileges. As a parent of such firms, for example, Petrobras included fifty-nine companies operating in many sectors that have nothing to do with petroleum. "Petrobras does not have a monopoly on all branches of the chemical industry. However, if you want to produce chemicals, it would be well to have a word with Petrobras."[10] The case of CVRD is similar. It has about fifty subsidiaries that have nothing to do with its basic business of mining. These subsidiaries are a barrier to foreign entry.

Economic concentration is also fostered by the administration of government subsidies. According to a study by Helson Braga, most subsidies are given to big business. In agriculture, most subsidies are received by rich farmers rather than by poor farmers. Braga found that in 1973, 1974, and 1975, the level of profits was positively correlated with the level of economic concentration.[11] About two-thirds of government subsidies are disbursed in the region of Sao Paulo and the southern part of Brazil. Geographically, industrial production is concentrated in the Sao Paulo metropolitan region, where the Federacao das Industrias do Estado de Sao Paulo (FIESP) members account for 60 percent of Brazil's total industrial output. In the rural northeast, concentration in landownership has increased markedly during the past several decades. According to the 1975 census, 1 percent of farm establishments account for more than 40 percent of all farm area. In contrast with the economies of large scale in industry, however, the comparative inefficiency of large Brazilian farms has long been acknowledged.

By means of interlocking relationships, as in Japan, conglomeration in Brazil's financial sector has contributed to the growth of concentration in its nonfinancial economy. Brazil has about a dozen major financial conglomerates, led by Bradesco and Itau, which have increasingly dominated private finance. They have done so with government encouragement and partly by virtue of their collaboration with the government. Concentration in banking, as concentration elsewhere, has received government sponsorship on the assumption that it would generate economies of scale. Typically, a financial conglomerate includes a commercial bank, an investment bank, a finance company, an insurance company, and a foreign trading company. As a government agent, it also may include facilities for the channeling of fiscal incentives toward the northeast, Amazonia, or designated economic sectors. Financial conglomerates are connected to industrial conglomerates, and—as in Japan—frequently they arrange transactions among their industrial affiliates. They promote "reciprocity" relationships that have an anticompetitive effect on financial intermediation.[12] The dominance of the top financial conglomerates over other financial institutions has been dramatized by bankruptcies among the latter. During 1983–1985, three leading privately owned building societies collapsed and three private-sector banks, including two of the country's largest, were liquidated.

Recapitulating the experience of the 1965–1968 recession in Brazil, federal enterprises and foreign enterprises in Brazil became stronger as a consequence of the debt crisis, especially in the "modern" sectors. To some extent, growth of government participation in the economy was involuntary. BNDES, for example, acquired many firms by foreclosure, including hotels, printing and publishing establishments, and small and medium-sized metal fabricating firms. In July of 1984, by a bookkeeping transaction, BNDES transformed a loan to Siderbras into equity. This was done for the purpose of complying with IMF "adjustment" requirements; however, it increased the government's role in the economy.

According to data compiled by *Visao*, in terms of value of output or net worth, the percentage of government participation in key sectors of the economy in 1982 was as follows:[13]

| | |
|---|---|
| Railroads | 100 |
| Telecommunications | 99 |
| Electric power | 98 |
| Warehousing | 75 |
| Mining and metals | 67 |
| Petroleum refining and distribution | 61 |
| Commercial banks | 57 |
| Steel | 55 |
| Shipping | 50 |
| Savings banks | 46 |

According to *Visao*, 60 percent of all investment was attributable to the government or to government enterprises in 1982.

A pessimistic comment on these developments by a government official was the following: "*Statismo*—overregulation, unfair government, and a progressively higher degree of government participation in the economy— this is not desirable, but it is incurable."[14] U.S. multinational corporations are criticized as well, but they are not as unpopular as they were in the 1960s. They too are being dwarfed by the federal enterprises. "The 'old story' about them was, 'They play the game of the U.S. government.' The 'new story' is, 'They are playing their own game.' "[15]

In addition to public- and private-sector monopolies and oligopolies, public- and private-sector cartels compound the anticompetitive effect of economic concentration in Brazil. There is a historical parallel between the rise of cartelism during the 1930s, with its price fixing and allocation of markets, and the rise of cartelism in the midst of the present debt crisis. Cartels flourished in the era of economic concentration and protectionism of the 1930s, as they do in the world economy today. Disorderly markets, rising nationalism, stagflation, and uncertainty of all kinds in present world circumstances give further impetus to the formation of cartels. In a world of cartels, Japan and Brazil are likely to be more economically collegial than Brazil and the United States. The foundation for the present trend in Brazilian economic concentration and cartelism lies deep in its past. Economic concentration is a euphemism for maldistribution of income and wealth. In attempting to account for the fact that many of the most successful developing countries have inadequate natural resource endowments, a World Bank official remarked, "Resources create economic rents; rents create vast inequalities; and inequalities create unprogressive vested interests." In Brazil, a virtual continent was divided into latifundia; its resources were monopolistically engrossed during the colonial period. Suspicion of the exploitative intentions of foreigners is a psychological result of Brazil's national consciousness of its colonial experience. Nevertheless, the institutional arrangements and the dualism of the colonial period survived as Brazil advanced beyond primary goods production to the output of secondary and tertiary products. In particular, a propensity toward centralization, economic concentration, and cartelism was institutionally established. The debt crisis accelerated this propensity.

Part of the institutional inheritance is the authorized legal status of cartels in Brazil. Even if there were an anticartel law, it would not necessarily be observed. A professor at the Fundacao Getulio Vargas remarked, "Law in Brazil is like a vaccination: sometimes it 'takes' and sometimes it does not. The antimonopoly clause in the Constitution, for example, is ignored and of no effect." Similarly, although Japan does have an antimonopoly law that prohibits cartels, as well as a Fair Trade Commission to enforce it, as of December of 1985, the Japanese FTC reported that there were 431 cartels authorized as "exceptions" to the law, covering 103 products and services. Japan also had numberless cartels that were unregistered and unauthorized. In Brazil, some cartels are explicit; others are implicit or underground, as in Japan. Many are maintained by the government. In countries where the government takes the lead in economic development, as in Brazil and Japan, bureaucrats have a propensity to establish monopolies and cartels which they can justify as being "in the national interest." The subordination of legislative to administrative authority in the implementation of controls in Brazil as well as in Japan helps account for the propagation of cartels in both countries. It is the administrators rather than the legislators who are in charge of the planning process and industrial policy. In Brazil as in Japan, it is the administrators who select key industries and key firms that will be eligible for infant industry protection. Their support is typically extended in the form of subsidies, tax benefits, and monopoly or cartel privileges. I found general agreement among Brazilian, American, and Japanese government officials, business executives, and academic observers that, as in Japan, the degree of economic concentration and the number of cartels in Brazil is increasing. In the opinion of a Japanese observer, however, there is a substantial difference between the effectiveness of Brazil's infant industry protectionism and that of Japan. In the informatics industry, for example, "Japan was able to successfully adopt protectionism and produce a mature, sophisticated, competitive industry. Brazil lacks the intellectual and scientific resources with which to do this. Brazilians are very flexible and unintellectual. They are energetic and have a mentality of progress. But they lack technique and training, and they don't know how to learn. Brazil will make itself backward by the informatics policy."[16]

One of the ways in which the Brazilian government creates cartels on behalf of its chosen instruments is by means of foreign exchange and foreign trade controls. This again is a faithful imitation of the Japanese model. In Brazil, with external controls completely in place, the debt crisis has effectively contributed to the acceleration of cartelism through restricted and privileged access to imports. Relatively small as the external sector is in Brazil, it looms large in the life of those industries which rely on import and export licenses, as well as related industries in the commodity chain and financial institutions by which they are accommodated. Hence external controls have served as a strategic instrument for the centralization and concentration of the Brazilian economy. Again, according to Senator Gomes, "Cartels exist in all countries. But elsewhere, there is democratic control of them. "Here. . . ."[17]

In accordance with their common acceptance and utilization of cartels, the Brazilians and Japanese have a collusive means of engagement with one another that the U.S.–Brazilian relationship lacks. Besides foreign exchange and foreign trade controls, Brazilian methods of establishing cartels include the "market reserve" policy, cartels mandated by government price controls, and government export-purchasing boards, as well as autonomous agreements among private firms. The ripple effect of SEI's market reserve policy in the production of microchips, for example, is to create cartels within industries that use microchips. The Telecommunications Ministry creates cartels in its allocation of contracts for new telephone exchanges to a restricted list of companies. Within Brazil proper, U.S. companies inadvertently or involuntarily may be parties to neocartel arrangements imposed by the Brazilian government. In the pharmaceutical industry—dominated by multinational U.S. corporations—a cartel is effectively established as a result of government price-fixing controls. In the tire industry—including Goodyear and Firestone—identical government-dictated prices are charged. In the electronics industry—likewise dominated by multinational firms—cartel behavior in pricing is apparent. In the automobile industry—exclusively composed of foreign firms, including General Motors and Ford—prices are changed in concert.

The tobacco industry is a government cartel for tax purposes. In sugar, the government effectively controls the entire crop by having a monopoly on the refining process. The government monopoly purchasing boards for sugar and coffee preempt private exports. Private-sector cartels or powerful oligopolies with a small competitive fringe prevail in shoes, textiles, food, soft drinks, beer, orange juice, small-scale steel plants, glass, cement, pulp, chemicals, and television and radio broadcasting. Also, as in Japan, "voluntary" export controls adopted under pressure from the United States result in implicit cartelization. After export quotas are negotiated, they have to be allotted to Brazilian suppliers and policed by an industry association or government agency. In December of 1984, for example, the United States and Brazil came to an agreement on "voluntary" export restraints to be applied to exports of Brazilian steel. In March of 1985, after acrimonious debate between government and private steel companies, the quota was divided and allocated among them. In July of 1985, Brazil's Federal Sugar and Alcohol Institute (IAA) announced that it was about to establish export quotas for the ethanol industry because of two antidumping cases brought in the United States under the leadership of Archer Daniels Midland Company.[18]

Although holding companies are illegal in Japan (having been abolished by the Occupation and never reestablished), in Brazil they are alive and well, both in the government and in private industry sectors. By the facility with which it generates joint ventures, the Brazilian *zaibatsu*-type holding company is preeminently suited to the promotion of economic concentration. With great flexibility, as in the former Japanese *zaibatsu* system, it allows the formation, re-formation, or dissolution of joint ventures within its framework. Votorantim of Sao Paulo is an example of an important private Brazilian holding company. Siderbras, which is the umbrella for all Brazilian government steel companies, is a typical government holding company. The flexibility of Brazilian holding company regulations makes them a versatile instrument of business response to the many aspects of instability in the nation. The increase in various forms of instability is one of the pronounced nonfinancial effects of the debt crisis in Brazil.

Concerning the internal debt, it has been proposed by Professor Maria da Conceicao Tavares that the government exchange part of the government debt in bonds and bills for preferred stock in the federally owned companies. This would both reduce the deficit and encourage economic growth. In performing the domestic exchange of debt for equity, moreover, increased ownership of the Brazilian economy would not accrue to foreigners. In the external sector, exchange of debt for equity would deliver ownership to foreigners. In so doing, however, it would reduce debt-service obligations. The savings could be channeled into productive uses. Accordingly, in 1982, incentives were introduced in the form of 5 to 10 percent tax write-offs for companies converting international loans to direct investment. Conversions were made at discounts of up to 30 percent of the nominal value of the equity exchanged. The incentives and discounts met with the disapproval of some Brazilian government officials, including President-elect Tancredo Neves. Furthermore, since about two-thirds of the external debt represented borrowing by federal companies, conversion of debt to equity would augment the position of foreigners in a way most offensive to nationalist sensitivities in Brazil. Finally, from a purely practical point of view, "The fact that the current account is heavily in the red makes the borrower boss. The Brazilian government wants the foreign banks to worry, so that they will lend more. If we reduce the debt, they will react by lending less."[19] For these reasons, in June of 1984, restrictions were placed on the types of loans that qualified for conversion and registration as authorized investments and minimum periods for maintenance of the resultant investments in Brazil were specified. In January of 1985, incentives for the conversion of debt to equity were entirely withdrawn. Approximately three-fourths of the US$800 million direct investment inflow received by Brazil in 1984 was in the form of debt conversion.

Expansion of countertrade activity has been another nonfinancial result of the debt crisis, with further implications for collaboration with Japan. Apart from socialist countries, Japan and Brazil are the world's leading practitioners of countertrade. In a sense, Brazil's BEFIEX program, inaugurated in 1973, constitutes a form of countertrade in that it exchanges import and tax concessions for investment-related export performance. In the recession following the second oil shock, whether or not the debt crisis was a crisis of "solvency" or merely of "liquidity," it was certainly lack of liquidity that drove Brazil further along the path of countertrade. To a large extent, it is the leverage exerted by huge federal enterprises such as Petrobras that have made possible the expansion of Brazil's foreign commerce in the form of countertrade transactions. After the relapse of OPEC in 1984 and the rise of countertrade, the Brazilians were tempted to believe that the "oil weapon" had changed hands. For example, any major purchase of petroleum by Petrobras is accompanied by pressure on behalf of reciprocal Brazilian countertrade exports by Interbras, its trading company affiliate. CVRD arranges similar deals. In so doing, these federal enterprises help justify their existence and thus provide an argument against denationalization. As an offset, however, it has been argued that the countertrade accomplishments of the state enterprises have been performed partly at the expense of potential sales by the private sector. The concentration of foreign exchange in the hands of the Central Bank in August of 1983 gave a powerful impetus to further countertrade initiatives within the private sector as well. Barter and its variations were methods of circumventing the government's restrictions on imports and also avoiding letter of credit difficulties. But it is noteworthy that when the foreign exchange concentration regulation was rescinded in March of 1984 and the domestic growth rate recovered in 1985, small and medium-sized firms preferred to work for sales expansion in the domestic rather than foreign market. This revealed that the burden of expanding Brazil's foreign trade lay chiefly on the shoulders of the major monopoly and cartel enterprises of the nation's economy. In the performance of that task, as in other aspects of Brazil's transition, the Japanese development model has been instructive. Japan's *keiretsu* groups and their *sogo shosha* have been engaged in countertrade and the like since they were reconstituted following the Occupation. In the future, collaboration of Brazil's major enterprises with the distribution networks of Japanese *sogo shosha* is virtually assured as countertrade transactions multiply in the world economy and as more nations, including the United States, adopt them as standard operating procedure. As bilateralism, managed trade, and countertrade arise in response to prevailing protectionist barriers, competitive export subsidies, exchange rate instability, and international financial disequilibrium, the summer season of the Japanese *sogo shosha* in Brazil is clearly at hand.

Privatization of state enterprises is another proposed response to the constraints and instability evoked by the debt crisis. For various reasons, including the fact that the very inception of many of these enterprises was inappropriate, very little privatization has been accomplished. While professing a policy of privatization, moreover, Finance Minister Dilson Funaro announced in November of 1985 that foreign loans to Brazil would in the future be exclusively directed by the government toward state companies, to help them roll over their external debt obligations. Brazil's failure to implement its privatization policy had the effect of enhancing economic concentration. The latter, in turn, was a result congenial to Japan. Because of its historical experience and institutional arrangements, Japan is better able than the United States to negotiate with a nationalized and centralized Brazil.

Prospects for privatization are poor, first, because the grandiose basic projects are clearly destined to remain in the public sector. Decapitalization in the private sector has made it difficult to denationalize even companies of modest size. Second, many of the state enterprises are inefficient, overstaffed, and have enormous debts. Heavy industry, for example, is greatly overexpanded. Domestic and foreign market prospects have been poor. State companies were able to show profits because prior to the currency reform, the law allowed them to include as revenue the inflationary profits derived from the excess of the monetary correction of their fixed assets over their net worth. If these adjustments and other subsidies were excluded, all major federal enterprises except Petrobras and CVRD would have shown a loss in recent years. Moreover, the state companies are not merely business organizations: they have become politicized. Politics enters into the determination of their budgets, the financing of their deficits, their personnel appointments, and their influence on appointments within the government itself. Many of the state companies have been located in inappropriate regions for political rather than economic purposes. Many state companies are dominated by left-wing politics. Although unions are prohibited in state companies, they have quasi-unions in the form of "clubs," many of which are run by opposition political parties. Any attempt to fire workers by privatization would meet with powerful resistance. By 1985, with almost no exceptions, only the smallest of the state enterprises had been privatized.

## Difficulties, Progress, and Reform

The crisis of the Brazilian economy in the first half of the 1980s is summarized in the fact that per capita GDP fell by at least 12 percent between 1980 and 1983. Industrial employment fell by about 23 percent between December of 1980 and March of 1984. Both external and internal events contributed to the crisis. Inappropriate and delayed response to the first OPEC price shock of 1973 placed Brazil in a highly vulnerable international position. In 1979, the economy was shaken by the second oil shock and also by soaring interest rates on external debt, world recession, and weak commodity prices. At that point, it was no longer possible to defer adjustment by further international borrowing or by increased import restrictions. In late 1980, drastic recessionary adjustment measures were imposed. These, however, failed to address the internal disequilibrium of the overgrown public sector and the large and increasing consolidated public-sector deficit. After the Mexican default in 1982, the virtual termination of lending by international banks forced the Brazilian government to attempt more drastic adjustment. With the advice of the IMF, this chiefly included expenditure reduction on the part of the public sector, particularly in public-sector investment. Ironically, the collapse of investment had repercussions in the form of inflationary supply deficiencies that subsequently jeopardized the adjustment process itself.

In the meantime, however, given that economic growth is the key to overcoming the debt problem, Brazil surprised its critics and even itself in the progress that was made following *abertura*. In the final years of the military regime, owing to economic adjustment efforts, the real GDP growth rate per capita had been −5.7 percent in 1981, −1.5 percent in 1982, and −4.9 percent in 1983.[20] In 1984, the last year of the Figueiredo administration, the overall real GDP growth rate was 5.7 percent. In 1985, the first year of the Sarney administration, it was 8.3 percent. The preliminary figure for 1986 was 8.2 percent. The improvement was partly the result of previous efforts on behalf of economic adjustment and partly due to the burgeoning of U.S. import demand. In the trade account, sharp improvement followed the decline in the world price of oil and reduction in the quantity of oil imports made possible by import-substitution programs. The latter included increases in alcohol fuel, hydroelectricity, and domestic oil production. The net cost of petroleum imports declined from US$9.4 billion in 1980 to US$3.9 billion in 1985. The balance of payments was helped enormously, moreover, by the decline in international interest rates that affected 80 percent of Brazil's medium- and long-term debt and virtually its entire short-term debt, which were priced on a floating rate basis. Brazil's trade surplus of US$13.1 billion in 1984 (third highest in the world, following Japan and West Germany) had enabled the authorities to grant large wage increases; the ensuing consumption boom was the basis for the record GDP growth rate in 1985. The trade surplus in 1985 (again third highest in the world) was US$12.5 billion.

The trade surplus, however, had its own problems. First, it was inflationary by virtue of expansion of the money supply. Second, it arose partly from import restrictions. These included barriers against foreign manufacturing equipment for which there were—or were supposed to be—domestically available equivalents. By 1986, many firms in major industries were operating at close to capacity. Because of low level of investment in the first half of the 1980s, there was no imminent prospect of further productive capacity coming on stream. Domestic demand was competing against the foreign market for available output. Exports, moreover, were threatened by the "new protectionism," especially in the United States, Brazil's principal trade partner.

In keeping with the "open" character of U.S.–Brazilian relations, the friction in their relationship is "open" as well. The many cases of overt confrontation between the United States and Brazil redound to the indirect advantage of Japan. (Indeed, overcoming the antagonist by indirection is a classic element of Japanese strategy.) Both sides have their complaints, but inasmuch as the trade balance has been in Brazil's favor, the loudest cries have come from the United States. As required by Section 303 of the Trade and Tariff Act of 1984, a catalog of U.S. complaints about Brazilian (as well as Japanese and other) import restrictions and export-promotion practices is published by the USTR in the form of an *Annual Report on National Trade Estimates.* As itemized in the 1985 issue of this report, sources of friction between the United States and Brazil may be briefly summarized as follows:

Brazil's multiple exchange rate practices in the form of a variable tax on purchases of foreign exchange.

High tariff levels on Brazilian imports of plasticizers, almonds, feed supplements, aluminum and fiberglass insect screens, textile and apparel products including polyester fabric, certain paper products, electric shavers, canned peaches, corn, and fruit cocktail.

Quantitative import quotas imposed by the Bank of Brazil's Foreign Trade Department (CACEX).

Import licensing and other administrative barriers. Virtually all Brazilian imports are subject to license. Regulations are complex. The "law of similars" applies to 90 percent of imports. These restrictions have been the most important factor in the decline of U.S. exports to Brazil. Affected items include steel products, process control valves, nonbulk agricultural commodities, general aviation, machine tools, roller bearings, batteries, and textiles and apparel.

Discriminatory apple and pear import licensing restrictions. Import restrictions based on rules concerning standards, testing, labeling, and certification. Most significantly affected have been seeds, including grain, sorghum, corn, and beans.

Government procurement, with special reference to the "buy national" policy.

Export subsidies for soybeans and soybean products. These include tax exemptions, preferential production financing, and preferential export financing. Brazil has dramatically increased its share of world markets for these products, mostly at U.S. expense. During the past decade, the U.S. percentage of world soybean meal and soybean oil exports has fallen from more than 70 percent to approximately 20 percent.

Lack of intellectual property protection. Patent protection is inadequate, and copyright piracy is a serious problem with regard to unauthorized motion picture performances, translation of literary works, videocassette and record piracy, and piracy of computer software.

Countertrade and offsets. Brazilian exports under such agreements cover the full range of manufactured products and raw materials, as well as construction services. Substantial U.S. exports to third markets of products such as poultry, soybean meal, chemicals, cotton, paper, and steel have been displaced.

Service barriers. Foreign companies, particularly construction firms, are prevented from providing technical services unless it can be shown that no Brazilian firm can provide the service. All technical service contracts must be approved by the Industrial Property Institute (INPI), where they are subject to substantial delays and other administrative difficulties. Telecommunications and data services may be subject to new controls under the informatics law's implementing regulations.

Insurance. Government actions effectively cause all Brazilian import insurance to be placed with Brazilian firms.

Data processing and telecommunications. Brazil requires that data be processed within the country, thereby depriving many data processors of using central processing facilities abroad. Foreign equity participation in information service industries in Brazil is limited.

Motion pictures. All color prints must be made in Brazilian laboratories. In addition, 16-mm black and white films must be printed in Brazil. Brazilian theaters must show Brazilian films at least 140 days a year.

Ocean shipping. U.S. chemical and mineral producers express concern over Brazilian government requirements for transportation of imports on Brazilian vessels.

Investment barriers. The BEFIEX program (Commission on Fiscal Incentives for Special Export Programs) grants tax benefits to firms that maintain a three-to-one ratio of exports to imports. [U.S. firms, however, are among its principal beneficiaries.] The United States has expressed concern about the trade-distorting effects of this program. By the end of 1983, actual exports under the program totaled US$12.9 billion.

General investment barriers. In some situations, Brazil limits foreign equity participation and imposes local content and export performance requirements, often tied to incentives. It restricts the transfer of earnings and capital and limits or prohibits entry of foreign investors in "sensitive" sectors such as electronics, computers, and aviation. The impact of these barriers has had the effect of reducing the proportion of U.S. direct investment in Brazil, while U.S. direct investment in Asia has substantially increased.

Informatics. The informatics sector is broadly defined to include not only computers and parts, but all other devices incorporating a digital instrument. Included are communications switching equipment, instruments, process controls, optoelectronic components, and software. A complex 1984 law authorizes import restrictions for a period of 8 years. It reserves production and sales of many products exclusively for Brazilian-owned firms. National firms are to be given preference in government procurement and access to special fiscal and financial incentives. Foreign firms operating in special export zones are to enjoy all export incentives but may not sell in the domestic market. Incentives and approval of investment proposals are subject to local content requirements. During the period 1978–1982, U.S. computer product exports to Brazil grew at a compound annual rate of 21 percent, while the Brazilian computer market grew at an 18 percent rate. From 1980 to 1982, however, U.S. computer exports grew at a rate of only 14 percent a year, while the Brazilian market increased 30 percent. The United States has consistently objected to Brazil's informatics policy and warned Brazil of the likely effect of the law's passage and implementation on Brazil's development and U.S. economic interests.

General aviation aircraft. Although Brazil can impose tariffs and other taxes equal to 65 percent of CIF value, licensing is the major deterrent to U.S. general aviation aircraft sales in Brazil. On the other hand, Brazil freely exports assembled aircraft to the United States, on which no tariff is imposed.

With few exceptions, such as the informatics dispute, it is apparent from the preceding summary that U.S.–Brazil conflicts of interest are largely concentrated in the primary goods and low- and middle-technology sectors. In 1986, Brazil was unresponsive to U.S. complaints. The nation was in a euphoric mood after celebrating the accomplishments of the civilian government on the anniversary of its first year in office. These included the world's leading growth rate of GDP as well as an astonishing surplus in the trade account. Moreover, it seemed (mistakenly) that inflation had been stopped in its tracks by the currency reform of February of 1986. These facts were flung at the IMF, whose standard remedies and whose surveillance Brazil by then had repudiated. They also served to convince Brazilians that their transition from self-sufficiency to dependence on the world economy did not require submission to U.S. demands. How did Brazil arrive at its prematurely euphoric mood?

To recapitulate, despite the reforms that had been attempted in the terminal years of the military regime, inflation had accelerated. During 1983, for example, it had continued to rise despite reduction of the consolidated real public deficit and increased restrictions on monetary and credit expansion. Contributing factors were the 30 percent "maxi-devaluation" of the cruzeiro in February of 1983, elimination of subsidies on petroleum products in June of 1983, and (temporary) reduction of the wheat subsidy. That these nominally desirable policy measures were nevertheless inflationary was an ironic aspect of Brazil's economic predicament. Brazil's break with the IMF in mid-1983, furthermore, was destabilizing, and the collapse of international commercial bank lending inflamed inflationary expectations. The predominant inflationary factor, however, was the comprehensive system of indexation that currently incorporated into wages and prices the inflation that had previously occurred. Thus, even after the removal of destabilizing factors on the supply or demand side, indexation served to ratchet inflation by validating inflationary expectations of further wage and price adjustments. Indexation together with accommodating monetary and fiscal policies made inflation self-propagating. In February of 1986, shortly before the Sarney administration's first anniversary, inflation was running at the rate of approximately 500 percent a year.

On February 28, 1986, President Jose Sarney announced a dramatic Economic Stabilization Program of currency reform and wage and price controls to overcome Brazil's "inertial" inflation. Its main provisions were as follows:

> An across-the-board freeze on most retail and wholesale prices and government utility rates.

> An 8 percent "bonus" for most blue- and white-collar workers, with wages and salaries frozen for 12 months. In the event of a rise of 20 percent or more in the cost of living since the previous adjustment, wages were to be increased by 20 percent. (This provided for more prompt and complete indexation of wages than had been authorized even before the February 1986 reform.)

> Reform of Brazil's currency, with the new cruzado replacing the cruzeiro at a ratio of 1 to 1,000.

> A 12-month freeze of treasury bond rates at the March 1986 value of 106.4 cruzados, thus effectively de-indexing financial, real estate, and other markets.

> A switch from indexed to free-floating interest rates for all financial instruments, with the exception of ordinary savings accounts. The latter were to be revalued quarterly with full allowance for inflation.

> Fixing of a "stable" foreign exchange rate of 13.8 cruzados to the U.S. dollar.

Supplementary measures announced in March of 1986 included creation for the first time of a modest unemployment insurance fund, labor law changes favoring collective bargaining, and a 12-month freeze on most mortgage and rental payments. A further important reform was the termination of the Bank of Brazil's residual role as a monetary authority.

Initially, the results were favorable. Between March and July of 1986, the cumulative amount of inflation was only 4 percent. There were important nonfinancial or real effects as well. Of fundamental importance was the stimulus to output of real goods. Whereas formerly many manufacturing firms had profited by financial manipulation rather than by physical production, this was no longer easy to do. Banks were hardest hit by the reforms, as investors left the money market in favor of physical assets. (As a primary result of the reforms, banks lost revenue on demand deposits that had been relent with monetary correction plus a substantial interest rate charge.) Moreover, the domestic price freeze made exporting more attractive. In both the domestic and external sectors of the economy, the triumph of stable prices enabled firms to make medium- and long-term plans. In conjunction with

Argentina's ("Austral") currency reform, it facilitated an agreement between Brazil and Argentina in July of 1986 for inauguration of a customs union. Thus, like the debt crisis, but for better reasons, the currency reform was conducive to internationalization of the Brazilian economy.

The strong recovery induced by the Economic Stabilization Program, however, soon induced renewed spending on the part of Brazilian state enterprises. Since public sector spending (including loans) was equivalent to about 60 percent of GDP, their increased spending was once again inflationary. Thus while the public-sector borrowing requirement was about 2 percent of GDP in 1985, it is estimated that it rose to 5 percent of GDP in 1986. Additional inflationary pressure was exerted by a powerful consumption boom as savers joined investors in switching from financial assets to physical products. By July of 1986, the black market value of the U.S. dollar had soared to a level almost twice that of the official rate. Another complicating factor was the legacy of unresolved price discrepancies bequeathed by the price freeze of February of 1986. For example, the prices of such items as milk, meat, gasoline, cars, refrigerators, and television sets were frozen at disproportionately low levels as compared with those of other products. While consumption of these products was stimulated, their production was inhibited, leading to shortages and new inflationary pressures.

As a means of restraining spending and increasing government income, President Sarney in July of 1986 announced a new 3-year development plan. In lieu of a sales tax, the plan would raise revenue through a system of compulsory loans from consumers. With clear political implications, these compulsory loans to the government were to be extracted mainly from the middle class, a minority of about 10 percent of the population. They were to take the form of price increases on luxury goods, such as cars, automobile fuel, and foreign travel. They were to be repaid in the form of tax credits within a period of 3 years. The price increases, being classified as "loans," were to be excluded from the cost of living statistics, and thus inflation was to remain theoretically under control.

In retrospect, the first 6 months following the reform of February of 1986 were as typical of a situation in which a resurgence of inflation was expected as one in which it had been conclusively overcome. The consumption boom touched off by the reform was instigated partly by fear of what would happen when price controls were lifted. Indeed, evidence of an underground thaw in the price freeze was the principal reason for the 3-year development plan announced in July. Private domestic investment and foreign investment remained totally apathetic. Contributing to the low level of investment were the very import restrictions that had been imposed in favor of domestic firms: they had difficulty in importing essential machinery, components, and replacement parts from abroad. Private investment also was constrained by uncertainty concerning legal and administrative policies of the New Republic.

Brazil's predicament lay partly in its need to achieve social reforms in the course of economic stabilization. The "social deficit," for example, called for land reform as well as reforms in nutrition, public health, basic education, and housing. Economic progress had been unbalanced among sectors of the economy, among regions and urban-rural locations, and among households. None of these can be resolved in the short run, and each requires the expenditure of an enormous amount of political capital on the part of the government. There is also the predicament of inconsistencies. Wage policy, which was shaped in accordance with social reform, was inconsistent with economic stabilization. Production and consumption subsidies that had been cut during 1983 and 1984 had to be restored in order to overcome shortages induced by the price freeze. But the disappointing rise in government revenue after February of 1986 left the government unable to finance these subsidies without deficit spending. During the 3 months following February of 1986, the deficit was reflected in an inflationary explosion of the money supply. This was exacerbated by inflationary wage policy and the public sector deficit. The government's budgetary dilemma was not helped by the fact that the program for privatization of public enterprises made virtually no progress. By the same token, the economy remained highly concentrated. Big-business oligopolies in the private sector remained sluggish and inefficient because for years they had received protection from foreign competition in accordance with the official import-substitution policy.

Despite the improvement in the growth rate and in the foreign trade account, Brazil's domestic economy was not open to foreign competition, it remained dominated by state enterprises, and its private sector was increasingly regulated. Price controls, credit controls, wage controls, and foreign exchange and other controls, plus an increase in bureaucracy, revealed that *abertura* had brought more rather than less government intervention to the nation. Moreover, despite the internationalizing influence of the debt crisis, Brazil remained one of the world's most closed economies. This anachronism was compounded by the fact that despite some diversification in the commodity composition of its exports, the geographic distribution of its trade remained heavily centered on the United States. (In 1985, the United States absorbed 28.6 percent of Brazil's exports and provided 19.9 percent of its imports. In the previous year, both figures had been almost as high.)

Thus the Brazilian predicament is one of many dimensions. In the attempt to cope with it, Brazil has become more centralized and controlled. For reasons mentioned earlier in the discussion of Japan's geopolitical strategy, a Brazil that is both increasingly controlled and increasingly vulnerable to the world economy is one that is increasingly susceptible to Japanese influence. Japan's international infrastructure can serve Brazil more effectively than that of any other nation. In its economic transition, Brazil conforms with Japan's headquarters country scenario.

## U.S. Relations with Brazil

> For my family—everything.
> For my friends—whatever is possible.
> For my enemies—the law.
> —Brazilian adage

When the trade-negotiating branch of the U.S. foreign economic policy establishment cites this adage, what it has in mind is the "law of similars," market reserve, and the like. Being subject to such laws, the United States feels itself to be the "enemy." According to my Washington informant,[21]

> From an American point of view, the law of similars is unfair. Furthermore, Brazilian law is often implemented in a haphazard, capricious, or arbitrary manner. It is unfair that Brazil should deny access to its market for the very commodities, such as informatics, where our comparative advantage exists and in which the United States is *not* a declining nation. Brazil is in a state of adolescence. It wants to be treated as an adult, but it declines to accept mature responsibilities. It clings to the privileges and immunities of an LDC. How can Brazil be made to see the rationality of market-opening measures? Removal of restrictions on foreign trade and investment would be productive. Is U.S. retaliation the only means of bringing Brazil to act in its own interest?
>
> Like the Japanese, Brazilians respond only to pressure. They have a zero-sum view of external relations. They believe that one party's gain is the other party's loss. Until faced with overwhelming pressure, they are unwilling to make concessions. Then, pragmatically, like the Japanese, they yield at the last minute.

Even if retaliation were indicated, the amount of leverage the United States could apply to Brazil is arguable. Moreover, while many sophisticated Brazilians agree that market-opening measures would be in Brazil's interest, they see the issues in a different perspective. Concerning informatics, I was told by a Brazilian economist at the IMF:[22]

> The United States places too much emphasis on this. Relatively, it is a very minor point. The more important point is Brazilian access to the U.S. market. This is the key factor. Second, Brazil should have more decision-making power in U.S. private enterprises in Brazil. U.S. firms do not employ Brazilians to be chief executive officers, as the Europeans do. German firms have Brazilian chief executives; Ford and G.M. do not. A foreign chief

executive cannot know the domestic market as well as a Brazilian. American chief executives stay a couple of years; than they are rotated elsewhere and some new man arrives. A Brazilian chief executive will also have more incentive to export. Volkswagen and Fiat are the leading automobile exporters; Ford and G.M. are a remote third. U.S. firms follow the leader in exports; they do not lead.

Concerning the debt problem, the United States should be more flexible. In the first place, the United States should try to arrange a restructuring of the debt. Second, it should put a cap on the real interest rate—2 percent would be appropriate. This would give the United States a good image in all of Latin America. But in Washington, no one is thinking about the U.S. image there. They don't give a single minute, even in the State Department, to thinking about U.S. public relations in Latin America. Everyone knows what U.S. policy is toward the Soviet Union, toward Israel, toward the Arabs. But no one knows what U.S. policy is toward Latin America. There is no policy.

Brazil is one of the strongest advocates of a high U.S. growth rate. If the United States has a low growth rate and becomes more protectionist, this will restrict Brazil's exports. In the short run, however, the most direct and effective way of improving the U.S. image in Latin America is to do something constructive about the debt problem.

A Brazilian economist in the World Bank spoke in a similar vein:[23]

The most important fact is this: the United States doesn't realize how much weight it has in relation to Brazil. It doesn't realize the effect on Brazil of changes in the interest rate, for example. When the United States sneezes, Brazil catches pneumonia.

Second, U.S. policy as it affects Brazil is inconsistent. Various agencies have a hand in it, and none of them is concerned with U.S. foreign economic policy as a whole. The various departments—State, Commerce, Treasury—have different philosophies. They also have different constituents. They respond to the influence of different lobbies. When the Department of Commerce negotiates with Brazil about a particular item, such as textiles, they represent only textiles, not the overall interests of the United States. Therefore, U.S. policy at large is sacrificed to the special interests of highly segmented pressure groups. These pressure groups even affect the vote of the United States on the Board of the World Bank. For example, on April 22, 1986, the board approved a loan of US$155 million to Brazil for the purpose of assisting the general development of Brazilian agriculture. It was Loan 2679-BR, entitled "Second Agricultural Extension Project." But the U.S. member of the board voted against it. This was because the American Soybean Association was opposed to it. They were afraid that even though the loan was designed for the improvement of Brazilian agriculture in general, that in 5 years time it would give some incidental benefits to soybeans. In voting against this loan, the United States violated the articles of agreement of the World Bank, which say that the mandate of the bank is to provide overall development assistance. Similarly, the United States voted against a Malaysian project because it would benefit palm oil, even though the benefit to palm oil was trivial in relation to the project as whole.

Furthermore, the U.S. agencies that affect foreign economic policy take a short-term view. Therefore, the United States fails to anticipate crises. It does not take measures to prevent the disease; it waits until the disease breaks out and then attempts to treat the disease. It waits until the last minute before taking action. The United States should have learned from its experience in Central America that during the past 30 years it did not provide enough development assistance. Now it has troubles in the Caribbean. Later, if the United States does not help Brazil to develop, it will have troubles in South America that will make Central America look like a flyspeck.

The United States should also be more flexible in its interpretation of Articles 201 and 301 of the Trade Act. These provisions are not applied consistently and equitably because of the different amounts of influence and pressure exerted by a mixture of lobbies on various U.S. government agencies. Concerning subsidies, incidentally, U.S. agriculture is far more heavily subsidized than Brazilian agriculture.

To say nothing of the Cerrado project, agriculture is indeed a case in point concerning the conflicts of interest between Brazil and the United States in Brazil's economic transition. In agriculture, for example, the United States pays its farmers to grow less, while Brazil pay its farmers to grow more. During the past decade, prospects of primary-product producers have gone from one extreme to another. At present, apart from Africa, the world is "awash in grain."[24] In agricultural trade, the U.S. surplus declined from $25.6 billion in 1981 to $11.4 billion in 1985. The U.S. government is giving up the attempt to maintain farm prices; instead, it is attempting to support farm incomes. In accordance with the 1985 Food Security Act ("Farm Bill"), the price of rice was reduced in April of 1986; this upset U.S. relations with Thailand, which heavily depends on exports of rice. In June of 1986, by reducing "loan" support, the United States lowered the price of wheat. The European Community, Australia, and Canada protested. As an offset, U.S. farmers received "export enhancement" subsidies to maintain their incomes.

During a 4-year period, the U.S. Department of Agriculture was authorized by the Farm Bill to spend $1 billion in "bonus" subsidies to farmers, in addition to about half that amount for "export promotion." The agricultural subsidy war that is mounting between the United States and rival nations threatens to precipitate retaliation in other commodity categories, such as steel, textiles, and high-technology products, as well as in noneconomic fields, such as security affairs.

Conflicts of interest among other nations open a path of opportunity for

Japan. This is the route along which Japan's geopolitical strategy will travel, in encouragement of Brazil and other U.S. economic rivals. Tradeoff negotiations among countries that subsidize exports and those which practice import protectionism places Japan in a position to benefit from both. For this reason, Japan's stake in the present GATT round of negotiations is different from that of the United States, despite their common position with regard to high-technology trade. From a Brazilian point of view, incidentally, there is no basis for a tradeoff between Brazilian access to the U.S. market for primary and middle-technology products in return for U.S. access to the Brazilian market for informatics. In October of 1985, a Japanese diplomat was told by an important Brazilian industrialist that inasmuch as Brazil has already paid exorbitant interest rates on its debt to the United States, it owes the latter nothing in the form of concessions on its market reserve policy in the field of informatics.[25]

In mid-1986, moreover, the Brazilian government was studying proposals to place additional economic sectors under the protection of market reserve. These included pharmaceuticals, chemical specialties, minerals, aerospace, and biotechnology. This was a further example of the trend toward increased government intervention, cartelization, and economic concentration in Brazil. The implications were not auspicious for U.S.–Brazilian relations.

In summary, as outlined below, current evidence suggests that in its various modes, the U.S. approach to Brazil may be described as bilateral, direct, or adversarial, while the contrasting modes of the Japanese approach may be described as consensual, indirect, or geopolitical. In each case, the respective modes of approach may be overlapping.

Although committed in principle to the unconditional most-favored-nation (MFN) doctrine, the United States has in practice qualified its adherence in a growing number of cases. These have included the bilateral memorandum of understanding (MOU), bilateral investment treaties, and bilateral "voluntary export restraints" and "orderly marketing agreements" with various trade partners. In accordance with the Multifiber Arrangement (MFA), negotiated as an exception to GATT, bilateral quotas for exports of clothes and textiles to the United States have been assigned to Brazil as well as to Japan. Likewise, in other arrangements as described earlier, bilateral quotas for exports of steel have been assigned both to Brazil and to Japan. In April of 1983, the U.S. Department of Commerce signed four MOUs with the Brazilian Ministry of Mines and Energy concerning specific Brazilian hydroelectric and thermal electric projects. A fifth MOU project concerned a coal gasification plant. These bilateral accords foreclose open competitive bidding and are expected to generate U.S. exports amounting to a billion dollars within an 8-year period.[26] To the disadvantage of Brazil, the East-West conflict also enters into Washington's suspicion of multinational agencies that may subsidize countries of which the U.S. taxpayer would disapprove. In particular, the World Bank has been subject to these suspicions. The effect has been to promote U.S. bilateral relationships.

In its "direct" mode of approach to Brazil, the United States asserts its own interests openly. This is to be contrasted with the "indirect" approach of the Japanese, whose self-interest is not threatened by Brazil's economic development. In practice, the contrast shows up in the U.S. preference for autonomous, wholly-owned direct investments as compared with the Japanese manipulation of joint venture arrangements, in the U.S. preference for directly productive activities as compared with the Japanese contribution to Brazilian infrastructure, and in the U.S. demand that Brazil conform to the U.S. concept of correct commercial policy as compared with the Japanese promotion of Brazilian activities that will indirectly favor the achievement of "comprehensive economic security" for Japan. Robert Blocker commented on the direct versus the indirect approach. "U.S. firms here," he said, "complain about controls, credit restrictions, and the like. The Japanese firms work around them."[27] Japanese indirection is illustrated also in a controversy concerning restrictions on imports into Japan of oranges and beef from the United States. For years, by resisting U.S. demands that these restrictions be removed, the Japanese have diverted the attention of the United States to relatively trivial issues while economic strategy of global salience was being contrived by Japanese bureaucrats offstage.

In U.S. relations with Brazil, the direct approach may assume an adversarial aspect. During the Carter administration, this was the case with regard to demands for control of nuclear proliferation, respect for human rights, and removal of barriers to trade. During the Reagan administration, the targets have shifted. By means of an advertising campaign, IBM waged an open publicity drive against the government's informatics policy—an action that would be unthinkable on the part of any Japanese firm. In effect, by its sins of omission and commission, Brazil became a scion of early postwar Japan which had been attacked by the United States for subsidizing production, dumping exports, restricting imports, and resisting the entry of foreign investment in financial and nonfinancial sectors. U.S. pressures, moreover, as in the case of pressures on Japan, have been inconsistent. While the U.S. government demands that Brazil remove its production subsidies, private U.S. investors in Brazil argue the opposite. President Edward Hagenlocker of Ford do Brasil asserted the need for establishing new export subsidies in Brazil when the BEFIEX incentives program expires in 1989. In order for Ford to successfully export from Brazil, "we must have our competitiveness guaranteed," he declared.[28] As perceived in Brazil, moreover, "the United States is unwilling to overcome its own government deficit by precipitating massive unemployment, but it is willing to see that happen in Brazil."[29]

U.S. direct pressures on Brazil, as in the case of Japan, may not only be inconsistent, but also counterproductive. By insisting on "voluntary export restraints," which require the assignment and policing of export quotas on the part of government or trade association authorities, the United States has contributed to the cartelization of industry in both countries. This makes the possibility of achieving economic liberalization in both Japan and Brazil more remote than it otherwise would be. In the meantime, Japan is the unintended beneficiary of U.S. pressure on Brazil by increasing Brazilian antagonism against the United States. More fundamentally, cartelization of the Brazilian economy is a counterpart of cartelization and economic concentration in Japan. "Cordial oligopoly" relations on the international plane are wholly consistent with the evolution of Japan as a headquarters country in the rationale of that scenario.

In October of 1985, the U.S. Treasury launched its proposal, known as the Baker plan, for relief of the international debt crisis. Besides further assistance from the World Bank and the Inter-American Development Bank, the plan called for international commercial banks to provide fifteen debtor countries, mainly in Latin America, with additional loans amounting to US$20 billion during the 3-year period 1986–1988. The plan was widely welcomed as a step in the right direction. It was also regarded as inadequate, thus reflecting the dilemma of the creditors as well as that of the debtors.

The Baker proposal combines elements of typical U.S. modes of approach to Brazil, including the bilateral, the direct, and the adversarial. Ever since the debt crisis became manifest in 1982, the United States has attempted to cope with it by concentrating on the difficulties of a selected group of debtors, especially Brazil, Mexico, and Argentina. The Baker plan is a key-country approach, in effect an enhanced *bilateral* approach. It does not propose a solution for the debt crisis in general, nor does it provide for any improvement in the international financial system. It takes no account of the deterioration in Brazil's terms of trade, nor of the problem of inflation-adjusted interest rates in the rollover of Brazil's external debts. It is a *direct* approach in that the U.S. government assumes direct responsibility for implementation of the Baker loans. It is *adversarial* in that it places pressure on the debtor for compliance with prescribed reforms as a precondition for disbursement of the loans.

The conditionality of the Baker plan implicitly incorporates the conditionality of IMF adjustment assistance. It requires adoption of monetary and fiscal policies that would be compatible with the liberalization policies it specifies. The latter include reduction of import restrictions, lowering of tariffs, removal of export subsidies, and goodwill toward direct foreign investment in Brazil. The prior adoption of monetary and fiscal policies that would be compatible with this prescription would be contractionary. The reason for this is the lack of symmetry in the prescription: it fails to mention any reforms for creditors. One of the reasons for the breakdown of the

Bretton Woods system of pegged exchange rates was the uneven impact of its balance of payments adjustment process on debtors and creditors. The new era of floating rates was supposed to give independence to all members of the IMF club in the determination of their domestic monetary and fiscal policies. It has not worked out that way. Under the Baker plan, as in practice (although not in theory) under the Bretton Woods system, the burden of monetary and fiscal policy reform is assigned exclusively to the debtor. Moreover, the Baker plan takes no cognizance of protectionist policies among the creditor nations. Can debtors produce a trade surplus sufficient to service their external debts in the face of trade barriers abroad while they abandon import restraints at home?

Given the prevailing state of the world economy, it seems likely that growth would be preceded by substantial economic shrinkage in the event Brazil fulfilled the preconditions of the Baker plan. Apart from this difficulty, Brazil's *abertura* would expose its government to enormous political opposition should it attempt to implement the plan's preconditions. In the past, moreover, debtor-creditor relations between the United States and Brazil have been conducted entirely between Brazilian and U.S. commercial banks in the private sector. By assuming responsibility for policing the implementation of Baker plan preconditions, the U.S. government further politicizes its economic relations with Brazil.

## Japan's Relations with Brazil

Schematically, in contrast with the U.S. modes of approach to Brazil, those of Japan may be characterized as consensual, indirect, or geopolitical. The interaction between the U.S. and Japanese modes of approach to matters concerning Brazil may give rise to competition, conflict, or cooperation between the parties.

Consensus between Japan and Brazil arises chiefly in the context of their common interest in economic development and in their common aim of reducing the degree of their dependence on the United States. In their mutual concerns, both nations are nonideological and pragmatic. They have interests, not "principles." Following the World War II, Japan is regarded in Brazil as having "written the textbook" on the technique of government intervention on behalf of economic development. Roberto Fendt remarked, "We definitely follow the Japanese model."[30] During 1964–1985, the period of military rule, the Brazilian government was highly interventionist. In this respect, Brazil had more affinity with Japan than with the United States. Despite the obvious and fundamental differences between Brazil and Japan, in terms of economic development, their strategies and policies have shared a number of characteristics in common. Both have deliberately utilized economic dualism as an instrument of development. Both have suppressed consumption in favor of production. Both rely on government administrative guidance to the private sector. Both are skeptical of the benefits of antitrust and anticartel regulations. Both rely on protectionist industrial policy for the promotion of infant industry. Both extensively employ the licensing and approval authority of the government as an instrument of industrial policy. In varying degrees, both sponsor direct government investment in industry. Both have employed subsidies and special tax measures. Both have assisted favored borrowers by rationing low-interest-rate loans from governmental or quasi-governmental financial institutions. Both are infatuated with the concept of "scale optimism." Both possess *zaibatsu* or *keiretsu* types of business conglomerates that dominate their respective economies by means of political as well as economic coordination. Both are controlled by hierarchies of elites. Both rely on a powerful popular consensus in favor of economic growth. On the international plane, both espouse the concept of "agreed specialization" among nations. Both aspire to be a link or intermediary between advanced and developing nations. Both are resolved to practice "autonomous diplomacy," especially in relation to the United States. Indeed, in many of the most important areas of common ground between Brazil and Japan, there lies a gulf between them and the United States. The consensual relationship between Brazil and Japan with regard to economic-development issues and their mutual desire to diversify away from overdependence on the United States may help account for the odd fact that in Brazil Japan is not criticized for protectionism or discrimination even though its policies are more restrictive than those of the United States.

Partly also, Japan may escape criticism because it often seeks its objectives by means that are indirect. In relations with Brazil, it has not applied pressure frontally; instead, it has attempted to mobilize for its own purposes those pressures to which Brazil is already exposed. It also has attempted to help Brazil make progress in ways that redound to Japan's advantage. Among the latter are reduction of Brazil's dependence on the United States, installation of Brazil's economic infrastructure, expansion of its primary-product sector, and development of its middle-technology industries. By indirection, Japan has manipulated the linkage between trade, finance, and technology transfer. This has been accomplished partly by its participation as a minority stockholder in Brazilian joint ventures. Partly it has been accomplished by the distribution services that Japanese *sogo shosha* have made available to Brazilian exporters. Partly it has been done by means of opening doors for Brazil through Japanese economic diplomacy.

In its geopolitical mode, Japan's approach to Brazil takes account of four trends that are conducive to Japan's emergence as a "headquarters nation." These are noticeable in the world at large and in Brazil in particular. They include (1) protectionism, a reaction against the principles of economic liberalization espoused by GATT, the IMF, and the World Bank, (2) economic concentration, promoted in the United States and western Europe by mergers, takeovers, and other forms of consolidation, as well as by financial deregulation, and in Brazil by various factors, including decapitalization and bankruptcy, (3) "agreed specialization" in international commerce, and (4) the rise of countertrade and its variations as a means of reducing the need for foreign exchange reserves in performing international transactions. In these departures from the nondiscriminatory, multilateral free-market system, there is a movement toward management of markets in the world economy. A managed system of this sort would be governed by political and strategic as well as economic tradeoffs. Because of its national experience and its institutional arrangements, such a world would be much more congenial to Japan than to the United States. The Japanese bureaucracy, resuming its historical role after having been flouted by economic liberalization, would intervene on the political level with foreign governments on behalf of Japanese big business. "Japan, Incorporated," would be gloriously restored.

Among the major industrial nations, protectionism has been a joint product of stagflation, the slowdown in the rate of expansion of world trade, supply-oriented exports on the part of Japan, and the welfare state. Supply-oriented exports are recessionary exports and are the equivalent of an export of unemployment. In 1983, exports accounted for all of Japan's economic growth; they accounted for two-thirds of its growth in 1984. Paradoxically, protectionism that has been partly precipitated by Japan itself is a causal factor in the scenario concerning its emergence as a headquarters country. According to Max W. Corden, the main characteristics of the "new protectionism" include lack of openness or transparency in the devices of protectionism, making it difficult to assess their extent; the trend from firm rules toward administrative discretion; and the return to bilateralism. Each of these characteristics is prominent in the practices of both Japan and Brazil, and they are a provocation to further protectionism on the part of their trade partners.

Protectionism and cartelism both at home and abroad complement each other in inducing Brazil's demand for "agreed specialization." Japanese authorities are wholly in accord with that demand. They fully appreciate that Japan's trading partners will no longer accept persistent deficits in every category of their commerce as a normal feature of doing business with Japan. Their strategy is to reserve an important position in the upper part of the industrial spectrum for Japanese industry. By deliberate industrial policy, Japan is systematically shifting the locus of its comparative advantage from the declining basic materials industries (textiles, paper and pulp, chemicals and petrochemicals, ceramics, steel, and nonferrous metals) to the rising processing and assembling industries (general machinery, electrical machinery, communications equipment, computers, electronic equipment, and precision instruments). In particular, Japan aims to excel in the high-technology services field, including international financial services and information processing. In contrast with the United States, which continues to claim a major stake in primary products and middle-technology goods that are in direct competition with Brazil, Japan is progressively removing itself from such competition. Japan's protection of its declining industries is mild as compared with its strong protection of those in the advancing high-technology field. Instead of fighting protectionism, the Japanese government employs it at home and accommodates to it abroad in pursuing a program of agreed specialization with Brazil.

The irony of "voluntary" export controls self-imposed by Japan is that they are voluntary in a sense of which the United States is oblivious. These controls help Japan to implement its own industrial policy. Japan's acquiescence in export controls is an expression of its allegiance to the principle of agreed specialization. The products subject to export restraints, such as steel, automobiles, textiles and clothing, and consumer electronics, are typically those which have been selected for offshore production by means of direct foreign investment. Japan's middle-technology industries are being increasingly transferred to places like Brazil, the United States, and western Europe. MITI estimates that by the year 2000, 10 percent of Japan's total production will be located abroad, as compared with 3 percent in 1985. The ratio would be much higher, of course, as a proportion of the output of the specified industries respectively. In addition to agreed specialization, a second reason for Japan's acquiescence in voluntary export controls is the mandate they confer on the government bureaucracy. In order to implement voluntary export restraints, quotas must be established, assigned, and policed. These quotas, together with the sanctions that enforce them, constitute government cartels, or "neocartels," to be distinguished form voluntary cartels organized by collusion in the private sector. As legal entities, they give the Japanese government bureaucracy a new raison d'être, broader turf, and more scope for intervention. New controls are a windfall to the bureaucracy after its involuntary self-diminishing approach to economic liberalization. The strategy of "overcoming trade friction" by voluntary export restraints is conducive to fulfillment of the headquarters country scenario, in which bureaucrats share power with big business in managing Japan's economy. In the meantime, from a Brazilian point of view, Japan's voluntary export restraints are a welcome contribution to progress toward "horizontal" division of labor in the world economy.

Unfortunately, however, the horizontal division of labor has further complications for Brazil. The expansion of its import-substitute program, augmented by the transfer of middle-technology industries from Japan, has the ultimate effect of increasing Brazil's foreign exchange vulnerability.[31] A new "external dependency" has arisen. The development of middle-technology industries within developing and newly industrializing countries, moreover, adds to competition among them, as well as to competition between them and the declining middle-technology industries of the United States. These effects compound each other and redound to the benefit of Japan. Brazil's new external dependence gives Japan leverage because more than any other nation, Japan possesses the international marketing and distribution facilities that can serve Brazil in expanding its exports. Among these facilities, Japan's *sogo shosha* have an unrivaled capability for performing both conventional and countertrade transactions. The latter have figured prominently in Brazil's recent response to its increasing foreign exchange vulnerability.

In its geopolitical approach to Brazil, Japan brings its rivalry with the United States to a focus. At present, in matters concerning Brazil, the rivalry is partly potential and implicit. It is masked by cooperation between the two nations in helping Brazil to avoid default on its external debt. Overtly, there is growing contact between the United States and Japan in their relations to Brazil as an export platform for competition in third areas, as in the case of automobiles. The potential and indirect effects of Japan's geopolitical approach, however, are more formidable. They arise from Japan's assistance to Brazil's export potential in primary products (as in its contribution to Brazil's development of the Cerrado and in the construction of fertilizer plants to serve the needs of the Cerrado) and middle-technology products (as in Japan's technology transfer to the capital goods industry), which will result in increased competition between Brazil and the United States in third markets as well as within the United States proper.

Rejecting the role of "locomotive," Japan aspires to *orchestrate* the world economy by means of its geopolitical strategy.[32] In assuming the role of orchestrator, Japan far transcends the simple notion of the complementarity of the Japanese and Brazilian economies. Geopolitical proposals for the Global Infrastructure Fund (GIF), including projects such as the Amazon area development project, construction of a superport at Tubarao in Brazil, construction of a second Panama Canal, the Asia port concept, and the proposal for removing the Andean rail gap in linkage between the Atlantic and Pacific oceans across Brazil, are among more than a dozen national projects under consideration in Japan. In economic terms, as well as in its concomitant political effects, the equity participation of the Japanese government in national projects and in lesser projects not so designated reduces the risk of foreign investment for Japanese private business. Besides equity investment, approximately one-third of Japan's loans to Brazil have been provided by Japanese government or quasi-governmental financial agencies. Government collaboration thus gives Japanese firms a political as well as an economic advantage over U.S. firms abroad. Recently, this collaboration has imparted a dynamic element to Japan's activities in Brazil that otherwise might be lacking. While many private Japanese firms have been skeptical about making further commitments in the midst of the debt crisis, the Japan Export-Import Bank has demonstrated government leadership by aggressively supporting further investment. Its reasoning is that the debt crisis creates an opportunity for Japan to expand its foundation for long-term advance in Brazil.[33]

Orchestration in the Japanese private sector may be applied in the form of pressure for improvement of its terms of trade. In the case of iron ore, for example, by a huge reduction in purchases from Australia in favor of purchases from Brazil, Japan has forced prices down and correspondingly has improved its balance of payments. In the case of soybeans, the same tactic is applicable by means of potential purchases from Brazil as an alternative to purchases from the United States. As Brazil becomes increasingly important as a world supplier of food and minerals, competition among third parties will result in lower prices to Japan for these commodities regardless of the actual source of its imports.

At the micro level, orchestration is evident in the policies of Japanese global firms. Subsidiaries of Japanese general trading companies in Latin America, for example, are coordinated by regional headquarters in Sao Paulo as well as by Tokyo. In contrast, the typical U.S. multinational corporation establishes autonomous and uncoordinated profit centers abroad (known as "strategic business units") which are relatively isolated. In the Japanese model, by means of central coordination, affiliates gain the benefits of the specialized services of their sister organizations throughout the world. They cross-subsidize each other by coordination of comparative advantage in production, technology, and distribution.[34] In the present era of declining terms of trade for primary products and overcapacity in middle-technology products, such as chemicals and steel, control of international distribution systems may come to be more important than control of production sources. These circumstances are ideally suited to the nature of Japan's global strategy.

Japan's geopolitical goal is attainment of a stable world environment within which it can achieve comprehensive economic security. Its policies concerning Brazil and other nations are systematically organized in terms of that objective. The United States, in contrast, appears to lack a clearly defined long-term policy concerning either Latin America in general or Brazil in particular. In approaching Brazil, Japan is advancing, not shifting, from its historic base in east and southeast Asia. With a clear understanding of its own national interests, with fixed purpose and flexible policies, Japan will be increasingly competitive with the United States in matters concerning Brazil. In its role as a headquarters nation, its direct and indirect impact on the United States will be greater than ever before.

Obviously, present trends are not being explained in these terms by the Japanese. However, "communication and mutual understanding" can arise from study of the facts, which here speak plainly. In its relations with Brazil, a U.S. advantage is that there is no mystery about Brazilian thinking and strategy. The same cannot be said of its relations with Japan. Prime Minister Yasuhiro Nakasone achieved the feat of winning U.S. acclaim merely by appearing to be straightforward. In the postwar period—beginning with the polite reception accorded to General MacArthur's troops when they entered the sacred homeland—every major development in Japan has come as a surprise to American authorities. The United States continues to underestimate Japan. Consequently, unwelcome surprises may lie in store. There should be no surprise, however, about the role of Brazil in the strategy that reflects Japan's pursuit of its national interests.

## Notes

1. The U.S. growth recession was dated by Geoffrey H. Moore, director of the Center for International Business Cycle Research, Columbia University, in June of 1986.

2. Interview with Professor Celso Luiz Martone, Fundacao Instituto de Pesquisas Economicas, University of Sao Paulo, in Sao Paulo, August 2, 1983.

3. Interview with Senator Severo Gomes, Federal Senate of Brazil, in Brasilia, August 10, 1983.

4. Interview with Tasuku Nagata, secretario geral, Camara de Comercio e Industria Japonesa do Brasil, in Sao Paulo, August 3, 1983. Mr. Nagata remarked further, "Japanese companies are accustomed to a degree of competition in the Japanese home market that is much more intense than in Brazil."

5. Interview with Kelly Joyce, commercial consul, United States Consulate General, in Rio de Janeiro, July 16, 1984.

6. Interview with Paulo Rabello de Castro, chief editor, *Conjuntura Economica*, Fundacao Getulio Vargas, in Rio de Janeiro, August 15, 1983.

7. Interview with Alexis Cavicchini, director, Suma Economica Publications, in Rio de Janeiro, July 18, 1984.

8. Interview with Roberto Fendt, Jr., director of studies and research, Fundacao Centro de Estudos do Comercio Exterior (FUNCEX), in Rio de Janeiro, July 20, 1984.

9. Interview with Masayuki Ikeda, director and vice president, Mitsui Brasileira Ltda., in Rio de Janeiro, July 17, 1984.

10. Interview with Brian Michael F. Neele, head, Trade Information Division, Ministry of External Relations, in Brasilia, July 11, 1984.

11. Interview with Helson Braga, assistant to Roberto Fendt, Fundacao Centro de Estudos do Comercio Exterior (FUNCEX), in Rio de Janeiro, August 16, 1983.

12. See Peter Knight, et al., *Brazil: Financial Systems Review* (Washington D.C.: World Bank, 1984), p. 139.

13. *Visao*, August 1983.

14. Interview with J. A. de Macedo-Soares, chief, Commercial Division, Ministry of External Relations, in Brasilia, July 12, 1984.

15. Interview with Carlos Alberto Amorim, Jr., coordenador adjunto, Ministerio da Fazenda, Coodenadoria de Assuntos Internacionais, in Brasilia, August 10, 1983.

16. Interview with Masayuki Ikeda, director and vice president, Mitsui Brasileira Ltda., in Rio de Janeiro, July 17, 1984.

17. Interview with Senator Severo Gomes, Federal State of Brazil, in Brasilia, August 10, 1983.

18. *Financial Times*, July 19, 1985.

19. Interview with Hiroshi F. Katayama, vice president, Citibank, N.A., in Sao Paulo, July 3, 1984.

20. Central Bank of Brazil, *Brazil: Economic Program*, Vol. 15, June 1987, p. 61. According to the Bank of Boston, the real GDP growth rate per capita was −1.6 percent in 1981, 0.9 percent in 1982, and −3.2 percent in 1983. Bank of Boston, *Brazil in Figures, 1985*.

21. Interview, August 18, 1986.

22. Interview, August 21, 1986.

23. Interview, August 19, 1986.

24. See Barbara Insel, "A World Awash in Grain," *Foreign Affairs,* Spring 1985.

25. As of August of 1986, U.S. demands concerning Brazil's informatics policy included the following: a more precisely specified definition of the products protected by "market reserve"; a maximum time limit within which applications for import licenses would be examined; publication of the specific criteria used by SEI, the agency in charge of granting such licenses; and establishment of an appeals procedure for companies whose license applications have been rejected.

26. U.S. General Accounting Office, *Emerging Issues in Export Competition: A Case Study of the Brazilian Market,* September 26, 1985, p. 13.

27. Interview with Robert H. Blocker, president, Blocker Assessoria de Investimentos e Participacoes, S.A., in Sao Paulo, July 3, 1984.

28. *Journal of Commerce,* July 16, 1985.

29. Interview with Dr. Felippe Arno, president, Arno Corporation, in Sao Paulo, August 4, 1983.

30. Interview with Roberto Fendt, Jr., director of studies and research, Fundacao Centro de Estudo do Comercio Exterior (FUNCEX), in Rio de Janeiro, July 20, 1984.

31. For further discussion of this point, see Albert Fishlow, "The State of Latin American Economics," included as Chapter 5 in Inter-American Development Bank, 1985 Report, *Economic and Social Progress in Latin America,* p. 128.

32. In 1977, Japan and West Germany were urged by the United States to adopt expansionary economic policies and thus to serve as "locomotives" in pulling the world out of its then prevailing recession. Japan reluctantly complied, with inflationary consequences that it bitterly regretted. (In Germany, similar results occurred.) In 1986, the same expansionary policies were again being urged on Japan and West Germany by the United States, this time in the name of promoting economic growth.

33. Interview with Wataru Aoki, chief respresentative, Export-Import Bank of Japan, in Rio de Janeiro, July 16, 1984.

34. For discussion of this point, see Gary Hamel and C. K. Prahalad, *Harvard Business Review,* Reprint 85409, July-August 1985.

# Index

# About the Author

**Leon Hollerman** is Husby-Johnson Professor of Business and Economics at St. Olaf College. Previously he was Dengler-Dykema Distinguished Service Professor of Economics at Claremont McKenna College and Claremont Graduate School. He has been a visiting research professor at Tokyo University and Hitotsubashi University. His books include *Japan's Dependence on the World Economy* and *Japan, Disincorporated: The Economic Liberalization Process* (1988). He is also the author of many articles on international economic affairs and a recipient of major research awards. His career as a Japan specialist was launched during the Occupation of Japan, when for 5 years he was an international trade economist on General MacArthur's staff.